Business in Networks

The IMP (Industrial Marketing and Purchasing) Group was formed in 1976 by researchers from five European countries. The group's first work was a large-scale comparative study of industrial marketing and purchasing across Europe. Results of this study were published by John Wiley in 1982, edited by Håkan Håkansson, under the title *International Industrial Arketing and Purchasing: An Interaction Approach*. The group's 'interaction approach' is based on the importance for both researchers and managers of understanding the interaction between active buyers and sellers in continuing business relationships. In a second study this interaction in single business relationships were systematically analysed as embedded into networks of relationships. This study was reported in *Developing Relationships in Business Networks* published by Routledge 1995 and edited by Håkan Håkansson and Ivan Snehota. Several other and related studies have been carried out focussing on different types of relationships and business networks. This work is published in numerous books and articles (see www.impgroup.org). A selection of this work can be seen in *Understanding Business Marketing and Purchasing* (3rd edition), edited by David Ford (International Thomson, 2001). The second edition of *Managing Business Relationships* (2003) by David Ford, Lars-Erik Gadde, Håkan Håkansson and Ivan Snehota and *Supply Network Strategies* (2001) by Lars-Erik Gadde and Håkan Håkansson have been published by John Wiley & Sons Ltd. These books encapsulate the research, teaching, consulting and writing experiences of the IMP Group.

The group hosts an international conference in September of each year which attracts a large number of researchers working in the areas of business marketing, purchasing and inter-company networks. The group publishes an on-line journal, *The IMP Journal*. This together with other output from the group and its conferences can be found at www.impgroup.org.

Business in Networks

Håkan Håkansson
David Ford
Lars-Erik Gadde
Ivan Snehota
Alexandra Waluszewski

WILEY

A John Wiley and Sons, Ltd., Publication

Library of Congress Cataloging-in-Publication Data
 Business in networks / Håkan Håkansson [et al.].
   p.   cm.
 Includes bibliographical references and index.
 ISBN 978-0-470-74963-0 (pbk. : alk. paper)
 1. Business networks.   Håkansson, Håkan, 1947–
 HD69.S8.B864 2009
 658′.044—dc22

                        2009018442

A catalogue record for this book is available from the British Library.

Set in 10/12pt Goudy by Aptara Inc., New Delhi, India.

CONTENTS

PREFACE

There are at least two ways to describe the story behind this book. One story started more than six years ago when the five of us jointly agreed on the need to articulate our experiences of the interactive business landscape and its consequences, which had emerged from our research in the IMP setting. This was an easy decision to take, but it proved rather demanding to accomplish. Although we started out with a similar basic understanding of the interactive business landscape and its main effects, the writing process revealed that we also had different opinions about more or less every aspect discussed in the book. The more that we attempted to articulate our own understandings, the more were the different ideas and interpretations that had to be explored and reconciled. Thus, our own interaction meant that the book was not completed, as planned, within a little more than six months but in rather more than six years. During this time, we had many meetings and intensive discussions that ranged from tiny details of expression to concepts as a whole. Although our differences mostly related to particular details, they forced us to articulate alternatives that we could all agree upon. The idea that interaction both takes time and produces effects over time is a key message of the book and is also a lesson that we have had to experience personally. It takes time to convince co-authors that a particular way of articulating a message is the best for the moment and it takes an even longer time to accept the demise of some of our own favourite ideas and to realize that a co-author's suggestion actually works better. However, after six years of these processes, we are prepared to take collective responsibility for the content of the book.

The second way that the story behind the book can be presented is as an even longer interaction process that has involved many more researchers and very many more discussions of how to articulate the phenomenon of business interaction. The first IMP project was started in 1976 and included researchers in five European countries. In 1984, we held the first international IMP Conference in Manchester and the 25th will take place in Marseille in September 2009. During this time, we have been involved in a number of joint projects across several countries. Furthermore, and as we present in the book, more than 120 IMP-related dissertations have now been completed. Researchers from Europe, Australia, the United States and Asia have participated and contributed to the development of ideas on business interaction. Some of these have been around for more or less the whole period of the IMP enterprise but we have also had the great opportunity to welcome a large number of young researchers, some of whom were not even born when it all started. It has been a fantastic journey and it is quite impossible to describe and give credit to all those who have influenced us during that process. In the book, we try to reference a number of the most important works but we sincerely apologize to all those that we have missed.

The book is our attempt to bring all this empirically-based research together into one picture of the business landscape. It is our picture and it is one that characterizes the business landscape that we have observed by using the metaphor of the rainforest. We start the book with empirical observations of interaction that are the basis for the whole IMP development and try to put these together into a picture of the rainforest-like business landscape. We then use this empirical base to conceptualize the process of business interaction and focus on the concrete aspects of that interaction, its 'substance'. This substance means that all interaction has important consequences both in time and across the wide space of the business landscape. The examination of these consequences for the basic elements of the landscape (resources, activities and business actors) form an important part of the book. It is the systematic evolution of the interdependencies within and between these elements of the business landscape that provide the strongest argument for us to characterize the business landscape as a rainforest.

In the third part of the book, we try to relate our conceptualization of the interactive business landscape to a number of important aspects of the business world. We discuss how a number of the prevailing business disciplines and the ideas of economics attempt to cope with business interactivity and we present a tentative approach to a structure of managerial activity in an interactive world. An interactive view of business also leads us to a re-interpretation of ideas of business evolution and the processes of business history. Finally, we examine some of the implications of the interactive business landscape for those involved in public policy-making and for those attempting to direct business enterprises.

We hope that you will find that reading these discussions is as interesting and challenging as we have found writing about them. We also hope that this book will be a useful part in our continuing and inevitably unfinished interaction around these themes.

We wish to thank the Norwegian Research Council for financial support through the research program 'Towards a New Understanding of Marketing'; the Swedish Governmental Agency for Innovation Systems (Vinnova); and the Tore Browalds, Jan Wallanders and Tom Hedelius Research Foundation. Finally, we thank all those students and co-workers within the IMP research setting who have contributed so much towards our ideas and our limited understanding of what happens in the interactive business landscape.

Håkan Håkansson
David Ford
Lars-Erik Gadde
Ivan Snehota
Alexandra Waluszewski

Europe, April 2009

A JUNGLE OR A RAINFOREST?

The business landscape is full of both mundane and surprising events. One way to illustrate the pattern of these ordinary and dramatic events is to use metaphors. Traditionally, the jungle metaphor is most frequently used in attempts to capture the soul of the business landscape. It is a metaphor that pictures a landscape characterized by deadly competition between the companies that populate it. An alternative metaphor, which we suggest in this chapter, is that of the rainforest. This metaphor gives quite a different picture of how companies are related to each other. The idea of the rainforest indicates that a basic feature of the business landscape is the intricate interdependencies between the companies that populate it. Thus, the rainforest metaphor suggests that companies are involved in many different forms of cooperation and are not simply rivals. We explore the rainforest metaphor in this chapter and identify three typical features that emerge from it: the variety, motion and relatedness of the business landscape.

The use of the rainforest metaphor also indicates the aim of this book. It is not to search for new aspects of the business world and to explain these with established theories. Instead, our aim is almost the opposite: It is to pinpoint the basic features of the business world that lie behind observed changes and to explain these with an alternative framework. Our point of departure is empirical observations from extensive business research carried out over the last 30 years, observations that definitely do not fit into the established frameworks of economic thinking. The common message from these observations is, frankly, that mainstream economic thinking and models have simplified away some fundamental aspects of business life and have, therefore, provided an incomplete understanding of the basic processes and structures of the business landscape. Thus, we argue, there is a need for an alternative framework that can provide descriptions, analyses and explanations of some of the basic features of business that mainstream theory has diminished or neglected. It goes without saying that this suggestion must, to some extent, contradict established assumptions and frameworks. In the next section, we articulate the claim for an alternative, why we find it necessary and what types of contribution it may represent.

Business in Practice and in Theory

What is 'normality' in business? What is it like to be involved in business? Well, first and foremost, business involves dealing with the ordinary and the day-to-day. For example, a construction worker installs a standard type of pipe into a building project; an equipment supplier delivers a piece of apparatus to a pharmaceutical research laboratory; a distributor submits its weekly order to its main wholesaler. However, the ordinary life of business is spiced with surprises, large and small. The construction company may inform the worker that he cannot buy the material he uses any more: Purchasing for the whole company is to be centralized. The pharmaceutical company may ask its supplier for immediate technical support as it suspects that there is contamination in the apparatus. The wholesaler invites its customers to a meeting because an aggressive environmental non-governmental organization (NGO) is directing a new campaign against one of their main products.

The surprises that spice ordinary business life indicate that the business landscape is full of changes. Sometimes these changes are very visible: A well-known company declares bankruptcy and has to close down; two multinational companies merge with each other; a bank collapses; a national government announces that a particular material cannot be used because of its negative environmental effects; national and trans-national governments announce new financial regulations. But, often, the changes in the business landscape are more or less invisible to those who are not directly involved in a particular affair. For example, a producer, a customer and some complementary firms may develop their technologies and their organizations to relate more closely to each other; a supplier and some of its sub-suppliers start to cooperate in order to improve a product; a producer invites its suppliers into discussions about what it should continue to do in-house and what it should outsource to the suppliers.

All the changes, both visible and invisible that intervene in ordinary business life have effects that are difficult to predict or to interpret, both for those who are directly involved in them and those who are more distantly related. For example, how will a particular bankruptcy affect other companies, organizations and individuals, in what places and over what time? How will cooperation in product development between a supplier and its sub-suppliers affect others around them? In contrast to what happens within a company, the processes that take place between companies and their effects are not captured by traditional accounting or information systems. Some of the formal arrangements that are concluded between companies are legally documented. But there is no system of accounting for all of the interdependencies across the business landscape and their effects on the multiple resources, activities and people in different companies.

The complexities of the business landscape mean that it is easy to understand why the ordinary and non-ordinary processes between companies and organizations are ignored, so that business can be captured in an abstract analytical language. This language, whether developed by academics or journalists, generally takes its starting point in what is most easy to observe; the activities of individual companies. This company-centric approach is well represented in internal company documents, strategic plans, management policies, annual reports, analysts' reviews and journalists' assessments. The processes between companies are more difficult to interpret and are traditionally boiled down to one particular phenomenon: they are assumed to be driven by antagonism or competition.

The early 2000s provide no exception to this view. We are told that competition between companies is more intense than ever and that this must spur each company to improve its internal efficiency and effectiveness. Increased globalization and the call to outsource and off-shore operations to low-cost countries are all part of this competitive world. The OECD argues that new patterns of resource allocation, efficiency and market performance are a result of more aggressive competition among firms.[1] Similar interpretations are made by trans-national, national and regional policy organizations all over the world, accompanied with initiatives to transform public knowledge and to develop new intellectual property that can be used as part of the competitive forces of new and established firms. Even the relations between companies that are located close to each other are assumed to be mainly antagonistic. If these companies prosper, then we are told that the main explanation is that they are located within a highly competitive cluster where rivalries spur them to beat each other and, thus, to develop.

However if we look again at business in practice, then another way that companies relate to each other stands out as normal. Numerous companies, including some of today's most dynamic and profitable, seem to be more interested in dealing with both the ordinary and non-ordinary aspects of business life by using, rather than trying to destroy, others. Companies such as IKEA, Dell and Toyota devote their energies to working out how suppliers, customers and complementary firms can be used to create efficiency and innovation. A common denominator between these companies seems to be the wish to create a decentralized structure that stretches over and between company boundaries. A consequence of this approach is that questions of efficiency and innovation have to be dealt with across companies rather than just within companies. When it is common for 70, 80 or even 90 per cent of the product value of these companies to stem from what their external suppliers can achieve, then the core of business is not what happens within a company, but what happens in the interactions between that company and others.

Thus, while business *in practice* is about coping with ordinary and non-ordinary phenomena through interacting with others, business *in theory* is about independent companies acting as individuals, spurred only by their competitors. These radically different views of business in theory and in practice have two potential outcomes for all of us who try to understand business life and its effects.

The first potential outcome is that the idea of interdependent companies interacting with each other is just a slight nuance of the phenomenon that the traditional analytical tools of business were developed to capture: How independent companies act in order to prosper in an antagonistic environment. If this is the case, then we can continue to rely on established analytical assumptions, frameworks and models and just adapt them a little to include interaction as another means that can be managed by the independent firm.

The other potential outcome is that the interaction that we say characterizes business in practice is not at all a nuance of the traditional analytical view of the nature of business. Instead,

---

[1]http://www.oecd.org/eco/structural/competition.

it is a completely different phenomenon. If this is the case, then we may conclude that the basic processes of business are different from those that are assumed in the traditional framework. In turn, this leads us to the following question:

> Is it fruitful to try to squeeze the phenomenon of complex interaction between interdependent companies into a framework that was developed to deal with the ideas of independence and antagonism?

This book starts by answering 'No' to this question. Instead, we aim to develop an alternative framework which can explain the intensive interaction that takes place between companies and organizations. Our point of departure is empirical observations stemming from extensive research carried out in the IMP setting since the early 1970s.[2] (This experience is thoroughly presented in Chapter 2.) The common message from these observations is that interaction is at the heart of business life and that mainstream economic thinking has simplified away a fundamental aspect of business in practice. Thus, if we claim that business in theory should reflect the basic processes and structures of business in practice, then there is a need for alternative frameworks which can provide descriptions, analyses and explanations of some of the main features that mainstream theory has diminished or neglected. In the following section, we articulate the claim for one particular alternative, why we find it necessary and what types of contribution it represents.

The Need for and Danger of Metaphors

The function and the consequences of doing business affect not only companies but all of us, as individuals and as society as a whole. All these stakeholders have a strong interest in interpreting what happens in the business world and in trying to work out what it means to them. What does go on among the companies that people work in, buy from, sell to or protest against? People in different positions in a company have to try to make sense of what happens internally in that company and between it and those around it. Those with positions within governmental and non-governmental organizations are also concerned with understanding the business world and with how to stimulate some effects and restrict others.

However, the enormous complexity of the practice of business means that no one can fully understand it, whether they are a celebrated business leader supported by a huge staff or the most well-informed business analyst, journalist or researcher. We all have to rely on simplifications, from self-generated rules of thumb to advanced theoretical models. What is most important is perhaps not the form of these simplifications, but the underlying assumptions about the business world on which they are based. One way of pinpointing these assumptions is to consider the basic metaphors they relate to.

The metaphors that are used, or the associations that are drawn with other phenomena that rest on similar assumptions, can provide striking illustrations of the features that are enlarged,

---

[2]The Industrial Marketing and Purchasing Group (IMP) is an informal network of researchers who have carried out numerous studies into the interactions and relationships between companies, see www.impgroup.org.

diminished or assumed to be irrelevant. These underlying assumptions provide the basis for frameworks and models and, consequently, for how research is carried out and interpreted. They have a huge impact on how particular phenomena are perceived and interpreted.

Here we consider two metaphors that are used to illustrate some of the basic features of the business world. The jungle metaphor was originally presented in the mid-eighteenth century and has been the dominating metaphor related to economic thinking since the nineteenth century. The rainforest metaphor is much less widely used, at least in relation to economic phenomena. A comparison of the metaphors highlights just how powerful underlying assumptions and simplifications are in leading our attention towards particular aspects, whilst others are diminished or even neglected.

Both metaphors portray the business world in relation to nature. Seeking inspiration from assumptions about biology to try to explain economic phenomena is a tradition that has coloured historical as well as contemporary theory development. The metaphors have at least two basic characteristics in common. They both portray the business landscape as being created by many: it is viewed as a decentralized structure. They also both portray the business landscape as populated with similar and dissimilar units. However, the metaphors differ radically in one aspect: the way that companies that populate the business landscape are assumed to relate to each other.

The Business World as a Jungle

What takes place in the business world is most often characterized in terms of rivalry in a jungle-like landscape. Since the story of the island of Juan Fernandez was first presented by Joseph Townsend in 1786, the view of a hard and antagonistic nature, where the weakest 'goats' and 'dogs' have to pay their debt to nature and only the fittest will survive, has become the dominant metaphor in modern economic thinking. Townsend's legend describes how the admiral Juan Fernandez let loose goats on an island off the coast of Chile in order to provide food for future visitors. The goats multiplied rapidly, but the visitors who benefited from them were unwanted pirates. The admiral released some greyhounds on the island in order to kill the goats. In the absence of any social order, a natural law or equilibrium was established under which the goats and dogs fought for survival. In the mid-twentieth century, Polyanyi (1944) revealed how Townsend's story, supported by Darwin, had become a cornerstone in the development of the idea of a market populated by autonomous actors fighting for the survival of the fittest. Today, the jungle metaphor seems more vivid than ever. It is used in contemporary thinking about business strategy, innovation management, marketing and purchasing to describe a business world dominated by fierce fighting between independent enemies.

This metaphor enlarges the idea of antagonistic behaviour between independent companies: It visualizes suppliers that are played off against each other by the customer. It describes how producers are outperformed and where the 'fittest' take market share from the weaker or even drive them out of business. It also focuses on the way that threatening complementary producers are disarmed through acquisitions or by hostile takeovers. Further, the metaphor captures how the fittest lay their hands on new knowledge through exclusive property rights. Thus, the jungle metaphor focuses on one central ingredient of the business world: the fierce fighting between rivals. This underlying assumption and its associated simplifications fosters attention in frameworks, models, empirical investigations and analysis on antagonistic behaviour between companies and organizations (Waluszewski 2004).

Furthermore, theoretical schools related to the jungle metaphor highlight fighting as the way to achieve not only efficiency, through competition between producers or in buyer–seller negotiations, but also successful business development. Rivalry among producers of goods and services is deemed the central development force in the business world. Accordingly, strategy, marketing, purchasing and technological development advice are formulated in order to direct managerial behaviour in this direction. If a producer is able to create even a small 'competitive advantage' in the parameters of price or quality then it is assumed that this will have immediate effect in terms of a rapidly expanding customer base (Porter 1990). Thus, in order to survive in the business jungle, each firm has to identify its competitors, analyse their characteristic behaviour, and then fight for a 'competitive advantage' in relation to these (Marglin 2008).

The jungle metaphor may have been around for so long and become so all-embracing because it relates so closely to Western ideas of modernity: A society populated by rational, calculating, self-interested individuals acting to fulfil their own unlimited wants and in which the relations between them are limited to market reactions (Marglin 2008). However, this simplification also implies that other types of relation to other types of business actor are less significant and they are given less attention.

The Business World as a Rainforest

What interpretation of the world of business is evoked if we replace the jungle metaphor with another simplification of nature? The rainforest metaphor isn't common in business discussions (Håkansson and Waluszewski 2002) and it leads to an almost completely different understanding of the interactions that take place among those who populate the business world. The rainforest metaphor doesn't view those who populate it as solitary entities who are totally occupied with fighting each other. Instead, all of them are interdependent. Each is vital to and dependent on others that it borders and overlaps. This interdependence implies that the characteristics of the rainforest are not defined by the entities that populate it, but by the interactions between those entities. These comprise the complex array of millions of individuals and species who are designed for a life in relation to each other.

The rainforest metaphor emphasizes the importance of interaction with others. The life of one company is dependent on others and vice versa. Companies evolve in relation to each other over time in processes that produce great variety. These processes are beneficial for both individual companies and the landscape as a whole. Hence, the assumption that underlies those economic frameworks that relate to the rainforest metaphor is that multidimensional interaction is a basic feature of the business landscape. The independency and rivalry of the jungle metaphor are replaced by interdependency and interaction. Thus frameworks related to the rainforest allow relations other than the antagonistic to come to the fore. Rivalry may still be observed, but it is not assumed to be the dominant way of relating to others. Companies that traditionally would be identified as competitors may also appear as complementary, cooperative counterparts.

The rainforest metaphor steers interest to the direct interactions between customers, suppliers and other related companies and governmental and non-governmental organizations, and to the interplay between other indirectly related parties. It focuses attention on the processes of both cooperation and conflict as products and services are produced and used. It highlights how tangible and intangible resources of many types, stemming from many different organizational units, are related, confronted and adapted in ways which are beneficial for those involved in the doing of business. Thus, strategic business thinking related to the rainforest metaphor takes as its starting point the interactive features of business in practice.

The underlying ideas on which this book is based relate closely to the rainforest metaphor. However the rainforest metaphor, like all metaphors, is a simplification. Hence a key question is, 'Which aspects of business are enhanced or diminished by a framework based on these assumptions?' The following chapters give an insight into these considerations and the empirical observations they rest on. The ambition is to provide a framework based on some salient features of business in practice that is, we hope, useful both for those involved in and those affected by the business world. But before that, let us conclude this chapter with a short introduction to how these rainforest-like features of the business landscape, which triggered our search for an alternative framework, present themselves.

Business in Practice: Recognizing and Using the Characteristics of the Rainforest

Two big multinational companies, one based in Sweden and one in Finland, operate in similar businesses. Traditional analysis would consider them as fierce competitors. The managers in the two companies share the same view. But when one of these companies recently carried out a 300-million Euro investment in a new production facility based on an improved production technology, the investment decision was preceded by close interaction with its neighbouring competitor. Why do these two giants, dependent on the same kinds of input, using the same production technology and delivering to the same types of customer, cooperate on technological issues? Why don't they keep their expensively acquired knowledge secret and use it to achieve 'competitive advantage'? Both companies claim that the benefits of sharing their experience outweigh those of keeping them secret. First, sharing technological experience enables both companies to learn more about which possibilities are within reach and which directions are less beneficial: 'We don't have to make all the mistakes ourselves.' Secondly, each company's ideas for development are more well-grounded if they are also based on the experience of the other producer and their customers. Thirdly, the two multinationals' production facilities are based on equipment from the same supplier. But each investment over time has been combined and adapted to earlier investments, so no plant is exactly like any other. Consequently, even if one of them simply tried to exactly copy the solution arrived at by the other, they would never achieve the same effect.

A highly specialized biotechnology-tool producer supplies equipment for the analysis of molecular interaction. Its customers are research laboratories in universities and pharmaceutical companies. Although some of its customers are very well funded, their ability to pay is not reflected in the tool producer's pricing. Instead, some of its most prosperous customers are often asked to take a new instrument for free. Why isn't the tool producer tougher in its price negotiations? Why does it not try to sell harder? This 'elastic' way of defining the company's boundaries has several benefits for the biotechnology tool company. First, it means that some of the most prestigious research institutes are effectively development departments for the company. Instruments are placed at these laboratories and biotechnology company personnel work side by side with the researchers to determine how the instrumentation can be used effectively in different investigations. Secondly, once a customer laboratory has succeeded in using the equipment in a new application, it then functions as a 'marketing channel' for the supplier. If a research institute manages something new with the equipment then this will lead to research publications and publicity for the biotechnology company's equipment.

A small Swedish tourist company, offering day tours in the mountains on Icelandic horses, has a competitor within the same region. Both companies offer Dutch and German tourists a similar experience at a similar price. Whenever one of the two companies has too many customers, they immediately contact the other in order to work out a solution. Competing is an alternative that neither of them can afford. Both consider it to be of greater importance to direct their efforts to the creation of an attractive tourist area for visitors to enjoy their experience, regardless of who the supplier is. In the long term, they believe that both companies gain from this as does the region as whole.

We will come back to some of these short empirical illustrations later in the book. The examples stretch from multinationals to family firms, from biosciences to horse power and from physical products to services. Each suggests that a particular ability is crucial for the companies' prosperity. This is the ability to relate to the world around them in a much more multidimensional way than the strictly antagonistic. This ability enables companies to take advantage of at least three different aspects of the business world:

- **Variety:** We saw how the biotechnology-equipment producer and its customers could benefit from variety in the business landscape. Variety in products meant that the equipment could be combined with a range of different resources to enhance its usefulness. Variety in counterparts meant that the equipment could be adapted and combined in ways that broadened its application and the problems it addressed.
- **Motion:** The multinational companies and their equipment suppliers and others in our examples were able to benefit from motion in the business landscape. By being open about their present and planned investments in production technologies and, not least, their struggles in relation to these developments, the two multinational producers and their suppliers could take advantage of the movement in their counterparts' development of technologies, methods, equipment and products.
- **Relatedness:** The horse-tour companies and their customers were able to benefit from relatedness in the business landscape. By sending customers to each other, the two companies could utilize their resources and activities in a more efficient way. This and other contributions to the creation of a positive image of the tourist region provided benefits for many related companies. More generally, the examples show how companies used the fact that products, production, and companies have specific effects on others to which they are related.

These three main features of business in practice relate closely to the features that are highlighted by the rainforest metaphor. A business landscape characterized by variety, motion and relatedness de-emphasizes the separateness of the individual. Instead, the rainforest metaphor implies that it is more or less impossible for a company to create benefits for itself or others by itself or through its own individual search for the 'right solution', whether it is the right organizational form, the right technology, or the right counterparts. But this insight into business in practice has not coloured mainstream economic theories. Instead there has been an almost mythological belief that a single company can act alone and can *manage* its environment, its suppliers, customers, stakeholders, competitors, societal interests, and so on. The idea of a business landscape built on such a universal agency has been and still is, 'such an important piece of the ideology of modernity and so central to economic thinking that it is easy to lose sight of the obvious' (Marglin 2008:58). However in studies that are based on empirical observations of business in practice, the lack of universal agency is so striking that it is more or less impossible to neglect it. This was one of the basic observations that triggered the IMP studies and the development of a particular framework for analysing a business world characterized by interdependency. In Chapter 2, we take a closer look at the background of these studies and some of the experience gained from them. In particular, we consider how the aspects of variety, motion and relatedness have arisen in these studies.

Content and Organization of this Book

This book is divided into three parts. The first part is a presentation of the characteristics and effects of business networks in action and consists of three chapters. In Chapter 2, we summarize some of the empirical results of 30 years of research focused on business interaction and relate it to the three key features identified earlier in this chapter: variety, motion and relatedness. Based on these findings, Chapter 3 is devoted to a conceptualization of the interaction process. We argue that business interaction has important 'substance' that affects the companies involved in it in several ways and thus becomes a central factor in forming the business landscape. We present a basic model for analysing business interaction. Chapter 4 brings the idea of interaction into the business landscape and discusses how companies can survive and develop within such a landscape. This chapter is built on a large case study and brings us close to the way that business takes place through interaction.

Part II of the book also consists of three chapters. Here, our ambition is to identify the consequences of the nature of the business landscape presented in Part One for three key elements of business: resources, activities and actors. Chapter 5 is focused on resources, which are used in a highly relative way in an interactive landscape. All resources are formed and used in relation to each other and their value is directly affected by the interaction between them. Thus the interfaces between resources become a crucial business issue and affect both how a company uses resources and how it becomes valued by others. Resources form the basis for business activities, which are discussed in more detail in Chapter 6. The interdependencies between activities performed within different companies become an important focus in an interactive environment. By creating and utilizing these interdependencies, companies can achieve advantages both in costs and time. Interaction is the major means through which a company's own activities are designed, developed and perform in relation to the activities of important counterparts. Finally, in Chapter 7, the consequences for how the business actor should be conceptualized are discussed. An interactive actor takes a very different shape compared to the classical market actor that is believed to be driven by its own personal attributes. The interactive actor is as much a result of the interaction as a subject in it. The consequences of this idea of the business actor are huge and the problems of conceptualization are considerable. Chapter 7 identifies a set of important issues related to how actors combine attributes originating from themselves and from the wider landscape.

In Part III of the book, we use the idea of the business network as an analytical tool to examine some important areas of application. The first of these areas is management. Chapter 8 describes how the existence of business relationships has been integrated in economic models that build on the market model. In the market model, business relationships have to be seen as some kind of market failure or as special cases that only appear in certain specific situations. This allows relationships to be integrated into the usual market model. In Chapter 9 we try to do the opposite: We start out from the assumption that business relationships are the norm and try to see the consequences of this assumption for the way that managerial problems are formulated and for the kind of solutions that are possible. The main result is a picture of management as a way of trying to cope in networks instead of trying to manage networks. In Chapter 10 we examine the use of the network model to explain the evolution of business. Instead of the current view that there have been distinct forms of governance at different times, from the invisible hand to the visible hand and onward to some 'network society', our analysis points to the interplay between these different forms. Chapter 11 continues the use of the network model for analysing the business landscape in terms of industrial policy.

The final chapter of the book focuses on the use of and the consequences of the rainforest metaphor. The use of this metaphor arose from our empirical research where we have observed how individual business relationships are multidimensionally *unique* in the resources and activities that are involved in them and in how they evolve in juxtaposition with those of others along a time continuum. A few of these relationships are individually of overwhelming importance for each company. They appear to be so important that by describing them we may arrive at a very accurate view of the companies themselves. These relationships are clearly connected with other relationships in a network; what happens in any one relationship is related to what happens in many others. Companies live in a business landscape where the number, the complexity and the extent of these interconnections are very similar to how a rainforest is usually described. In the final part of Chapter 12, we try to portray how five important roles are affected by this landscape: the entrepreneur, the CEO, the accountant, the consumer and the politician.

BUSINESS NETWORKS IN ACTION

In this first part of the book, we try to paint a picture of business networks in action based on our empirical studies. In Chapter 2, we concentrate on characterizing the nature, development and use of individual business relationships and we relate the concept of the business relationship to the three key features of the business landscape that we identified in Chapter 1: variety, motion and relatedness. The business landscape outlined in these empirical studies is characterized by companies relating to each other in a very systematic way. What might be even more important is that this way of systematic relatedness seems to be a possible way of handling variety and motion. One conclusion is obvious: There are reasons to take interactions seriously. It is so substantive that it affects all those involved in it in a number of different ways. Thus, there is a need for development of a conceptualization of interaction.

This is done in Chapter 3, where the empirical base is used as a platform to develop a more comprehensive conceptual scheme of interaction and important influencing factors. Three time factors and three space factors are identified and analysed in relation to interaction. Finally, in Chapter 4, the three basic dimensions identified in Chapter 3 – interaction, time and space – are brought into the broader picture of analysing developments within the business landscape.

INTERACTION AS A WAY OF DEALING WITH RELATEDNESS, VARIETY AND MOTION

2

In Chapter 1, we characterized the business landscape by using a rainforest metaphor. This was an attempt to draw attention to three main features of the landscape: its variety, motion and relatedness. But why give these three features so much attention? This chapter gives the background to how a 'rainforest-like' view of the content and function of the business landscape emerged. Basically, it was our empirical experience of companies' interaction and the development of business relationships that triggered interest in the basic structures and processes of the business landscape. Along with expanded empirical investigations, we searched for alternative theoretical sources and the development of a framework specially designed to deal with these issues.

The main content of the chapter is an overview of how companies engage in direct interaction with each other in order to deal with variety, motion and relatedness and how these features are expressed in terms of time and place specificity.

The Need for a Different Theoretical Approach

Why have we devoted so much attention to the rainforest-like features of the business landscape? Our attention was triggered by a stubborn, recurrent, empirical message that seemed to clash with established business theory. This message is that the development of long-lasting business relationships between customers and suppliers is the normality of business life.

An early expression of this message appeared in a thesis that focussed on the export patterns of Swedish steel companies in the early 1960s and started out from traditional economic assumptions. This thesis included a short section about an empirical observation that could not be explained within the available framework: In practice, business took place among the same producers and customers over a very long time (Johanson 1966). These business relationships were 'impossible' in terms of established economic thinking and challenged a group of researchers to delve deeper into their existence, background and causality. The search for an explanation of

Table 2.1 Important theoretical roots for the IMP project.

Field	References
Marketing	Alderson (1954)
	Alderson (1957)
	Alderson (1965)
	Twedt (1964)
	Mattsson (1969)
	Stern (1969)
Business economics	Penrose (1959)
	Richardson (1972)
	Alchian and Demsetz (1972)
	March and Simon (1958)
	Cyert and March (1963)
Organizational and social sciences	Homans (1961)
	Blau (1964)
	Levine and White (1961)
	Litwak and Hylton (1962)
	Evan (1966)
	Thompson (1967)
	Van de Ven et al. (1975)

the empirically observed phenomena of interaction and relationships became the starting point for the development of a new field of research.[1]

This field subsequently became labelled 'Industrial Marketing and Purchasing' (IMP). It had the basic structures and processes in the business landscape as its common research interest and was concerned with the basic question: Why do producers and users hold on to each other over years and even decades, instead jumping around between different counterparts, playing with the price mechanism?

The need for a framework that could capture the content and effects of long-term interaction became obvious at an early stage in the research. Our starting point was a research model inspired by sociologists and anthropologists engaged in studies of social interaction (see Table 2.1). From this basis, we approached industrial buying and selling as similar phenomena that intimately affect both parties and their social and technological assets.

From this point of departure, analysis of the processes between buying and selling companies pointed to the importance of interdependence. Instead of acting as universal agencies, the companies that we investigated appeared to interact closely and deeply with their main counterparts, working with both organizational and technological issues and making significant adaptations

---

[1] In the text, we have chosen to describe the development from the Scandinavian researchers' point of view but a similar development took place in other European locations. In Sweden, some important sources were Forsgren and Kinch (1970), Guillet de Monthoux (1975), Håkansson and Wootz (1975) and Håkansson and Snehota (1976); in the UK, Blois (1972), Luffman (1974), Cunningham and White (1973, 1974) and Ford (1976); and in Germany, Kutschker (1975).

in relation to each other. Thus, business in practice appeared to be a process of creating benefits through voluntarily relating and adapting to each other.

These were early indications of a business landscape that had more in common with a rainforest than a jungle. However these observations led to another question: Is the rainforest metaphor only relevant for a few Scandinavian producers and their international customers, or is the phenomenon of interactive problem-solving between companies a generic feature of business life, despite the increased interdependency with which it is associated? This question was the starting point for a trans-national study of marketing and purchasing in five European countries. The first IMP project started in 1976 and included investigations of the content and effect of more than 1000 supplier–customer relationships (Håkansson 1982; Turnbull and Valla 1986).

The outcome of the study can best be described as a 'discovery', or as overwhelming testimony that to do business is to create benefits together with others. The most immediate finding from the research was that the relationship pattern across the European business landscape appeared to be very stable and the average European business relationship was over 12 years old. But under this un-dramatic surface, another picture emerged. This pointed to the fact that the resources exchanged between companies and the activities they carried out were constantly being developed and adapted in relation to those of directly and indirectly-related counterparts and that each actor's economic benefits were dependent on how this pattern evolved. Thus the long-term interaction between major counterparts appeared to lead to 'co-evolution' between producers and users. In other words, business in practice appeared to be almost opposite to how it is described in the economist's model of the world, in which independent business actors are assumed to engage in ad-hoc affairs and to be separate from each other. These empirical findings led to a number of challenges to the prevailing view of marketing and purchasing that were expressed in the first joint IMP report, as shown in Box 2.1.

Box 2.1   Three Challenges Identified in the IMP Project

Firstly, we challenge the concentration of industrial-buyer-behaviour literature on a narrow analysis of a single discrete purchase. Instead we emphasize the importance of the relationship which exists between buyers and sellers in industrial markets.

Secondly, we challenge the view of industrial marketing as the manipulation of the marketing-mix variables in order to achieve a response from a generalized and, by implication, passive market. We believe it necessary to examine the interaction between individual buying and selling firms.

Thirdly, we challenge the view which implies an atomistic structure in industrial markets. This view assumes a large number of buyers and sellers, with ease and speed of change between different suppliers for each buyer and ease of market entry or exit for those suppliers. Instead we stress the stability of industrial market structures.

Source: Håkansson, H. (ed.), 1982. *International Marketing and Purchasing of Industrial Goods: An Interaction Approach*. John Wiley & Sons Ltd. Reproduced by permission.

Table 2.2   Important sources of inspiration during the development of IMP.

Field	References
Social network theory	Cook and Emerson (1978)
	Aldrich and Whetten (1981)
	Axelrod (1984)
	Granovetter (1985)
	Burt (1992, 2004)
Transaction cost theory	Williamson (1975, 1979, 1985)
	Reve (1990)
	Heide (1994)
Organization theory	March and Olsen (1976)
	Powell (1987, 1998)
	Brunsson (1989)
	March (1999)
Marketing	Arndt (1979)
	Webster (1979)
	Achrol (1991)
	Achrol and Kotler (1999)
Economic development	Freeman (1982, 1991)
	Dosi (1982)
	Dosi et al. (1988)
	Arthur (1988)
Innovation management	von Hippel (1976, 1978, 1988)
	Van de Ven et al. (1989, 1999)
Relationship and service marketing	Gummesson (1979, 2002)
	Grönroos (1984, 1997)
	Vargo and Lusch (2004)
Economic history and anthropology	Rosenberg (1982, 1994)
	David (1985)
	Wilk (1996)
	Gudeman (2001)
Science, technology and society studies	Hughes (1983, 1987)
	Latour (1984)
	Bijker (1987)
	Galison (1997)
	Jasanoff (2004)

These challenges were fuelled by empirical observations in the first IMP research project. They were also inspired by other 'dissident' scholars and their struggles in dealing with empirical observations of exchange that contradicted the assumptions of the traditional models of the business world (see Table 2.2).

These studies provided support for the empirical observation of interaction as a significant part of business and organizational life. Other scholars also underlined that interaction was not something that could be depicted as only a Scandinavian or European phenomenon. Some inspiring observations of the role of interaction in supposedly more 'rugged' business landscapes were made by scholars outside Europe, from the US, Asia and Australia.[2]

The authors of this book have been concerned with the phenomenon of interaction since the first IMP empirical observations that business in practice is far removed from the assumption of universal agency in an atomistic market.[3] Over the past 30 years, the challenge of how to make sense of an interactive business landscape has triggered a whole series of research projects, seminars, workshops and conferences in which different aspects and effects of interaction and relationships have been examined. This shared interest is also behind the development of the IMP Group into a larger, informal research network, involving some hundreds of researchers around the world. (See www.impgroup.org for a presentation of the IMP Group and, for example, Ford (2002) and Håkansson and Waluszewski (2002, 2007) for an overview of the research field.) An important part of the research has been carried out within a large number of doctoral projects. The authors of this book have benefited from being involved in a number of these research projects as supervisors and committee members or as interested readers. A less than complete list of more than 100 doctoral dissertations dealing directly with interaction and relationships in the business landscape is presented in the appendix.

The following section is an attempt to summarize some of the output from this empirical research. The aim is not to provide a complete review of all of the studies of business interaction that have been carried out within the IMP setting. Instead, we try to present some of the main characteristics of the business landscape and suggest how these characteristics lead to the development and use of extensive business relationships.

A Business Landscape Populated by Interacting Companies

Why do companies interact and why do they develop business relationships, when this obviously increases their dependence on others and decreases their freedom? How companies relate to each other in business and the functions and effects of relating are common to the wide variety of empirical studies carried out within IMP. We can summarize some of the main empirical findings by relating them to the three basic characteristics of the business landscape introduced in Chapter 1: relatedness, variety and motion.

---

[2]Studies based on the US are Dwyer *et al.*(1987), Frazier *et al.* (1988), Van de Ven *et al.* (1999), Wilson and Mummalaneni (1986), Anderson and Weitz (1989), Anderson and Narus (1990, 1991), Miles and Snow (1992), Piore and Sabel (1984), Han *et al.* (1993), Dabholkar *et al.* (1994), Mohr and Spekman (1994), Spekman *et al.* (1998), Bowman and Narayandas (2001) and Narayandas and Rangar (2004). Studies from Australia include Welch *et al.* (1996), Wilkinson (2008), Wilkinson and Young (2002), and Young and Wilkinson (1989, 1997). Studies from Asia include Sahal (1980), Takeuchi and Nonaka (1986), Teramoto (1990), Hamilton (1996), Wilkinson and Yeoh (2005) and Wiley *et al.* (2006).

[3]Ford, Håkansson and Snehota were all involved in the formation of the first IMP study in the 1970s; Gadde and Waluszewski became engaged in this thinking in the early 1980s.

Interaction as a Way of Dealing with Relatedness

A striking finding from the first IMP project is the long-term nature of the relationships between suppliers and customers, with many spanning twenty or thirty years. Many subsequent studies have given support to the idea of long-term and complex relationships.[4]

But why do companies do business with their main counterparts over such long periods of time and what effects do these long relationships have on the larger business landscape? Our empirical investigations underlined that relationship continuity is favourable for both customers and suppliers in relation to companies' attempts to achieve both stability and change. Thus, repeated transactions produce efficiency benefits that are usually greater than their costs. A long-term orientation is also important for development: Empirical investigations revealed that established relationships are the most important source of innovation for both buyers and sellers (Håkansson 1989). For buyers, a long-term orientation is a prerequisite for making the best use of a supplier's resources in order to achieve gains in efficiency and development. A long-term orientation also enables sellers to create or rationalize efficient supply systems and to capitalize on development opportunities. Continuity is also valuable in helping to reduce some of the uncertainties that both parties face in doing business with each other (Ford et al. 2003). These uncertainties may centre on exactly what a customer should seek from a supplier and what a supplier should offer to a customer. Both customer and supplier are also likely to be uncertain in the early stage of their relationship about whether their projected transactions will actually occur, whether they will be on time and whether they will meet their respective expectations. Continuity can also extend a supplier's knowledge of the context in which its offerings are used. This information will positively affect the supplier's problem-solving ability (Skarp 2006).

Continuity not only affects the relatedness between individual customers and suppliers. It also profoundly affects the character of the business landscape as a whole. When the norm is for companies to develop deep and long-lasting relationships with their main customers and suppliers, the business landscape is characterized by a pattern of inter-connected relationships. For each company in this pattern, their relatedness is directed towards relatively few counterparts, each of which is of considerable financial importance to it. For example, a Swedish survey of more than 100 companies showed that, on average, their top 10 suppliers accounted for about two thirds of their total purchases and their top 10 customers accounted for a similar proportion of their own sales (Håkansson 1989). If we look more closely at particular companies, we find a similar pattern. For example, 35 suppliers account for 80–85 % of Hewlett Packard's purchasing spend. One of the main reasons for its concentration on a small group of suppliers is Hewlett Packard's reliance on them for technology development (Carbone 2004a). The economic significance to companies of a small number of suppliers also seems to be increasing. For example, the importance of Motorola's top 25 suppliers increased from one third to half of its total purchases over a two-year period (Carbone 2004b). Sun Microsystems have gone from building 100 % of their systems themselves to building 10 % of these systems internally in a span of three years

---

[4]The importance of long-term relationships is a major theme in all IMP research; see Håkansson and Östberg (1975), Möller and Wilson (1985), Gadde and Mattsson (1987), Håkansson (1989), Helper and Levine (1992), Anderson et al. (1994), Holmlund (1997), Holmlund and Törnroos (1997), Keep et al. (1998), Ritter (1999), Möller and Halinen (2000), Zolkiewski (2004), Araujo et al. (2003), Gadde and Ford (2008) and Wilkinson (2008).

(Hannon 2004). These examples indicate that companies voluntarily increase the relatedness of the business landscape.

But why do companies increase their dependence on a few main counterparts? Firstly, empirical research shows that strong relatedness has important *structural* effects in the business landscape. If one of the involved companies is successful in some way then this inevitably affects others to which it is related. If a company is prospering then this is likely be positive for its suppliers and sub-suppliers. If it is in trouble, others are affected and they may well be forced into a common problem-solving process. Thus, relatedness also has important *dynamic* effects in the business landscape.

These structural and dynamic 'team effects' were early and continuing observations of IMP studies. The team effects are an outcome of relatedness and could not be achieved by any company individually. By working together over time, the people involved in a business relationship can develop a shared understanding of what is going on both inside and outside that relationship, facilitating stability and development. In the following sections, we see that team effects are important in the variety and motion of the business landscape. But let us first take a short look at how relatedness can be used to create benefits.

How to Create Benefit from Relatedness

The use of direct relatedness between companies is often rather obvious. For example, suppose a paper company needs to use a stronger pulp in its production process. Interaction between the paper company and its pulp producer leads to an increased input of electricity in the pulp process leading to a stronger mechanical treatment of the wood chips. This produces a stronger pulp, from which both the producer and user benefit.

However, there is also an indirect and less visible relatedness between companies which is still of great economic importance. An advertising agency wants to use the space they have bought in a newspaper for colour advertisements. But this means that the paper is exposed to more liquid in the printing process and consequently needs to be stronger. Through indirect interaction, this requirement is communicated from the advertising agency via the newsprint publisher and its paper supplier to the pulp producer. Again, the pulp producer works out a method of increasing the input of electricity and the mechanical processing of the wood chips and this produces a paper that can better resist the liquids it is exposed to in the printing process (Waluszewski 1989; Strömsten and Håkansson 2007).

Relatedness as an Organizing Force

The empirical observations made in the IMP setting underline that interaction and business relationships are of key importance in creating benefits from relatedness. Interaction, whether in an established relationship or a new one, where neither of the counterparts yet knows each other means that different business solutions are related to each other across company boundaries. Thus, any business solution consequently has an effect on related solutions. This relatedness has not only been observed in the IMP sphere, but was recognized almost a century ago by Marshall (1920: IV.VIII.2): 'any disorder in any part of a highly-developed organism will also affect other parts'.

Relatedness means that any greater or lesser change in the business landscape produces reactions. As soon as two companies adapt in relation to each other by changing a product, a process or an organizational routine then the effects are distributed to other related solutions of other producers, users and complementary firms. Thus, the effects of any new solution are distributed and meet other technological and organizational solutions which are already related to each other in specific ways. This 'friction' between different business solutions created by relatedness leads to the co-evolution of business solutions (Håkansson and Waluszewski 2002:189). The business solutions that are already embedded across company borders will force new developments to take particular directions. Hence, the main investments that have already been made by related businesses are provided with some basic protection from external change. This protection can have a profound effect on any attempt to embed new solutions or to create innovation in the business landscape. We discuss this issue further in Chapter 5.

Thus the empirical findings made in the IMP setting provide a very clear message about relatedness: Companies seem not only to accept relatedness, but voluntarily to engage in developing and using it systematically. Relatedness is a significant and unavoidable aspect of the business landscape that is used by companies to create benefits for themselves through the development of efficient and innovative relationships. However, we see in the following sections that using and managing relatedness is not easy.

Interaction as a Way of Dealing with Variety

Another important message from the first joint IMP project concerned variety within the business landscape. Business relationships are multidimensional. In order to benefit from a relationship and to achieve increased efficiency or innovation, the participants have to relate to each other over time and also in a number of dimensions. First, they have to find technological solutions that accord with their existing technologies and with those that are used in their other relationships. Secondly, they have to find administrative routines that are compatible with their overall organizational structure and with those of their counterparts. Thirdly, they have to find financial solutions that relate to their own economic logic and to that of their counterparts. This variety, 'where tiny initial differences produce enormously different effects' (Waldrop 1992:31), means that business relationships rarely involve only marketing and purchasing staff. Most often they raise issues that have to be addressed by those with knowledge of each others' production technologies, development possibilities, administration, logistics, finance, and so on.

How can mutual benefits be created despite this variety? The basic approach seems to involve a particular kind of development, involving adaptations made in relation to each other. The importance of mutual adaptations was one of the main findings of the first joint IMP project and also in a number of subsequent projects.[5] These studies underline that the adaptations made to cope with variety in the business landscape can take two rather different forms.

---

[5]The use of relationships to facilitate adaptation was reported and analysed in Ford (1980), Håkansson (1982), Turnbull and Valla (1986) and Hallén *et al.* (1991). More recently the role of adaptations has been investigated and discussed by, among others, Blankenburg-Holm *et al.* (1996), Brennan and Turnbull (1999), Brennan *et al.* (2003), Håkansson and Waluszewski, (2002), Gadde *et al.* (2002), Forbord (2003), Leek *et al.* (2003), Hjelmgren (2005), Baraldi and Strömsten (2006), Skarp (2006), and Harrison and Waluszewski, (2008).

Adaptations can be carried out in order to *decrease* the variety of material and non-material solutions, for example through development of standards and routines. Attempts to decrease variety can be made in order to make the working procedures across company borders smooth and efficient. For example, production processes and products can be standardized, in order to decrease the need for continuous adjustment and development, as was nicely exemplified in a study of construction companies (Bengtson and Håkansson 2007). Administrative work within business units can be adapted in relation to specific business partners, for example in terms of routines for price negotiation, meetings, ordering, deliveries, invoicing and payment. Such inter-organizational routines are typically developed through day-to-day experience, but may also be the outcome of more systematic investigations aimed at performance enhancement as a study of the supplier relationships to an international distributor exemplified (Bygballe 2005). Adaptations may also involve specific adjustments in relation to individual business partners, so that a particular customer or supplier is treated in a more or less unique way.

Adaptations can also be carried out in order to *increase* variety, through technological and organizational development (Håkansson and Waluszewski 2002:134). For example, a customer trying to develop its own uniqueness might encourage a supplier to increase its knowledge of a particular application of its technology and both parties may benefit from adaptations based on this enhanced understanding. Similarly, companies may develop new organizational solutions, such as systems for the exchange of information or services and the costs and benefits of these adaptations may also be shared with other counterparts. New physical solutions may be developed, such as new production processes and new products, and the costs and benefits of these may also be shared by other counterparts.

These adaptations, aimed at increasing or decreasing variety in order to create efficiency or innovation may take the form of major one-off measures or smaller successive steps over time. Major adaptations generally involve changes in both physical and organizational resources and are likely to require strategic assessments. Hence, major adaptations are often visible and easy to observe both internally and for outsiders. Successive adaptations are most often handled locally and are consequently much more difficult to observe. Because they are hidden, these adaptations may be underestimated from an outside perspective. However, over time these hidden struggles with variety may have significant results. Under a surface of apparent stability, the interacting parties may change substantially in terms of renewed production technologies, product design and organizational structures.

How to Create Benefit from Variety

Variety can be natural or man-made and both forms can be used as business opportunities. All business operations, even those traditionally regarded as simple and standardized, have a variety which can be utilized (Håkansson and Waluszewski 2002:197–8).

There is huge variety in nature. For example, the variety of the tree genome consists of about 30 000 genes. This provides a challenge to those companies related to the supply and use of forest-based products. The key question is how this variety can be utilized in the production of seeds and plants, in order to achieve increased growth, longer fibres and reduced lignin content, properties that are highly valued by both producers and users (Waluszewski 2006). For example, a supplier of exclusive magazine paper has used the variety created by the micro-climate where trees grow in order to fulfil the quality demands of fashion magazines such as *Vogue* and *Elle*. Both the producer and user of high-quality magazine paper can utilize the fact that pulp from trees grown in the bottom of valleys is easier to bleach than pulp from trees which have grown up on the hills.

Man-made variety, expressed in tangible, as well as intangible, ways is no less impressive and can be utilized in many ways. In the biotechnology example we used in Chapter 1, the equipment producer faced severe problems in developing a large enough customer base for a new molecule investigation product. In order to deal with this problem, it started a systematic search for variations among the users that had started to work with the product. This variety was used by the producer as a base for the development of new software and consumables and a growing number of users. The users could benefit from an increased number of standardized applications as well as specially adapted tangible and intangible varieties to support them.

Variety as a Source of Opportunities

The empirical observations made in the IMP setting underlines that although variety provides challenges, it is also an important source of opportunities in the business landscape. The existence and effects of a 'rich and bewildering diversity' (Basalla 1988:2) has also fascinated anthropologists, historians and technology historians for decades (Basalla 1988; Gudeman 2001). Although the economic effects of variety have generally been ignored in mainstream economic thinking, taking advantage of variety is, as Edith Penrose said, 'the mother of the heterogeneity assumption'.

> The fact that most resources can provide a variety of different services is of great importance for the productive economy of the firm. [...] Not only can the personnel of a firm render a heterogeneous variety of unique services, but also the material resources of the firm can be used in different ways, which means that they can provide different kinds of services.
>
> *Penrose 1959:75*

The IMP empirical findings emphasize the importance of interaction and business relationships in benefiting from variety. Ways of exploiting variety include attempts to decrease variety in order to reach efficiency and attempts to increase variety in order to create innovation. The existence of variety is an important opportunity in the business landscape. Variety is both an important starting point for all interaction and an end result of it.

Interaction as a Way of Dealing with Motion

The third striking observation in the first joint IMP project was that the business landscape is characterized by motion. An early but important indication that doing business involves living with motion was the limited use of formal agreements and contracts between companies.[6]

---

[6]The importance of trust is a central aspect in all relationship building; see, for example, Blau (1964), Macaulay (1963), Håkansson (1982), Hallén (1986), Young and Wilkinson (1989), Huemer (1998), Young (1992), Halinen and Törnroos (1998), Forsström (2005) and Johnsen and Ford (2008).

Our studies found that formalized procedures and contracts are common in regulating short-term business exchange, i.e. where the space for motion is limited. However, the greater the motion, the more difficult it is to use formal contracts in order to deal with unexpected but normal effects such as uncertainties, conflicts and crises. Informal mechanisms, such as trust and confidence were considered by managers to be more important than formal contracts in handling the unexpected effects of motion. These findings underline that social interaction and the development of trust is an important way to deal with motion in the business landscape.

But the role of social interaction and development of trust is not primarily to exclude the uncertainties created by motion, but rather to ensure that it is handled fruitfully. Skills in social exchange are critical for this; it is individuals who interpret different situations and act as agents within the relationship. Over time, individuals form attitudes, perceptions and social bonds on the basis of their experiences, memories and expectations. However, companies sometimes continue to interact with each other through a number of threatening conditions in the apparent absence of any trust at all. Their straightforward explanation is that in many cases there are only a very few suppliers and customers available so they simply have no choice other than to move along with their 'enemy'. Other reasons for continuing with a counterpart may be because they are tied to each other through earlier investments made in relation to each other. For example, in a study of customer–supplier relationships in the German automotive industry, Backhaus and Büschken (1999) observed 'the paradox of unsatisfying but stable relationships'. Despite the fact that companies were notoriously unhappy with their business partners these relationships continued, due to site-specific investments undertaken over time.

Dependency and power represent another crucial dimension of how the effect of motion can be dealt with through interaction and relationships. Sometimes the customer is in the more powerful position, sometimes the supplier. In most cases, however, the occurrence of mutual interdependences means that companies are able to actively influence their relationship in ways that are beneficial for both parties (Tuli et al. 2007). Moreover, the short-term exploitation of bargaining power may severely hamper the realization of long-term benefits (Kumar 1996; Rokkan and Haugland 2002). Therefore, an increasing reliance on long-term, high-involvement relationships influences the way power is used between companies. Rather than being applied co-ercively (Frazier and Antia 1995), the power that is exercised in high-involvement relationships is increasingly used in a constructive way (Gadde and Håkansson 2001). Or, as was concluded in Håkansson and Snehota (1995:8), 'companies appear to be tied together by apparently long-lasting, broad, relatively balanced and informal relationships'.

Although companies tend to develop a balanced way to deal with dependency and power in their business relationships, there will always be conflict. The parties in a relationship will have different interests and their operational and financial interdependence will be affected by motion in that relationship and across the business landscape. This means that conflict is an inherent feature of business relationships. Any conflict is multidimensional and will have functional as well as dysfunctional attributes. Conflict is an important ingredient in the promotion of innovation and hence is a dynamic force in business relationships (Gadde and Håkansson 1993). The functional aspect of conflict is important to consider in the development of social interaction and trust. A central aspect of trust is whether it allows the interacting parties to express their conflicting views in processes that might be valuable sources for development of new solutions.

Contrary to popular belief, high-involvement relationships also breed more conflicting views than arm's-length relationships, which are much more anonymous and silent. The more that two companies try to work together, the more conflicting issues will be discovered, as extensive case studies of single relationships reveal (e.g. Forsström 2005; Awaleh 2008). Thus, collaborating firms cannot escape conflict and the absence of conflict would be an indication that the two companies have made insufficient efforts to exploit the effect of motion. Furthermore, living with the effects of motion emphasizes the importance of teaching and learning processes in business relationships. People representing different company functions of both parties have to be involved in interaction in order to deal with the never-ending motion of a business relationship and its consequent conflicts, threats and uncertainties. Motion forces people to learn from and to teach each other. The ways that these processes of learning and teaching evolve over time is central both to relationship development and each company's prosperity (Gadde and Håkansson 2007).

The ability to benefit from motion is related to a company's ability to utilize another in its development. Many companies become very skilled in drawing on each other's resources in technological, organizational and commercial development, as indicated by the Hewlett Packard example above. Numerous studies illustrate how, over time, suppliers have emerged into crucial technological development resources for their customers manifested, for example, in joint development of tangible items, such as components and systems, and intangible services.[7]

Studies focusing on the customer side also highlight the important role of the user in development issues. Numerous studies have shown how critical in the 'innovation journey' are demanding and skilled customers. These customers have the deepest understanding of the use of a supplier's offering and can provide important insights about more and less possible development paths. Joining forces can result in benefits for companies by rationalizing their day-to-day operations and by larger changes in manufacturing, logistics and other functional areas. Customized production that adapts facilities to the requirements of a particular customer can benefit both parties. Joint efforts in coupling the manufacturing or service operations of two companies may lead to short-term productivity gains for them as well as long-term reorganization of larger-scale structures involving other companies. Coping with motion through joint development with specific counterparts is similar to dealing with variety. It does not reduce the motion but changes its direction and form. These changes may in turn create new types of interdependence. Business in practice is less about trying to get rid of interdependencies and more about trying to utilize

---

[7]The dynamic development aspect of interaction and relationships, especially in relation to technological development, has been discussed in, for example, Ford and Hardwick (1986), Håkansson (1987, 1989), Waluszewski (1989), Laage-Hellman (1989, 1997), Axelsson and Easton (1992), Henders (1992), Forsgren *et al.* (1992), Lundgren (1994), Ford and Thomas (1995), Dubois (1998), Tunisini (1997), Raesfeld (1997), Wynstra (1998), Araujo (1998), Buttle and Naude (2000), Walter *et al.* (2001), Holmen (2001), Axelsson and Wynstra (2002), Baraldi (2003), Bengtson (2003), Gressetvold (2004), Wedin (2001), Hulthén (2002), von Corswant (2003), Ritter and Gemünden (2003), Håkansson *et al.* (2004), Fredriksson and Gadde (2005), Jahre *et al.* (2006), Möller and Svahn (2006), Ford and Håkansson (2006a), Helander and Möller (2007), Vercauteren (2007), Johnsen and Ford (2007) and Harrison and Waluszewski (2008). The importance of supplier relationships has also been observed by other scholars, with supply management literature providing the most obvious example (see Wheelwright and Clark (1992) for an overview).

and create benefits from them over time. Increased interdependency through technological and organizational adaptations may be utilized by the directly involved parties together, by each of them and their other customers and suppliers, and by these customers and suppliers in their other relationships. Thus, motion that is coordinated by participants across the business landscape can, over time, result in both increased efficiency and innovativeness.

How to Create Benefits from Motion

Motion in the business landscape is a source of opportunities even when it may appear threatening. For example, the purchase of Atlantic salmon obviously involves doing business with companies representing fishermen working on the Atlantic sea; i.e. the Canadian, Norwegian and Icelandic fishing industries. However, Atlantic salmon is today one of the most important export products of producers located thousands of kilometres away, on Chile's coast to the Pacific Ocean. How did the established producers react to this movement that initially appears disadvantageous to them?

When the breeding of Atlantic salmon started in the late twentieth century, a dramatic shift occurred in the types and locations of companies that could provide this type of fish. Suddenly companies representing salmon breeders on the opposite side of the globe became an alternative source. Some Chilean companies showed that the Pacific Ocean was also a suitable location for the breeding of Atlantic salmon. A whole new industry emerged, involving everything from the development of feeding to the distribution of Atlantic salmon to customers in the US. From a traditional perspective, this motion could only provide severe challenges for the established producers of Atlantic salmon in Canada, Norway and Iceland. However, the possibilities that this motion provided by offering new combinations and development opportunities for established producers' technologies led to another view emerging. Some of the companies that were challenged initially by the Chilean development were able to benefit from it by providing feed, equipment, know-how and ownership (Huemer *et al.* 2009).

Motion in a Moving World

The importance of the everyday struggle to take advantage of the motion of the business landscape has not only been observed in the IMP setting, but was stressed more than 60 years ago (Hayek 1945). These 'constant small changes', the 'deliberate adjustments' and 'new dispositions made in the light of circumstances not known the day before' are those that 'economists are increasingly apt to forget about' (Hayek 1945:523–4). The motion of the business landscape affects all companies. Each company tries to develop in a direction that appears to be beneficial to it. But while it is struggling to move in that direction, others are also moving, sometimes in supportive directions and sometimes in directions that hinder. Any movement that a company makes is among companies and organizations that also are in motion. Thus, to be in business in a rainforest-like business landscape is to move in a world that is also in motion. This interconnected motion emphasizes the close connection that exists between the development of relationships and attempts to create benefits from motion in the economic landscape.

Interaction and the Larger Business Landscape

The experience we have presented from the last three or four decades of empirical research on interaction and business relationships is mainly drawn from studies concerned with those directly involved or closely related to particular relationships. Most of the research carried out in the IMP setting has focused on how single companies interact and handle relationships, and the benefits and drawbacks that this creates for those directly or closely involved in them. These studies have also contributed important findings on the basic structures and processes of the larger business landscape. A conclusion of the first joint IMP study about the effect of the interdependencies that arise from mutual adaptations in technology, organization and knowledge was that, 'the result of this for the whole market system is that it will tend to be rather stable. Instead of free moving units within a market we have companies with very little freedom to move' (Håkansson 1982:394).

However, the observation that companies had restricted freedom to move on the basis of their individual decision-making did not equate to the idea of a business landscape in stagnation – quite the contrary. But instead of companies moving in any direction they wished, or in a direction that political decision-makers wanted, it was our conclusion that the motion of the business landscape is shaped by interaction as 'the mechanism in the existing system' (Håkansson 1982:394). These observations led us to consider the connection between the existence of business relationships and the basic structure of the business landscape. During the last decade more systematic research on how interaction and business relationships are related to the larger business landscape has been carried out.[8]

This research has indicated, on one hand, that the ways that companies interact and relate to each other have important consequences for the business landscape, regardless of institutional characteristics such as the amount of state coordination and the extent of decentralized public and private decision-making (Whitley 1994, 2000); on the other hand, institutional characteristics, the people that are involved and the functions that they represent also influence the interaction processes going on between companies (Håkansson and Waluszewski 2007).

However, before we go deeper into these patterns, we will stop for a while and devote the next chapter to considering the content and function of the process that is fundamental for each company's life as well for the larger business landscape: interaction.

---

[8]See, for example, Hägg and Johanson (1982), Johanson and Mattsson (1986), Håkansson and Snehota (1989), Snehota (1990), Axelsson and Easton (1992), Anderson *et al.* (1994), Young and Wilkinson (1997), Håkansson and Ford (2002), Håkansson and Waluszewski (2002), Ford and Håkansson (2006b), Harrison and Waluszewski (2008), Waluszewski *et al.* (2009), Gadde and Håkansson (2008) and Håkansson *et al.* (2009b). Network studies by others within IMP include Ford (1990), Grabher (1993), Håkansson and Johanson (1993), Halinen and Törnroos (1998), Halinen *et al.* (1999), Möller and Rajala (2007), and Wilkinson (2008). Social network studies include Granovetter (1985), Powell *et al.* (1996), Uzzi (1997), Castells (1996), Podolny (1994, 2001) and Burt (2004).

ANALYSING BUSINESS INTERACTION

3

In this chapter, we take a deeper look into the nature of business interaction. We suggest that business interaction can be interpreted as a process that occurs *between* companies and which *changes* and *transforms* aspects of the resources and activities of the companies involved in it and the companies themselves. The substantive nature of business interaction gives it a particular existence in time and space, which in turn has important consequences both for the structure of the business landscape and processes within it. In this way, interaction is at the heart of business development.

The Idea of Business Interaction

The idea that interaction between individually significant companies is a primary characteristic of the business landscape is a basic observation in IMP studies. The implication of this observation is that it is not what happens *within* companies but what happens *between* them that constitutes the nature of business. The idea that interaction is central to economic life is not a surprise to any economic researcher. However, there is an important difference in how interaction is approached in theories influenced by mainstream economic thinking and the view that has emerged in the IMP setting. In approaches coloured by the traditional market assumptions, interaction is treated as a simple *mechanism* that facilitates exchange. This exchange is carried out by independent firms in processes which are instant and free from friction and which can be generalized (Wilk 1996). Thus, market theory has contributed the common understanding that exchange takes place within 'a system that not only regulates itself but also regulates ourselves, a process that shapes and forms people whose relationships with one another are circumscribed and reduced by the market' (Marglin 2008:2).

The empirical studies presented in Chapter 2 outline a view of interaction that is far from this simple mechanism. The basic difference is that the interaction that has been observed between companies in IMP studies has *substance*. The substance of interaction means that it leaves traces behind in several ways. Interaction always affects the resources and the people that are involved in it and the activities that they perform. Interaction always involves costs for each actor engaged in it. But even more important than the cost of interaction is that its benefits seem to outweigh the costs in enough cases to make it impossible for any company to disregard it. It is the costs and benefits for both parties involved that make interaction such a central economic process.

From an economic point of view, interaction can be interpreted as a multidimensional process between companies that change and transform aspects of the resources and activities of those companies and the companies themselves. For example, interaction may lead one of the companies to modify the product and service offering that it supplies to a counterpart whilst it may lead the counterpart to reorganize aspects of its operations in order to accommodate that offering. But interaction isn't just a dyadic process. All companies simultaneously interact with many others and interaction between any two companies affects their interactions with these others. This *network* of connections between interaction processes leads to modifications to activities, resources and companies across many organizational boundaries. The connections between interactions give the business landscape a shape that can be depicted by the rainforest metaphor.

This description implies that interaction isn't just one of the activities of a business. Instead it appears to be the major means through which companies systematically relate and combine their activities and resources with each other. Interaction affects all of the activities and resources that are spread widely in a network across the business landscape and all of the companies in the network. It is through interaction that the benefits of these resources and activities flow between and into the companies in the network. Being a ubiquitous process, interaction also forms a working structure for the network and provides an element of stability to how different companies relate to each other in the network. Being the means through which companies address their respective problems, interaction may also generate problems for companies and conflict between them. Interaction may lead to change and dynamism in companies as well as leading to inertia and stability. Interaction is driven by, and produces a world full of different and often conflicting interpretations of the meaning of the particular business behaviour of different actors. It is often difficult or impossible for those involved in this networked world to separate the individual actions and reactions of each actor or to trace their causes, effects and outcomes. In this way, interaction presents numerous problems for all people working in, affected by or trying to affect companies, as well as for those trying to research companies.

Thus there is a considerable gulf between the concept of more-or-less frictionless market exchange and the concept of business interaction. This gulf means that, in order to understand the business world, we have to investigate a number of the different dimensions of interaction as well as its outcomes and drivers. This investigation involves abandoning the market theory's assumption of interaction as a market mechanism and substituting an understanding of interaction as having a substance that changes both the human and the physical world. This investigation sheds a different light on traditional business research areas: purchasing, marketing, innovation, strategy and policy.

The next section of this chapter describes some of the characteristics and the range of what happens in interaction between companies. Then we try to conceptualize interaction in order to be able to use it as a framework for analysis. This means trying to develop a model that can help us to characterize, categorize and explain some aspects of business interaction. To do this, we relate interaction to two key dimensions of the interactive world (time and space) and seek to demonstrate that these dimensions have to be brought to centre stage in researching interaction.

Interaction Processes Between Companies

Interaction takes a wide variety of forms in the business landscape. Some interaction processes have a very long history; others are more spontaneous. Some relate to the continuous movement of large volumes of physical products, others to individual purchases. Some interaction processes include complicated technical problem-solving, whilst others are very simple. The differences are immense. We can try to portray some of this variety by starting with the category of interaction that we believe is the most central from an economic point of view: the processes that become so significant to the companies involved in them that they acquire some quasi-organizational features. In other words, the interaction process becomes a business relationship (Blois 1972). This type of interaction process can extend over many years and involve many resources, activities, individuals and different types of problem solving, as described in Chapter 2.

In a typical development, the production, delivery and use activities of the two companies may have been closely adapted to each other. Both physical and human resources may have been adapted and combined in specific ways. There may be hundreds of people from each side that have more or less frequent contact with a similar number of people on the other side. The two companies may have accomplished a number of projects together and there may be one or more continuing at any one time. The interaction may have become quite structured and specialized, involving specifically designed offerings and procedures by either or both of the companies. Some parts of the interaction, such as the coordination of deliveries or service events may have become standardized or automated. Other parts may relate to a particular problem of one or more of the participants; may be project-related and involve considerable change, uncertainty and resource investment for those involved; or may be restricted to a specific time period. Other parts of the interaction may involve detailed negotiation and development to integrate different activities and resources or even to subsume the actors into a joint organization or company. The interaction processes may be sufficiently critical to one or both of the companies from a volume, profit or technological perspective that they are closely monitored and systematically evaluated by them.

Each of these interaction processes is unique. They are very 'heavy' from an economic perspective, i.e. they involve significant investment, costs and revenues and they change substantial aspects of the activities and resources of each of the companies. A limited number of these interaction processes may dominate a particular company's operations and can realistically be said to have determined the nature of that company.

In contrast, the business world also contains many much more limited interaction processes that are either ad hoc or short term. Some of these processes may still be intense and involve important problem solving, or they may leave significant imprints on the companies concerned, such as large construction projects. Other interaction processes may be less significant or intense but may still be valuable. For example, they may involve a supplier and customers that buy from it only occasionally, but with whom the interaction can be standardized to reduce costs.

Another example of ad hoc interaction is the case of a supplier that is able to contribute a specific technical solution that is crucial for a particular customer at a particular point in time.

There are also a large number of interaction processes that involve more costs than benefits for one or both of the counterparts, despite (or because) of the efforts of those involved. Others may be in their early stages and may or may not develop into long-term and important interaction processes. It is often difficult to evaluate these developments and most companies have to engage in a large number of such interaction processes just to find the few that are worth developing further.

Because interaction is a process over time, it is likely that connections will develop between different interaction processes in which the two companies are involved. These connections may be more or less systematic and more or less conscious. But their outcome is that, through participating in a single interaction process with a single counterpart, a company becomes related to a set of many others about which they may know little or nothing. In this way, business interaction is a process in which ideas, solutions, technologies, problems and interdependencies are transferred across a network of companies.

Interaction between companies enables each to take advantage of an economic world characterized by continuous change, but with many potentially cooperative or at least mutually beneficial counterparts. Continuing interaction with others provides some kind of stability in a world of unpredictable outcomes and unknowable influencing factors. In this way, interaction is both a dynamic and a stabilizing force.

An Initial Conceptualization of Interaction

In order to develop an initial conceptualization of interaction, we use two very simple diagrams to describe the major difference between classical market exchange and business interaction. Market exchange (Figure 3.1) is based on the transfer between actors[1] of unchanging entities: products, services or money. Exchange can take place without there being any significant intervening process between the counterparts. An example of such exchange can be the auction systems that are used for some raw materials or that have become popular when using e-business. Thus we can interpret exchange as a 'mechanism' that connects the actors for the time of the exchange, but which does not have any content of its own. In general terms, this mechanism is discussed as the 'market mechanism'. The idea of this mechanism, leaving no trace on the involved parties, is a

Figure 3.1   Market exchange.

---

[1]The process of business interaction is observable between companies, operating units, functional areas or individuals. For the sake of simplicity, we refer to all of these as Actors. However, we devote Chapter 7 to a full discussion of the complexity of the idea of the business actor and its wider implications.

very powerful theoretical construct that works as an invisible hand. It assumes that the objects that are exchanged between the counterparts are fixed entities.

However, the typical situation that we have observed in the business landscape is rather more complex than this picture of market exchange suggests. There appears to be some sort of *transforming* process that occurs between business actors. From an analytical point of view, this process and its content may be separated from the two actors. The conceptualization in Figure 3.2 suggests that interaction is a process that occurs between companies over time and gains all its content from the two parties, but which develops in a way that is not fully controlled by either of the two, or the two together. It suggests that the interaction gains a life of its own. In this way and over time, interaction affects what each company contributes to and receives from the other and also affects the companies themselves and their activities and resources.

The spiral at the centre of Figure 3.2 is a representation of the process of interaction over time from which emerge products, services, deliveries, developments, adaptations and payments, each with particular characteristics and timing. The arrows *to* A and B *from* the spiral represent A's and B's interpretation, assessment and outcomes of what has emerged from the interaction and what has been their counterpart's intentions and approach to it. These interpretations relate each actor's assessment of its own approach to their problems and aspirations, to their resources and activities, and to their other interactions and their positions in the wider network.

Figure 3.2   Business interaction.

The form taken by the evolving outcomes of interaction is affected by how both parties act and react. The arrows *from* A and B *to* the spiral represent the approaches of A and B to the interaction between them. These approaches may be manifested in many forms, such as the 'quality' of a service delivery; the effort (or lack of it) that is devoted to a product adaptation; the stance taken in a negotiation; the timing of a payment or the commitment to a joint development. Some of these approaches to interaction may be in line with a clear intent or strategy by one or both of the companies. But some or all may be unconsidered or inconsistent, or they may be the result of inertia and simply continue the status quo. These approaches may be oriented towards a single episode of interaction. They may be unique to a particular counterpart or be part of an attempted common approach to a number of counterparts by either of the companies. It is likely that there will be inconsistency in the approach to interaction with a single counterpart, both between different individuals in a company and by that company over time.

The spiral indicates that interaction is an evolving process. It has no single identifiable outcome or end-point because each output is an input into the continuing process and will be interpreted differently by each counterpart involved in the interaction and by others. The effects of interaction may be both immediate and long-term; current interaction is affected by what has taken place previously and by the perceptions and expectations of future interaction held by the actors. Interaction is a process that takes place between actors and its content is always produced by more than one party. The two arrows in Figure 3.2 between each of the actors and the interaction show that the connection between the approach of each actor to the interaction between them and the outcomes of that interaction is beyond their individual intentions or control. Instead, the interaction between business actors is influenced by their approach or intentions and by the process of interaction itself. This creates an outcome for each actor which, in turn, is interpreted by both counterparts.

Each actor probably has a view of the activities and resources they wish to contribute and the approach they wish to take to the interaction. Each probably also has a view of what they want to gain from the interaction. But there is no reason to assume that the wishes of both actors will be the same. Each actor has some initial control of its own activities and resources. But the form that these activities and resources subsequently take and how they affect what are delivered to and received from the counterpart is affected by the way that they interact with those of the counterpart. Interaction is an intervening variable between the activities and resources of the two companies as they come together. Interaction changes both what is contributed and what is received by the two companies. Successive interaction over time can lead to outcomes that mean that the activities and resources of the companies and the companies themselves are transformed through interaction.

The process of interaction may occur routinely, without conscious effort or planning by any of the actors involved. In contrast, it may involve extensive planning, development, negotiation, bargaining or conflict. But irrespective of how the process develops, the interaction of resources, activities and actors means that no single actor is or could ever be in control of what emerges from its interactions or be independent in the world of business.

No company ever interacts with just one counterpart. The typical situation is that interaction occurs in several parallel continuous processes in which two actors are involved, as portrayed in Figure 3.3. Each actor is taking part in several of these processes in order to address their

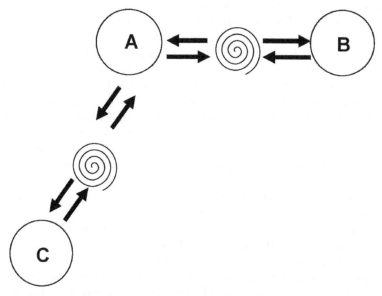

Figure 3.3   Business interaction among three counterparts.

individual problems and each dyadic interaction will be affected to a greater or lesser extent by those to which it is connected.

This description leads us to the following initial conceptualization of interaction:

> Interaction is an important economic process through which all of the aspects of business, including physical, financial and human resources, take their form, are changed and are transformed.

One important consequence of this conceptualization is that business interaction is not simply communication or negotiation, even if these may be important aspects of it. The greater the involvement of a company in a particular interaction, the greater will be the effects on its activities, on its resources and on the company itself. Interaction is a cumulative process over time. Hence, the characteristics of actors themselves and of their activities and resources are as much an outcome of interaction as they are an input to it. The actors, activities and resources of business are defined by interaction. This view of business interaction has been refined in the ARA model.

ARA Model

The Activity–Resource–Actor (ARA) model (Håkansson and Johanson 1992) provides a conceptual framework of the process and outcomes of interaction, based on empirical studies in the IMP research stream. The model suggests that the outcomes of an interaction process (or the content of a business relationship) can be described in terms of three layers between the counterparts: activity links, resource ties and actor bonds (Håkansson and Snehota 1995).

The model also suggests that the three layers are inter-connected: Each affects and is affected by the constellation of resources, pattern of activities and web of actors in the wider network.

- **Activity Layer:** This layer relates to the links between the activities of two actors. Various activities such as production, logistics, administration, deliveries and information handling may be more or less integrated and linked together. In this way, the two companies' activity structures can become more or less systematically and tightly linked (Richardson 1972; Dubois 1998; Torvatn 1996; Gadde and Ford 2008). The relative strength of specific activity links, or their absence, in a business relationship has been shown to have substantial economic effects on the actors involved.
- **Resource Layer:** This layer relates to how the two actors' resources may become more or less adapted and more or less mutually tied together as their interaction develops. Specific mutual adaptations may concern tangible resources such as physical items of plant or equipment, but may also include intangible resources such as knowledge. Resource ties arise as the two parties in a relationship confront and mutually adapt their resources over time (Hallén et al. 1991; Waluszewski 1989). Resource adaptations can make resource usage more efficient. But more importantly, the systematic combination of resources also underlies the development of new joint resource combinations in the process of innovation (Håkansson 1987, 1989; Biemans 1992; Lundgren 1994; Laage-Helman 1997; Holmen 2001; Håkansson and Waluszewski 2002, 2007).

- **Actor Layer:** Broadly speaking, this layer relates to the interpersonal links developed between individuals in the involved companies through interaction. This layer is built on the degree to which the individuals see, know and feel close to each other; how they trust, appreciate and influence each other and become mutually committed (Wilson and Jantrania 1994; Wilkinson and Young 1994; Huemer 1998). Bonds that arise between individuals may be more or less strong and will influence to varying extents what the individuals involved in a process perceive as possible and feasible directions for that interaction. Actor bonds are important for the 'learning' and 'teaching' of counterparts about opportunities and solutions, as pointed out in some of the studies of learning in relationships (Dahlquist 1998; Håkansson and Johanson 2001).

These three layers of buyer–seller relationships are not independent and there is important interplay between them: Activity links may limit or facilitate resource adaptations; resource ties may limit or favour the possibility of activity co-ordination and actor bonds may open up the possibility of developing activity links and resource ties.

The ARA model also takes into account another aspect of business relationships, namely that actor bonds, resource ties and activity links have consequences that go beyond the specific relationship in which they arise. They result from and have effects not only on what is happening between the actors but also within the actors themselves and within their other relationships. The content of a particular relationship can be used by the counterparts to affect their organization, use of resources and structuring of their activities. Conversely, the content of a relationship also reflects the characteristics of the two actors in the same dimensions. Additionally, third parties to a relationship may also take advantage of developments within that relationship. For example, other actors that have relationships with the two actors involved in a particular relationship as well as those in the broader network of businesses can affect and be affected by the ways in which the content of the particular relationship develops (Snehota 1990; Easton and Lundgren 1992; Blankenburg-Holm *et al.* 1996; Gadde and Snehota 2000; Pedersen *et al.* 2008). Every relationship is a more or less important connection in a number of webs of actors, constellations of resources and patterns of activities that stretch across many other businesses.

The role of interaction means that it is not enough to look inside a company for explanatory factors in the development of that company. If we want to understand the development of a particular business actor, or its activities, or its resources, or the economic logic between these elements, then we have to understand the interactions in which that actor, activities and resources are currently and have previously been involved. Our unit of analysis must be each specific process of interaction and how it occurs between particular combinations of companies. Similarly, an analysis of the development of business in an interactive world must centre on the evolution of specific interaction processes rather than on the apparent changes that occur in any single company. These company changes are more likely to be the outcome of those processes than the determining factor in them.

The substantive nature of business interaction also means that it will be analytically important when and where a particular episode of interaction takes place. The substance created by interaction will have a certain location in both the time and space dimensions. These variables form the themes for the next two sections.

Interaction and Time

Interaction in a business relationship is strongly connected with time. At a specific point in time the interaction between two companies will be dealing with particular issues. For example, the interaction may be related to the planned rationalization of day-to-day activities, to a specific problem that has arisen, or to attempts to exploit innovation opportunities. In early IMP research, these elements of interaction were considered as 'episodes' within more or less continuous interaction processes.

Each episode follows its own logic; it involves specific actors, it deals with particular aspects of business and takes place in a particular context. However, because each episode is part of a continuing interaction process it is affected also by a time-horizon that is much more extended. Both parties involved in an interaction episode link the current issues to their experience of previous interaction and the adaptations that have been made. This history will impact on their options, attitudes and behaviour. Both parties will also have expectations about their future interaction which will colour the current episode. Obviously, an actor's approach to interaction will be affected by its view of whether a counterpart is likely to be a central feature of its future or to decrease in importance over time. Any two companies are likely to make different interpretations of both history and future and this in turn leads to ambiguity in the assessment of the current episode. Figure 3.4 illustrates the impact of time on interaction.

The role of time and how sequential episodes of interaction are related to each other is a central issue in the conceptualization of interaction. A potential way to deal with this issue is to consider that episodes are linked together over time in a development process. Such a process comprises a lifecycle embracing a number of stages through which the relationship between the two actors is evolving. When this approach is applied, an episode is viewed as part of change processes that involve learning, adaptation, commitment and distance-reduction over time (Ford *et al.* 2003). This and similar stage models tend to infer that the development of relationships is a rather deterministic, unidirectional and linear process leading to 'an ever closer union'.

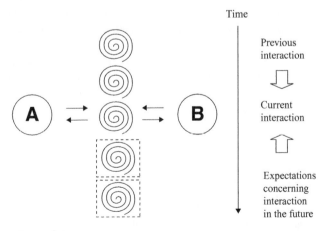

Figure 3.4 Interaction and time.

However, our empirical research has demonstrated a huge diversity between relationships that become inert after only a few months and those that continue to develop over many years (Ford and Rosson 1982).

Another perspective on time and interactions is to assume that business interaction produces a cumulative effect over time. Interaction is considered to be an investment process. Through the development of the business relationship and its associated interaction, companies are perceived to be investing in each other. An investment view indicates that a company's activities should be steered in ways that develop and capitalize on these investments (Johanson and Wootz 1986). The investment logic puts an emphasis on long-term relationships since initial costs can only be balanced by revenue generation over time. Such a long-term view of business processes is advocated also by researchers in other fields, because this perspective makes it possible to understand interaction effects that may only become apparent over an extended period of time.[2]

The approach taken in this book is to handle time as a combination of these two views: Business interaction is considered as a process consisting of episodes over time, where time is embedded into the process in several ways. Time comprises major opportunities as well as major problems for all of those involved in interaction, whether as participants or analysts. Time provides suitable conditions for learning, adaptations and relationship development. However, these increasing investments over time constrain the behaviour of companies in other respects. Time largely defines the nature of interaction as a process in which sequential episodes are related to each other.

In practice, it is difficult to delimit the connection between time and interaction. Thus, it is always difficult to characterize what defines a single episode of interaction or to find a neat way to identify its boundaries or when it starts or finishes. No matter when or where we observe interaction, what we see is the continuation of things from the past. This applies just as much to the interactions surrounding the start-up of an apparently entirely new company as it does to the interactions involved in the latest delivery of a continuously purchased component to a long-established customer. In both cases, it is difficult to trace the real starting point for these interaction processes. In the same way, it is never easy to identify the final completion or outcomes of interaction. Each interaction episode affects subsequent interactions between the participants and others. The problem of predicting the future direction of a series of interaction episodes is increased because each of those episodes can affect subsequent interaction in multiple directions.

A second problem in the analysis of interaction and its effects is that interaction is not evenly distributed over time. Interaction is likely to be 'lumpy', so that there are periods of more frequent and intense episodes of interaction, while other periods are characterized by less involvement between the parties. Moreover, there is huge variation in the intensity of interaction in different

---

[2]The importance of time and a long-term view on business have been recognized by many other researchers in related areas. Examples include those in the history of technology (Hughes 1983; Lindqvist 1984), history of science (Galison 1997; Collin and Pinch 1999), science in action (Latour 1984, 1996; Law 1994) and economic history (Rosenberg 1994; David 1985). Other researchers, such as Nelson and Winter (1982), Pasinetti (1981), Penrose (1959), Nonaka (1991), Zajac and Olsen (1993) and Kauffman (1995), work in areas where change, growth or evolution have been central questions. Organizational studies, such as March (1988) and Powell et al. (1996), deal, for example, with organizational learning.

episodes. Episodes are important to understand in themselves, but it is even more crucial to understand how single episodes are related to each other. Thus, the interdependence of episodes means that a single episode that is apparently marginal itself may have a huge impact on other episodes that are considered to be more important. Also, many of the preoccupations of managers are in trying to manage effectively *within* a particular episode. The way that an episode is handled may be important itself. But it may also have an impact either positive or negative on other episodes, whether orders, meetings, deliveries, developments or financial transfers. One way for analysts to cope with 'lumpy' interaction of varying intensity is to identify 'significant events' or 'critical incidents'. This approach takes historical information into consideration, but is characterized by boundary problems similar to those of episodes. More importantly, the idea of critical incidents may also involve assumptions about simplified causality of outcomes that are likely to be unwarranted in a situation of complex, multi-party interaction.

The interaction between two actors will evolve over time through experience and learning. But interaction at any one point in time is not pre-determined by what has happened before. Interaction will also be affected by the concerns or problems of the actors as they arise and by influences on them from their parallel interactions or those from elsewhere in the network.

Most interaction episodes, such as those comprised of individual deliveries, payments, communications, and so on, are relatively insignificant among many others. A series of episodes will, in many cases, simply be continuous and perceived as 'normal', such as a normal flow of orders, normal terms of payment, and normal deliveries. These episodes are part of everyday life for those involved in them and existing business relationships and routines play an important role in providing a basic structure to business activity. Most interaction episodes are not identifiable as critical incidents. Many are not significant in themselves at all, although they may have impact on other episodes that are critical.

An interaction episode is not just an island of significance in a sea of ordinariness, if for no other reason than that its significance is impossible to assess at the time. Interaction episodes, together with the various actors' interpretations of them, define the life of the individual or corporate actor. These episodes may be interrelated in an obvious or a confusing way but, taken together, they comprise the relationship between the participants. A single episode affects each of those involved in it differently and is also likely to be interpreted differently by each of them and by others around them.

Any interaction episode impacts on both participants, since it provides some newness into the relationship. Each single element of newness in an interaction episode simultaneously constrains and expands the opportunities for future interaction – in this relationship and in others. In fact, any kind of newness may have multiple sequential effects in many directions which will be discussed in the next section, about interaction and space. These multiple processes of restriction and expansion lead to two problems for both actors and analysts:

- It is difficult to make sense of the potential alternatives that become available through interaction. The actors involved may not be aware of how their options have been broadened or narrowed due to the outcome of previous episodes. Similarly, the multiplicity of simultaneous interactions, both between and outside of any dyad, makes it effectively impossible to construct distinct causal links between particular episodes and outcomes in interaction.

- It is difficult for the actor to anticipate and cope with the chain of events in the interaction process. Things happen in accordance with some logic of causality; however, owing to network complexity, this causality is not possible for an analyst or manager to interpret. Each actor has a view of a preferred or probable sequence and interacts with an eye to future interaction. These subjectively preferred or predicted sequences mean that a researcher seeking to explain interaction over time will have to be interested both in the changing views and perspectives of the actors and how activities and resources are actually evolving.

Interaction and Space

Interaction between two organizations takes place not only at a certain point in time, but also in a specific space. The narrow part of this space is represented by the two companies and the relationship between them. But it is important to widen the horizon of the space dimension, in the same way as with time. As indicated in Figure 3.5, both actors in a focal interaction are simultaneously involved in interaction with other business partners. The focal interaction affects and is affected by what is taking place in these other interaction episodes elsewhere and all these parallel episodes raise memories of interaction history and expectations of the future.

The space dimension is the second important characteristic of interaction.[3] It positions each single interaction in relation to others and provides the focal interaction with an extended context. The relative position in space of an interaction process provides the starting point for each episode and has consequences for what happens in it. This position in space affects the resources, such as knowledge, that are mobilized; the activities that are performed; and the intensity of the interaction among actors. Every single interaction episode affects the relative positions in the space dimension. What happens between two companies may bring them closer to some other interaction processes and more distant from others and thus change positions in

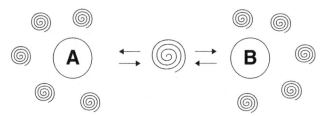

Figure 3.5 Interaction in space.

[3] As with time, space has been an important research topic within IMP and other research areas. Important contributions within IMP are Johanson and Mattsson (1985, 1992), Mattsson (1989), Törnroos (1991), Henders (1992) and Baraldi et al. (2006). A closely related area is research on internationalization, such as Johanson and Vahlne (1977, 2009), Welch and Welch (1996), Andersson et al. (1997), Kogut (2000), Forsgren et al. (2005) and Barkema and Drogendijk (2007). Another related research area that has been important is economic geography, with contributions from Rogers and Larsen (1984), Saxenian (1991, 1994), Storper (1997), Malmberg and Maskell (2002), Maskell et al. (1998) and Storper and Venables (2004).

the business landscape. In this way, all interaction affects how actors, resources and activities are positioned in relation to each other (Johanson and Mattsson 1992; Henders 1992). A consequence of this relativity in space is that we cannot explain what happens in a single interaction episode in isolation from others to which it is connected. Nor can we realistically describe an interaction process except as relative to the other interactions that may exist in parallel or in sequence with it.

Connections in the space dimension lead a particular interaction process to become more or less closely related to other interaction processes, in some of its aspects. For example, the efforts of two companies in joint technological development may lead to increasing interactions between one of them and some other contacts of its counterpart. These contacts may provide support technologies or may be potential applications for the technology. In this way, a company, through its counterpart, may become related to actors which were previously unknown to it. Interaction with a specific counterpart indirectly but systematically relates an actor to a whole set of other actors. Interaction is a way for ideas, solutions and technologies to travel across several actor boundaries. The facilitation of these connections is the classic role of distributors, such as wholesalers and export–import agents, and financial intermediaries, such as brokers.

The interacted business landscape is characterized by a large and increasing number of companies with a few highly specialized internal activities or resources that operate almost solely on the basis of their ability to access the activities and resources of others. Hence these companies operate on the basis of their ability to interact on behalf of counterparts. This role is illustrated in Figure 3.3. The position of Actor A between B and C gives it a special opportunity to act directly as an interacting mediator between two or more adjacent actors that do not interact with each other. This mediating effect in the space dimension may extend to other more distant interactions across the network and is commonly seen in the cases of, for example, search engines, import houses, trade organizations, financial service providers, information brokers and logistics service providers.

Interaction provides companies with opportunities to take advantage of an economic world that is characterized by diverse, distant and often unknown but potentially cooperative counterparts. Interaction creates stability in a landscape that is continuously in motion. This stability is necessary in a world that is full of influences that are unknowable by any individual actor. The space dimension of interaction relates a single company to particular others that, in turn, are related to others. In this way, every actor in a network has a specific position and its interactions and assets reflect this. In the short term, these positions provide the multiple and relative contexts for interaction. In the long term, continuing interactions successively change these positions and this structure.

The space dimension endows interaction with a couple of important consequences: Firstly, actors deploy their resources and develop their interdependencies differentially in space. This is because the resources of an actor will be valued differently in the different interactions in which they are employed. Heterogeneity in space applies to all aspects of business in an interactive context. Thus we cannot make sense of a single interaction process in isolation, but only in relation to others that exist in parallel or in sequence with it. Another important consequence of the space dimension is that there are no general rules enabling us to determine what interaction is appropriate in a particular situation. What is good at one point in space may not work in another. What is right for one company given its position in space may be wrong for another.

These problems of diagnosis multiply when the time dimension is taken into consideration: what is right in the short run may be wrong in the long run and what is perceived in a positive way by one counterpart may later be viewed negatively by the same actor.

The ability to analyse and cope with changes in the space dimension is a key issue for actors. These changes involve relative movement between one particular interaction process and others, implying that some of them become increasingly important while others lose significance. These effects follow from responses to two critical questions for those involved in analysing interaction:

- Who should a particular actor prioritize in its interactions and who should it not?
- Which resource or activity should be focused in a particular interaction and which should not?

The space dimension of interaction creates a dynamic structure in which an actor becomes related to particular others that, in turn, are also related to particular others. In this way, every actor has a specific position within the network through its interaction. In the short term, these positions provide the multiple and relative contexts for interaction. In the long term, continuing interactions successively change these positions and this structure. The space dimension has two major effects on the interaction:

- The evolution of an interaction process is not determined by the aims of either of those involved in it. Instead, it emerges from a combination of the relative intentions of the counterparts in the process and of the positions they have in the space. Hence, the direction and content of connected interaction processes influence the development.
- Interaction may lead a particular company to systematically adapt towards a specific counterpart, i.e. to get closer to it in one or several dimensions. This adaptation is manifested as changes in the companies' resources, activities and relative interdependence. But at the same time, the counterpart may be moving toward some other counterpart and that counterpart may also be moving in relation to others and so on. Companies evolve in relation to each other and the evolution is a case of movement within a moving world!

An interesting paradox of this moving world is that its structure and dynamics may be rooted in the development of rather mundane routines. A considerable proportion of an actor's interactions are likely to be more or less routine within its various relationships, involving such things as 'normal' deliveries, services, payments, terms of trade, and so on. This normal interaction may be contrasted with interaction that, consciously or unconsciously, changes the characteristics of a particular relationship or its connections with others. Routine interaction may lead to the development of formal or informal rules between specific companies and across the wider network, so that each knows what should be done and what they can get away with. It is common for the effects of these rules, both formal and informal, legal and illegal, to extend over many participants in a network and to produce a contrast between the relative interactions of 'insiders' and 'outsiders' (Kriesberg 1955; Palamountain 1955). Common examples of these rules include professional ethics, trade association rules, contract law and dispute resolution, common terms of trade, market sharing and price fixing.

Routines have an important effect on interaction. On one hand, routines create predictability and trust between counterparts and can increase the efficiency of a relationship by reducing many of the costs of handling that relationship, such as making deliveries, payments and other day-to-day activities. However routine interaction may also become 'institutionalized' so that ways of working are unquestioned and inefficiency and other problems can develop.

A final but important consequence of the time and space dimensions is that there is no such a thing as a new network. When we recognize the existence of a particular network for the first time, then we are simply isolating part of a pre-existing network that would have been visible if another space horizon had been applied. Similarly, neither a newly discovered actor nor a newly developed relationship creates a new network. Instead, new actors, new resources, new activities and new relationships always emerge from something that pre-exists them and there is always a history behind them. Each new actor (or relationship) is always related to others that already exist. A new actor, resource or activity will have some, but probably a rather limited, effect on the existing network. The new actor's interactions with others will be affected by and will affect the continuing and future interactions of those around it. A useful analogy here is of the introduction of a new product into a supermarket. The supermarket is not constructed around the new product, nor is there empty shelf-space waiting for it. Other existing products will have to move sideways to accommodate it, although the effect on each one may be small. Some of these existing products may benefit and others may lose because of the entry of the new product. In the same way, a new actor's interactions will affect those around it, but those interactions will be built upon the previous experiences of those involved in the interaction and those of the others around it. Each actor brings its own baggage from the past. This phenomenon is familiar from technological studies where 'path dependence' has been identified as a key issue but here that path dependence is considered within a wider context. Path dependence means that the analysis of interaction must always look behind current patterns of interaction to what has preceded them and framed their evolution.

A Model of the Interaction Process

The previous two sections have described how the variables of time and space are important in understanding business interaction. We can now build on these sections to develop a descriptive model of the interaction (Figure 3.6) in which these connections are made more specific.

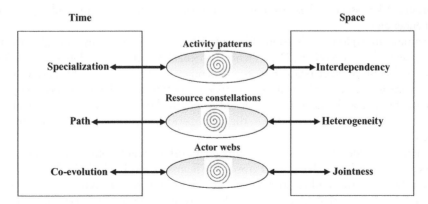

Figure 3.6   A model of business interaction.

The model is based on the idea of interaction as a multidimensional process involving the three layers that form the basis of the ARA model: the *activities* and *resources* of each of the counterparts in the relationship and the counterpart *actors* themselves, each with their associated hopes, expectations and approaches to each relationship. The model indicates that each of these three layers is involved in the interaction process and each is modified and shaped by it.

Each of the three layers of the interaction process combines particular aspects of the space dimension with particular aspects of the time dimension. One effect of this combining is that the structural dimension that positions interaction in space becomes a dynamic force for interaction and the time related processes become anchored in that structure. But more importantly, this combination means that all the structural features as well as the time related processes become integrated into business interaction as influential business factors or parameters. Interaction occurs within and between each layer. Each layer of interaction takes place in the context of wider *activity patterns*, *resource constellations* and *actor webs*.

Activities and Space

An important feature of activities in an interacted world is that they are *interdependent*. The activities may take place in different geographical locations; they may arise from different problems; be for specific or wide application; be more or less extensive or involve different types of costs and benefits. Even if some of these activities may appear to be independent, they are always connected to others in a variety of ways. Interdependence of activities is both a pre-existing structure of interaction and an outcome of interaction and the development of business relationships. Interdependence both affects and is affected by interaction.

The interdependence of activities is an unavoidable consequence of the distribution of activities across the business landscape which in turn is directly related to interaction. This distribution of activities develops over time in order to gain the benefits of division of labour. These interdependencies are both important and complex and interaction will be strongly influenced by the possibilities and problems that arise from them. But the complexity of interdependencies may mean that actors are not aware of the existence of all of them, nor may they appreciate their implications. A key aspect of business interaction is the building, managing and exploitation of interdependencies.

Companies can exploit the division of labour in a more extensive way through seeking and accepting dependence on others. Dependence also enables them to develop and exploit other activities and achieve efficiencies. But interdependencies also increase the degree to which companies are directed toward specific counterparts over time as well as the relative importance of their interaction with them. Companies also seek to build the dependence of others on themselves in order to achieve stability in their interactions over time with consequent gains in efficiencies.

The interdependencies in an actor's existing relationships simultaneously empower and constrain its ability to achieve change and growth (Håkansson and Ford 2002). Thus, a company relying on the activities of others increases its freedom to invest its own resources in more productive activities within that relationship or elsewhere and provide the basis for it to develop in new directions. But at the same time, an actor's dependence in its existing relationships restricts its freedom to act in the directions of its own choice and requires it to invest in interaction within its existing relationships.

Activities and Time

In a continuously changing world, each single activity and the activity patterns of which it forms part evolve over time. The model refers to this evolution as a process of *specialization*. The activity pattern involving several actors are likely to become increasingly specialized as individual actors build specialization into their activities relative to others as their interaction develops. Specialization involves adjustments and adaptations by each actor in their activities in order to find solutions that are acceptable for different counterparts and for their own cost and revenue criteria. Many of these adjustments are step-wise changes in order to successively reduce costs in daily business. The costs and benefits of these specializations are continuously assessed by the involved companies as their relationships develop, their interdependence grows and their activity base evolves. The adjustments necessary for specialization involve significant costs for the actors, but are critical for the development of particular relationships or for combinations of relationships. Specialization is neither a simple nor an uncontroversial process. The adjustment of a single activity may affect (either positively or negatively) many other activities across different activity patterns. Adjustments in one interaction process in order to increase specialization in one activity pattern frequently lead to problems in another pattern.

Resources and Space

An important feature of the resources in the interactive landscape is their *heterogeneity*. A resource that is homogeneous would be expected to have the same value irrespective of which other resources it is combined with. But interaction provides the possibility to exploit heterogeneity. Interaction enables the usefulness and value of a single resource to be increased through finding better ways to combine it with other resources. In other words, the location of a resource in relation to other resources can be changed in a systematic way to affect its value. Interaction enables resource heterogeneity to be exploited as a means of value creation across company boundaries. Conversely, a company can increase the value of a single heterogeneous resource such as a product or a machine through interaction with one or more counterparts. Thus, interaction can 'move' the location of resources towards or away from each other in a number of aspects of the space dimension: geographic distance, problem orientation, technology, and so on. This movement is not at all random as we see in the next section.

Resources and Time

The development of a single resource or a combination of resources; physical, human or financial into particular abilities or technologies often follows an identifiable *path* over time. These paths have been observed in a number of studies of technological development and have been referred to as 'path dependency'. The development of a resource along a path is strongly affected by the interaction which can be observed in the use of that resource and in its combination with others in an evolving resource constellation. This path often involves the use of particular resources in different applications in sequence. For example, the technological resource of electronic control was, over time, applied in different applications, such as petrol pumps, taxi meters, domestic appliances and vehicle engines, by combining it in different resource constellations with other technological as well as physical, financial and human resources.

The development of single resources or constellations of resources over time, whether depicted as path dependencies, technology trajectories or lifecycles seems to be based on two basic features of resources: the resource's potential to be developed, which is only partly known at any one time, and how this potential is related to other resources. For both these reasons, the path followed by a particular resource is highly dependent on the interaction that takes place where multiple problems are addressed in constellations with other multiple resources accessed by multiple actors. The evolving resource path is also affected by changes in the specialization of activity patterns that are difficult to reverse. For example, when resources are committed to a relationship with a particular counterpart, it takes that resource down a path within a particular constellation that may involve significant investment by the company in development activities. Conversely, a decision not to invest in a particular resource may well be difficult or impossible to reverse at a later time after others have made similar investments. Resource decisions may effectively be once-and-for-all decisions.

Actors and Space

The space dimension has similar implications for the actor layer and these are based on the differences between actors in their various interactions. Each actor acquires a particular identity and features through its interactions with particular counterparts. An actor is not a self-contained entity and it cannot exist in isolation. An actor is always linked to others and is formed by its interaction with those others. We refer to this linking as *jointness*. Jointness is a way of characterizing the specific relationship between any two actors in relation to all others. Jointness is a central feature of an economic world where interaction is a key attribute and it has a number of aspects.

Even if interaction appears to take place between only two actors, the intentions of those actors, the content of their interaction and its outcomes will not be limited just to them. Any actor interacting with a specific counterpart depends on the intentions, resources and activities of all the others with which it also interacts. Clearly, any company that supplies another does so by using its own activities and resources. But it also uses the activities and resources of its own suppliers as well as those of the customer and its other customers. In this way, all business interaction has important 'joint' content. Thus a business company cannot be adequately described in terms of its own internal activities and resources. A company is more accurately described as a 'node' at which the activities and resources of others come together with its own, through its interactions with those others.

Jointness can be manifested in various organizational forms such as when actors take part in joint technological development, joint logistics or the development of joint sales or procurement. We can identify jointness in the design of resources or in the performance of activities as well as in the holding of similar ideas about the context of interaction. An important effect of jointness is that it limits the autonomy of an actor. Jointness reduces the importance of an actor's own intentions in determining the direction of its development and increases the importance of the combined intentions of interacting parties in their development.

The underlying logic of jointness is that the space dimension in interaction makes it both possible and necessary to create joint positive results with others. In the long run, any company in an interactive world is dependent on the success of its counterparts. The interaction between two actors is related to interactions with others and it may be influenced, mediated or facilitated by these others. This is seen clearly in the context of a 'distribution channel' or 'supply chain'. In both of these cases, it is the interdependencies of activities and interaction between the actors, rather than the plans or control of any one of them that jointly allow goods and services to flow between them.

The concept of jointness fundamentally questions the meaningfulness of analysing a single business alone or a single action in itself. We cannot separate and isolate any action by an actor from the preceding and following actions of counterparts. All are part of the continuing interaction between multiple actors. An actor exists in the context of its network and is defined by its relationships and through its interactions in that network. An actor's interactions effectively determine its characteristics, its capabilities, its scope, its freedoms, its obligations and its restrictions. Each actor and each interaction will depend on and be based on the actor's own resources and those of others who stand with it, behind it and against it.

Actors and Time

Actors evolve in an interactive landscape. Business companies successively change in terms of the activities they perform, the resources they control and their jointness in relation to important counterparts. The existence of jointness means that the evolution of each single actor is not an individual process but one that takes place interactively with others. We call this *co-evolution*: An actor seeking to cope with its own problems or opportunities has to do so by coping with the problems of its counterparts. Co-evolution does not infer that any two businesses necessarily evolve by becoming closer or more similar to each other or that relationships have a deterministic life leading to ever greater mutuality. Instead, co-evolution is a multidimensional process that takes place within two or more actors in parallel as each seeks to relate its own problems, resources and activities to those of others. In this way, co-evolution can actually lead actors to become more different from each other.

Conclusion

The model of business interaction that we have presented is focused on some important aspects of interaction. First, three layers of the interaction process are identified: Interaction links activities performed by different actors to each other and creates activity patterns that evolve over time. Interaction also ties resources owned or controlled by different actors to each other, creating resource constellations that develop over time. Finally, interaction bonds actors to each other into larger actor webs that also change over time. Each layer is interactively defined, both in itself and in its connections to the other two. Thus each layer can only be understood in terms of the others, from both an analytical and a managerial perspective.

Secondly, the model identifies the role of interaction in relating structural or space-related features to time-related processes. In this way, interaction has an organizing effect on economic activity. The interaction is decentralized and involves all actors together in shaping and changing basic economic conditions.

The model indicates that business interaction is a major force both in creating and exploiting business conditions. Interaction affects all of the activities performed in the network, how those activities link to each other as well as how these links develop over time into specialized activity patterns. Interaction also affects all of the resources that are used and produced through business activities and how they combine over time. Interaction also affects actors as it relates and embeds them in each other creating an evolving actor web which also affects the way that activities are linked and resources are tied.

This way of conceptualizing interaction as the central business process leads to some interesting consequences. It indicates the importance of interaction in knowledge creation. Continuing interaction is an important source of knowledge for every actor and learning and teaching are two important sub-processes within it. Interacting actors produce something together that is embedded with history and future expectations. All actors are able to benefit from what has happened previously in the network as well as what they learn from counterparts. Previously created knowledge and continuous learning in interaction can be incorporated in the design, planning or forecasting of future interaction. Memories of interaction with others can be used as a device for prediction and as a planning tool. Each actor can also bring experiences from their other interaction processes as input into interactive development of technologies and operations.

Secondly, this way of conceptualizing interaction suggests that it plays a key role in the 'construction' of value and thereby the way companies economize. The substance of interaction has a key role in affecting activities and resources and directly influences their economic outcome. Thus, interaction is a way for actors to co-create the physical and economic context of business. Of course, this development may lead to negative as well as positive outcomes for companies by leading them into uneconomic activities or unproductive investments.

Thirdly, this way of conceptualizing interaction also gives managers the possibility of creating at least some stability and predictability in their lives. We can illustrate this with the example of 'supply management'. Through systematic interaction with suppliers, a customer can successively increase the specialization of the activities performed by itself and its own suppliers, and also by other related companies such as the suppliers to its suppliers and the other customers of its suppliers. Interaction can also be used to find new and better ways to combine the resources used by involved companies. In this way, interaction can successively decrease costs or increase revenues.

DOING BUSINESS: EXPLOITING TIME AND SPACE

4

We suggested in Chapter 3 that interaction is the dominant feature of the business landscape and that the most important business processes are not those within companies but those between companies. If this is the case, then each single company is faced with some particular challenges: It has to survive, develop and prosper in a business landscape where it is in control of only a tiny proportion of the processes on which it depends. Other processes, taking place at other times and elsewhere in space, influence its inputs and determine the value of its outputs.

What can a single company do when its structure and the processes in which it is involved are influenced to such a large extent by external structures and processes? The suggestion discussed in this chapter is that even in these circumstances an individual firm can still take advantage of time and space. The discussion in this chapter will be illustrated by examples from a larger case study (Håkansson and Waluszewski 2002) of how a number of different companies and organizations were suddenly made to face an environmental issue by non-governmental organizations (NGOs), by environmentally concerned governments and later by their customers. We trace the way in which some companies that were connected to the evolving situation in different ways (as sub-suppliers, suppliers, producers and users) tried to turn the disadvantage of being involved in the environmental debate to an advantage. Each of these companies was dragged into the environmental debate by others. However, as we see, it was through interaction with others that each, in their own way, built on their established investments in order to turn disadvantage into new business opportunities. But before we look more closely at these examples of how time and space can be used, let us consider some general features of these processes.

Chapter 3 suggested that the process of interaction is the manifestation of companies' attempts to take advantage of what happens over time and in space. There are at least three different ways in which interaction can be used to create and develop human and physical resources by exploiting time: it can initiate new processes and give them a particular direction over time; it can revisit processes that took place at an earlier time; and it can connect contemporaneous processes. By initiating and connecting time-specific processes, interaction produces effects that are direct and indirect, planned and unplanned.

There are also at least three different ways that space can be exploited through interaction: in geographical space, it can connect separate resources and activities; in technological space, it can connect capital investments such as technological facilities; and, in knowledge space, it can connect different bodies of knowledge.

'Normality' in traditional economic theory is a business landscape populated by autonomous actors that exchange homogeneous or totally knowable resources. If this really was the normal situation, then the use of time and space specificities would be rare exceptions from the normal way in which economic activities are organized. But empirical observation shows the important role in business life of the systematic exploitation of time and space. This presents a challenge to some of the basic assumptions of traditional economic thinking that was already argued more than half a century ago, by Nobel laureate Friedrich Hayek. He underlined the importance of 'the knowledge of the particular circumstances of time and place' (Hayek 1945:522). Specific knowledge about material and immaterial resources or 'goods and services' is created at different times and in different spaces depending on the way that this knowledge is used in relation to other resources. Or, as Hayek (1945:524) puts it:

> The continuous flow of goods and services is maintained by constant deliberate adjustments, by new dispositions made every day in the light of circumstances not known the day before, by B stepping in at once when A fails to deliver.

Hayek's message is that we need to take seriously the experiences of the 'practical businessmen' about those 'constant small changes which make up the whole economic picture', but which 'economists are increasingly apt to forget about' (Hayek 1945:H.15). Once we start to rely on these practical experiences then the business landscape takes on the form of 'a constantly evolving market process rather than the movement towards an optimal equilibrium'. In the next section, we take a closer look at some 'practical experiences' of companies and organizations trying through interaction to increase their knowledge about time and space and to utilize this in their business.

Taking Advantage of Development over Time

To exploit movement over time involves moving in relation to others, at least for a company that wants to survive and prosper. To move in a way that is beneficial for some of a company's main suppliers and customers is a prerequisite for its prosperity. This would be easy to achieve if all suppliers and all customers were moving in the same direction. But uniformity of motion is rarely, if ever, the case. So how to exploit development over time becomes a challenging issue. Addressing this issue involves considering a number of questions: How are key suppliers and customers moving? What are the movements of related companies and organizations, representing alternative technological, organizational and commercial approaches, legislative or environmental pressures? The answers to these questions demonstrate that a company and those around it are rarely moving along smooth, parallel paths. But still, the individual company has to find out a way to take advantage of these often contradictory but related movements over time.

Interaction and the establishment of stable business relationships seem to comprise an economically critical means of directing, organizing and exploiting development over time. Interaction provides the means to take advantage of different effects of development over time: linear, cyclical and other non-linear changes. In this section, we take a closer look at each of these types of time-related effects.

Dealing with Linear Change

Interaction over time, often manifested in long-lasting business relationships, is a way to take advantage of *linear* changes in the business landscape. Step by step, each counterpart gains a deeper understanding of its own, its counterparts' and related counterparts' role in the business process. The parties learn from each other about the direct process in which they are involved as well as other processes that are related to it. Thus, interaction over time is a way to exploit each party's own history and their common history. From an economic perspective, interaction may be seen as an investment process, where linear effects can occur in both the short and the long run. Let us take a look at how these linear effects appear in the first part of our empirical illustration.

In the late 1980s, Greenpeace carried out a spectacular action in order to shed light on an identified environmental problem related to the supply and use of paper-based products. Greenpeace members dumped 1.5 tonnes of dead fish at the entrance to the office building of Sweden's largest producer of chlorine-bleached pulp, Södra Cell. The action was very visible, not only to Södra Cell: as intended, it attracted considerable media attention and thus became known to both the general public and related businesses.

Greenpeace's message was that the industry's use of chlorine to produce white, strong paper resulted in the discharge of chlorinated waste water, which is very harmful to natural life. Chlorine had been an established ingredient in the bleaching process for at least four decades and was regarded as a necessary treatment for pulp used in paper products, from exclusive magazines, catalogues and advertisements to hygiene products. This did not bother Greenpeace and their message to the industry was clear-cut: Stop using chlorine. The message to the consumer was also clear-cut: If the industry cannot use chlorine-free bleaching processes, then choose non-bleached products.

Behind this loud campaign was another learning process, quieter and more hidden. When Greenpeace identified two main environmental threats related to the supply and use of paper-based products (the discharge of chlorinated waste water from pulp-bleaching mills and the surplus waste caused by increased use of packaging and other paper materials), the Pulp and Paper Campaign was organized by Greenpeace activists across the world. They were trying to learn as much as possible about the development of processes and products which were less environmentally harmful than the established ones. They were interested in new solutions under development within universities, research institutes and companies. Gradually, this interaction with knowledge producers all over the world created a picture of the technological possibilities that were within reach. Greenpeace's gradually emerging picture of environmental opportunities proved to be valuable not only for their own planning of public actions, but also for one of the world's largest producers of catalogues.

IKEA produces more than 100 million catalogues and supplements annually and is a very prominent user of chlorine-bleached catalogue paper.[1] IKEA is a very public company with a

---

[1] IKEA was using 'lightweight coated' (LWC) paper. This consists of a very thin base paper which is coated with clay at an average speed of 1500 metres per minute in order to make it extra bright and glossy.

deliberate policy of staying 'on the customer's side' and it is very vulnerable to the effects of all kinds of environmental issues related to its activities. As the head of the IKEA catalogue group put it, 'We must consider the fact that IKEA is a very public and successful company – the ideal target for journalists and/or "green" organizations.' When the environmental debate became directed to damage caused by the production and use of paper products, IKEA tried to investigate the kinds of environmentally acceptable solutions their suppliers could provide. 'When the public debate focuses on cutting down trees, or on waste disposal problems, or maybe in the near future on the air pollution created by our printers, it is closer at hand for the public to think of IKEA, being much more present in the minds of the people than the companies in the paper and printing industry.'

When IKEA's search for environmentally acceptable catalogue paper became known to Greenpeace, the leader of the Pulp and Paper Campaign contacted the management of IKEA's catalogue group. Both organizations were curious about the other's view on environmental threats and opportunities and this became the starting point for informal discussions. Greenpeace learned about the established methods of pulp and paper production in which IKEA was involved. IKEA learned about development projects for the reduction of chlorine as a bleaching chemical and the increased use of recycled waste paper, or secondary fibre, that Greenpeace had knowledge about. In practice, this meant that IKEA learned not only about development opportunities among their direct suppliers of magazine papers, but also about what was going on among related suppliers, i.e. pulp producers, producers of bleaching chemicals and equipment and producers of de-inking equipment (de-inking is a process in which ink is washed out to make pulp bright enough to use). With this knowledge in hand, IKEA started to work out a new environmental policy for catalogue paper, which was *not* based on the paper that their suppliers told them was possible, but on what a whole network of knowledge developers had within reach. Greenpeace on the other hand, saw the interaction with IKEA as offering the possibility to get one of the world's most public companies to take a similar standpoint to itself.

This empirical illustration is typical of how interaction is used by companies and organizations over time to take advantage of linear effects. Through their interaction experiences, several companies and organizations are related to each other systematically and each company tries to build on specific others in order to create both cumulative and integrating effects. All types of knowledge, including the tacit knowledge of others, may be mobilized in this way, not just at one moment in time but again and again as that knowledge develops. The process does not include all of the experiences or knowledge of others. Instead, only specific experiences of others are used and these specific experiences are different for each involved company and organization. Each company builds on specific others and each company creates its own 'truth', or its own way to approach technologies and commercial solutions. One consequence of these specific processes is that there are different linear effects but they are also combined with each other over the long term.

Dealing with Cyclical Change

Interaction over time is also a way to deal with *cyclical* changes. These cyclical changes can emerge for a number of different reasons. First, there are natural or socially created variations in the supply and use of things, over weeks, months, and seasons. Secondly, there are cyclical changes in how technologies develop from new to well established and mature. Thirdly, there are cyclical changes in the economy in a region, a country or across the world. Some examples of how interaction is used to deal with these types of cyclical changes are given in the next instalment of our empirical illustration.

IKEA purchases about 50 000 tonnes of magazine paper per annum for its main catalogue. In combination with its involvement in paper and printing technology, this makes it a very prominent magazine-paper customer. But not all suppliers dreamed of having IKEA's catalogue group as a customer. SCA is one of Sweden's largest producers of paper products. It took its first step into the production of magazine and catalogue paper in the early 1990s,[2] but IKEA was not even on its list of its preferred customers for a number of reasons. First, IKEA demands a large volume of paper concentrated on only a few occasions each year, when the main catalogue and some thinner seasonal catalogues are printed. SCA saw this as far too difficult a schedule to achieve economically. Secondly, SCA had invested about 240 million Euro in the latest magazine paper technology. But despite its decades of experiences of producing simpler qualities such as newsprint, SCA was a beginner in the field of high-quality magazine paper. The new investment meant that SCA had to master a new production technology. Furthermore, SCA had to master the technological demands of new kinds of users, the publishers and printers of fashion magazines, such as Vogue and Elle; the producers of catalogues such as IKEA's and the producers of advertisements are of different kinds. What these users had in common, besides the traditional demand for strength and 'run-ability' of the paper in the printing machines was a demand for enhanced brightness and high-quality picture reproduction in the end product.

In order to overcome these obstacles, SCA favoured a special type of customer: publishers that had their own printing facilities, produced frequent publications and were financially stable. By interacting with this type of customer, SCA was able to maintain a stable production level throughout the year, to ensure viability during economic down-turns (when compared to printers that specialize in advertisements) and, finally, to learn from and solve technological problems directly with publishers' own printing staff.

This shows how companies interact to avoid too large cyclical changes. Entering a new type of production and consequently a new user situation was challenging enough for SCA. But dealing with cyclical changes was best avoided until the company became more experienced in this new area. Thus, by interacting with middle-sized, stable customers, SCA could both avoid cyclical changes and learn and adapt to its new business situation. This is just one example of how cyclical changes can be handled through interaction. Another example is the way in which companies with highly seasonal sales try to find other counterparts which have an opposite seasonal variation.

Interaction can be used to both influence and take advantage of cyclical effects. This can be achieved either by choosing to interact with particular counterparts or by interacting over time with one counterpart. These approaches are particularly important for companies involved in areas with high seasonal variation, such as agri- and aqua-culture, but also in communication and transportation.

---

[2]SCA's newsprint mill, Ortviken, located in Sundsvall in northern Sweden, totally modernized to become a production facility for LWC magazine paper.

Dealing with Other Non-Linear Change

Interaction over time is a way to create co-evolution among other *non-linear* development paths. Through interaction, the parties involved in a particular technological or organizational development can relate processes that hitherto had been separate. The parties involved can utilize each other's engagement in other contemporaneous processes and connect these parallel changes with earlier development processes. Let us continue with the empirical illustration.

SCA was one of Sweden's largest forest owners, but also used re-cycled paper to produce products for which brightness was required, such as packaging materials. SCA's ships left Sweden with finished packaging materials and returned with waste paper from Europe that was broken down and used in the production of new packaging materials, in combination with fresh pulp.

Many paper producers are located in areas with a restricted supply of fresh wood fibre, such as southern Sweden, the European continent and the UK. The collection and de-inking of old newspapers and magazines had long been an important ingredient for these producers in the production of basic printing paper, such as newsprint. However, although secondary fibre was an important complement to fresh wood fibre, it was also considered to be of 'second quality', especially by producers and users of more exclusive magazine paper. Consequently, the use of secondary fibre tended to be a 'hidden input' or restricted to more 'simple' paper products, such as newsprint and packaging material, that do not have the same requirement for brightness as, for example, magazines, catalogues and advertising products.

The ability to recycle old newspapers and magazines became connected with the environmental issue of how to reduce the waste mountain. This changed the status of this source of fibre from 'secondary' to 'green'. Governmental and non-governmental groups pressed for an increase in the collection and use of secondary fibre. A bill put forward by the German Minister of the Environment in the early 1990s proposed that all packaging (and, later, all newsprint and magazines) sold in Germany should be recycled into new materials and this became the starting point for increased European collection of post-consumer waste paper. Large European non-governmental environmental groups, with Greenpeace and Friends of the Earth at the forefront, campaigned for an increase in the collection and use of secondary fibre. Paper-using companies, particularly those close to the final consumer, such as Coca Cola, McDonalds and SAS, became sensitive to the environmental debate and started to communicate that their printing and packaging material were based on secondary fibre.

This change in attitudes had a considerable effect on companies related to the collection, de-inking and use of secondary fibre. What previously had been necessary to hide suddenly became valuable to publicize! SCA for example, started to announce their use of secondary fibre in packaging material as a part of their environmental responsibility. Many users of paper materials started to print 'based on recycled fibre' on their packages, advertising materials etc. A consultancy engaged in the development of de-inking technology characterized this development as follows: 'Before the environmental debate, when representatives of publishers and printers visited a production plant with a de-inking facility, this was passed as quickly as possible. But since secondary fibre became "green", the de-inking plant is shown first.' As well as communicating what they were doing, companies engaged in the production or use of products based on secondary fibre started to interact with established and new types of user about the possibilities of increasing the use of re-cycled materials in established and new applications.

This shows how the use of resources is dynamic and how closely this dynamism is related to interaction. A feature of a resource that had previously been seen as an indicator of low quality, suddenly became something positive by being connected to other development processes. The resource did not change in itself, but how it was perceived by the interacting parties changed. Interaction provides the possibility of taking advantage of this kind of non-linear effect and creating new resource combinations based on how specific resources are considered. In this way, interaction is both a reason and a way to deal with and take advantage of such non-linear surprises.

So far the case study presented above has illustrated how interaction can be used to take advantage of linear, cyclical and other non-linear effects of time. In the next section, we take a closer look at how interaction can be used to take advantage of spatial development.

Taking Advantage of Spatial Development

We have already noted that a single company can take advantage of several aspects of network space. We can now examine some of these in turn and relate them to our case study.

Relating Economic Activities Across Geographical Space

Interaction provides a way for companies to relate particular economic activities in different geographical places to each other. This means that particular processes and structures at two or more places may become connected. However, interaction is also an opportunity to make something special out of these connections and take advantage of unique place-related features of the business processes of purchase and supply. In the next section of the case study, we see how interaction is used to take advantage of specific geographical places.

SCA's investment in the production of advanced magazine paper in northern Sweden was an important step in the company's approach to exploiting geography. When the environmental debate increased and secondary fibre became 'green', SCA could benefit because it was already using secondary fibre in its production of packaging materials. But the fact that one of the company's newsprint mills located outside London was using secondary fibre as input provided another important opportunity. Here, SCA had a production unit experienced with de-inking technology. Also, the London mill was located in the middle of what was called 'the secondary fibre forest', an area with a surplus of post-consumer waste paper.

The main part of SCA's newsprint production had hitherto been located at the Ortviken mill in northern Sweden, with good access to fresh fibre, but with restricted access to secondary fibre. As we mentioned above, most of the secondary fibre that SCA combined with fresh pulp in the production of packaging materials was imported on returning paper transport from Europe and the UK. To develop newsprint production in northern Sweden based almost completely on post-consumer waste imported from Europe to northern Sweden was regarded as an economic impossibility.

In order to take advantage of the access to fresh wood fibre in Sweden and to the 'secondary fibre forest' around the London newsprint mill, SCA decided to change the use of these geographical locations. The investment in magazine paper production in northern Sweden was one important part of this change. Magazine paper production was dependent on access to fresh wood fibre and it was thought that this would guarantee that SCA would be free from demands for it to use secondary fibre at this geographical place. Another important move was for SCA to concentrate all its newsprint production at the London mill, which was modernized to increase production capacity based on post-consumer waste as the main fibre input.

This outlines how variations in economic activity at two places can be exploited in order to create benefits for both parts of the business. By adapting the production structure of each place, the variation in supply of the two inputs could be utilized.

Business in practise involves taking advantage of place-related features and this process is expressed in the way that companies are organized. For example, many companies develop their marketing or sales organization on a geographical basis in an attempt to respond to variations in customers' buying and usage behaviour.

Creating Connections Between Bodies of Knowledge

Interaction takes place between two (or more) specific bodies of knowledge that are separate from each other. All companies and organizations develop their own body of knowledge. This body of knowledge is partly the outcome of the tangible resources in which the company has invested. It is also a function of the company's internal history, the kind of people that it has recruited, and the teaching and other knowledge development processes in which they have been involved. But the body of knowledge of any company is also to a large extent dependent on the body of knowledge of other organizations with which it has interacted and the people who have represented those organizations. Thus each company represents a specific and unique body of knowledge which is separate from other bodies of knowledge but which is oriented towards some particular and significant counterparts. Interaction is an important means of relating and influencing knowledge and where it is situated. Thus through interaction companies can influence how the knowledge development processes are structured, separated and directed. This is illustrated in the following part of the case study.

Just as SCA's mill in northern Sweden was beginning to achieve a stable production of magazine paper based on fresh wood fibre that was bleached with chlorine, it received a shock. IKEA's catalogue group presented its new environmental policy. IKEA's message was that within one year they would only buy catalogue paper (LWC paper) based on totally chlorine-free pulp and containing at least 10 % of pulp from post-consumer waste.

IKEA's idea about how magazine or catalogue paper should be developed and produced was almost the opposite of SCA's. IKEA was not a customer of SCA and neither of the parties had the ambition to develop a business relationship. For SCA this was because of IKEA's difficult delivery demands and for IKEA it was because of SCA's lack of experience as a supplier of catalogue paper. But IKEA's new environmental policy was still regarded as a severe threat. SCA's marketing people feared that IKEA's demand would serve as a guideline for other influential publishers and printers. This was indicated by a number of customer declarations. The sales manager of SCA expressed it as follows, 'The message from IKEA undoubtedly pulled the cork out of the bottle. Afterwards several of our customers declared that they were going to buy only from environmentally adapted producers.'

However, SCA's research and development manager argued that they should stay cool and that IKEA's development idea was just too unrealistic. One of the main quality characteristics of magazine and catalogue paper was its high brightness and strength and, hitherto, this had been impossible to achieve without a treatment with chlorine. Also, SCA thought that it was practically impossible to produce magazine paper using pulp based on post-consumer waste with all its associated contaminants.

This was not only the view of SCA, but a shared understanding of almost all producers of this advanced magazine and catalogue paper. Thus, when IKEA presented the idea of 'green' catalogue paper to their suppliers, none of them applauded. IKEA's largest supplier, the German company Haindl, totally refused. But IKEA held on to the idea even though none of its main suppliers could promise to deliver such a solution and even though its demand led to the breakdown of its relationship with its main supplier Haindl.

How did IKEA dare to ask for a solution that neither its existing supplier nor any other thought was realistic? As we mentioned above, IKEA had been interacting with Greenpeace. Through this interaction, it had acquired a sound understanding of what knowledge actually existed about how to decrease the use of chlorine and increase the use of secondary pulp, not only among pulp and paper producers but also among their suppliers of equipment and chemicals. Although none of IKEA's suppliers could present a ready application based on its definition of a 'green' catalogue paper, there were several development projects in the laboratory and in pilot plants on a large scale that pointed to the possibility of uniting these pieces of knowledge into such a solution.

Through Greenpeace, IKEA contacted a supplier of de-inking equipment, Sulzer-Escher Wyss, and learned that an input of 10 % post-consumer waste into catalogue paper could be realistic in combination with an intensified de-inking process with its associated reduction in yield. Also through Greenpeace, IKEA contacted one of the world's largest producers of bleaching chemicals, Eka Nobel, and one of the world's largest producers of bleached pulp, Södra Cell, and an interesting development of knowledge was outlined: When Greenpeace actions against chlorine affected the companies involved in the supply and use of chlorine-bleached paper products, all kinds of knowledge about how to reduce the use of bleaching chemicals became valuable. Despite their loud objections to Greenpeace's idea, they had themselves been attempting to reduce the use of this chemical for several decades. For example, in order to reduce the use of bleaching chemicals and energy, a large pulp and paper producer, an equipment supplier and Chalmers University of Technology had been engaged in the development of 'low-level' chlorine bleaching in the early 1970s. The 'classical' bleaching method based on chlorine gas was replaced with a chlorine-dioxide-based method that relied on the idea that a large amount of discolouring substances could be taken care of in the closed part of the pulp process, before the final bleaching step. Besides reducing the need for chlorine and energy, the new method meant that the discharge of chlorinated waste water was reduced by 50 %, from about 8 to 4 kg per tonne of produced pulp.[3] This improvement was not appreciated, either by the pulp producers or their customers and interest in the new method was restricted. However, when the reduction of chlorine became a 'green' issue then this aspect of the new bleaching method was suddenly recognized. Thus, in the wake of the environmental actions against chlorine, the knowledge

---

[3] Measured in adsorbable organic halides (AOX).

about the chlorine-dioxide method and the possibility of pushing the limits for the discharge of chlorinated waste water became interesting to several types of company and organization related to the supply and use of bleached paper products. 'Despite the fact that the oxygen-bleaching method was available in the middle of the 1970s, it did not get its real breakthrough until the late 1980s, when a low discharge of organically bound chlorine became valuable to industry', says the research and development manager of the equipment supplier, Sunds Defibrator.

This part of the case study illustrates how interactions are an important way of relating bodies of knowledge to each other in a systematic and systemic way. Interaction is also a way to integrate knowledge situated in different locations into a development process. Thus, interaction between companies and organizations must also be seen as interaction between specific bodies of knowledge. This also illustrates the fact that the economic value of particular bodies of knowledge is dependent on the counterparts' possibilities of using it. The bodies of knowledge must be compatible. When the knowledge of how to reach a low level of chlorine bleaching was presented, it took more than a decade before it became really interesting to users. The development of a new body of knowledge can be useful in the eyes of those that finance the work if it leads to scientific publications and patents in universities or research and development institutes. However, in order for knowledge to be embedded in a business setting by producers and users, the new body of knowledge must have a positive impact on established bodies of knowledge. Regardless of how new or unique a body of knowledge is, it is not useful until others have developed complementary bodies of knowledge that can use it. The new knowledge must fit into established producer and user settings. In the example above, we saw that as long as the producers and end users did not care whether or not their paper-based products were bleached with chlorine, a new body of knowledge about how to decrease the level of chlorine made no sense. It was not until the body of knowledge about low level chlorine bleaching became possible to utilize in relation to bodies of knowledge concerning environmental issues, that it acquired value in a producer–user setting.

Creating Connections Between Capital Investments

Interaction is also a way of connecting capital investments to each other. Larger investments in facilities, machines or systems always have some specific attributes or features. Through interaction these specific features can be systematically related to each other and taken advantage of by those involved. Thus, interactions and business relationships may be seen as 'pipelines' between specific capital investments. In this way, each capital investment and its unique features becomes part of larger resource constellations which increases the economic value that it can create. We illustrate this in the following part of our case study.

One particular mill had some very strong reasons to try to push the limits for how much the discharge of chlorinated waste water could be reduced through the chlorine-dioxide method. Sweden's smallest producer of bleached pulp, Aspa, was brave enough to present a request to increase its production capacity and, consequently, its discharges of chlorinated waste water at a time when the protests against chlorine peaked. Aspa was located at Lake Vättern, which also supplied the drinking water for several smaller cities and so the request became a hot political issue.

The Swedish environmental authorities, whose actions were closely observed by the environmental NGOs and media, answered with their toughest demands ever. The maximum level of discharge of chlorinated waste water was to be no more than 1.5 kg per tonne of pulp within five years for the general industry. However, if Aspa wanted to continue with their business at Lake Vättern, they were forced by the Swedish environmental government to show that they were able to achieve a discharge of no more than 0.5 kg per tonne of pulp within the same timescale.

Aspa was suddenly in a rather desperate situation. With limited financial and research and development resources, the only thing Aspa could do was to experiment with the established chlorine-dioxide method. Its technicians managed to reduce the discharge to about 1.5 kg per tonne without losing strength and brightness in its paper, but this was as far as they could go. Thus, a new bleaching method was necessary, but how could it be achieved?

Aspa's delicate situation was reported in the media and became familiar to both camps of the chlorine debate: to companies engaged in the supply and use of chlorine-bleaching methods as well as to environmental NGOs and users that wanted to get rid of chlorine. One company that followed the chlorine debate especially carefully was Eka Nobel, one of world's largest suppliers of the bleaching chemicals, chlorine and sodium chlorate.

If an environmental acceptable bleaching method was to be developed, Eka was keen that it should be based on chemicals that it produced and knew about through many years of extensive research and development. Consequently, rather than aim for the total exclusion of chlorine, Eka engaged in pushing the limits of the chlorine-dioxide bleaching method. Its ambition was to create a low-level-chlorine-dioxide bleaching method in combination with peroxide, another chemical that Eka also produced. Peroxide was regarded by the environmental NGOs as more or less harmless. The goal was to reduce the discharge of chlorinated waste water to a level below 0.5 kg per tonne of produced pulp. This was not enough, argued Greenpeace, but Eka relied on the chlorine-free definition of another influential environmental NGO, the Swedish Society for Nature Conservation. In order to stimulate the industry to engage in environmental issues, the latter argued that a 'green' definition should be based on what it was actually possible to achieve. To encourage companies to develop alternative bleaching methods, the Swedish Society for Nature Conservation defined 'chlorine-free' to mean a process in which the discharge of chlorinated waste water was no more than 0.5 kg per tonne of pulp. Since no official European definition of 'chlorine-free' existed (the issue was discussed within the EU but no decision was taken), the Swedish Society for Nature Conservation's definition of 'chlorine-free' became used by European producers and users of bleached paper products.

Aspa was exactly the 'guinea-pig' that Eka needed: a small, flexible mill, already equipped with chlorine-dioxide bleaching, which could be used for large-scale trials. When Eka approached Aspa with the suggestion of carrying out large-scale trials together, Aspa left all other alternatives and agreed. The first trials resulted in a full-bright pulp and a discharge of chlorinated waste water that was below 0.3 kg per tonne of pulp. Aspa could report to the governmental environmental authorities that it had succeeded in the development of a discharge below 0.5 kg per tonne of pulp and was, consequently, allowed to increase its production capacity. Eka could launch the new bleaching method, which was named 'Lignox', as chlorine-free according to the definition of the Swedish Society for Nature Conservation.

This shows how a specific feature of one capital investment, the Aspa mill and its restricted production capacity, became advantageous for Eka in its search for a production unit for large-scale trials. A specific feature of Eka's capital investments, its heavy reliance on production of chlorine and the need to base an environmentally acceptable bleaching solution on this capital investment, became advantageous in Aspa's struggles. In order to be able to utilize its capital investment in the future, Aspa was forced to find an environmentally acceptable solution and Eka's idea was the one that was most easy to combine with its existing investment. This part of the empirical case study underlines that interaction between companies connects specific features of capital investment and points to their use in solving specific problems. However, a particular capital investment is never related to a particular supplier in isolation. It is also related to other capital investments and used in similar or dissimilar problem-solving processes. In the next section, we see some of the consequences of this indirect relatedness between capital investments.

Combining Space Dimensions

The Lignox concept became a success for Aspa and Eka Nobel and both companies were able to develop new features and new benefits from their established facilities. However, some of Aspa's customers had customers that were very concerned about environmental issues. These customers asked if it was possible to go a step further. Was it possible to produce a pulp without any chlorine at all? The customer was prepared to go for such solution, even if it meant that they had to accept a somewhat lower brightness. Aspa agreed, but did not involve Eka Nobel in this continued development of the Lignox method. Instead, it developed a new chlorine-free bleaching process, based on the increased use of peroxide, in relation to its pulp customer. In early 1990, Aspa was able to tell its customer that it could produce a totally chlorine-free pulp. Although it did not reach full brightness, it was in line with the requirements of more basic graphic products. Aspa's totally chlorine-free pulp was particularly appreciated by a few of its customers, mainly German and Austrian paper producers that had made the 'green' issue part of their profile. However, the development did not attract any greater attention among other pulp suppliers or within Eka Nobel. The fact that one of the world's smallest mills, at the request of one of its customers was able to produce very small quantities of chlorine-free pulp was more or less neglected. However, the breakthrough at Aspa's mill received some unexpected publicity.

People in the Greenpeace Pulp and Paper campaign had closely watched the Aspa and Eka Nobel development of Lignox and Aspa's development work on a chlorine-free version of the concept and they viewed the latter as a real breakthrough. Greenpeace was determined to let the world know about the possibilities that existed for chlorine-free bleaching. Greenpeace approached Aspa with a request for delivery of chlorine-free pulp for a rather special purpose. Greenpeace' idea was to produce a spoof of the German magazine *Der Spiegel* which, in contrast to the original, was based on totally chlorine-free pulp.

Aspa initially hesitated. Although it had developed a chlorine-free solution, the step to interact with Greenpeace was still considered to be radical. 'We were two different camps', as the technical manager at Aspa expressed it. However, after considering the possible effects of the unexpected support, Aspa agreed. Aspa's pulp was transformed into chlorine-free magazine paper in one of Haindl's paper mills and then, through Greenpeace and a printing company, transformed into *Das Plagiat*. It was impossible to distinguish with the naked eye that it was printed on a paper based on totally chlorine-free pulp. The headline of *Das Plagiat* was 'Umweltkiller Druckpapier' and several pages of content were devoted to Aspa's mill and its totally chlorine-free, pulp-bleaching process. The publicity went beyond anything Aspa had experienced – *Das Plagiat* was distributed to thousands of European purchasers of printing papers, at printers, publishers and advertising agencies.

This part of the case study illustrates how the development of capital equipment is a continuous process. The fact that one supplier found a way to utilize the capital investment of a customer does not restrict the customer from searching for new ways of increasing its use of the same investment in relation to other counterparts. However, this search can have both positive and negative effects.

Aspa had been successful. Its relationship with Greenpeace and the *Das Plagiat* spoof meant that their knowledge of how to produce totally chlorine-free pulp became familiar to all kinds of companies and organizations involved in the production and use of magazine paper. However, this knowledge proved to be of restricted usefulness. When potential new customers approached Aspa, they realized that there was only one supplier that could deliver this quality and that this supplier only had one production line. Their interest in converting to the new quality soon cooled. Aspa understood that in order to make use of their process it had to be shared with others. Aspa already shared customers with one of the world's largest producers of bleached pulp, Södra Cell. So Aspa approached Södra Cell and asked them to join the totally chlorine-free project.

Södra Cell's research and development department reacted with interest. They were convinced that the vigorous chlorine debate would force at least some of the large pulp and paper producers to initiate development projects in this direction. Aspa's adapted Lignox concept suddenly put Södra Cell on this track. However, when the first large-scale tests were made using Aspa's adapted Lignox concept, the result appeared to be a complete failure. The company's general management heard about the development project and stopped it. Besides the failure, their argument was that no one would ever pay more for a pulp of worse quality and with less brightness and strength than the standard chlorine-bleached product.

A short time later, a customer approached Södra Cell's management with a request for test samples of chlorine-free pulp. The management realized that the customer and the customer's customers were deeply interested in such a product. Södra Cell decided to rejoin the chlorine-free track, but with the ambition that this pulp must achieve all standard quality parameters. As one of the largest producers, it also had the resources to mobilize support for this development. Södra Cell involved research institutes in Sweden and France, six large suppliers of equipment and chemicals related to the bleaching process, and three paper producers as pilot customers. After 18 months of intense development work, Södra Cell decided to invest in a new bleaching facility for totally chlorine-free pulp. Both Aspa and Södra Cell could benefit from the new situation. With capacity for substantially greater output and two different suppliers, customers could be sure of the long-term supply of the new pulp.

The use and development of capital investments, bodies of knowledge and geographically related features are each likely to occur in interaction between several companies through which the numbers, types and combinations of these investments are changed. The process is one of constant trial and learning in which the knowledge of how to combine the elements changes over time. Through this process, the investments are 'moved' in relation to their function and in relation to each other.

Södra Cell not only produced a new totally chlorine-free pulp, it communicated its success to its direct customers, their customers and also to politicians, journalists and environmental groups. To emphasize the zero discharge of chlorine, Södra Cell named the pulp 'Zero' and its marketing activity exceeded anything that it had carried out previously. Södra Cell enlarged the traditional range of communication channels from trade journals to the general media. Besides its own marketing activities, Södra Cell also had valuable support from Greenpeace, among others. After some initial hesitation from the customers, the Zero pulp rapidly developed into a real success. During the first years of production, both Södra Cell and Aspa broke their own production records and were able to achieve a 10–15 % price premium for the Zero pulp. Södra Cell's general manager concluded, 'We can also claim that the Zero venture has contributed to a considerable improvement of our company's financial situation. At a time when most other industries have been forced to record a drastic deterioration, Södra Cell has turned the trend around.'

Södra Cell started its large-scale production of Zero pulp in the autumn of 1992, the same year as IKEA presented its requirement for magazine paper based on totally chlorine-free pulp. This makes IKEA's move more understandable. IKEA's knowledge of Aspa and Södra Cell's endeavours was provided firstly by Greenpeace and later by direct contact with several of the involved companies and this facilitated its decision to go chlorine-free. IKEA was able to use the Södra Cell solution as evidence of the feasibility of creating a full-bright, totally chlorine-free pulp. Södra Cell also became a supplier to one of IKEA's providers of catalogue paper, the Italian company Cartiere Burgo. With the help of totally chlorine-free pulp bought from Södra Cell and secondary-fibre-based pulp bought externally, Burgo was one of IKEA's first suppliers that could fulfil the new environmental demands. These moves led IKEA, Södra Cell and Aspa together to influence other companies to take the same route of development.

The route taken by Aspa and Södra Cell in their technological development was not an isolated phenomenon. When IKEA declared its new environmental policy this was taken seriously not only by the Italian company Burgo, but also by its Finnish suppliers. The Finnish marketing organization, Finnpap, reacted positively when IKEA launched its new requirement despite none of their mills having any such catalogue paper in production at that time. The product development manager of Finnpap did not agree that the chlorine-free solution was best for the environment but declared that 'if IKEA needs a magazine paper based on totally chlorine-free pulp and secondary fibre to become "green", they shall certainly have it'. All the chlorine-bleaching units and their suppliers of chemicals in Finland were subject to the same environmental demands as Aspa and Södra Cell and almost all were already working with low levels of chlorine bleaching that could be used in the 'zero' process. However, to adapt to a single lead user was an economic challenge. One of the mills that managed to supply IKEA with its 'green' catalogue paper, Kaukas, had to take secondary-fibre-based pulp from its sister mill in France and transport it to a production unit in Laapeenraanta in the south-east of Finland, where it was mixed with totally chlorine-free pulp specially designed for IKEA.

Through the solutions supplied by Södra Cell and Burgo and through Finnpap, IKEA could present a new catalogue based on totally chlorine-free pulp and 10 % secondary fibre in the year after the new environmental policy was launched. The quality was more or less impossible to distinguish from that of traditional paper. Or as the IKEA's head of the catalogue said, 'the catalogue is more beautiful than ever'.

Beautiful or not, the new catalogue paper was a logistical nightmare for the Finnish producer, Kaukas, and this was realized by IKEA. A year after the new paper was presented, IKEA decided to go for a simpler solution, supercalendered (SC) paper, produced by a larger number of suppliers. This meant that IKEA would take a larger amount of the 'green' catalogue paper from producers located closer to the 'secondary-fibre forest'. One of the new suppliers was a mill in Austria, Laakirchen. Located in an environmentally sensitive area, Laakirchen was more or less forced by the Austrian government to develop a 'green' profile. Laakirchen had invested in the latest technology for de-inking secondary fibre and was combining this with Zero pulp from Aspa and Södra Cell. The choice of this supplier also meant that two companies that had declared that neither was interested in working with the other became connected: IKEA and SCA. Laakirchen is owned by SCA. When it started to deliver magazine paper based on secondary fibre and totally chlorine-free pulp from Södra Cell to IKEA, this had effects on the investments in its sister mills located some hundreds of kilometres away. The same year as Laakirchen started to supply this solution to IKEA, SCA decided to invest in totally chlorine-free pulp in its pulp mill in Sweden. Thus, instead of using Södra Cell, Laakirchen could use its internal SCA supplier again. At the time of writing, SCA has become one of IKEA's main suppliers with a 'green' catalogue paper that neither IKEA nor SCA had initially thought of (see Figure 4.1).

The final part of the case study exemplifies most of the aspects of time and space that we have discussed earlier. It shows that two companies that started out with totally different goals and views of the technological development became business partners but with a different product and in a different location from the ones that either of them thought about at the beginning. The case study is an example of both the complexity of network evolution and also the absolute logic of the process. In fact, it may be wrong to talk about companies 'using' the three different aspects of time and of space. These factors are so strong and economically important that no single company can avoid them. Each *has* to work within them.

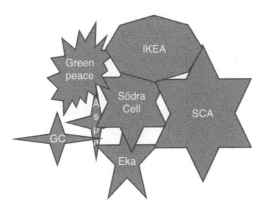

Figure 4.1 Actors involved in the case study.

The Company in the Interactive Business Landscape

In this chapter, we have started to outline a business landscape where interaction between companies is the central process. We have also tried to demonstrate how this interaction is closely related to time and space and how it can be a way to take advantage of variation in these dimensions. The business landscape is dynamic and we can identify two different but connected organizing processes within it: One process takes place *within* companies, and they each try to develop internal operations through it; the other process takes place *between* the companies, which successively develop ways of using each other. These two organizing processes are multidimensional and intimately related and changes in one of them will always affect the other.

When the business landscape is examined with an eye to the rainforest metaphor, then interaction and business relationships with the characteristics that we have described appear as distinct economic phenomena. The role of business relationships might even have become increasingly significant over time (Gudeman 2001). An increased reliance on external partners for issues of both efficiency and innovation means that the majority of a company's current activities and its future development is to a large extent dependent on others.

A company's interaction pattern is a way to characterize how the company is embedded in the business landscape. Each company is part of something bigger than itself and is embedded into this larger whole in many different ways. There are thousands of threads between each company and its environment that relate what is happening within the company to particular happenings outside it.

All these interaction processes position a company relative to the processes and structures within the business landscape. A company is embedded in both time and space in a number of different ways. It is through interaction that it tries to take advantage of those dimensions and, even more, tries to adapt to important changes in them.

This does not mean that engaging in business relationships is an automatic guarantee of benefits. There are substantial costs involved in developing and maintaining relationships and each engagement also leads the development of each participating company in a particular direction. For a supplier, to engage in co-development with a customer can create benefits in terms of increased innovativeness but it can also be a dangerous adventure if other customers are not interested in that particular development path. To be deeply embedded into a structure of stable business relationships can be beneficial. But if counterparts start to face economic problems, the same situation can become a dangerous trap (Waluszewski 2006). Successful business development is not something that a company can create by itself. Nor can a company assume that its relationships with suppliers and customers will automatically achieve it either.

ELEMENTS OF BUSINESS NETWORKS

The previous four chapters have given a detailed account of the characteristics of a rainforest-like business landscape and have explored what it is like to do business in this interactive world. The empirical picture that we have drawn has been combined with theoretical concepts that are built on the idea that interaction is a basic process in business. Our aim in the next three chapters is to examine how we may conceptualize three basic elements of the economic structure of this business landscape: resources, activities and actors. We are concerned with two questions about these elements: What are the main characteristics of each element and how do these characteristics affect the way that they should be analysed and used? What is their role in the creation of economic value and in economic development?

Chapter 5 deals with resources and how they are handled within an interactive landscape. The focus here is on how resources are combined through interaction, how interaction places the interface between resources at the centre of attention and how this affects the ways in which resources are used and valued. Chapter 6 takes a similar approach to activities. The interdependencies between activities are perhaps the most significant feature of the business landscape. These interdependencies affect how single activities are designed and also the total configuration of activity patterns stretching across the boundaries of many companies. Chapter 7 examines how we can conceptualize the business actor in an interactive world. In this chapter, we see that the characteristics of the actor are as much an outcome of the interaction process as they are an influencing factor in it.

Each of the three chapters includes discussions of the consequences that this framework has for our understanding of the development of the business landscape and how that process can be influenced by the companies involved in it.

INTERACTION AND RESOURCES

5

The interactive landscape is full of very different resources, both tangible and intangible, which are affected by the process of interaction. One effect of interaction is that the characteristics of different resources relate closely to each other. This relativity between resources affects how they are developed, how they are produced and how they are used. We start this chapter by examining how resources were analysed in earlier IMP studies. Our aim here is to give an overview of how resources may be viewed, analysed and handled in an interactive landscape.

We suggest that the value of resources is created in the ways in which they are combined with other resources. The characteristics of resources are formulated in some basic propositions at the start of the chapter. Each proposition is discussed in detail and exemplified. The interfaces between different combinations of physical and organizational resources come to the forefront in this analysis. Through these interfaces, resources are combined into *resource collections* within companies and also into *resource constellations* across company boundaries. We can trace the process of resource development in these interfaces and also see the tensions that arise from this development. We show the special role of business relationships in this resource development process. Finally, we systematically relate the role of the resource interfaces to the dimensions of time and space that we outlined in Chapter 3.

Economic Resources in the IMP Framework

Economic resources provide the building blocks for the structure and process of business. Resources may consist of raw materials, physical facilities, components, operating systems and finance as well as human knowledge, ingenuity and ability. The IMP framework is based on the idea that, by itself, a single economic resource is passive and without value. It is the ways that a resource *interacts* with other resources that define the nature of that resource and have the potential to generate economic value. Interaction over time combines many resources both new and old from many different locations.[1]

---

[1]This chapter summarizes the research about technological development within networks, such as that in Waluszewski (1989), Lundgren (1994), Laage-Hellman (1989, 1997), Håkansson (1993), Ford and

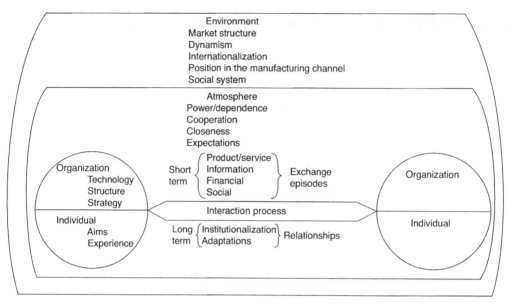

Figure 5.1 The interaction model.

Source: Håkansson, H. (ed.), 1982. *International Marketing and Purchasing of Industrial Goods: An Interaction Approach.* John Wiley & Sons Ltd, p. 32. Reproduced by permission.

Through this process, resources are changed, recombined, developed, used and re-used. In Chapter 3, we used the term 'path of resources' to refer to the process through which combinations of resources evolve.

The IMP theoretical framework places interaction across company boundaries at the centre of business development and value creation. An important consequence of inter-company interaction is that the nature of a company's resources is not fixed. In Chapter 3, we referred to the variability of resources in different contexts as their *heterogeneity*. Thus, the characteristics, usefulness and value of a company's resources depend on how they are combined with the resources of particular counterparts and how that combination interacts with other related combinations of resources elsewhere in the network. The nature of resources in business networks is defined by interaction. We can consider the issue of interaction and resources more closely by examining how resources are defined in three different but related IMP models.

The interaction model (Håkansson 1982) took the social interaction between suppliers and customers as its starting point (see Figure 5.1). This research model formed the basis for investigating how short- and long-term interaction affects the human and technological resource structure of the dyad. Thus the basic assumption in the interaction model is that resources are heterogeneous. Their features and economic values are assumed to be dependent on the

Saren (1996), Holmen (2001), Håkansson and Johanson (2001), Håkansson *et al.* (2001), Wedin (2001), Gressetvold (2004), Raesfeld (1997), Baraldi (2003), Bengtson (2003), Vercauteren (2007), Awaleh (2008) and Brekke (2009).

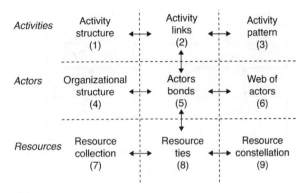

Figure 5.2 ARA model.

Source: Håkansson, H., Snehota, I., (eds) 1995, *Developing Relationships in Business Networks.* International Thompson, p. 45. Reprinted by permission.

interaction processes that they are exposed to. This basic assumption is also embedded in the ARA and 4R models.

The ARA model that we referred to in Chapter 3 was based on the idea that resources may become more or less adapted and more or less mutually tied together as their interaction develops (Håkansson and Snehota 1995). But this model took a wider perspective on resource interaction in two important ways. It formed the basis for study of how interaction connects resources over multiple organizational boundaries in a larger network. The ARA model, and the IMP 2 Research Project that was based on it, examined three layers of business interaction: activity links; actor bonds and resource ties (see Figure 5.2). The ARA model highlights the importance of the interplay between the interactions that take place in each layer; for example, it considers how the interactive resource ties that develop between companies may be reflected in the actor bonds that the companies have developed.

A central idea of the ARA model is that a single resource is combined with others on three levels: in a *collection* with others in a company; with others in the interaction with a specific counterpart in a *business relationship* and with a set of resources in a larger *resource constellation* of the network. Thus a single resource simultaneously exists in a number of different contexts where it is combined in different ways. These different contexts inevitably expose the single resource to tensions. These are likely to create problems in the use of a resource, but also provide opportunities for its development.

The interaction model and the ARA model take established business relationships as the starting point for resource analysis. But the 4R model (Håkansson and Waluszewski 2002) opens up direct and indirectly connected resources for investigation, regardless of whether or not they are associated with established business relationships. The 4R model (see Figure 5.3) encourages investigation of the interplay between resources themselves and how those resources are affected by being embedded in other resources across company boundaries.

The 4R model distinguishes between four types of resource as follows:

- *Products:* These are usually combinations of tangible resources produced and used by different units in the business landscape. Products can be moved around and therefore relate to several different resource structures.

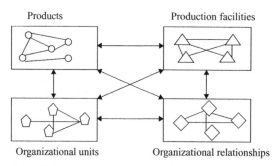

Figure 5.3 The 4R model and the interplay between resources.

- *Production facilities:* These are also combinations of tangible resources, but are more permanent than products. Their relative stability in time and place makes them important interfaces for other different and successive resource combinations. Facilities are normally controlled by one organization.
- *Organizational units:* These include the knowledge and experience of individuals and groups and their skills in handling particular resource combinations.
- *Organizational relationships:* These are a combination of tangible and intangible resources. They cross company boundaries and affect other intangible combinations, such as routines and procedures, and tangible combinations, such as products and facilities. Organizational relationships are much more complex than the other types of resource and this complexity creates both problems and opportunities.

Thus, the 4R model is based on the assumption that current and historical interaction processes shape single resource items by embedding them into many others and giving each resource item its specific features.

A Business Landscape Full of Resources

The basis of the framework we have presented is that the usefulness of a resource, whether product, facility, organizational unit or relationship is determined by its interaction with the resources of other companies.[2]

---

[2]We have been inspired by many other researchers who have studied knowledge or technological development. Some important examples are researchers within the fields of history of technology or economic history, such as Rosenberg (1982, 1994), Hughes (1983, 1987, 2004), Lindqvist (1984), David (1985), Arthur (1988) and Kaiser and Hedin (1995); researchers who have advocated the importance of the user in technological developments, such as von Hippel (1976, 1988, 1998) and Lundvall (1988); researchers who have investigated the development process such as Van de Ven *et al.* (1999); researchers who have used the Actor Network Theory for studies of science, such as Latour (1984), Callon (1980), Latour *et al.* (1979) and Law (1992); researchers with a special interest in knowledge and knowledge creation, such as Shapin and Schaffer (1985), Pinch and Bijker (1984) and Bijker (1987); researchers who have focused on the interplay between tacit and explicit knowledge, such as Nonaka (1991) and Nonaka and Takeuchi

Therefore a critical question for the usefulness of a single resource held by a company is how *other companies* can use it and combine it with their own. The considerations of these other companies will range from the usefulness of a single resource such as a product, machine or some particular knowledge held by a company to the usefulness of the collection of resources that the company represents.

The same resources are constantly being combined within companies, between pairs of companies, and between these pairs and other single or combinations of companies. One important consequence of combining resources is that any single resource is always exposed to several more or less different 'logics' and has several different identities in different contexts. First, each single resource has to function with other internal resources of the company in order to become a totality that may be useful to others and profitable for the company. Secondly, the same resource has to function in relation to *specific* counterparts: suppliers, customers or other direct and indirect related companies. Finally, the single resource has to fit into the larger resource constellations that it is related to, such as supply and distribution networks, technological networks and environmental networks. Each resource acquires its economic value in this world of constant and changing combinations. These multiple contexts give the resource its specific features, its multiple identities and its multiple, but different values.

Resources and Business: Basic Propositions

We now present a number of basic propositions that provide some ideas for practitioners and researchers on how resources can be approached in an interactive business landscape.

1. The value of a resource is dependent on connections to other resources.

In an interactive business landscape, the economic value of any resource is not a given but is dependent on its ties to other resources which are created through interaction.

This is a basic, but far-reaching, proposition that has important implications for how resources should be analysed and used. In an interactive business landscape, the value of each resource is dependent on the effects that it has on other resources, i.e. on the types of interface it has with these other resources. It is only when a resource is useful in combination with other resources that it has economic value. The issue of combination has at least two implications. The possible economic effects of any resource are impossible to foresee, since new interactive effects appear when it is combined in new ways. It is always possible to influence the value of a single resource through interaction with others. Thus, interaction with other resources in the business landscape can, in principle, be a value-creating mechanism for any resource.

(1995); and, finally, economic researchers interested in the use of science and technological development from a society's point of view, such as Dosi *et al.* (1988), Lundvall (1992) and Nelson (1993).

2. A resource changes and develops characteristics over time.

The effects of previous interactions are expressed in specific resource features and resource interfaces that strongly influence how each resource can be used.

Every resource that is in use in the interactive business landscape has developed through its relations with a wider combination of resources. Previous interactions both make possible and restrict the use of each single resource. These interactions have adapted and directed tangible and intangible resources into particular combinations. In this way, each resource and the way it can be used is a product of its history.

3. Every resource is embedded in a multidimensional context.

In an interactive business landscape, every resource is part of several resource combinations and hence develops features that are partly contradictory.

Any single resource exists in a number of different combinations and contexts: In the resource collection within a company; in direct interactions with particular counterparts; and within a larger resource constellation among many companies across the network. These different resource combinations each have their own logic and influence the single resource in directions that are at least partly contradictory. Each of these combinations have positive and negative effects on its development and usefulness in other combinations. The longer the history of a resource, the larger the set of other resources it has been related to and the more it is exposed to different influences on how it is combined.

4. All changes of a resource create tensions.

Any change of a resource in an interactive business landscape will produce tensions in related resources, creating a number of possible reactions.

All changes to a resource have positive and negative effects and these effects always impact differently on the economic outcomes for different actors and different resource combinations. Changing a single resource involves costs. But all resource changes also affect the costs of using other related resources. Thus, any change of a resource means that both it and related resources in multiple contexts have to adjust to a new economic logic.

5. Interaction intensity influences the effects of a change in a resource.

The greater the intensity of interaction between resources, the greater the effects of a specific change of a resource.

Interaction is the process through which changes to resources are initiated and completed. However, interaction is also the process through which these changes are reacted to and in which numerous partly contradictory effects occur. The intensity of the interaction between resources (and between the associated activities and actors) is directly related to the development of resource interfaces and to the outcomes of a change.

One important consequence of this proposition is that it is not the change in a resource itself that creates the most important effects, but the way that those changes interact with other resources. Intense interaction between resources multiplies consequences and multiplies the number of resources affected. It increases costs but also potential benefits. Further, increased interaction can lead to new solutions and can mobilize counterparts that may be affected positively.

6. The broadness of interaction influences the number of resources affected by a resource change.

In a specific resource change, the broader the interaction (in terms of the number of counterparts or managers involved), the greater is the number of resources affected.

Interaction processes vary in breadth. Those involved can bring more or fewer resources into the interaction with a specific counterpart. They can raise different issues or involve different types of manager and specialist. They can also relate several different interaction processes to the same change, by involving several counterparts. One important consequence is that the broadness of interaction always affects the number of resources involved. The broader the interaction the more resources are activated. If broad interaction continues over a period of time, there are more changes affecting more related resources. This extension inevitably increases costs, but also the potential benefits for the increasing number of counterparts.

We use the propositions (summarized in Box 5.1) to examine the major issues surrounding business resources and illustrate them with empirical examples.

An Interactive World Full of Resources

Proposition 1 (see Box 5.1) emphasizes the importance of related resources. Every new resource, both tangible and intangible, has to confront a world full of existing resources. There is no empty space waiting for a new resource. Each has to generate its own space and find its role in relation to existing resource combinations. Or, putting it more simply, there is never a demand for a new product. Any demand has to be created.

The second consequence of this proposition is that the value of any resource, ranging from a single component to a whole company, can be influenced through its interaction with other resources. For example, the value of a supplier to a buyer is affected by the direct and indirect

---

Box 5.1   Propositions about the Nature of Resources

1. The value of a resource is dependent on its connections to other resources.
2. A resource changes and develops characteristics over time.
3. A resource is embedded in a multidimensional context.
4. All changes of a resource create tensions.
5. Interaction intensity influences the effects of a change in a resource.
6. Interaction breadth influences the number of resources that are affected by a resource change.

interactions that take place between their resources. This implies that every customer can increase the value of every supplier that it uses and vice versa. This, in turn, implies that simple comparisons of suppliers, customers or other counterparts as fixed entities are more or less meaningless. Instead a major issue facing companies is how to economically use the potential that exists in each counterpart through resource interaction. Thus the choice of the 'right' counterpart at a particular time may be less important than what is done with that counterpart to develop how its resources are used in relation to other resources. In the same way, the value of a single resource can be influenced by how it is combined with other tangible and intangible resources: products, facilities, knowledge, experience and established relationships.

The business landscape is full of resources developed and used in relation to each other, but also in relation to previously existing resources. Both single resources and the interaction in which they are involved are firmly rooted in the past. This historical context is as important for intangible resources, such as organizational skills, as it is for tangible ones, such as machinery or buildings. This legacy of resources and interaction forms the basis for current and future interaction but it simultaneously constrains interaction and the use and development of resources. In many ways, this legacy can be an 'iron cage'.

For example, when a new mobile phone with a new design and features leaves the last assembly station at a Nokia production line, it is distributed, sold and used in a world already containing 1.6 billion mobile phone subscriptions.[3] When a new model of car leaves the last assembly station on a GM production line, there are already about 450 million cars travelling the streets and roads of the world.[4] When IATA registers a new type of aeroplane among its member airlines, there are already more than 10 000 aeroplanes in service.[5] When an accounting firm signs off the audit of a new customer's accounts that audit joins millions of other audits that chart the performance of that particular company and the rise and fall of millions of other companies, and the collective wisdom and folly of generations of financial managers. When a new salesperson or a design engineer is recruited by a large company, they join hundreds of people that are already employed in the company. Finally, when a company establishes a relationship with a new customer, this relationship becomes part of its wider portfolio of established customer and supplier relationships.

Almost regardless of what business area we look at, the basic pattern is the same: In comparison with the resources that in some way are perceived as 'new', the total number of existing resources in use is huge. Furthermore, these existing resources do not work in isolation from each other, but have been developed to function jointly and are used together in very systematic ways. Thus, if the new mobile phone is to be used, it has to fit into a thoroughly developed telecommunications system. The new car and the new aeroplane have to be designed to work in a complex system of traffic control, servicing and maintenance in order to be useful. The new audit has to fit into a legal framework and provide information in a standardized form to fit with the processes of company reporting and valuation. The design engineer and the salesperson have to work within the procedures established within their respective departments, between departments and in

---

[3] www.who.int.
[4] *World Book Encyclopaedia*, 2001. Chicago: World book.
[5] 31 December 2003, www.iata.org.

relation to other organizations. The new business relationship must fit with the relationships to other customers and suppliers and also in relation to the company's internal departments. Any new resource has to become part of a much larger combination in which its interfaces with the other resources in the constellation are crucial.

A single resource has no value and cannot be considered a resource from an economic point of view unless it can be embedded in larger resource combinations. A single resource is never used in isolation. The actual combining of resources may be more or less conscious, more or less active and more or less successful. We use an example to illustrate the importance of this combining of resources and its effects in terms of developed interfaces. Figure 5.4 illustrates a resource combination that could be seen as a single item, but in fact consists of numerous interfaces between single resources.

It shows the interdependent components and sub-systems that relate to each other in the instrument panel of a car. The components that make up the instrument panel system intersect with the combination that comprises the car's electrical system and its climate control system, showing that some components are also parts of other resource combinations. For example, the wiper control arm is part of the electrical system and the sun sensor is part of the climate system. These combinations, in turn, are connected to the resource combination that comprises the engine. In this way, resource combinations are embedded in each other so that numerous resource interfaces have to function appropriately together both physically and functionally.

The tangible resources that constitute the instrument panel also have to fit with the intangible resources involved in the design and manufacture of the panel. These resources consist of the capabilities of people in companies. The fit between physical and design resources is particularly acute when, as so often happens, physical resources are designed and manufactured by different companies (Araujo *et al.* 2003). These resource interfaces have to relate to the overall product architecture at a higher level of aggregation.

Combining New and Existing Resources

Proposition 2 (see Box 5.1) suggests that previous interactions determine the features of resources and how they are used and interface with others. Consequently, earlier interactions provide the basis for the current interactions of a single resource or the resource collection of a company. For example, a customer's earlier interactions with a supplier are embedded in its current interaction, in how the two sides operate as well as how they see each other. The result of these earlier interactions can be seen in such things as their corporate knowledge and routines and the developed features of their products and facilities. The resources have been used and tested as part of particular combinations, which has influenced their characteristics and usefulness and, in turn, will affect wider aspects of the involved actors. Even if the 'pictures' that the counterparts have of each other are old and inaccurate, they still affect how the counterparts interact. Historical interactions are important from an economic perspective and can be interpreted as investments that have the possibility to be exploited in the future. For this reason, it is important to examine historical interactions in all attempts to describe and understand current interactions.

For example, a particular product may have been central to a long-term supplier–customer relationship. If the supplier then attempts to develop a relationship with another customer,

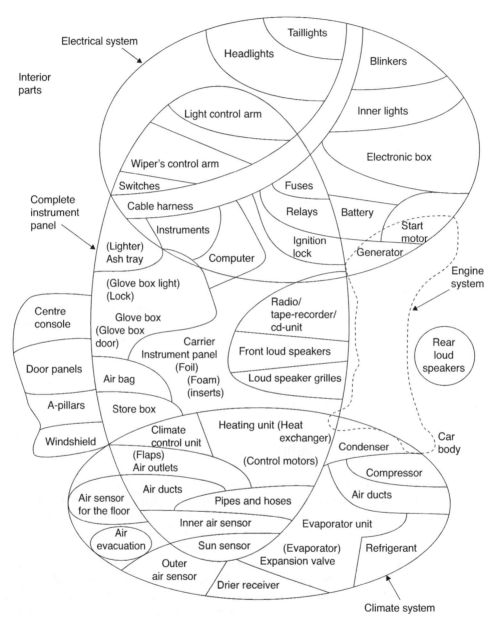

Figure 5.4 The instrument panel of a car.

Source: Jellbo, O. (1998). *Systemköp: en definitionsfråga.* Licentiate dissertation. Gothenburg, Sweden: Division of Industrial Marketing, Chalmers University of Technology, p. 55. Reproduced by permission.

that resource will have to be used in a somewhat different combination with other resources. The supplier as a whole, its product and the customer's resources will all be influenced by their previous interactions in different contexts. This may result in development patterns that are partly overlapping but could also be contradictory to the interactions with the existing customer or detrimental to business with the new one.

All resource combinations have their roots in an evolving pattern of interactions where resources are confronted, adapted and combined. Thus the development of a resource, for example a new product, does not take place in a vacuum but, for better or worse, draws from and affects all the resources of existing products, design and development skills, and material sciences as well as those resources associated with the use of the product, such as the skills of technicians, the assessments of safety and regulatory authorities and customer feedback.

We have used the car instrument panel (Figure 5.4) to illustrate some aspects of resources in an interactive economic landscape. However, as soon as we look at what appears to be a single combination of interrelated resources, we find other combinations that are related to it in a complicated way. For example, in the production of cars we can identify different resource combinations developed for handling the supply of special parts such as textiles or leather for car seats. If we look at the use of cars we find different combinations of resources that address for example, financing the purchase, leasing or renting of cars. Each combination has to relate to the overall resource constellation involving what Margaret Thatcher called the 'great car economy', but must also relate to other resource constellations involving textiles or banking.

Thus, a business landscape is full of resources that neither look nor function as they do by chance. Each has been developed interactively through the systematic work of thousands of people. But each resource has been designed and developed in ways that fit them into the *different* combinations of which they form part. The multiple and separate interactivity of resources always produces tensions in their function and form. These tensions produce costs for those involved in them but also provide opportunities for further change. The processes that resources go through in their development and relation to others can be described by two variables: the specific weight of investment in development and adaptation that each resource carries with it; and the number of other resources to which each resource is related and the consequent variety in the use of the resource.

These two resource characteristics are important for all new combinations. Any attempt to combine resources in new ways has to cope with the weight of previous investments made in them and the nature of their interfaces with others. There are many examples of this issue. For example, current computers use keyboards, the top line of which reads QWERTY, and so on. This order of letters was introduced to typewriters over a hundred years ago due to mechanical design problems regarding the bars, which in turn slowed down the typing. Everyone who has learned to type and every company that has word-processors has made an investment in using these keyboards and the system is effectively unchangeable. Similar examples have produced legal battles over embedded resources in the MS-DOS operating system and Windows software for personal computers. Thousands of single resources are so embedded into other resources that they are extremely difficult to change in any dramatic way. In contrast, the possibility of using a resource in new ways increases if that resource has previously developed interfaces in a number of different combinations. Common examples of this are seen in the area of business software. The use of a package in a new application is likely to be much more straightforward if that package has already been used in a variety of combinations with different operating systems.

All resources become 'heavier' through their developed interfaces with others. However, the full extent of this heaviness may not be apparent until attempts are made to change the resource or its interfaces. All resources have the capacity for a variety of uses that arise from their previous interactions with other resources. But the resources used in an interactive business landscape can never achieve optimum efficiency or effectiveness, as the set of resources it is related to is never fixed, but endlessly varying. Each resource is exposed to attempts to improve it, leading to tensions with established and new resources. The use of an individual resource is thus dependent on a multidimensional development of interactions and in these processes it is related to an increasing set of other resources over time.

Hence much business activity in an interactive landscape involves companies in wrestling with their existing resources, trying to combine physical and organizational resources in their own internal collections with those of other companies in new ways and integrating them with newly developed resources.

Resources and Multiple Contexts

Proposition 3 (see Box 5.1) suggests that every resource exists in multiple contexts. In the previous section, we explored some of the implications of this idea for the interplay between new and existing resources. Another important aspect of this multiplicity is the difference between the context in which a resource is produced and that in which it is used. These different contexts are readily apparent for products, such as cars, TV sets and mobile phones, but they also apply in the case of operating facilities, such as machinery, systems and equipment.

Context of Use

We illustrate the use aspect of a resource and the phenomena of pre-existing and evolving resources by taking the example of a particular logistics resource. A physical resource, a load carrier, was developed and introduced by a Norwegian dairy company, Tine, and used in its milk distribution system. The load carrier is perfectly designed to carry 160 one-litre containers of milk and is used throughout the distribution process: The carrier is used in internal transportation within the dairy; in handling in the warehouse; in loading the trucks and in transportation to retail stores. The load carrier is also used in retail stores to display the milk cartons. The load carrier is thus designed to work in combination with a number of other resources within and outside Tine, such as distribution terminals, other load carriers and the resources for internal logistics in stores (see Figure 5.5).

Tine's logistics department has taken the interfaces to these other physical resources into consideration in the design of the load carrier. Its relationships with the major retail chains provided crucial inputs about the interfaces between the load carrier and the resources of the retail store. The interfaces between these resources in the use dimension of the load carrier have created a very efficient logistics resource used in its thousands. The performance of a resource element used within a particular combination depends on how well it fits with other

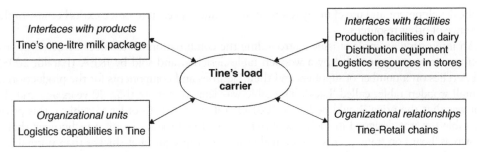

Figure 5.5 Central interfaces in the use of Tine's load carrier.

resources. The more those resources are adapted to each other, the better the performance of the combination as a whole. But, on the other hand, the features of the single resource are then determined by this particular combination. This means that problems may appear when conditions change.

Over recent years, Tine has expanded its product range and the standard one-litre milk container has accounted for a successively smaller share of its total sales. The load carrier can be used for the new products but is not as perfect for them as for the standard one-litre container. Tine has also developed an alliance with other retail store suppliers for joint distribution and the load carrier is not at all suitable for some of these products. Hence the resource no longer has the perfect interfaces with other resources that it had previously.

This example illustrates a very important feature that applies to all resources. The use of a single resource is related to a whole set of other resources, both tangible, as in the case of the resources in the distribution system, and intangible, as with the knowledge and capabilities of the people involved in the operations. These other resources are related to yet other resources. Any change in the combination of the resources and their interfaces affects the use side of the resources. These effects are difficult to foresee since combinations of the use of resources are often complex. Consider, for example, the resource constellation related to the use dimension of a car. This constellation is impossible to capture within any simple, clear-cut boundaries. However, it is possible to identify patterns of related problems, solutions and interdependencies that build on the use of resources from a wide array of locations, such as the resource constellations related to roads and streets, fuel, maintenance and repair, to mention a few. This complexity indicates the problems that would have to be faced if a new propulsion system for cars was widely introduced, based on hydrogen as fuel or using innovative batteries.

Context of Production

It is also possible to outline a general resource constellation that relates to the production of a car, although again we would not be able to identify any clear boundaries for it. Although this constellation includes resources that are also involved with other areas of the business, we find that its main tangible resources, such as factories, and non-tangible resources, including the knowledge of how things are or should be done, are systematically related to the resource constellation for the production of cars. We also see that a particular resource can be involved in the development and use of many resources over time and each resource exists because of the presence of other resources.

An interesting example of issues surrounding the combination of resources involved in producing a resource is provided by a wooden table designed and sold by IKEA (Baraldi 2003). IKEA relies on a number of suppliers and their facilities and components for the production of a small wooden table, called 'Lack'. The table was launched more than 20 years ago and the aim was that the price should be below 100 SEK (about € 10). In order to achieve this price, the table top was designed in such a way that it could be produced with a technology that is known as 'board on frame'. This design made the table top somewhat thicker than normal and this has become a noticeable feature of the table. Over the 20 years that it has been produced, IKEA has conducted more than 100 development projects together with about 20 different suppliers, including producers of furniture components and materials and suppliers of production equipment.

The aim in all these projects has been to find more efficient ways to design, produce and distribute the table top and the four legs. Some of these projects have led to the table legs now being hollow to save materials and weight. Others have substituted printed plastic surfaces for wood veneers. These collaborations with the suppliers have systematically developed all the resources involved in the table and their interfaces with each other. The process has related components to each other, to the materials used, to the way they are produced and to their distribution. The price of the table after 20 years is still 99 SEK and IKEA sells two million of them each year (Baraldi and Waluszewski 2007).

The resources involved in this interactive process can be analysed on a number of different levels. Fundamentally, the counterpart companies and the technologies they possess are themselves resources and so are the development relationships between IKEA and the suppliers. Within this overall constellation of resources, the evolving components and materials of the table are also resources that, like the companies, have been adapted to each other. These resource interaction conditions have also led to a widening range of furniture using the same technological resources of design, material and production. This process over time has taken place in parallel with developments in processes, materials and design which may have had their genesis and application in other contexts or combinations. Finally, the process has occurred through the development of relationships between the companies in which their individual skills have been combined.

Connections Between the Production and Use of a Resource

We can illustrate some aspects of the connections between the use and production of resources by looking at a Swedish supplier of steel (Skarp 2006). SSAB is quite small in comparison with other steel producers and thus finds it difficult to be cost effective in the production and marketing of standardized products that are produced and supplied in large volumes. Therefore, SSAB has prioritized the development of unique and customer-adapted products of specialized steel. However each of these customers buys only a small volume of each of the steels. This is a problem for SSAB because economic usage of manufacturing facilities for a steel supplier requires high utilization of capacity. For this reason, SSAB has developed a basic standard product that can be manufactured at reasonable economies of scale. This standardized product is then adapted to the specific user requirements of particular customers.

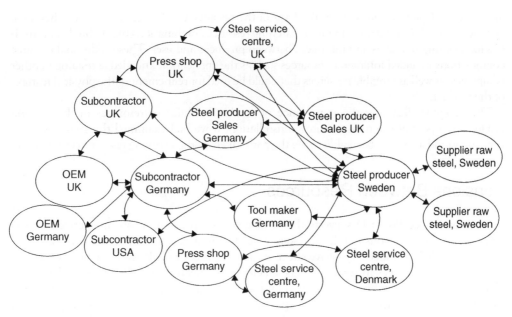

Figure 5.6 Business relationships involved in combining resources.

Source: Skarp, F. (2006). *Adaptations of products to customers' use contexts.* Doctoral dissertation. Gothenburg, Sweden: Division of Industrial Marketing, Chalmers University of Technology, p. 107. Reproduced by permission.

In some cases, it is possible for SSAB to adjust the standard product by recombining its own resources by, for example, shifting between its two internal sources of raw steel. In most cases, however, adaptations to resources require the active participation of the customer in frequent meetings and discussions. This involves interaction between the intangible resources of commercial and technical expertise from different functions in the two organizations. The tangible resources of the new steel and the equipment employed by the user are subject to a series of testing procedures. A typical outcome of these experiments is the joint adaptation of the features of SSAB's product and the customer's manufacturing facility where the product is to be used.

Sometimes the joint efforts of SSAB and the customer are not sufficient to adapt the product to the customer's context. In these situations, other resources have to be mobilized. Figure 5.6 illustrates the organizations involved in the process of adjusting the features of the standard product to the context of a subcontractor to a large OEM in Germany.

Adapting the steel product to the use context of the German subcontractor required the active participation of intangible resources in the subcontractor's organizations in the UK and USA. The customer of the subcontractor was represented by the German and UK operations of the OEM. The knowledge of various functions within SSAB was mobilized in adjusting to the new interfaces of the steel. A steel-service centre was needed for local processing of steel and a press shop was involved in manufacturing applications and sub-assemblies for the customer. These operations required specific production tools to be supplied by a German toolmaker. It would have been extremely costly and unprofitable for both SSAB and the subcontractor to make these adaptations entirely on the basis of the resource combinations in which they were already involved. Careful assessment of matching resource combinations highlighted opportunities for adapting resources and interfaces between producer and user. These additional resource combinations included intangible resources such as the application knowledge residing in other companies, as well as tangible resources that could be used for refinement of the physical features of the product.

This example illustrates the importance of combining different resources in the use and production aspect of the total resource constellation. If we had examined the same case over time, we would also have been able to see the path taken by the evolving resource combination.

Tensions Between Resources

Proposition 4 (see Box 5.1) suggests that a change to a resource in an interactive business landscape induces tensions in related resources leading to a number of possible reactions. Any change intended to produce a positive effect in some resources will also produce negative effects for some other resources in terms of costs, efficiency or effectiveness. This makes all resource changes troublesome and it is very easy to find striking illustrations of this two-way effect. For example, changes to airport flight paths to provide benefits for the airport, airlines and passengers may produce very negative effects for people who own property under the new flight paths.

Similarly, if a customer and supplier are successful in adapting a resource in a way that is beneficial to both of them, this may create problems for some of their other counterparts. For example, a supplier and some of its major customers may be able to achieve cost savings by investing in equipment that enables them to bypass distributors and operate direct deliveries. However, this move may mean that the operations of the supplier's distributor are no longer economic for the reduced volume of their trade. The negative effects on third parties of resource changes may produce reactions from them: They may attempt to hinder the development of the resources or the actors involved, or may develop their own interests in alternative resources. Thus the distributor may refuse to handle the supplier's sales to its other smaller customers or may switch its allegiance to other suppliers.

Because all resources are a part of several resource constellations, the tensions created by a resource change are distributed widely. For example, the development of collateralized debt obligations enabled mortgage banks to lend more freely and provided profits for at least some of those that traded in them. But this resource development has had profound implications for the business constellations that encompass almost all other businesses. There are always reasons to develop a resource in relation to every resource combination of which it is part. But there are usually contradictions between these potential developments as we have all seen. There are often differences between what makes a resource easier to produce and what makes it more useful. Furthermore, there might also be differences in what makes it more useful for one customer compared to another.

Systematically relating resources to each other produces resource combinations of economic importance. The complexity of these combinations means that important resource interfaces within them are rarely simple or standardized. This means that innovation and change are demanding processes. Interfaces have to be developed for a new resource and related resources may also have to be changed, creating effects in other related interfaces. The concept of 'friction' has been suggested to give insight into this process (Håkansson and Waluszewski 2002).

For example, when a resource is subject to pressure for change, it produces a reaction or *friction* because of tensions in both the focal and related interfaces. The effects of this friction are both distributed and transformed across the resource combination. How this distribution and transformation appear depends on how the resource interfaces exposed to the effect have been developed and on how important each resource is to the larger resource combination. Friction in a resource combination has an economic logic. It systematically relates every suggestion for something new to existing investments in resource interfaces. One consequence is that friction effects can both hinder and facilitate change, depending on how much the new solution can be positively related to earlier investments or to parallel changes.

The tensions between resource interfaces create a constant pressure to develop resources and a constant pressure to keep them as they are. However, all tensions have a particular direction and are part of a pattern of tensions stretching across each resource combination. Some changes will be more in line with the potential development of other resources or of the combination as a whole. This is where intangible resources play a special role. They are often quite flexible and can be used to integrate more inflexible tangible resources. In these processes, business relationships are of particular importance, as we see in the next section.

Business Relationships and Resource Development and Use

Intensity of Interaction

Proposition 5 (see Box 5.1) suggests that the greater the intensity of interaction between resources, the greater the effects of a specific change of resource.

For example, it is common for a company to reduce the total number of its suppliers as part of a plan to involve the remaining suppliers more closely in development projects. These developments are likely to increase the interaction between the resources of the supplier and those remaining counterparts and lead to more changes in resources. Increased interaction is a way to increase the economic effects of any resource change, but it also increases the overall costs and complexity of changes.

Breadth of Interaction

Proposition 6 (see Box 5.1) suggests that the greater the breadth of interaction between resources, the greater the number of resources that are likely to be changed. One form of broadening is to broaden the type of resources and issues addressed in a single relationship. For example, a customer and a supplier may adapt their offerings to each other's requirements. They could also establish further resource ties between themselves by jointly adapting their operating facilities to achieve greater efficiency. A second form of broadening is to systematically relate the resources employed in a particular relationship to those in other relationships. So, for example, the two companies involved in a relationship could integrate their product or operational adaptations with those of the customer's customers or supplier's suppliers. In both cases, the costs of the interaction will increase but the potential benefits will also be greater as more resources are involved.

A business relationship is a very particular type of resource. On the one hand, it is a single resource for both of the participants, although it is always the case that the two counterparts have a different view of its purpose or value. On the other hand, a business relationship is also a resource combination. The value of a resource in the interactive business landscape is dependent on the effects it has on other resources and business relationships play a crucial role for the development of all resources. Relationships can be interpreted as a set of resources, each of which is related to those in another resource collection in a counterpart company. Relationships are interactive processes over time in which some of the resources of the two counterparts are adapted towards each other. As we discussed in Chapter 3, the process of interaction does not take place in isolation in each relationship. Resource interaction in a relationship can be restricted or enhanced, prioritized or marginalized by the companies involved in it, based on their view of that relationship when compared with others.

Image Level and Activated Level of Interaction

Resources can take two roles in business relationships: Resources are frequently the *subject* of discussion in the interaction between individual actors in the related companies; resources may also be *objects* that are changed and activated by their interaction with other resources. We can formalize this distinction by separating an *image level* from an *activated level* of interaction (Håkansson and Waluszewski 2002:72ff).

At the image level, ideas about single resources as well as combinations of resources are discussed. These ideas are often represented by images such as drawings or formulae. Resources can be systematically related to each other on this image level following a theoretical logic. Here there can be lots of ideas, creativity and many possibilities.

On the activated level, resources are adapted and used interactively. There is direct contact and the result is much more practical rather than theoretical. The resources may work in the way assumed at the image level or they may not! The activated level may behave in quite unexpected ways due to imperfections on the image level. If the discussions on the image level are always firmly rooted in the activated level, there is unlikely to be significant difference between the two. However, this is not always the case: The activated structure may work despite the fact that it cannot be explained on the image level or the solution may appear to be correct from what is known on the image level, but it may not work on the activated level.

The activated structure and the image structure of resources have at least partly different logics: Everything that happens in the activated structure cannot be translated to images. The image structure, on the other hand, can include knowledge that has not yet been used in the activated structure and it can also include contradictory solutions. For example, a customer company may have a clear image about how to make more environmentally acceptable a product that it buys. However, the supplier company's image of these possibilities may be rather different as these are based on its experiences of dealing with the activated structure. This situation is characterized in the scenario where IKEA tried to force their suppliers of catalogue paper to adapt to their image of a 'green' or environmentally acceptable product (Håkansson and Waluszewski 2002:72ff). The suppliers had quite different images because of their different context.

Interaction within a relationship can centre on a tangible product or an intangible service but it often also includes a wider combination of resources, including those related to product production or service fulfilment and those involved in transport and distribution. Resource interaction often involves or relates to a number of different resource combinations or company resource collections. The content of a relationship is developed through interaction over time. Any interaction has to develop in relation to what is happening in all these connected resources. But interaction is also influenced by both sides. Each side can attempt to vary both the breadth and the intensity of the interaction. Each side can try to increase or decrease the number of different resources or issues dealt with and the number of individuals or functions involved. In other words, each side can vary their own, and attempt to vary their counterpart's, resource investments in their relationship. For example, some resources may be dedicated to a single counterpart and form part of a unique resource combination. Others may be changed so that they relate to a number of different relationships in a standardized way.

Issues of standardization relate to the creation of economic benefits in different resource interfaces. One situation where standardization becomes important is when it is necessary to relate a product resource to other resources such as production equipment. Resource interaction commonly involves a combination of resources that are highly dependent on the efficient operation of some particular resource.

The interaction in a single relationship between two companies involves supplies from many other companies that are used in development or operations. It is common nowadays for at least 70 % of a company's costs of producing an offering by to be accounted for by purchases from others. Interaction may involve a single item or a collection of thousands of individual items in a catalogue. In this latter case, it is the ability of a company to access or accumulate resources from many locations that gives value to its product for others, rather than any transformation of those resources undertaken by it. The use of input products from suppliers in any interaction with customers is an example of the use of resources based in other companies and this is likely to be a dominant aspect of business in networks. There are always important resource interdependencies across company boundaries and this is why its business relationships are an important part of the total resources of a company or a business unit.

Figure 5.7 illustrates the crucial role of relationships as resources. Company A has over time developed some joint resources in its relationship with Company B. This relationship provides access for A to the resources of B. In addition, Company B serves as a connection to other resources through its direct and indirect relationships with other firms.

A company consists partly of very intangible resources, such as the knowledge of single individuals as well as of groups that are involved in handling more tangible resources such as physical products and facilities. One type of resource is technological knowledge that can be applied to produce and use a number of different resources. Organizational resources also include the abilities of individuals to achieve synergistic benefits through interaction with each other. The importance of being able to interact effectively with counterparts means that organizational resources are not limited by the physical boundaries of an organization or to those employed by a particular actor. Instead, an organizational resource may span organizational boundaries within business relationships or through individual connections. Through these organizational resources

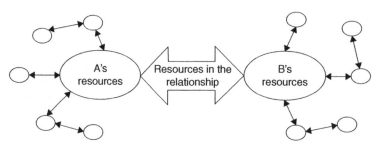

Figure 5.7   Business relationships as resources.

a company's tangible and technological resources may also be based in other companies. The combination of internal and external resources that enable a company to operate is developed over time in a number of different ways, such as through mergers or the acquisition of other companies. But the dominant method of resource development is in a large number of smaller steps in interaction with different counterparts, both suppliers and customers.

Resources in Time

Time has been a central aspect in our discussions of resource interaction. The content of interaction develops over time. It is manifested in business relationships and in changes to individual resources over time. The value of resources arises from how they are combined with other resources and this implies that the separate and collective interaction history of those resources is important. This importance can be described and characterized in terms of the existence and importance of the resource *paths* that we discussed in Chapter 3.

The content of the interaction, the development, combining and using of resources, can be interpreted as an investment process (Johanson and Wootz 1986). A key characteristic of an investment is that there is an observable pattern in outward and inward economic flows. Investments are paid out before income starts to arrive. The main effect of this pattern is that the lifetime of an investment has great influence on the creation of a positive economic outcome. For interaction, this means that it is important to achieve stability over time. This stability has to be combined with a path of changes in at least a partly organized pattern.

When a large investment is made in resources, for example in production or logistics facilities, it is obviously advantageous if these can be used over a long period of time. The same conditions apply for intangible resources, such as brands, patents and knowledge and experience about the company's operations and about how it can work well with other organizations. Similarly, building effective relationships is demanding of resource.

The case study of SSAB in the steel industry described how the company worked for more than three years with a particular customer without any commercial outcome. Lots of people from various departments and functions were involved in costly interaction with the customer and with other, related actors in the network. The customer also put huge resources into the change project. Changing input material in a production process such as this is a complex undertaking (see Figure 5.8). Replacing a specific input may impact not only on the operations of Customer A. The output of Customer A is most likely to be affected, in turn causing consequences for its

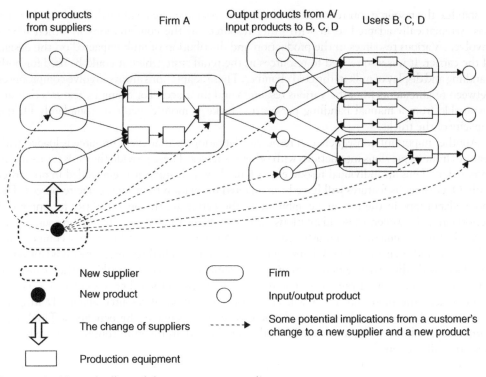

Figure 5.8   Network effects of changing an input product.

Source: Skarp, F. (2006). *Adaptations of products to customers' use contexts.* Doctoral dissertation. Gothenburg, Sweden: Division of Industrial Marketing, Chalmers University of Technology, p. 28. Reproduced by permission.

customers B, C and D. Also other suppliers' inputs to Customer A may be affected by a change to the new material. Investing in a new resource may impact on the whole resource constellation. It goes without saying that there must be considerable expectation of future benefits in order to involve and mobilize both the customer and the supplier in similar change projects.

A key aspect of resource handling is to take advantage of this total stock of resource investments by using single resources and resource combinations. This can be achieved by making complementary investments in both physical and organizational resources, to combine existing resources within and across company boundaries and to influence others to make complementary investments in order to create a path.

A second reason for the importance of resource paths is the need for actors to learn. Interaction over time provides opportunities for learning where and how resources can be adapted themselves and adapted to each other. These adaptations can produce changes in resource interfaces and improve the performance of a resource combination. Learning requires change in order to become useful, but it also requires a measure of stability in order to be productive (Håkansson 1993).

Adaptations are undertaken to improve the performance of a single resource in relation to specific others. These adaptations change some of the features of the single resource through developing its interfaces with other resources. In this respect, the individual resource is destabilized since its features are affected. However, changes at the individual resource level tend to stabilize the resource constellation in which these resources are combined. Tine's load carrier was systematically adapted to fit with other resources in the combinations in which it was involved. Various resources in the production and distribution of milk impacted on the design of the carrier. It was also related to resources in the retail store where it could be used for both handling and display of milk in the cold chamber. These adaptations always involve compromises between requirements from the various resources and interfaces. For example, features that are favourable from a manual handling perspective make it more difficult to completely fill the capacity of the trucks.

Another important consequence of resource adaptations is that every resource is loaded with features from its previous interactions with other resources. These provide the basis for its future interaction. Thus an individual resource is coloured by its history: it is embedded in an earlier path. Over time, its features will have been adapted in relation to other specific resources. The more adaptations in the resource combination, the better are the opportunities for enhanced performance. However, these adaptations make it difficult to change individual resources. For example, the instrument panel illustrated in Figure 5.4 is a complex combination of components, subsystems and their interfaces. Changing one of these individual resources means adapting its interfaces with the other resources. Some improvements may be impossible if they cause too much disruption to other resources. The more adaptations to the other resources in a specific combination, the more difficult it will be to use the individual resource efficiently in other resource combinations with different characteristics. For example, the benefits of Tine's load carrier were reduced when it was used for other products than the milk containers for which it was originally designed.

Paths are also created with connected interactions that relate the changes in one resource to changes in other resources and thus make them more useful in specific combinations. During these processes, old features may be used in new ways or new features may be developed. Even a resource that loses its connections in a business setting has the potential for development of new economic value. For example, when the Uppsala-based biotechnology equipment company Biacore started to produce analytical equipment for on-line investigation of molecule interactions in the mid 1990s, the management searched for personnel from among the former employees of LKB, a similar company that had closed down in the late 1980s. The staff of this company were known for their skills in work with a combination of biochemistry, fine mechanicals and automation. The management of Biacore found that these workers were no longer in the biotechnology industry but in a company producing military equipment. Although this company had a completely different product range, it became the first supplier of some key components to Biacore through its resource of former LKB employees (Harrison and Waluszewski 2008).[6]

---

[6]The development of resource paths is also important for technical development (Arthur 1988; Hughes 1983, 1987; Lindqvist 1984; David 1985; Kaiser and Hedin 1995). Studies show that the development of technological systems, particularly large ones, seems to follow particular patterns. Technological trajectory and path dependence are concepts used to illustrate these development patterns (Dosi *et al.* 1988). The argument has been that every technological system has some 'internal' characteristics that influence its development. The system is always defined in relation to some basic principles that make some development patterns much more likely than others.

The Lack case study presented above illustrates the importance of how these interactive and technological development patterns are intertwined. The efforts to keep the price of the Lack table constant required systematic efforts in changing the features of its components and input materials. These adaptations impacted on the interfaces between the resources. Some of these resources, for example the board-on-frame technology, had to be more or less accepted for technological reasons. Others, such as the lacquers, could be strongly adapted to the specific requirements for the table top in terms of colour, luminescence and resistance. But, most importantly, Lack was perfectly adapted to the total resources of IKEA. From the beginning, one of the main factors leading to low price was a low weight that fitted well with IKEA's distribution system. This requirement impacted on the original design of the table and has continued to impact on the product features even when transportation cost became less critical. The low weight of the table offers other benefits in logistics, such as reduced transport damage and user-friendly handling across the entire logistical network. However, achieving full truck loads in transportation interferes with requirements concerning service levels in the stores. Thus there are tensions between various types of adaptations and different resource features.

The reason behind the problems for the Tine load carrier relates to the same phenomenon. There is always a tension between adapting specific resources to different resource combinations. There are always those who are interested in stabilizing a resource combination and others who want to change it. This is especially the case for resources activated in different resource combinations or in combinations that stretch over company boundaries. These resources are exposed to different development patterns which may be contradictory. For example, Tine's combination of distribution resources was not fully utilized. Two other suppliers to the same stores had similar problems. Therefore, a logistic alliance between these three companies considerably reduced their total distribution costs. These gains were considered to outweigh the negative effects of the development on the perfect fit between the load carrier and the products for which it was developed.

Resources in Space

The content of interaction influences the position of resources in multidimensional space: how closely related they are physically, whether they are directed towards each other, and the extent to which knowledge about them and their use is different between counterparts. Resources are not combined in a passive way; resource combinations are not just tried out but also successively developed. This development affects the economic value of the different resources. This can be illustrated by the following example.

Before the environmental debate took off in the 1990s, companies producing a lot of waste paper, such as retailers, had to pay to get waste paper collectors to take care of it. When environmental organizations, paper producers and users started to regard waste paper as a 'green' input to paper production, waste paper was collected for free or could even be sold to the collectors. Thus, a change in how one resource (the waste) was combined and related to some other resource increased its value and the value of the total resource constellation in which it was embedded (Håkansson and Waluszewski 2002).

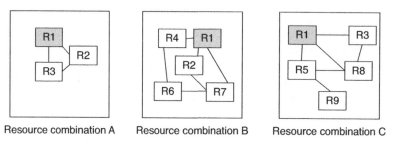

Resource combination A   Resource combination B   Resource combination C

Figure 5.9 The value of resource R1 is dependent on its combination with other resources.

A major reason why it is possible to affect resources economically is that they are, or at least can be treated as, heterogeneous. A heterogeneous resource is economically dependent on the other resource with which it is combined. This is not the case for a homogeneous resource. In space terms, we can say that space does not matter for a homogeneous resource (or that it always has the same distance from other resources). But the value of a heterogeneous resource is highly related to the other resources with which it is combined and to how this combining is done. A typical example used in economic literature is the existence of 'team effects' when individuals are combined (Alchian and Demsetz 1972). A particular individual A is of different value when combined with B compared to when combined with C because the characteristics of B and C affect A's motivation and capabilities. It is the same for the waste paper above: Combined in a certain way it was worthless but in another combination it attained a positive value. Figure 5.9 illustrates how resource R1 appears in three combinations with other resources. The value of R1 is different in each of these combinations in the space dimension. The value depends on which resources are combined and on the principles of resource combining across space. In Chapter 4, we discussed how interaction provides opportunities for benefit in terms of connections between geographical places, bodies of knowledge and capital investments.

The space dimension of a resource is central. Over time, resources move in relation to each other or become more or less directed towards each other. Some resources are combined in several ways and they successively become closer either physically or in terms of the knowledge held of their design or use. Other resources move away from each other. These changes in distance can happen between individual resources or companies as a whole. For example, the growth of business relationships has been described as a process of distance reduction between aspects of the companies' resources or the companies themselves (Ford 1980). It is interaction that creates these movements and it means that the same resource can be exposed to contradictory demands.[7]

To continue with the waste paper example, even as apparently simple a resource as waste paper must go through a process of being thoroughly combined and related to other resources

---

[7]The importance of the space dimension for the development of resources has also been argued by researchers interested in economic geography, such as Storper (1997) and Malmberg and Maskell (2002); researchers interested in economic development and international trade, such as Krugman (1991), Krugman and Venables (1995) and North (2005); researchers interested in the internationalization of companies, such as Johanson and Vahlne (2009); and researchers interested in the function of multinational companies, such as Andersson *et al.* (1997) and Ghoshal and Bartlett (1990).

before it can be used as a resource in a business setting. In order for waste paper to be collected from households and businesses, sorted and distributed to a paper mill, there are combinations of technical and organizational resources that have to be related to each other. For example, before the waste paper can be used in the paper production process for newsprint, it has to be de-inked. However, the de-inking process may require adaptation to the paper-making process. This produces a typical example of the tensions that arise when a resource is combined in several resource combinations across organizational boundaries. On the one hand, the producer of the newspaper wants a final product from which the ink does not come off on the hands of the reader. On the other hand, the producer of the newspaper wants to decrease costs and show its customers that it is printing on an environmentally acceptable paper, i.e. that it is using de-inked waste paper. So it wants an ink that can be washed off in the de-inking process. Thus, although resources are exposed to interaction processes where they are systematically related to each other and in which interfaces with specific attributes are created, these are often contradictory to each other.

Varying combinations of tangible resources provide useful development opportunities. However, these opportunities are multiplied when they are combined with intangible human and organizational resources. The development and repositioning of these resources can be used to develop, combine, produce, investigate, adapt and use tangible resources. Intangible resources, embedded into organizational units and organizational relationships, are in some aspects similar to tangible resources: They have been developed over time and are thus heavy from an economic point of view and it is even more difficult to know how they interact with other resources. Reducing the distance between the knowledge or technologies of counterparts through learning and teaching is one of the primary routes to relationship development and the development of specific resources.

If we treat resources as heterogeneous, we can understand the importance of interaction for enhancing the value in them by changing their position with respect to other resources. This is in contradiction to the view of the business landscape that follows from an assumption of resource homogeneity, i.e. where all resources are totally known or where they have the same value independent of the other resources with which they are combined. In this case, interaction would be meaningless. However, it is costly or impossible to treat all resources as heterogeneous and this is the reason for the importance of standardization. Standardization of resources is a way to create homogeneity in relation to specific other resources. Resource standardization may have cost benefits for the development and operations of the company doing the standardizing, but disadvantages for those subject to it. The cost effects of standardization must be set against its possibly negative effects on the important resources of the business relationships in which it takes place.

Resource heterogeneity provides the potential for new value to be developed just by changing the ways resources are combined. Thus in some contexts, used newspapers and packaging products are an important 'green' material for paper production, while in others they are just waste. A more extreme example is provided by ice; in many parts of the world, ice is something that simply creates problems for boat traffic. However, ice has also led to the development of an important export industry from Boston to the Caribbean, Europe and India for the smart set to use in their drinks. When a pile of ice on a frozen river in Northern Sweden is put into the hands of a number of sculptors and house builders are flown in from different parts of the world, it results in an ice bar or an ice hotel. When these constructions are combined with the physical and organizational resources built up by a number of tourist offices and travel organizers who sell 'experiences' to visitors who live a great distance from ice and snow, then a resource that previously only generated costs becomes a very useful resource in a business setting.

The space dimension in interaction is important as it exploits the heterogeneity of resources. This has at least two important consequences: The first is that, regardless of whether a resource is used in one or several business settings, it has a number of very specific more or less elaborate interfaces with related resources. In this way, each resource has a particular position and direction in the space dimension. The second consequence is that behind each interface between two resources, there are several other resources, that also have interfaces with them and that are dependent on the existence of the focal interface. Thus, when a resource is related to other resources it gains an economic value, but it is also 'loaded' with tensions and dynamics due to the forces of resources with which it interacts. Thus a resource can be said to incorporate time through its history and to be located at a moving point in multidimensional network space through its heterogeneity.

One important consequence for practitioners is that there is always an economic potential in finding new ways to improve the combination of a specific resource with all others. The economic value of any resource can always be improved. Another more problematic consequence is that when a resource is combined with a new resource there may be severe effects on already existing combinations creating strong reactions from other involved actors.

A major problem for practitioners is that there are so many resource combinations, especially when we consider all the different combinations that occur in connected resource constellations. It is impossible for any single actor to know more than a tiny part of all these combinations. This reinforces the importance of interaction as the way in which actors can work together and build on each other's tangible and intangible resources.

Conclusion

This chapter has described the interactive nature of business resources. Interactivity means that resource utilization is not a process that can centre on a single resource or be restricted to a single company. Interactivity forms the basis for capitalizing on the heterogeneity of resources and is the means through which resources can be combined, developed and exploited.

An interactive view of resources concentrates on the ways that they become activated through interaction with others. The propositions that we have introduced underline that resource interaction is an evolutionary process. No new resource is ever context-free and no developed resource is ever free from the interfaces in its past. Resource evolution is a process that affects the nature both of single resources and the resource collections of companies, their relationships and the total resource constellation. Resource combination leads to a never-ending set of possibilities for further evolution and recombination with other new and existing resources. However, the propositions in this chapter also point out that these processes are full of tensions and struggles due to connections with existing interfaces. The value of a single resource varies both in time and in the combinations in which it is used. Each resource has a particular set of interfaces with other resources and these interfaces are in turn embedded into a larger pattern of related interfaces. Individual resources interact with each other and this means that they are constantly adapted in relation to each other. All these interactions affect the use, and thereby also the value, of each resource. The interfaces between resources, which can be located within and over organizational borders, have distinct effects on the current economic use of a resource, as well as on its future development.

All of this means that, when we examine resources, we need to be aware that they exist at different levels of aggregation, from the individual resource through combinations with single other resources to smaller resource collections that are part of a larger constellation.

This chapter has concentrated on interaction between resources and to a lesser extent on interaction about resources. But in Chapter 3, we emphasized that each layer of interaction, activities, resources and actors also interact between themselves. The next two chapters investigate the nature of interactive activities and the interactive actor.

INTERACTION AND ACTIVITIES

6

In this chapter, we focus on how business activities are influenced by being parts of an interactive world. Activities bring life to a network: Goods are produced, delivered and displayed; services are provided, accounts are calculated and bills are paid. All these and millions of other activities affect and are also affected by the actors and resources with which they are associated. The activities in a business network are both part of the process of interaction and the outcome of the network. Activities are interdependent. Even those activities that appear to be carried out entirely within a single company and out of sight, or without the knowledge of others, are dependent on and interact with things that are done by other companies and organizations and, in turn, they affect the activities of others. Each activity forms part of the patterns of activities that extend within and over company and organizational boundaries and stretch across the landscape of the network.

Activities not only interact with others spatially across the landscape of the network. They are also related to each other over time. A single activity is affected by what takes place contemporaneously, since it is carried out at a specific time. But that activity also has a history. It will have evolved from earlier activities and when it is performed, it creates effects that appear immediately as well as those that emerge over a period of time.

In this chapter, we examine the interaction between activities and how that interaction relates to the need for change and stabilization. We begin by illustrating the complexity of the activity patterns in which firms are involved by using a set of propositions. We conclude that interdependencies and time are central features of activity patterns and examine the relationship between these central features. Configuring activities is a core issue for companies and we offer a framework for configuring activities and activity patterns. The final part of the chapter is devoted to a discussion of the dynamics of activity patterns related to three large companies.

A Business Landscape Full of Activities

Our focus in this chapter is on the activities of companies and on how those activities are affected by being part of an interactive world. It is the interaction between activities that brings life to a network and which characterizes the actors that perform them. Goods are produced and transported, services are completed; new technologies and products are developed; information is exchanged; money is transacted. The activities of each company are interconnected with those of many others. All these activities affect and are also affected by the actors and resources with which they are associated. The activity patterns in the business landscape are essential elements in the processes of interaction in business relationships. The complexity of these patterns is substantial. For example, in the construction industry the characteristics of house-building have been expressed in the following way:

> The physical substance of a house is a pile of materials assembled from widely scattered resources. They undergo different kinds and degrees of processing in large numbers of places, require many types of handling over periods that vary greatly in length and use the services of a multitude of people organized into many different sorts of business entity . . .
>
> For any given house the parts of the process must be well enough performed and coordinated so that all the separate pieces come together. These pieces must arrive at reasonably acceptable time, in a tolerable sequence, and at bearable prices upon the particular small piece of ground where a builder and his contractor combine them into a house.
>
> Cox and Goodman (1956)

The authors continue by saying that despite the fact that the complexity related to the operations in this activity pattern 'looks impossibly formidable, it is in fact solved over and over again as new houses go up in their millions'. Moreover, it is argued that these issues in house-building are handled and solved so often that we come to take the solution for granted and tend to forget how much effort and ingenuity have gone into it.

At any construction site, numerous activity structures and resource collections of various firms intersect. These patterns cross the boundaries of several organizations: main contractor, material producers, subcontractors, distributors, installation firms, and so on. The combined efforts of these actors in building the house require numerous interaction processes. Interaction is important because the separate parts of the process must be 'coordinated so that all the separate pieces come together' both during work at the site and in the planning conducted before it. Interaction is also required in order to coordinate what takes place at the site with what is happening in the manufacturing facilities for building materials, in the warehousing of these materials and in their transportation to the site. Another complication is that each of the actors involved at a particular construction site is simultaneously involved in other projects at other sites with other business partners, further emphasizing the need for interaction.

These conditions are prevalent in any activity pattern in the business landscape. Undertaking a particular activity is strongly contingent on other activities. To an increasing extent, these activities are undertaken in different companies implying that interdependencies stretch across the boundaries of firms. Figure 6.1 illustrates interdependencies in an activity pattern involving one buying firm, three of its suppliers and sub-suppliers, one of its own customers and another buying firm. The direct interdependence between the buying firm and one of its suppliers is denoted by 'e' in the figure. However, this interdependence is, to a large extent, derived from the connections to other companies involved in the pattern. These indirect interdependencies stem from: the connection between two suppliers ('a'); the connection between the buying firm and a sub-supplier ('b'); the connection between the buying firm and a customer ('c'); and the connection between the buying firm and another buyer ('d'). In reality, the complexity is even

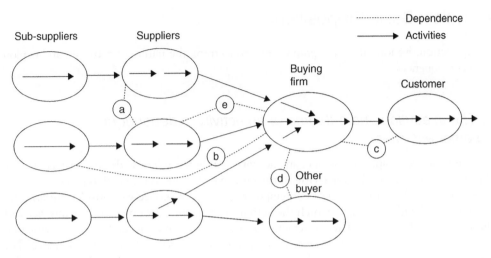

Figure 6.1 Interdependencies in activity patterns.

Source: Gadde, L.-E. and Håkansson, H. (2001), *Supply Network Strategies.* John Wiley & Sons Ltd, p.75. Reproduced by permission.

greater since indirect interdependencies also occur through the supplier's connections to other customers and sub-suppliers as well as the customer's connections to its customers and to other suppliers than our buying firm.

In this way, the activity patterns that criss-cross the business landscape are both highly complex and significant for economic life. These features become obvious if we try to imagine all of the activities behind the supply and use of any everyday product or service. For example, when a Norwegian fishing-vessel in the North Sea lands a catch on the boat, the fish is sorted, frozen and placed in a cold-store on the boat. After it is landed, the frozen fish may be transported to a fish-processing business in China, where it is de-frozen and hand-filleted by young Chinese women. Then the fish is re-frozen and sent to the UK for final packaging. After this it is distributed to wholesalers and retailers. Some days later, the frozen and packed fillets appear as a special offer in a supermarket chain in UK. Similar patterns of activities, stretching across the borders of several organizations, industries and geographical areas can be identified behind the provision of almost any product or service, whether it is based on natural resources or is the outcome of advanced industrial operations. For example, a steel component in the safety system of a car goes through a huge number of related operations. These activities span the boundaries of a steel mill, the factory of a component supplier and the assembly line at the car producer. Service operations involve similar activity patterns: Logistics service providers, such as Federal Express and DHL, make alternative activity patterns accessible to their clients. Transportation activities based on the efficient utilization of trucks, aircraft, ships and other vehicles connect logistic hubs across the globe, making it possible to dispatch goods overnight to companies over most of the world.

From this background, we can formulate some basic propositions about activities and activity patterns as we did for resources in Chapter 5.

Activities: Basic Propositions

In this section, we formulate five propositions concerning the nature of activities and explore their consequences.

1. The execution and outcome of an activity is dependent on other activities.

In an interactive business landscape, any activity is interdependent with other activities. The current configuration of these activities is the outcome of previous interaction processes.

Almost regardless of the kind of contemporary product or service we consider, we find that it is associated with patterns in which the activities undertaken by one company interact with those conducted by others. These interaction processes create interdependencies evolving from the efforts of companies to synchronize their operations in order to improve performance. This synchronization is achieved through the linking of activities that are in some way related to each other, e.g. the manufacturing, warehousing and transportation of a product. These links between activities may, over time, become manifested in connections that are very visible, such as when operations are located in close connection to each other. For example, many car manufacturers require their most important suppliers to establish manufacturing facilities in supplier-parks immediately adjacent to their assembly lines. In other situations, related activities may be located far away from each other, making it difficult to identify the linkages between them. But even in these cases, closer examination makes it possible to observe inter-connections and dependencies of various types. For example, the catching of krill fish in the North Sea is related to a Swedish-based biotechnology company's activities because a particular substance obtained from the krill is used in the production of an enzyme.

2. Adjustments between activities improve their joint performance.

In an interactive business landscape adjustments between activities provide the means of handling interdependencies and enhance performance in the activity configuration.

By adjusting two activities in relation to each other the joint performance of the two is improved. These adjustments may involve, for example the synchronization of production activities in and between companies, adjustments to transportation services, scheduling of service provision and fine-tuning between production and logistics activities. Some business transactions are characterized by an immense exchange of documents. In these situations, adjustments of administrative routines for offering, ordering, confirmation, delivery notification, invoicing, etc., may contribute substantially to enhance the functional and economic performance. Other examples include joint efforts in product design and technical development. In most cases, adjustments concerning information exchange are prerequisites for these gains. Adjustments between activities impose costs for those involved. The aim is that over time these costs will be outweighed by long-term benefits. However, the potential advantages provided by mutual adjustments are accompanied by increasing interdependence among the activities.

3. Adjustments between activities create interdependencies.

In an interactive business landscape, adjustments between activities impose interdependence. There are different types of interdependencies and changing one of these will impact on the others.

Adjustments are not only ways of handling interdependence, they also impose interdependence. For example, designing just-in-time (JIT) deliveries in cooperation with a particular vendor may be a way for a customer to reduce potential availability problems related to its previous dependence on the discretion of a number of more or less anonymous suppliers. Once a JIT solution is put in place, however, other types of interdependence will appear. The customer company is now dependent on the delivery reliability and continuous flow of inputs from this specific counterpart. In the same way, the supplier has made commitments and investments that constrain its other activities. In the analytical part of the chapter, we identify three types of interdependency and illustrate how changes of one type of interdependency impact on the other two.

4. A single activity is part of several activity configurations.

In an interactive business landscape any activity is part of many activity chains and configurations. These conditions impose tensions for the design and the potential changes of the single activity.

Although it is often possible to trace a clear activity configuration surrounding a particular product or service, few if any of these arrangements exist in isolation. There are always connections between one configuration and others across the network so that a single activity may also be part of other configurations leading to production and distribution of other products or services. For example, the activities involved in the development, production and delivery of titanium components for military aircraft connect at many points (and over time) with the activities involved in the production of golf clubs and bicycles. A company involved in the undertaking of one of these activities interacts with manufacturers and users of bicycles, golf clubs and military equipment. Each of these have their own specific requirements of the particular activity – how it should be best performed and what changes might be called for – and these, in turn, lead to tensions that must be handled.

5. As two activities become adjusted to each other, the better they function together.

In an interactive business landscape, mutual adjustments between two activities improve their functionality in relation to each other. These adjustments also make the two activities increasingly useful for the larger activity pattern of which they form part, since increasing interaction leads to the discovery of new potential applications within this broader context. At the same time, however, this increasing specialization will make it difficult to utilize these activities effectively in other patterns that have followed other routes of specialization.

This proposition follows from propositions 2, 3 and 4 (see Box 6.1). Adjustments improve the joint functionality of two activities. The more adjustments, the more fine-tuned the two become in relation to each other and the better their performance. Therefore, in our example above, the functionality of an activity related to the manufacturing of golf clubs is improved the more that the activity is adjusted to other golf-club production activities. These adjustments require enhanced interaction in relation to the 'golf-club configuration' which in turn may result in discovery of new potential applications in this context. Increasing attention and adjustments to this configuration may also provide opportunities for involvement in hitherto unexploited activity configurations with the same characteristics as golf-club production. On the other hand, adjustments to golf-club-like applications will impact on the features of the activity. These changes may make the activity less useful in relation to those activities involved in manufacturing bikes and military equipment that, in turn, are subject to specialization. This proposition is similar to others in that there is a clear link to the resource structure. One example of this link is the load carrier designed by the milk producer Tine that we described in Chapter 5. The load carrier was an efficient means of undertaking activities related to the distribution and display of the milk cartons of Tine. However, these activities could not be undertaken in the same efficient way in the activity configurations of Tine's partners in the logistics alliance.

The Activity Layer

The five propositions (summarized in Box 6.1) together form the basic point of departure for our analysis of the activity layer of business interaction. Activities are integral parts of the processes of interaction in a business network; a single business activity is isolated from others and each would be useless on its own. Any activity is related to different but simultaneous patterns in concert with other activities. These patterns occur whether or not they were planned or designed by any of the many actors that are involved in them, or are affected by them, or whether those patterns appear to be incidental to their own operations. A single activity, whether it occurs at one point in time or is continuously performed has more or less identifiable effects on other specific activities, on resources and on actors. A single activity enables or leads other activities to take place and provokes reactions and re-reactions to occur. The interaction model in Figure 3.6 illustrated the connections between activities and their central dimensions of time and space. Table 6.1 recapitulates these characteristics and shows the central issues in the two dimensions that are to be explored in this chapter.

We have identified the key issue for activities in space as the *interdependence* between them and this has been expanded on in our propositions. Even those activities that appear to be carried

---

Box 6.1   Propositions about the Nature of Activities

1. The execution and outcome of any activity is dependent on other activities.
2. Adjustments between activities improve their joint performance.
3. Adjustments between activities create interdependencies.
4. A single activity is an integral part of several activity configurations.
5. As two activities become adjusted to each other, the better they function together in the larger activity pattern in which they are involved.

Table 6.1 Central characteristics of the activity layer.

Dimension of interaction	Impact on activities	Central issues
Space	Interdependency	Activity linking Coordination across boundaries of firms
Time	Specialization	Adjustments over time Stabilizing and modifying

out entirely within a single company and out of sight, or without the knowledge of others, are dependent on their interaction with other activities in other companies and organizations. In turn, these activities affect the activities of others. Each activity forms part of the patterns of activities that extend within and over company and organizational boundaries and stretch across the landscape of the network. The efficient undertaking of an individual activity is therefore dependent on its linkages to other activities and the coordination of these linkages. Increasingly, interdependent activities are located in different firms, because of recent attention that has been devoted to outsourcing. Coordination of activities therefore requires joint boundary-spanning efforts by companies. This requirement may be especially problematic and cause tensions when an activity is about to be changed because these changes may require the modification of a multitude of other activities, many of which may be undertaken by other firms.

The key issue for activities in time is their *specialization* with respect to each other. Every activity has a history inherited from its role or that of its precursors in previous activity configurations. The activity will have evolved from interaction processes and through this interaction the single activity will have become adjusted to other activities in order to be conducted efficiently. The five propositions illustrate the importance of these adjustments which refine the individual activity in itself, but also increasingly connect it to other activities in its particular subset of the overall pattern. In the model in Figure 3.6, we identified the time aspect of the interaction processes for activities such as specialization. The prevailing specialization in the activity pattern will favour some types of change while constraining other modifications.

Specialization and interdependence imply that a single activity and the patterns of which it forms part are exposed to two forces. One of the forces strives to stabilize the activity and develop routines for its performance by adjusting it to other activities. This specialization will enhance the performance of the activity pattern. At the same time, however, changing conditions will provide opportunities for modification of the activity in order to further improve its performance in some dimension. Thus, this force calls for changes in the activity pattern. Therefore, even apparently repetitive activities are not static but are constantly evolving – in small or larger steps. The direction of this evolution is the outcome of interaction between the actors in a network and changes in the meanings that they attribute to an activity.

Activities in IMP Research

The role of the activity layer in business networks has become increasingly emphasized in research within the IMP framework. In the first IMP project (Håkansson 1982), activities are not clearly visible in themselves. Primarily they appear as important aspects of the episodes between the two companies in dyadic relationships and mainly relate to product and information exchange. Once these short-term episodes evolve into long-term interaction processes within relationships, activities change in character. Various types of adjustment among activities become crucial causes and consequences related to relationship building. Activities and their roles were important in the design of the first IMP study as the manufacturing arrangements of the companies were the point of departure for the sampling of firms. Therefore, activities and their patterning also form the basis for many of the conclusions of the first IMP study.

In later IMP research, (for example the ARA model in Håkansson and Snehota 1995), the role of activities in business relationships is explicitly acknowledged and specific concepts for analysis of activities are developed. 'Activity links' is here identified as one of the main substances of a business relationship. Activity links are associated with 'technical, administrative, commercial, and other activities that can be connected in different ways to those of another company' (Håkansson and Snehota 1995:26). In this book, we are not only concerned with activity links in relationships between companies, but also with activity links within individual companies. In the 1995 model, the activities undertaken within the company were grouped together under the label 'the activity structure' of the firm. Because all companies are involved in many relationships, the links between any two companies connect with their links to the activities of others. These linkages relate the activities of many companies in what are identified as *activity patterns*. The activity structure of a company is thus a subset of the activity patterns in the network and individual activities are connected through activity links.

In this chapter, we build on these earlier IMP concepts and introduce another: 'activity configuration'. An activity configuration consists of the activities that are involved in the creation of a particular product or service. For example, we can talk about the activity configuration underlying a Toyota car, a logistics service of DHL, a Nokia mobile phone, an information technology service of Motorola, and so on. An activity configuration is thus characterized by interlinked activities and the actual configuration is a subset of the overall activity pattern and involves parts of the activity structures of various firms.

The first consideration in the analysis of an activity configuration, is to determine what activities are needed to create a particular outcome, such as an end product. This involves identifying appropriate mechanisms for coordinating single activities in order to handle their inherent interdependencies as we discussed in Proposition 1 and analysing the potential benefits and drawbacks of adjustments in accordance with Propositions 2 and 3 (see Box 6.1). These considerations relate to the activity layer and concern *what* activities are needed in order to create a particular outcome from the activity configuration. For example, in order to satisfy particular customer demands a supplier may choose between relying on large-scale manufacturing and the associated speculative inventories or designing a system for build-to-order production. In most cases, a huge number of options are available and the activity configurations utilized by different suppliers of the same product are normally characterized by considerable variety. In specific time periods, however, some configurations may dominate because they are considered to represent 'best practice'.

Obviously, the configuration of activities is affected by the two other network layers. Even if the activity configuration for an end product is more or less a given, there is a crucial issue concerning the allocation of these activities between various actors. This means that *who* is

Table 6.2 Bases for value generation in the activity layer.

Standardization	Differentiation
Cost efficiency	Variety
Scale economies	Customization and uniqueness

going to undertake the activity has to be determined, thus bringing issues related to division of labour to the forefront. In this respect, the capabilities of the actors and the resources they can access will have considerable impact. Recent decades have been characterized by outsourcing and disaggregation of activity patterns. These changes mean that the coordination of activities increasingly crosses the boundaries of firms. The causes and consequences of these changes in the configuration of activities are explored in Dubois (1998). Moreover, the efficiency and effectiveness of an activity configuration is strongly dependent on its connection to the resource layer of the network. Alternative activity configurations exploit existing resource constellations differently. Furthermore, current constellations of resources may be recombined, in turn exaggerating the opportunities for differentiation of activities. These conditions make the question of *how* to utilize the resource constellation in the network an important issue. The potential for differentiation and the consequences of variety in activity configurations in the PC industry are explored in Hulthén (2002).

The above questions related to what, who and how cannot be decided by a company in isolation. They require interaction among many companies since any activity configuration involves the resource collections and activity structures of a huge number of actors. The resulting configurations have profound economic and financial implications for the actors, whether they are involved in creating the products and services or are the recipients of them. In the evaluation of the economies of various configurations, actors strive to balance two considerations (Håkansson and Snehota 1995:53): economizing by standardization, which leads to an emphasis on increasing the scale of activities; and economizing on differentiation leading to an emphasis on uniqueness and adjustments between activities (see Table 6.2).

A particular activity configuration is an intersection of the activity structures of various actors, each with its own interpretation of what would be an appropriate balance between standardization and differentiation. The actual determination and the consequences of an activity configuration are therefore a problematic issue which is explored in the rest of the chapter. We begin with an example where we relate the activity structure of a specific company to the overall activity pattern to which it is connected.

The Activity Pattern Around

In order to illustrate critical issues in activity configurations, we will use the example of a company involved in making shirts. The shirts designed and marketed by this company are 'up-market' offerings with some particular features, for example they are wrinkle-free. The range in textiles and apparel is generally enormously varied in terms of product types, models, fabrics, qualities, colours, patterns, and so on. These features in combination with a short lifecycle imply high volatility and low predictability of demand for specific shirt variants. Thus clothing retailers have to deal with the uncertainty of what shirts will actually be demanded by consumers. Fast-changing fashion adds to these problems. Retailers need to be able to modify their preliminary orders during a particular fashion season to relate to the actual buying patterns of consumers. A shirt maker thus has to cope with onerous requirements for modifications of preliminary orders from its retail customers. These conditions put great pressure on the activity structure of the shirt maker.

For our shirt maker (henceforth referred to as SM), demand follows this typical pattern for the apparel industry, i.e. huge variety, short product lifecycles and fluctuating demand. These conditions imply great problems for SM's activity configuration in order to exploit available resource constellations in the best way. Some activities are concerned with producing standardized shirts that are supplied to retailers from five distribution centres. The manufacturing of these shirts is based on forecasts and so they are produced speculatively. These activities are planned entirely by SM and this makes possible the efficient utilization of procurement, manufacturing and distribution. On the other hand, there is uncertainty concerning the actual demand for these shirts. Because standard shirts are included in the assortment for several years, this uncertainty is somewhat reduced by experience gained over time. Another type of activity configuration is required for fashion shirts which are launched for a specific upcoming season. In this case, decisions concerning the configuration of activities and the capacity required constitute major problems since there are no previous reference points for demand.

The overall capacity requirements for shirt production are almost the same irrespective of fabric and model. Thus, there is little need to adjust manufacturing capacity because of variations in the demand for different shirt models. However, the features of the shirt models impact on the sequencing of manufacturing orders. For example, in contrast to single-coloured fabric, checked and striped fabrics require additional activities for pattern matching, which increases throughput time. Setting up the thread is another time-consuming activity that affects the requirement for efficient batch sizes and lead times.

In order for SM to handle these issues efficiently, retailers have to order shirts (both standard and fashion) several months in advance. Owing to these conditions, SM is able to plan its activities in terms of fabric procurement, sewing and other operations. However, the orders from retailers are only preliminary and include part of what they need for the coming season while the remaining part will be ordered during the season on the basis of actual demand. Moreover, once the season starts, sales figures will show that some shirts sell better than expected while others do not match predicted levels of sales. Consequently, retailers seek to modify their orders. These order changes are problematic for SM to handle as they require both volume flexibility and the forecasting of demand changes during the season. The volume flexibility is secured through a mix of its own facilities and subcontracting operations, which together make it possible to match capacity requirements with demand even at peak time.

The main problem for SM concerns the handling of the requirements for rapid alterations to changes in quantities and delivery dates. Over time, SM has made great efforts and been able to adapt to these conditions by the way that it organizes its activities. SM has developed the capability to handle frequently changing production plans and manufacture limited batches and this is considered one of the main benefits in SM's relationships with retailers. However, the costs of creating this flexibility are substantial. Due to long lead times and the large batch sizes required by suppliers, SM has to hold huge inventories of both fabrics and finished shirts.

Maintaining these inventories in the face of rapid changes in models and in fashions is risky since stock may become obsolete before it is sold. Therefore the activity configuration for these shirts entails considerable costs. These costs can be traced primarily to the unwillingness of SM's suppliers to support SM's adjustment to the requests from retailers for changes in delivery times and quantities. As a consequence of these frustrating conditions, the managing director of SM posed the question: 'Why can't the fabric supplier be more flexible in dealing with our orders?'

The answer to this question resides in the characteristics of the intersecting activity structures of the various actors in the overall pattern of activities. We will come back to and explain why suppliers are reluctant to adhere to SM's request for adjustments. But to be able to do so, we need to deepen the discussion of the central features of activities.

Central Features of Activities

Activity patterns underlie and provide for the activity configurations of products and services. But whereas products and services are identifiable and quantifiable, interconnected activity configurations and patterns are largely hidden from view, are difficult to trace or to measure and hence difficult for firms, governments and regulators to monitor or control. Activity patterns are constantly evolving through interaction; they have no equilibrium point and there is no reason why they necessarily operate for some notional public good. It is the *outcomes* from these arrangements that are received as services or products by customers at any point in the network. But the particular configuration of activities within those patterns is what customers are actually paying for and on which they are dependent.

The complexity of the activities leading to and from any single activity is a defining feature of the interactive landscape. As illustrated in the shirt-making case, these activities do not exist as part of a simple one-dimensional chain or channel. Each single activity is likely to be a junction for a number of different activity configurations leading to and from various offerings that have this single activity in common. Examples of such junctions are the warehousing activities in a logistics hub, the final machining activities in a mechanical engineering company's workshop, and the cheque-clearing activities of a bank. Another aspect of this complexity is that in striving to make the activity configurations underlying these different offerings both efficient and effective, numerous reconfigurations of activities will take place. Activities, rather like resources, have divergent characteristics as expressed in Propositions 2 and 3 (see Box 6.1). On the one hand, adjustments of activities in relation to each other are carried out in order to handle interdependencies, for example the manufacturing activities of a supplier and the transportation activities of a logistics service provider. On the other hand, the routines and adjustments that are established in this way contribute towards increased interdependencies, so that the activities carried out by different companies at different times and in different places become more and more integrated with each other.

Consequently, the most important features of activity patterns are the sequential effects that occur because no single activity is independent of others or completely stable over time. Every activity is exposed to attempts to make minor or major changes in order to make it fit with other activities carried out internally or externally. It is through these adjustments and routines that activities become linked to each other. This is what we referred to as specialization in the interaction model in Chapter 3. Specialization is a continuous process and concerns both individual activities and the links between activities. Since every activity is part of several activity configurations, the call for specialization stems from various sources which may often conflict with each other (Proposition 4). Hence, activity configurations are always exposed to modifications and adjustments because changes of one activity will impact on other activities, both within and across company boundaries. Over time these changes affect the way that patterns of related activities evolve, similar to the paths in the development of resource constellations discussed in Chapter 5. Thus, interdependency and specialization are two crucial factors in the development of activity patterns and affect each related actor's ability to create and exploit benefits through its efforts to stabilize or develop activities and their connections. We examine interdependence and specialization in more detail in the following sections because these features of activity patterns have consequences for what activity configurations are feasible.

Activity Patterns and Interdependencies

Because no activity is isolated from others, activity patterns are characterized by several interdependencies stretching in various directions. These interdependencies occur between production, distribution, and service activities and many others.

Some of the activities in a specific pattern may be carried out entirely by a single actor and out of sight of others who may still be affected by them. These activities form part of other activities at a more aggregate level, such as the way that a printing process is part of the pattern of activities for the production of a particular magazine or billing services are part of a utility operation. Conversely, broad categories of activities may be disaggregated. For example, the activity configuration for the production of a specific Toyota car model may be disaggregated to the manufacturing of gear boxes at a supplier factory and further disaggregated to the operations of a specific mechanic on the assembly line. The more that an activity configuration is separated into sub-activities, the more obvious are the interdependencies between those sub-activities. It is not the intrinsic characteristics of business activities that form the basis of interdependency and interaction in the network. Instead, business interaction takes place on the basis of the idiosyncratic and often widely varying views of different actors of the meaning, value, connections and importance of particular activities. For example, an insurance company may consider the purchase of cleaning services as a useful and cost-efficient way of making its office complex pleasant to work in. In contrast, a food company may consider similar cleaning services provided by the same company as vital for the safe continuation of its operations.

The current interdependencies among activities are part of an evolving arrangement of activities within and between firms. Through this evolution, some of the interdependencies between activities will have been handled, others will have become strengthened, and others will have been neglected, either consciously or unconsciously. We come back to these issues when we discuss activities in relation to time. Because activities are not isolated from each other, they impact directly and indirectly, in both the short and the long term, in ways that may not be fully understood by any of the actors in the network. What we observe in business networks are outcomes of patterns of activities that have evolved in different ways.

Some activity patterns may appear easy to characterize. For example, we may say that they constitute or form part of a supply chain, value chain or distribution channel. But all of these

Figure 6.2 Activities in shirt-making.

classifications run the risk of limiting our perspective concerning the actual characteristics and the consequences of interdependencies. This is because they are not based on a view of the entire activity pattern in the network, but on an artificially determined, subset of activities, usually seen from the perspective of a single company. Unfortunately, these limited stereotypical sub-sets frequently determine the actors' views of the interdependencies in which they are enmeshed and of how those interdependencies should be handled.

In the following sections we explore three types of interdependence in activity patterns.[1] The first of these is *serial* interdependence which is a characteristic of most industrial activities, implying a predetermined order of activities, e.g. that activity A has to be completed before activity B can be started. Secondly, *dyadic* interdependence occurs when two activities are adjusted in relation to each other. An example of dyadic interdependence is the adjustments between the outbound logistics activities of a supplier and the inbound activities of a customer. Finally, *joint* interdependence is at hand when two activities become dependent because both are related to a third activity, such as the physical delivery activities of two suppliers in relation to the same buyer.

Serial Interdependence

The idea of supply chains and distribution channels both highlight *serial* interdependencies between activities. These typically occur in interlinked manufacturing and distribution processes such as those for consumer durables, paper-making, shipbuilding and process industries. Serial interdependence comes about in situations where a specific activity cannot be performed until another one has been completed. In practice, the activities may take place simultaneously because both are carried out continuously. In the shirt-making example, the activities undertaken by SM are preceded by other activities (see Figure 6.2).

All these activities (each consisting of numerous sub-activities) are characterized by serial interdependence. The first of the main activities is cotton-farming. The fabric used for SM's shirts require cotton with specific features to make them appropriate for SM's application. These features are determined by the length of the cotton staples, in turn requiring cotton that has grown in particular soils. Cotton is then spun into yarn and it is the features of the cotton that determine what type of spinning activities are necessary. After the spinning activities, yarns are supplied to companies involved in weaving. Weaving includes five main steps from warp preparation to quality control and the whole process from yarn to fabrics takes approximately four weeks. Woven fabric is then sent for finishing, which is the last activity before SM's sewing

---

[1]This discussion is considerably inspired by Thompson (1967). Thompson primarily dealt with intra-organizational issues and identified three types of interdependencies (serial, pooled and reciprocal) derived from the characteristics of the basic technology in which the firm is involved. On the basis of the nature of these interdependencies, Thompson identified appropriate mechanisms for coordination.

operations. Finishing involves a huge number of sub-activities that provide the fabric with its particular visual appeal and required properties, e.g. in terms of being wrinkle-free. The finishing activities take on average 15–20 working days to complete.

Fabrics delivered to SM have gone through another activity that is critical in determining its features. Fabrics for shirts have to be coloured and there are two opportunities for the dyeing of fabrics each involving particular types of activity patterning. One option is to use 'piece dying' where whole lots of fabric are dyed before finishing. The alternative is to dye the yarn, implying that coloured yarn is used in the weaving activities. In both cases, the activities are serially interdependent, but dyeing may enter the activity chain in different ways.

Serial interdependencies also occur within a single company between two or more machine operations or service processes. This type of interdependence characterizes all patterns where activities have to be performed in a step-wise manner. This form of interdependency is reinforced through increasing process integration using techniques such as just-in-time deliveries, build-to-order production and efficient consumer response (ECR). Serial interdependencies normally span the activities of several specialized firms in identifiable activity configurations in wider patterns. Because of its temporal features, the coordination of serial interdependencies may be planned and thus rely on activities that are more or less standardized.

Recent developments of activity patterns in terms of just-in-time manufacturing and build-to-order production increase interdependencies and the need for coordination. For example, an order from a buyer for a customized product has to be coordinated with the procurement of raw materials and components for the manufacturing and assembly of the product, which may also require pre-made subsystems to be delivered from a warehouse. Similarly, service visits need to be coordinated with the customer's operations and delivery schedules need to be decided in cooperation with a logistics service provider.

Dyadic Interdependence

Other types of interdependencies need to be handled in the particular ways determined by their characteristics. Examples of these include interaction for the provision of business services where production and consumption activities occur more or less simultaneously. The outcome of such a 'service meeting', for example between a business consultant and its client, is never standardized. It is determined by the interaction between the respective activities of the customer and the supplier of the service. The output from the activities of one of the actors serves as the input for the activities of the other and vice versa. We identify this as *dyadic* interdependence, which is important not only in services. Dyadic interdependence is always present when two activities are specifically adjusted to each other. Joint action in the design of a new offering, involving the supplier and a prospective customer is another illustration of this type of interdependency.

Dyadic interdependency may also be less direct. For example, the activities involved in the aircraft operations of an airline and those of a provider of maintenance service for engines are characterized by dyadic interdependence: The demand for services generated by flying operations provides the input to the maintenance activities, in the same way as the output of the maintenance activities makes the flying operations possible.

In the shirt-making example, cotton farming and spinning are characterized by both serial and dyadic interdependence. This is because a specific type of cotton requires its own particular spinning activity and different types of spinning facility require particular types of cotton. Furthermore, SM's activities are characterized by dyadic interdependence in relation to finishing because the various qualities of the shirts require their own particular finishing operations. Developments toward increasing customization and individualized offerings add to this type of interdependence which is characterized by mutual adjustments of activities. Therefore, activities involved in just-in-time deliveries are not only serially interdependent. In many cases they also feature dyadic interdependence because the logistics operations of customer and supplier need to be related to each other. Mutual adjustments of activities are both the origin and the outcome of dyadic interdependency as suggested in Propositions 2 and 3 (see Box 6.1). These adjustments, in turn, are based on substantial interaction and information sharing.

Joint Interdependence

A third type of interdependency occurs when the performance of one activity is dependent on another, because both of them are related to a third activity. For example, the activities of two suppliers become jointly interdependent when they together supply the processes of a common customer, such as an assembly line or a chemical plant. If the activities of one of the suppliers are not adequately performed, this affects the activities of the other since the processes of the customer, to which both suppliers are related, are disturbed. This *joint* interdependence is very common in industrial processes and can be handled through rules, routines and standards. Standardization assures that an individual activity is undertaken in a way that is consistent with the way that other activities are performed.

The joint interdependency in networks increases with enhanced specialization so that companies focus on a limited part of the activity patterns in which they are involved. The disaggregated activity patterns that follow from these efforts have to be coordinated and integrated for the activity arrangement as a whole to solve the problems of customers. For example, the components of a PC are the outcome of the manufacturing activities of many firms. These components have to become integrated into a functioning product or service for the buyer. The individual activities must thus be coordinated in a way that shapes a configuration that can lead to a valuable solution. Therefore, new types of actors have evolved in many activity patterns in manufacturing and services, each with a particular competence in these coordinating activities. These firms are often recognized as 'system builders' or 'system integrators'. Similarly, the need for integration of logistics services characterized by joint interdependence has become a breeding ground for the expansion of firms such as FedEx, DHL, and other logistics service providers.

In the shirt-making example, the activities in weaving and finishing are jointly interdependent since they both influence and are influenced by the activities of SM. Similarly, what goes on between the weaving company and SM is jointly interdependent with the connections between the weaving company and other shirt makers. Therefore, any adjustments between the weaving company and SM will impact on others (see Figure 6.2). One of the most typical examples of joint interdependence is the activities at a construction site as we illustrated in the introduction to this chapter. Here the activities of numerous materials suppliers, huge cadres of installation firms and others are jointly interdependent, involving severe consequences for the others if one of these activities fails, is delayed or in other ways does not meet expectations. These situations require extensive interaction between the various actors. The consequence of these adjustments is that activity patterns over time become increasingly specialized.

So far we have discussed the three types of interdependencies in isolation. However, as soon as we examine activities in the business landscape we find that all three types are present simultaneously. Any activity is serially related to others in some way within the overall activity pattern because it always comes between other activities. Similarly, any activity is involved in joint interdependence, because any activity in relation to a specific business counterpart affects and is affected by other activities. Finally, all activities are characterized by dyadic interdependence because they are part of complex interaction processes. The richness of the business landscape and its enormous capability for development and variety arises from the constant evolution of interdependent activities and the seemingly infinite potential for new and innovative configurations. We explore these opportunities further after we have introduced the framework for analysis of activities.

Activity Patterns and Specialization

We argued above that the current interdependencies in an activity pattern have evolved over time. This evolution is the outcome of various actors' ambitions to increase or decrease the extent of specialization of the activity patterns in which they are involved in order to make them more efficient and effective. These ambitions take many forms, for example in terms of routines and adjustments which are discussed below. The consequences of these efforts are that activities become increasingly connected and in this way they manifest particular sub-patterns within the overall pattern of activities. Individual activities within these configurations are refined in order to function as effectively as possible and fine-tuned in relation to other activities. This is what we have identified as specialization. Specialization provides similar long-term consequences to the resource paths that we discussed in Chapter 5. Here the implications are that particular activity configurations may receive widespread attention and become known as 'best practice'. For example, most car manufacturers today share a common view of what is the most effective activity configuration for the production of cars. In the same way, many companies subscribe to common principles for efficient logistics design and product development processes.

There are strong economic reasons for a company to increase the extent of specialization through adjustments. One way to achieve this is by making activities repetitive. In order to achieve the benefits from investment in physical and human resources, activities have to be repeated over and over through procedures that evolve into routines. Organizational routines provide economies of scale in operations and enhance learning, both within and between companies. A routine is shaped by history and represents a pattern of behaviour that is followed repeatedly. In this way, routines stabilize behaviour and make it possible to economize on limited capabilities. Moreover, routines serve as reservoirs of tacit knowledge. Therefore, the undertaking of an activity at a certain point in time is affected by routines established previously. Thus routines stabilize activity patterns, but they do not make them static. The stability they provide is relative since new conditions may make a current routine less appropriate than it used to be. However, the potential for the modification of a routine is to some extent built into the routine because the past has a strong impact on current arrangements. Expectations concerning future conditions may also be a reason for modifications to routines. Changes in routines affect

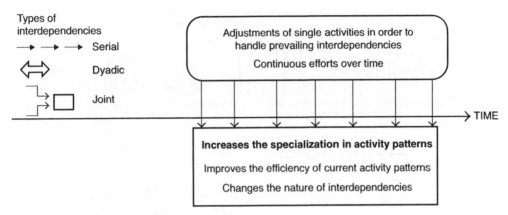

Figure 6.3   Over time, activity patterns become specialized.

the way that individual activities are carried out, as well as the functioning of whole activity patterns. Adjustments of routines at a particular point in time will provide both constraints and opportunities for the future.

Adjustments are a way of handling all three of the types of interdependencies discussed in the previous section: For example, serial interdependencies in activity patterns for just-in-time deliveries may be handled through fine-tuning of logistical activities. In the case of joint interdependencies, for example between two companies in the supply network of a common customer, the customer may require both suppliers to adjust their activities in relation to the internal activities of the customer. Dyadic interdependencies between the service operations of a supplier and its customer sometimes can be handled by technical adjustments between the activities of the two companies. Various types of adjustment are important ways of improving the performance of administrative activities. For example, we argued above that in some business transactions a multitude of information has to be exchanged between buyer and seller in terms of requests, quotations, orders, delivery notifications, invoices etc. Adjustments in the processes of information exchange in these relationships can enable both supplier and customer to rationalize their administrative activities. The consequence of these adjustments is that activity patterns become increasingly specialized over time, as illustrated in Figure 6.3.

We have already described how the specialization of a single activity at a specific point in time is contingent on how it is related to the overall configurations and patterns of which it is part. The current situation is influenced by how these activities were arranged previously. In the activity pattern in which SM is involved, the actual patterning related to spinning and weaving over time have been subject to substantial specialization. This specialization has evolved over hundreds of years and is strongly embedded in this history. In the same way the current configuration of activities will have strong influence on future configurations. What is possible to modify in spinning and weaving is constrained by the current specialization of these activities in relation to other activities. In the same way, expectations about the future will impact on the interaction concerning current attempts at reconfiguration.

Activity patterns of the past are thus reflected in the way activities are organized today. Some aggregated activity patterns are stable over long periods of time, as in the textile industry. A

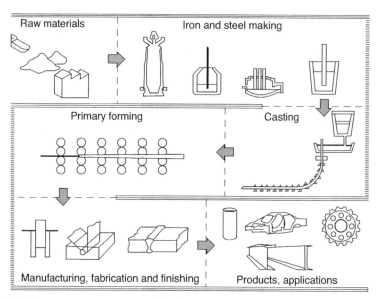

Figure 6.4   The basic activity pattern in steel making.

similar example can be found in steel making, where the basic activity pattern has remained the same for a long time. Figure 6.4 illustrates the overall activity pattern for steel processing; each of the main activities then can be disaggregated into a huge number of sub-activities.

Modifications of an individual activity in these patterns must always relate to the way the overall pattern is organized. This does not imply, however, that steel processes are the same today as they were 100 years ago. On the contrary, the activity pattern and the organizing of specific activities in casting, hot and cold rolling (examples of primary forming), and steel manufacturing, have changed enormously even though the overall pattern has remained much the same. Similar conditions characterize other process industries, such as papermaking and chemical production. The longevity of these basic patterns requires that modifications and changes to individual activities are adapted to the actual specialization of the total activity pattern. What can be done in terms of changes is strongly dependent on how this pattern is arranged and this is, to a large extent, contingent on the past. These conditions provide a basic stability to activity patterns since they have to be developed within the context of these evolving adjustments. Over time, however, these successive modifications may change the activity pattern considerably.

Sometimes changing conditions will call for modifications to these overall patterns. These situations primarily tend to occur when technological developments provide opportunities for major re-structuring. To realize these opportunities, the current connections among activities have to be changed. New activities are introduced and adjusted to each other and the linkages between remaining activities are modified or dissolved. These changes may in some ways break with the logic of the established activity pattern. Examples of these radical changes are the introduction of self-service in retailing and the assembly line in manufacturing. More recent illustrations are provided by Internet banking and the principle of build-to-order applied for example, by Dell. Another example of these changes is just-in-time deliveries, in which warehousing activities can be eliminated through changes in the patterns of transportation and communication. These re-arrangements of activity patterns may then spread among companies and eventually serve as role models for others.

When considering all the efforts that over time go into the organizing of activities in relation to each other, it is tempting to assume that it would be possible to successively develop an activity pattern that achieved the optimal situation and was totally harmonized. Unfortunately this is not possible since the conditions characterizing an optimum pattern will have changed before this state is reached. This means that, despite the basic requirement for stability in the activity pattern, adjustments and modifications will always be required. Hence, opportunities for such changes have to be built into the activity configurations when they become established. There are two main principles that provide an explanation for this.

First, the linking of any two activities is never 'seamless'. It is always a compromise between different forces. What would constitute a perfect link based on the features of one activity is seldom perfect for the conditions of the other, since both are linked to other activities and thus involved in other configurations. The resulting link is a compromise between two sets of requirements and therefore allows for some modifications that do not affect the actual activities themselves. Thus the link between two activities provides flexibility by functioning like the shock absorbers in a vehicle.

Secondly, the links between any two activities have been established in interaction through compromises made between the actors involved in them. This means that the actors performing the two activities, whether they represent the same company or not, are aware of the nature and the consequences of these links. Because of this mutual dependence, each party, consciously or unconsciously, takes the perspective of counterparts into account to some extent when considering modifications to activities.

The linkages between activities are not always obvious and attempts to accommodate some activity links frequently conflict with other links as suggested in Proposition 4 (see Box 6.1). Sometimes these linkages are simply overlooked or forgotten, thus creating future problems for some actors' ambitions to handle interdependencies. Regardless of whether the actors are aware of it or not, every activity is interdependent with other activities and a key issue is how these interdependencies are handled over time.

A Framework for Activity Pattern Analysis

The interdependencies between myriad network activities and their continuously changing specialization make the configuring of activities a major issue for those involved in business. The way that activities are organized within an activity pattern has direct consequences for the efficiency of that arrangement, for the participants involved in it and for recipients of its outputs. This is the case whether the configuration surrounds the production of a single identifiable product or a range of services. The design and coordination of individual activities emerges through interaction between participants and this interaction must handle the various interdependencies between many activities. For this reason, both specific configurations and the overall patterns are in constant flux.

A company must take all three types of the simultaneously existing interdependencies into consideration when organizing its activities: First, by coordinating serially interdependent activities it will be possible to economize on integration through planning and scheduling. This coordination may be achieved, for example, by just-in-time manufacturing or integrated delivery systems. Secondly, the configuration also has to handle dyadic interdependence, for example through mutual adjustments of some of the activities involved. The more adjusted that two activities become, the more efficient their performance in relation to each other will be. However, adjustments to activities are always costly and those costs will bear differently on the parties involved, in both their amount and timing. Therefore, monitoring and considering the effects of one's own adjustments and those of others is a central issue in the organizing of activities. Whatever temporary balance is arrived at will impact the differentiation and variety in the activity pattern.

Thirdly, the actual configuration has to take care of joint interdependencies. Issues related to this interdependence may be handled through standards, such as the ways in which suppliers deliver to a retail store or the assembly line of a car factory. Standardization is often preferred for economic reasons as it supports repetition and thus increases the economies of scale in operations. Finally, the actual configuration within a particular activity pattern inevitably affects the activities in other related configurations and patterns, whether or not this is taken into account by those involved. If some activities are standardized with positive effects on directly related activities, this may have detrimental effects elsewhere because of indirect effects. For example, replaceable modules used when servicing equipment may be beneficial to producers of the equipment, service suppliers, replacement parts stockists and most users, but problematic for customers with non-standard types or rates of use of the equipment.

Managers have to handle the complexity of the activity patterns in which they are involved even though each single activity is connected to many others in an activity configuration. Different configurations evoke their particular types of interdependencies, lead to variety in the forms of specialization and have their particular effects on performance. Below we introduce two conceptual tools that may help in the examination of the characteristics of activity configurations and the potential consequences of changes in these conditions.[2]

We begin our exploration of these concepts by taking the serial linkages of an activity into consideration. This is dealt with by the idea of the *sequentiality* in activity patterns. We continue by bringing in dyadic and joint interdependencies where we discuss the interplay between *similarity* and *diversity* in activity patterns. On the basis of this exploration, we conclude that a critical issue in the organizing of activities is the 'balancing' of activity patterns with regard to time and space.

---

[2]These concepts are inspired and partly derived from the seminal article authored by Richardson (1972). Richardson analysed parallel and serial dependence in activity configurations and suggested 'similarity' and 'complementarity' as appropriate concepts. These concepts were later combined with the IMP framework in Dubois (1998).

Sequentiality

Cotton farming, spinning, weaving, finishing, and shirt making are characterized by serial interdependence because they have to be undertaken in a predetermined order. For analytical purposes, we identify activities with these features as *sequential* activities.[3]

Activities that are sequentially related are not necessarily characterized by strong interdependence. Storing inventories of semi-manufactured parts and finished products in serially interlinked manufacturing activities represent configurations of activities that reduce the extent of interdependency between the various production activities within the overall pattern. These inventories function as buffers. They are produced speculatively and may normally be used interchangeably in relation to the activities that involve the customers of a company because speculation must be based on some form of standard.

In the shirt-making case, the features and quality of the various types of yarns are primarily dependent on the length of the cotton staples. The characteristics of these fibres in turn determine the type of spinning activities that can be employed. This means that cotton farming and spinning are sequentially related and thus have to be undertaken in a specific order. Moreover, a specific activity arrangement in cultivation requires a particular spinning activity, and vice versa. Two activities with these characteristics are described as *tightly sequential*. The output of an activity that is tightly sequential has a particular direction in its linkages to other activities, such as those found with a customized PC from Dell, a tailored suit from Armani, or a customer-adapted information technology service from Motorola. The activities in these processes are dedicated towards a specific end product or service or a specific customer and therefore can only be used in combination with other individualized activities. Activities are thus characterized by different intensity in terms of their 'sequentiality'.

Recent developments in the configuration of activities have had the effect of increasing the tightly sequential nature of activities. This is primarily owing to a shift from an approach based on 'speculation' toward 'postponement'. These approaches are based on activity patterns relying on different levels of sequentiality (see Figure 6.5).

Activity configurations built on speculation aim at exploiting the potential economies of scale in manufacturing and distribution activities. The outcomes of these sequential activities are standardized offerings, the quantities and qualities of which are based on plans and forecasts of demand. In these configurations, offerings are made available to customers mainly through inventories at various locations. In contrast, the principle of postponement involves the final characteristics of the offering being determined and fixed as late as possible. The ultimate form of postponement is build-to-order where the individual customer order initiates the processing of the offering. In this case, efficiency in information-exchange activities and activity patterns

---

[3] Analysis of sequential activities is central in several streams of research. The early literature on marketing channels focused on interdependencies between the distribution activities undertaken by various firms, such as producers, wholesalers and retailers. Moreover, this literature also involved the connection between distribution and manufacturing activities, for example, Alderson (1965) and Bucklin (1965). Today, sequential activities are central to the logistics and supply-chain frameworks in the analysis of flow efficiency in activity configurations. See, for example, Christopher (2005) and Stock and Lambert (2001).

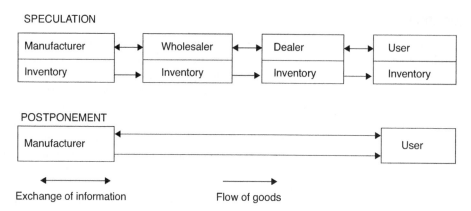

Figure 6.5   Speculation and postponement models.

in logistics are substitutes for storing and warehousing, thus making it economically feasible to make adjustments to the special requests of individual customers. Activities in these patterns become tightly sequential and this requires extensive coordination of activities.

Deciding on the extent of sequentiality is thus an important issue in any configuration of activities. Tightly sequential activities are based on adjustments of activities and these configurations involve costly coordination arrangements. On the other hand, the costs of warehousing and inventories in these activity configurations are substantially reduced and individualization in relation to specific business counterparts is made possible.

Diversity and Similarity

We have used the concept of sequentiality to analyse the characteristics and consequences of serial interdependence. We also need concepts for the examination of the two other types of interdependencies: We have already noted that dyadic interdependence is handled through mutual adjustments. Therefore, it is important that each activity is adjusted to the particular features of any activity to which it is related in a dyadic way. This is the case in a logistics service, a manufacturing process, an accounting consultancy service, the design of an offering, and so on. Resource constellations are characterized by heterogeneity and the requirements of various business partners are characterized by variety. Therefore, adjustments to activities have to take different forms in order to handle dyadic interdependencies in the most efficient way. Thus these conditions require *diversity* in the configuration of activities. Diversity provides the means for handling the particular requirements of specific counterparts in terms of customized products and individualized services. The activity configuration behind SM's high-fashion shirts is an example of such an arrangement that is different from the configuration for standard shirts. Similarly, SM handles service levels and assortment policy differently between clothing retailers, also indicating diversity in this part of the activity pattern. Thus, diversity in activity patterns provides advantages when it comes to handling dyadic interdependencies. But diversity is costly and also causes problems in handling of joint interdependence, which is further explored below.

Diversity in activity patterns follows from adjustments of activities aimed at handling dyadic interdependencies. The more a single activity is fine-tuned in relation to another activity in order to function effectively, the greater the dyadic interdependence. As we suggested in Proposition 5 (see Box 6.1), this fine-tuning provides considerable benefits for the functioning of the specific activity in its current context. However, these adjustments may also constrain the usefulness of an activity in relation to other activities with which it may be jointly interdependent. Another consequence of adjustments to relate to different business counterparts in order to handle dyadic interdependence is the increasing variety in the activity structure of the company. The greater this variety the more difficult it is to benefit from economies of scale in carrying out an activity. Therefore, the call for diversity in an activity pattern is always accompanied by requirements for increasing the *similarity* in the way activities are undertaken. Similarity in the activity pattern is achieved through standardization, which makes it possible to economize on the scale of operations. For example, the weaving company in the shirt-making case study makes standard collections that they offer to many customers in order to benefit from similarity in its activity structure. They also design unique fabric that is offered to particular shirt makers and these customized offerings lead to diversity in the configuring of activities. In this way, the weaving firm exploits both similarity and diversity. In doing this, it is necessary that weaving activities are planned so that orders from different customers can be combined as effectively as possible. This planning makes it feasible to reap the benefits of similarity by making the most efficient use of its production facilities.

Similarity and economies of scale in activity patterns are obtained when one configuration of activities can be used for multiple orders and form part of multiple activity patterns, through the exploitation of the same resource constellation. Similarity may involve activities that use the same machinery and equipment, the same work-force capabilities, the same transportation facilities, and so on. Thus, increasing the similarity in a pattern of activities provides cost advantages. Similarity among activities in terms of routine is central to all activity patterns whether in manufacturing, banking, logistics or consultancy services. Efficiency in activity patterns is thus contingent on the combined effects of similarity and diversity – or standardization and customization. Figure 6.6 illustrates a supplier's combining of standardized and customized activities in relation to three of its customers. The activity structures of these customers have different features and thus call for variation in the linkages in relation to the supplier. Besides the standard activities applied in relation to all three customers, the supplier has to customize some of its internal activities in relation to Customers 1 and 2. Customer 3 exploits only standard activities within the supplier company. The exchange operations between Customer 1 and the supplier are customized.

We now have analytical concepts that can help to explain the reason for the reluctance of SM's suppliers to deal with requirements for modification of orders. The problem for the companies on the supply side of SM in responding to its requests is due to their overall ambition to benefit from similarity in their activities. Similarity among activities may be captured in various ways in different facilities, for example by combining yarn qualities with similar requirements in spinning, or by combining fabrics needing the same treatment in the finishing. The long lead-times and large batch sizes in the activity pattern are thus explained to a large extent by the efforts of suppliers to increase the similarity in their activity structures by combining orders from many customers. Fully complying with requests from buyers for

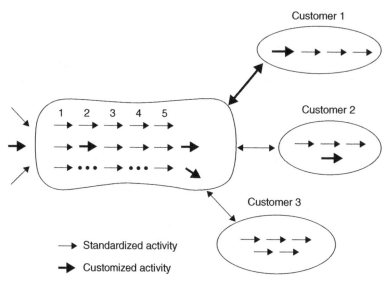

Figure 6.6 A supplier's combining of standardized and customized activities.

adjustments of plans and schedules would lead to increased diversity and thus interfere with these ambitions.

Moreover, serial interdependencies work much in the same direction and this further constrains customization and variety. Many of the specific features of the fabric needed for non-iron shirts are not created until the finishing operations start. However, these features depend to a large extent on the treatment of the fabric in the weaving facilities and require cotton fibres with specific characteristics, which in turn demand specialized spinning techniques. This means that even if a weaving firm is capable of working on a broad range of fabrics, the possibility of adjusting quickly to changes demanded by their customers are severely restricted because lead times are long; the activities involved are tightly sequential and the same configuration of weaving activities are used in relation to many customers. Therefore, once weaving activities have been scheduled for a planning period it would not be economically justifiable to adjust the continuing operations to keep up with changing requirements from individual customers. Even if SM is considered to be one of the most important customers by its suppliers, its share of their turnovers is only about 5 %. Therefore, if suppliers adhered to the flexibility demands of the shirt manufacturer, the economics of their operations would suffer considerably as the extent of similarity would be reduced. This would impact on the costs of their activity structures and thus affect all their customers, including SM.

Interaction as a Means of Handling Interdependence

Our exploration has highlighted some of the issues involved in organizing activities across company boundaries. An individual company must simultaneously consider the potential consequences of changes in sequentiality, similarity and diversity. At the same time it is connected to business counterparts that face the same issues. If each company tries to handle these issues in isolation it seems obvious that efficiency and effectiveness of activity patterns as a whole will suffer. Our claim is that some of these problems can be addressed by examining the interaction between the activities of the various parties.

The inherent problem in this case, as in many other situations, is to handle the combined requests for variety (diversity) and cost efficiency (similarity). The more variety in the requests from different customers, the more difficult it is for the supplier to reap economies of scale and consequently the higher the costs or longer the lead times and requirements for large batches. If all buyers take the decision of what to order in isolation, without interaction with the supplier, their orders will most likely lead to considerable diversity in the supplier's activity structure. On the other hand, a customer in close interaction with the supplier may adjust the features of what to buy in order to enhance the similarity of the operations of the supplier. Adequate information about the characteristics of the supplier's manufacturing facility, and other buyers' exploitation of it, may lead the customer to adapt its requirements to better coincide with the technical features of the manufacturing facility and the demands of other customers. Through enhanced interaction between the various actors and their activities, it may also be possible for the supplier to make room for special requests by directing the customer towards features that have only minor adverse effects on the similarity of its operations. If the customers' scope of interaction is expanded to include interaction with other customers then even better conditions may be created. Based on their interaction, a group of customers may together come up with joint plans for improved exploitation of a supplier's activity structure.

The shirt-making example shows that customer–supplier relationships and individual company supply chains should never be considered in isolation. The economics of the configuration of activities in one relationship are contingent on how this particular configuration interacts with other relationships and the rest of the activity pattern. In the same way, efficiency in undertaking activities in a particular supply chain depends on how this configuration relates to the configurations of other chains. Thus the organizing of activities requires balancing the benefits from economies of scale and similarities on the one hand and the advantages associated with individualization and diversity on the other. The task is one of balancing the economics of standardization with the economics of differentiation (Håkansson and Snehota 1995). We now explore the characteristics and consequences of this balancing in relation to the space and time dimensions of interaction.

Balancing Activities in Space

Companies are continuously involved in attempts to modify their own activities and are affected by changes originating from others. All these efforts are contingent on restructuring of the resource and actor layers of the network and impact on the interdependencies among activities. This means that, whatever the main motive behind a particular reorganization may be, it affects all three network layers. Moreover, a change originating from any of the three types of interdependence also influences the other two. Every modification of an activity configuration thus spreads in the spatial dimension. Further analysis of the efficiency and dynamics of activity patterns therefore will require an exploration of the relationships between sequentiality, similarity and diversity.

Table 6.3 Balancing similarity and diversity in the design of offerings.

	Product dimension	Service dimension
Offered as standard	Numerical control	Delivery
	CRT terminal	Installation
	Drive motors	Physical setup
	Basic software	Basic training
Offered as options	Program panel	Three-year guarantee
	Interactive screen	Advanced training
	Advanced hardware	Field engineering
Offered as customized	System package	Vendor-managed inventory
		Running the operations

The main issue when dealing with similarity is the balance between exploiting the variety in resource constellations and achieving economies of scale. Handling this issue appropriately requires a network perspective since resource collections and activity structures of other actors must be taken into consideration. Outsourcing and insourcing are important ways of changing the similarity of activities. Sometimes benefits may be gained through outsourcing activities to suppliers that work on a larger scale; in other situations, insourcing may provide similar benefits. As soon as the similarity of one activity is changed, it impacts on the possibility of obtaining similarities in other activities. For example, a manufacturer striving to increase the similarity of its production activities may negatively affect the opportunity for gaining similarities in the logistics activities of its distributor.

Increasing similarity in activity patterns may constrain attempts to change the level of sequentiality in relation to particular business partners. Too much reliance on standardization in order to reap economies of scale may interfere with efforts to provide customers with tailor-made and synchronized delivery solutions. Thus it is difficult to exploit the potential benefits of increased sequentiality because this reduces the similarity of activities.

The relationship between similarity and diversity works in much the same way. The more that the similarity of activities is increased in order to economize on resources, the more difficult it will be to exploit the diversity in the demands of individual business partners. Most companies and both parties in a business relationship would like to benefit from both of these things simultaneously. A supplier will try to solve this dilemma by developing offerings in which some features are standardized, while other features are optional. By combining standardized and optional features in various ways, customers are provided with offerings that are partly individualized. Table 6.3 illustrates the various building blocks of the offering of a supplier of information technology services.

Some elements of this offering in the product and service dimensions are standardized and form part of the offering to all customers. The optional elements are chosen by some customers while others rely on the standard elements only. Finally, some customers may prefer more or less completely customized solutions. The offering elements are characterized by different levels of similarity and economies of scale. Because all customers have to take the standard elements, they are characterized by substantial similarities and no diversity. The optional elements are only available in one variant each. The economies of scale are lower because only some customers select these elements. The diversity is restricted to the customer's choice to take or not to take them. Finally the customized solutions are, by definition, characterized as being of low similarity and providing a considerable amount of variety to the offering. Designing offerings in this way makes it possible for a supplier (and a customer) to combine some of the benefits of similarity and diversity.

The situation is somewhat different when it comes to the third combination: the relationship between diversity and sequentiality. An activity pattern is characterized by considerable diversity when activities have been adjusted to the requirements of individual business counterparts. In many cases these adjustments to handle dyadic interdependencies make activity patterns tightly sequential (for example in terms of just-in-time deliveries or build-to-order production). Therefore, it is not uncommon for diversity and sequentiality to exist together in activity patterns. Increases in one of these dimensions are often accompanied by increases in the other. But, as we discussed above, the problem with this combination is that both diversity and tight sequentiality reduce the similarity among activities. Therefore these configurations are costly. Again we are confronted with the need to consider the three interdependencies in activity patterns together. Going far along the direction of diversity and tight sequentiality may erode the opportunities for achieving similarity. Thus there are certain interdependencies among the interdependencies!

An interesting example of the interdependence of interdependencies can be observed in the processing of herring. The processing of different fish shows considerable similarity as the same physical and human resources can be used in most cases. This applies during the herring season in late autumn when the processing companies concentrate on that fish. At this time, inspectors from major Japanese customers set up camp inside the processing factories in Norway. Initially the activity pattern of processing is not tightly sequential, as the herring go through the same early processes and inspections for a variety of end uses. If the Japanese inspectors reject the herring at either of the first two stages of processing then it can be shipped to Poland for canning, although at lower prices. Up to this point, the activity pattern is also characterized by diversity. In the third stage of processing, the activity pattern for Japanese customers becomes tightly sequential and loses its diversity because after this processing the herring is only usable for sushi. At this point, the Norwegian processors hold their breath! If the herring is rejected by the Japanese customer it is useless for canning and has no value for human consumption.

Balancing Activities in Time

Balancing is also important in the time dimension. Here the obvious concern is about balancing the extent of specialization. Specialization in activity patterns arises from the continuous refinement of activities in relation to each other within a particular configuration. Specialization improves the performance of this particular activity pattern both in the short term and the long term.

Fine-tuning and specializing activities increases efficiency in a particular resource constellation and increases the possibilities of using these activities in other configurations relying on the same constellation of resources. At the same time, however, specialization may make it difficult to rearrange activities in response to more radical changes in basic conditions such as new opportunities provided by developments in other resource constellations. Therefore it is important that the effects of the current extent of specialization is continuously monitored and reflected upon.

The outcome of these examinations may be that some aspects of the current configuration are perceived as problematic for the future and therefore will need attention to modify the extent of specialization in a particular direction. For example, many companies today are reconsidering the configuration of their activities in relation to the evolving activity patterns in energy production and consumption. Similarly, the call for sustainability in industrial activities tends to lead companies in new directions in terms of raw material supply and logistics solutions. Another outcome from assessments of the extent of specialization may be that the long-term well-being of a company will require it to be better connected to new emerging patterns that are perceived as important for the future, as biotechnology is considered today.

Modifications in the configuration of activities occur either through changes to individual activities, or through changes in the linkages between activities. In many situations, these changes tend to take place at the same time. This is because modifications to a single activity may require, or lead to, changes in the way activities are configured in relation to each other, and vice versa. These activity adjustments derive from changes in the constellations of resources and the webs of actors. For example, technical developments may make it possible to improve both single activities and patterns of related activities. We have mentioned the significant reconfiguring of activities that may be achievable through the combined effects of technical developments in manufacturing, logistics and information exchange. Information technology has a particular role in this respect because the speed and reliability of information exchange is improved as the control and coordination of manufacturing and distribution are enhanced. However, no activities are refined by technology alone, nor do activities configure themselves. These adjustments require the direct involvement of actors.

This involvement requires actions to affect similarity, diversity and sequentiality in order to improve performance in activity configurations. Actors are always involved in these efforts in their day-to-day operations. Even if these modifications are only minor and taken in small steps, they will have a considerable impact in the long term. The combined effect of numerous small modifications may lead to major changes in a pattern of activities over time. Most of the changes thus take place within the current overall activity pattern through modifications of the extent of specialization among activities.

Now and then, however, activity patterns undergo major reconfigurations that are perceived to be revolutionary. We previously mentioned internet banking, the introduction of the assembly line into manufacturing, and self-service in retailing as examples of revolutionary changes. The introduction of the assembly line was undertaken by firms well established within existing activity patterns and was part of the increasing specialization of these patterns. In many cases, however, new activity configurations are organized by firms previously not directly involved in the particular pattern. For example, it was neither IBM nor Hewlett-Packard that introduced build-to-order assembly in the PC industry and it was the 'newcomer' IKEA and not established furniture retailers that organized an activity pattern based on flatpacked furniture and heavy consumer involvement in operations. These cases exemplify a general understanding that many radical changes seem to be undertaken by firms perceived to be 'outsiders'. These innovators are outsiders because they were not previously involved in the activity pattern that is transformed. In most cases, however, they are not real newcomers. Instead, these companies provide links between the activity pattern and resources that were earlier exploited in other patterns and that are therefore unknown to the established web of actors. In this way, the reorganization of activities is as much a recombining of resources as 'pure' innovation.

There are several reasons why it is sometimes easier to innovate from the outside than from the inside of an activity pattern. Sometimes established firms become blinkered by the current ways of doing business and lack the ability to see the potential for reconfiguration of activities. But there is another and more important explanation. Companies that are established in current patterns have invested heavily in order to make their activity configurations efficient and effective. Moreover, interaction within these configurations will have led to modifications to improve the performance of the arrangements. Their efforts have involved numerous adjustments in relation to other companies. These modifications and adjustments may also be seen as investments and companies are likely to seek to exploit these investments as completely as possible. The need for resource exploitation motivates companies to continue with the same activity configuration as long as possible. Furthermore, adjustments over time and the subsequent specialization induces specific interdependencies between activities. Therefore the prevailing specialization and the motivations of companies may make it difficult to adjust to new conditions. A company coming from the outside is less constrained in these ways and is not burdened by being heavily embedded in the current pattern. In contrast, new conditions may improve its opportunities to exploit the resources that are accessible to it.

Balancing Activity Patterns: Three Illustrations

All companies in the interactive business landscape are involved in changing the configuration of activity patterns by designing new activities, redesigning or closing some activities, and changing the linkages between others. These processes in a single company are impacted by interaction with modifications and reconfigurations undertaken by other actors. All these changes affect the similarity, the sequentiality, and the diversity of activities in a very complex interplay. They also affect the extent of specialization. In this section, we try to illustrate this interplay through three examples. The first is from the car industry and centres on Volvo Car's attempts to cope with the three types of interdependencies in the efforts to offer customized vehicles to car buyers. The second example is from SKF and shows how the activity patterns for production and distribution of bearings have been modified over time in a more or less continuous reconfiguration within an established activity pattern. The third example deals with a more radical change by analysing the entry of IKEA into the activity patterns and resource constellations of furniture retailing. In presenting these cases, we concentrate on the activities and resources of the three main actors. However, what these companies were able to do could not have been done without interaction between their own activities and resources and those of counterparts. We discuss this after presenting the three case studies.

Volvo Car: Build-to-order Production

It is important for companies to find a balance between diversity and similarity when suppliers and customers organize and adjust activities in relation to each other. It might be tempting for both parties to think of offerings that are adapted to the particular requirements of the other. But the adjustments of activities that these solutions require are always costly because they tend to constrain the opportunities for similarities in the operations of both the supplier and the customer.

The range and variety of offerings have increased enormously in many industries, for example in the manufacture of mobile phones, PCs, cars and in fashion. This expansion stems partly from the broadening of standardized assortments. However, in many cases, it also follows from suppliers' ambitions to offer solutions that are individualized to the requirements of specific customers. This increasing diversity of activity configurations is problematic for the economy of company operations. For example, car buyers are now provided with the opportunity to become partially involved in the design of their vehicles. In order to design such activity configurations economically, cars have to be assembled to order because it would be a financial disaster to produce them speculatively, since each car is potentially available in a huge numbers of colours, engines, transmission alternatives, left or right-hand steering, interior trim, wheel variants etc. For example, one Volvo Car model is theoretically offered in more than one million variants. Tailoring each car in accordance with individual customer demands requires a flexible and well-organized activity configuration in manufacturing and distribution.

The overall activity pattern in car manufacturing is characterized by strong serial interdependencies; the assembly line actually represents an archetype of this form of interdependence. Over time 'modularity' has emerged as a recipe for handling this interdependence. The principle of modularity is based on pre-manufactured subsystems and modules that are combined in a final assembly to fit with a specific customer's requests. These modules must be available in huge numbers of variants in order to match the variety in consumer demands, which calls for diversity in the activity pattern. Most modules are physically large and represent considerable capital investment. The cost of buffering all the potential modules would thus be extremely high in terms of both capital and space. Many car manufacturers therefore require that module suppliers are located in supplier parks close to the assembly line. The module suppliers preassemble components and subsystems delivered from their own large-scale manufacturing plants into ready-to-install modules that are supplied just-in-time. Owing to the serial interdependence, they have to be delivered in pace with the assembly line of the car manufacturer and in the same order that individualized car bodies enter the assembly line. These activities are thus tightly sequential.

Through this activity configuration, car manufacturers are able to supply car buyers with individualized vehicles at reasonable cost, despite the low level of similarity between the final consumers. The key to these economies is that module suppliers function as buffers between the activities on the customer side and those on the supplier side. This is achieved through the decoupling of the tightly sequential activities between the assembly line and the consumer from upstream activities. In this way, production of components and subsystems can benefit from the similarities through manufacturing in large-scale centralized supplier plants (see Figure 6.7).

The diversity in the activities of the car assembler in relation to consumers is huge since to some extent the consumers are allowed to decide on the design of their cars. The activity pattern of the global component supplier on the left of Figure 6.7 is characterized by moderate diversity. These suppliers normally serve a number of car assemblers. Some of these customers rely on individualized solutions, while others prefer standardization. The activities of the module suppliers located close to the assembly line are characterized by low diversity in terms of customers

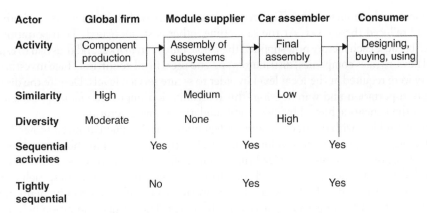

Figure 6.7 Similarity, diversity and sequentiality in the customization of cars.

since they normally serve only one assembly line. On the other hand, there is diversity in what is delivered to this assembly line since the modules have to fit with the requirements of individual car buyers.

An activity configuration like this is very dependent on interaction between the companies concerned. This interaction concerns the long-term development of the car in relation to the various components and modules that comprise the car. In the short term, the fine-tuned activity configuration is extremely dependent on continuous interaction to secure that the assembly line is supplied appropriately in relation to the specifications of the individualized cars. This requires efficient exchange of information between the car assembler, the module suppliers and other suppliers. This information exchange involves detailed planning and scheduling of activities, but must allow for rescheduling to handle revisions of plans and priorities concerning the specific cars to assemble.

SKF: Dynamics within Established Activity Patterns

SKF has been the world's largest supplier of roller-bearings for almost a century. To be able to maintain its position, the company has reconfigured the activity pattern for production and logistics on several occasions. In this section, we describe three major changes to their European operations. From its base in Sweden, SKF established manufacturing operations in a number of European countries. Each of these factories produced almost the whole of the company's product range and supplied domestic customers and those geographically close. This organization minimized transportation costs but severely constrained opportunities to exploit potential economies of scale in manufacturing because all products were manufactured in all plants. Technological leadership secured SKF's position as the number one bearing manufacturer for a long time. But other suppliers gradually reduced this leadership and this required SKF to focus increasingly on cost efficiency. Therefore, in the 1970s, SKF reconfigured its activity structure for bearings in order to increase similarities in its manufacturing operations.

In order to achieve the objective, the various factories focused on different parts of the product range. Within this partial assortment, the factory was made responsible for both technical development and manufacturing. This reorganization increased the similarities in both operations and reduced these costs. At the same time, other costs increased. Transportation costs increased because each factory now supplied the whole European market and thus had to establish material flows to sales companies, distributors and end users in all countries. Huge investments in inventory were required at the local level in order to secure service levels. Despite the disadvantages in transportation and warehousing, this reorganization improved efficiency substantially because of the benefits achieved by increasing similarity in manufacturing.

The main problem with the new activity configuration was that fluctuating customer demands made it difficult to predict sales volumes in specific countries, despite huge investments in advanced forecasting systems. Long lead times in manufacturing and distribution escalated the need for local inventories and the synchronization of transportation activities, each of which operated on quite a small scale. These conditions and increased efficiency requirements initiated the next reconfiguration of activity patterns in the 1990s. The ultimate ambition behind these efforts was to increase the similarities in transportation and warehousing without sacrificing service levels in relation to customers, despite the fact that local inventories were reduced. This was made possible through the centralization of inventories in a European distribution centre in Belgium, which considerably increased the economies of scale in warehousing operations. Also, similarities increased in transportation because the output from the various factories were now transported in bulk to the distribution centre rather than individually to the various sales companies and customers. When customers were serviced from the distribution centre, transportation could again benefit from increasing scale. Rather than each factory individually supplying its limited product range, the distribution centre supplied the whole assortment through a single transport.

The financial impact of economizing on transportation and inventory reductions was considerable. The interesting thing is that these benefits were not attained through a trade-off with service levels. Despite the fact that inventories were centralized, service levels and lead times were improved. First, the whole assortment was always accessible in the distribution centre, while it previously would have been too costly to store all bearing items in the local inventories. Secondly, information technology developments made possible considerable reductions in lead times in the information flow from request to delivery notification as well as providing more reliable information exchange, which in turn reduced uncertainty. Thirdly, more efficient logistics equipment improved the speed as well as the reliability of the materials flows.

Through this step, SKF was able to exploit similarities in both manufacturing and distribution. Customers' requests for diversity in the product dimension could be reasonably satisfied through rapid developments of manufacturing technology. These developments allowed customization without too great a sacrifice in terms of economies of scale. When it came to distribution services, the activity configuration required that all deliveries were handled in the same way. Any package from any of the factories to any customer in any place in Europe had to follow the same route; from the factory to the central warehouse in Belgium, to the distribution hub in the local country and to the end customer. This configuration was inflexible and could not meet customers' requests for variety in distribution services. These conditions paved the way for the third reorganization, the outcome of which is illustrated in Figure 6.8.

The role of the central warehouse is changed in this distribution network. It now serves only small customer orders and buyers with irregular consumption patterns. In addition, the central

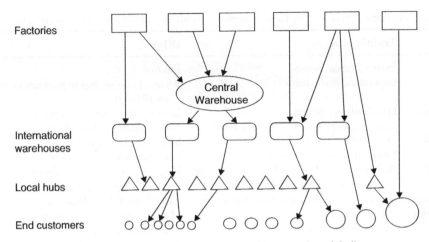

Figure 6.8   SKF's distribution network after the third transformation (simplified).

warehouse has become the after-market service centre of SKF. Because the warehouse now handles small orders it is no longer efficient to deliver to the local hubs as before. Instead the company has established five international warehouses in Europe that work on a larger scale for transportation to local hubs. Orders for large volumes are delivered directly to the international warehouses and never pass through the central warehouse. These orders are then distributed through the local hub or directly to the end customer. Finally, some orders bypass even the international warehouse and are sent either to the end customer or to the local hub for further delivery to end customers.

As shown in Figure 6.8, the distribution network of SKF is characterized by substantial variety when it comes to the servicing of customers. In reality, the variety is even greater because the largest customers may be handled differently. One of SKF's customers is Volvo Car. The distribution arrangement in relation to this customer follows the principles presented in the previous example. Other large customers may be handled quite differently since they do not rely on modular supply.

The SKF example illustrates how a company may redesign its activity configuration over time in order to improve efficiency by exploiting new conditions. The modifications to this activity pattern primarily deal with balancing different types of similarity. However, the strong emphasis on reaping similarities in the first two transformations had to be balanced with increases in diversity in the third.

IKEA: The Dynamics of Alternative Activity Patterns

IKEA's entry into furniture retailing was based on the configuration of an alternative to the activity pattern in which established retailers were involved at the time. Table 6.4 summarizes a comparison of some of the main differences between the activity patterns of 'traditional' retailing and the pattern configured by IKEA.

Table 6.4 A comparison of activity patterns between traditional furniture retailers and IKEA.

	Traditional retailer	IKEA
Design	External design houses	Internal
	Focus on aesthetic features	Focus on cost savings in production and distribution
Production	Handicraft production	Large-scale operations for economy
	Small-scale operations and 'exclusivity'	New materials and suppliers
Assembly	Often built to order	Mechanized processes
	Labour-intensive operations	Final assembly by consumer
Logistics	Bulky furniture giving problems in handling and necessitating costly transport	Flatpack kits giving streamlined, consumer-packaged distribution
Marketing and sales	City-centre location and many staff giving huge costs	Cheap out-of-down location
		Mass communication of Scandinavian image
Service	Extensive 'free' service	Self-service concept in store
	Expensive small-scale delivery	Transport from store by consumer

IKEA's configuration of activities is an interesting example of modifications in similarity, diversity and sequentiality, in comparison with the activity patterns of traditional retailing in the middle of the twentieth century. It also highlights the impact of specialization in the evolving activity patterns. The business mission of this Swedish firm was 'to provide cheap furniture to ordinary people'. Low cost was thus the main strategic driver in the development of the activity pattern and it was attained through high similarity and low diversity. Diversity was almost non-existent for a long time and, particularly in its early days, IKEA paid very little attention to the possible variety in consumer tastes and behaviour. Limiting activity diversity was a prerequisite for achieving similarity in production through standardization and reliance on modularity and mass manufacturing. Mechanized processes replaced many labour-intensive handicraft arrangements in assembly operations. Similarities in logistics and marketing were attained through the large scale of the operations in comparison with previous configurations.

On the other hand, similarities were considerably reduced in the final assembly and transportation to homes as these operations were shifted from producers and retailers to the individual consumer. Consumers were willing to take on this change in the division of labour because doing so provided opportunities for buying furniture at really low prices. Changing the activity pattern in this way was made possible only because of changes in the resource constellations of the network. Consumers required transportation resources and IKEA's entry into furniture retailing took place at a time when cars were becoming common in Swedish families. This resource was also useful in another respect. The fact that consumers could go by car to the retail store made it possible for IKEA to locate out of towns, with corresponding cost advantages in comparison with traditional retailers' expensive 'high street' establishments.

The serial interdependence in the activity pattern was increased compared with previous arrangements which were based on the distribution of bulky furniture. The flatpack logistics principle applied by IKEA not only reduced bulkiness, it also made possible an enhanced coordination of these activities. Most furniture was now packaged for the consumer at the manufacturing site and these flat packages remained unchanged all the way through the inbound transportation to

IKEA's store, through its warehousing and display activities, and in the outbound logistics to the final consumer. Secondly, obtaining these benefits required a complete change in the design and manufacture of the furniture. These modifications increased the serial interdependence between production and logistics and created opportunities for both enhanced manufacturability and cost-efficient transportation and materials handling.

Design was critical for IKEA's strategy to become successful so the decision was taken to insource this activity, in contrast to other retailers, which had traditionally relied on outside design houses. IKEA's design activities were strongly connected to all the other activities in Table 6.4. Furniture was designed to be 'production friendly' and also to make it possible to utilize alternative and non-traditional materials and suppliers. The furniture designs also had to relate to logistics by allowing for flatpack transportation. Finally, in marketing, its in-house design resources made it possible to create the IKEA brand awareness, to a large extent relying on a Scandinavian image. The reconfiguration of activities and recombination of resources paved the way for the unique activity pattern behind IKEA's solutions, and also had a huge impact on the web of related actors, both suppliers and other furniture retailers.

The IKEA case exemplifies what is usually identified as a 'revolutionary' reconfiguration of activity patterns. Such changes can take place when technical development impacts on the opportunities for resource combining and subsequent activity reconfiguration involving a multitude of adjustments. As we have argued above, it is not uncommon in these situations for actors not previously involved in the established activity pattern to be in a better position to grasp these opportunities than those that are heavily embedded in the established pattern through long-term adjustments. The established furniture retailers had made considerable investments in their resource collections and activity structures. Their main mission was therefore to exploit these investments. IKEA started more or less from scratch and could therefore more easily take advantage of evolving opportunities.

Discussion of the Illustrations

The three examples illustrate how activity configuration in practice relates to specialization and interdependency in activity patterns. Any activity pattern is characterized by all three interdependencies. The three concepts of analysis that we have introduced were instrumental for understanding the changes in the three cases. As we suggested in the analytical framework section, companies need to balance similarity, diversity and sequentiality in order to get the most out of the activity patterns in which they are involved. Balancing is crucial also when it comes to the time dimension and to the extent of specialization. It is important for a company to increase the extent of specialization of activities because it leads to performance improvements. However, too much specialization may interfere with opportunities to reconfigure activities when new conditions arise.

We also need to add that Volvo Car, SKF and IKEA could never have achieved the changes we described in isolation. The reorganization of activities required the resources of the companies themselves and their counterparts. The efficiency and effectiveness of the activity arrangements required adjustments and linkages to activities in other companies. Finally, the aspirations of the three companies to reorganize their activities fitted well with objectives of other actors, the actions of which then supported the change initiatives.

Volvo Car would not have been able to organize its activity configuration without active support from the global component suppliers that located their modular assembly units close to its assembly line. But Volvo is a small producer of cars and it would not have been possible for it to get its suppliers to make the necessary changes. The reason that Volvo was able to succeed in their reorganization efforts was that a number of other, much larger automotive firms also developed the same requirement. So what Volvo actually did was to exploit opportunities that became available when large players in the web of actors were changing the overall pattern of activities.

The development of the infrastructure for physical distribution and information exchange was crucial to SKF's efforts to reorganize its distribution network. Even though the forecasting systems designed in the first transformation did not fully live up to expectations, they were necessary for taking this step. Without fleets of truck operators crossing the European continent, SKF would have been unable to reorganize in the way that it did. Other manufacturers' successful centralization of inventories served as an inspiration for SKF's second transformation. The development towards a united Europe also led many suppliers to locate their central warehouses in Belgium and Holland, which in turn generated logistics competences in this area that were exploited by SKF. Finally, in the third transformation, SKF could benefit from the ever increasing fine-tuning of the logistics networks in Europe following on from customers' increasing requirements for differentiation of distribution services.

IKEA was able to gain its position in furniture retailing because it could involve the consumer in its activity configuration. Changing the division of labour in terms of final assembly and transportation was attractive to both IKEA and consumers since it reduced costs and thus prices. One of the reasons behind this shift was that the resource constellations around consumers had changed because they now had access to their own means of transportation. Furthermore, IKEA localized and mobilized suppliers that were interested in supplying flatpack furniture. Some of these were previously suppliers to customers in other industries and saw an opportunity to increase the variety of their customer bases. Through this background, they provided IKEA with new materials and technologies that were important for IKEA's future product development.

Conclusion

The main characteristic of activities and activity configurations in the business landscape is that they exist in a much larger context than a single business. In this larger context, activities are formed through interaction where every activity is organized in an active interplay with a number of other activities. In this way it becomes part of a larger activity pattern involving numerous interaction processes. These processes are complex and vary in intensity, but constantly change the characteristics of the activity patterns in the business landscape. The space aspect of activity interaction primarily concerns the interdependencies among activities.

We have identified three types of interdependencies, each providing particular opportunities and constraints for activity configuration. Balancing the impact of these interdependencies is a significant issue in the design and redesign of activity configurations because each of the interdependencies impacts on the economic performance of the activity layer as a whole. The time aspect of interaction highlights the successive specialization adjustments in activity patterns carried out to improve their performance.

The more intense the interaction of activities, the more substantial will be the content of interaction processes and the more difficult it will be to change an individual activity without affecting other activities. On the one hand, changes in the configurations of activities emerge and evolve through the processes of interaction. On the other hand, the more interaction that occurs, the more any single activity will be enmeshed and interdependent with others. Because of this increasing extent of specialization in the activity pattern, it will be difficult to change any single activity unilaterally.

It might seem that our discussion has centred on activity patterns related to the manufacturing and use of industrial products. However, the interdependencies identified in these examples are equally valid for the analysis of activity patterns in service operations. Service providers such as banks, insurance companies and telecommunications operators are continuously striving to improve the economies of their activities by expanding their client bases. In order to achieve these benefits they have to increase the similarity of their operations. Standardization is one of the most important ways to handle the configuration of these as the activities of a service firm and its clients are characterized by joint interdependence. But some customers may have specific requirements for the services they buy. Depending on the size of the customer and the nature of diversity required, the service provider may be interested in mutual adjustments with a customer, which then leads to dyadic interdependence.

Furthermore, our examples have concentrated on activity patterns that are more or less repetitive over time. In many cases, however, activity patterns are consciously temporary, which is illustrated by our example from the construction industry in the introduction. These patterns become established for a specific undertaking and, when this aim is achieved, the activity pattern is dissolved. In some situations, these temporary activity patterns may involve numerous complex activities and be configured for quite a long time. The design and installation of a power station or a chemical plant are typical examples, as are major infrastructure projects in communication and transportation. The time aspect of the activity pattern is different in these cases, while the space aspect is similar in many respects to those that we have discussed.

INTERACTION AND ACTORS

7

In Chapters 5 and 6, we focused on business resources and activities. In this chapter, we take a closer look at actors. Business actors are also part of the interactive landscape. Just like activities and resources, they affect the landscape and are affected by it. However, there is a striking difference between actors and resources and activities: Although the resources of a business and the activities performed in it have human dimensions, it is only actors that from intent. This intent is based on knowledge of the resources, activities and other actors, on views of their evolution over time and of their location in network space. Following their intent, business actors interact with others to combine resources and link activities. Thus, actors have some very particular features in relation to resources and activities and consequently to the business landscape. From an analytical perspective, these features create some key problems for us in trying to understand the nature of the business actor.

In this chapter, we approach actors from the perspective of how they act in interaction. Actors do not exist in isolation. They are only actors for others, which means when they are acknowledged as such by some others. They need others because they draw on what others have as resources and carry out as activities. They need others that need them in order to acquire an identity and thus come to existence as actors. Every actor is thus situated in a wider web of interacting actors.

We begin this chapter by examining the variety of actors in business networks and the different forms they tend to assume. We then discuss how past IMP research came to the conclusion that actors need to be considered from the perspective of their interactions and how the very idea of actors changes when we look at actors from the perspective of their acting in interaction with others. The distinctive features of actors as they appear in interaction are then examined and, in particular, we discuss the *jointness* of actors in space and how they *co-evolve* in time. In the final part of the chapter, we formulate six propositions about actors that reflect the interaction perspective. We argue that conceptualizing actors from the interaction perspective can better explain certain phenomena and behaviours in business networks.

A Business Landscape Full of Actors

The first notable feature of actors is their variety. Any view of the interactive business landscape shows a great number of different actors, all trying to accomplish various tasks, from very simple ones to the most complex. There are many individuals in a company who each follow a particular agenda to accomplish more or less consciously planned tasks. Others seem only to follow prescribed routines. These individuals may be agents for a resource, such as a facility, a product or an activity pattern, or they may represent a department or a business unit. A view of the interactive landscape may also show teams or departments in a company composed of many people that meet to achieve a particular task, such as delivering a product to a client by a specified date. The same view may show a company that has committed itself to the expensive development of a new service package for a particular customer. We may also see a large multinational corporation announcing plans to withdraw from a large geographical area. There is an endless sea of more or less conscious interaction within and between millions of apparently separate organizations involving huge numbers of transactions. If we look at any business we may see individuals, groups, teams, whole organizations or even groups of organizations that behave in a coordinated way and attempt to accomplish particular outcomes: Or perhaps we should say, more precisely, that all of these *appear* to be acting in a particular way and *appear* to be dedicated to accomplishing particular tasks.

Some of the actors in the business landscape may appear to be inspired by ideas that they try to pursue. Others may seem to be reacting to what they see as problems that need attention. Everything that these actors do involves resources and activities and has consequences for other actors. A glance at the business network may show a few individuals trying to set up a new business, convinced that it will change an industry. At the same time, a division of a large company may acquire a small business because it has some competence that will be useful for the operations of the division. Perhaps a deal is being negotiated to set up a joint venture or to carry out an acquisition or a team of technicians from a supplier company is trying to solve a problem with business software installed at a customer's site that is not performing as it should. Everything that actors do affects different resources and activities directly or indirectly. Without actors, business networks would not be dynamic.

The variety of the business landscape and of the actors within it leads to our first problem in trying to understand the concept of the business actor: The form of the actors in a business network is not fixed or pre-determined and there are many actors other than formal organizations and individuals.

A second feature of business is that none of the actors in it is isolated from other actors. Whatever they do and try to accomplish directly draws on and affects some other actors and indirectly affects many others. Each actor interacts directly with some of those that are close to it in network space in terms of geographical proximity, knowledge or interdependence. Teams and project groups work for and with other teams; individuals interact with other individuals within and across company boundaries. Their work is of interest to others that are not directly connected to them and it may possibly interfere with their own work or that of other organizations. Each company interacts directly with a specific set of other companies, including its customers and suppliers and those involved in similar activities or that have similar resources. But with others it interacts only indirectly, through intermediaries.

All these interactions between actors form a *web* that stretches across the business landscape and that encompasses the links and ties between their respective activities and resources. There appears to be some continuity over time in the ways that actors relate to each other within the relationships that they build between them. In principle, each actor is free to relate to any other actor in the way and at the time that it chooses. But, in practice, the ways that actors are related to each other is rather selective. We suggested in Chapter 3 that there are a limited number of actors available to each actor and with which it can interact to achieve some compatibility. For example, there are likely to be only a limited number of suitable customers, suppliers or development partners for each company. All actors tend to interact with some continuity with their important counterparts. These individually important counterparts are important for what an actor can do and will become. All actors are unique and the particular form of their interactions with each specific counterpart is a function of mutual and separate learning and development over time. Over time, these interacting actors become mutually interdependent and the role of the individual actor becomes difficult to isolate from its interacting counterparts.

This leads us to our second problem in trying to understand the concept of the business actor: The boundaries of the actors in the business landscape appear to be blurred or unclear. It is difficult to establish where an actor ends or begins.

These two problems (the changing form of actors and the blurred boundaries) not only affect researchers seeking to describe and conceptualize business actors in the interacted landscape. They are also problems for the actors themselves: Blurred boundaries mean that it is difficult for actors to maintain a clear view of themselves, of what they are doing and what they should be doing. It also means that it is difficult for the collective actors that comprise a company to keep together that company and those in it. The problem of the variety of actors also means that it is difficult for an actor to identify the most appropriate counterparts with which to interact and to determine the form that it wants that interaction to take.

In Chapters 5 and 6, we discussed how resources are combined and activities linked to each other for the purpose of business development. It is always actors that do this combining and linking. It is actors that enact, learn and acquire knowledge about the effects of combinations and links. It is actors that carry out re-combinations, look for new possibilities and fix problems as they come. It is actors that control, spread and use their collective knowledge of the different aspects of the highly complex network. The interacted landscape is a continuously emergent construction of activities, resources and actors in which the actors are the main organizing force.

The structure of the business landscape that we have described indicates two very different situations in which actors take part at the same time: The first is direct interaction with a few counterparts. For a company as actor, these may include immediate major customers and suppliers, bank representatives, or those with which it is involved in technological development. Each actor is likely to know a lot about these direct counterparts and about how to combine resources and configure activities with them. This can be depicted as the actor's own 'small world'.[1] All actors have a small world that makes sense to them.

---

[1] The notion of 'small worlds' is related to the classical studies of social networks in which there are a limited number of steps from one actor to any of the other actors (Milgram 1967). The small world is the context as seen by an actor looking out into the network. The context becomes very different when this particular actor is looked upon from others only two steps away. In the first context, the world is shrinking and becoming smaller. In the second, it is expanding very fast and multiplying into very large numbers.

The second situation in which actors are involved is with the large number of actors in the wider network. Each actor is connected to specific resources and activities in this 'wider world', indirectly via some of its particular counterparts. The actor knows much less of this wider world. The actor is much less influential and much more uncertain about the consequences of changes in activities, resources and other actors. In this situation, the actor is dependent on the resources and activities of those that act as intermediaries for it in this wild wide world. The wider world is more difficult to make sense of because it consists of many small worlds with their own 'logic'.

In both of these worlds, actors attempt to balance two forces: The necessity of reacting to the actions of others; and the possibility of influencing others. Actors need to balance these two forces in order to secure their existence as actors; that is, to be seen and acknowledged as an actor by others. Living in such a context is demanding because the possibility of interpreting what is going on in the business landscape is always limited and the outcomes for each actor depend as much on the actions of others as on its own actions.

Analysing actors from the interaction perspective involves us in addressing these two situations simultaneously. We are especially concerned with how an actor develops associations or 'bonds' with its direct counterparts and with the role and impact of these bonds on the life of the single actor and the effects of the bonds on the dynamics of interaction on companies, business relationships, and the business landscape as a whole.

In this chapter, we discuss these two situations that we have been struggling with as researchers. The situations are far from being fully understood because they raise some very complex questions. However, we are convinced that developing the conceptualization of business actors from the interaction perspective can help us to understand and explain at least some of the empirical phenomena that characterize the business landscape and which do not seem to be explicable using conventional frameworks.

Actors in the IMP Framework

Most of the studies of business relationships in the IMP research have only addressed the issues of actors indirectly. For example, many of the studies have examined the approaches and outcomes of interactions as they are seen through the eyes of individuals. At other times these studies have examined the interactions and interpretations of individuals as *representative* of companies and others have used multiple interviews in particular companies to try to interpret some idea of consensus. In other studies, an orientation towards an examination of activities and resources has meant that the actor dimension is reduced almost to the category of a 'residual' explanatory variable. There have been few empirical studies that have centrally addressed the nature of the business actor, its discretion, motives, or its effects on others explicitly and systematically. As a consequence, the actor dimension has on the whole, been less well developed than ideas on business resources and activities. The observations of actors in IMP research points rather clearly to the need to approach the conceptualization of actors from the interaction perspective. But our observations of actors have also highlighted some of the difficulties involved in developing an alternative conceptual framework for actors.

When we started our research, we found that the companies that operated in what we called 'business markets' seemed to work in different ways in each of a limited number of important relationships. The main aim of the first IMP research project was to explore the content of the relationships between customers and suppliers. Companies were assumed to be the actors, although this assumption was not made explicit. However, in designing the project, we found it important to devote time to examining the particular relationships between individual 'operatives' as representatives of their companies in relationships with a customer or supplier.

One of the important findings of the first IMP project was that episodes of 'social exchange' between individuals from the two companies were essential for developing long-term relationships between customer and supplier companies. It was clear that the experiences of these individuals form the history of their interactions and are crucial for the formation and development of business relationships. We also found that we could identify a relationship 'atmosphere' defined in terms of the perceived social, cultural and technological 'distances' between the individuals, the commonality of their expectations and levels of conflict between the individual actors in the relationship (e.g. Ford 1980; Hallén 1986). This atmosphere was an important intervening variable that mediated the impact of the technological and commercial factors on the development of the relationship between the two companies. A third finding was that the dimensions of individual companies, such as their strategy and structure, impacted on relationship formation and development. In other words, social exchange between individuals, taking place within a particular atmosphere, and a structural fit between the organizations were important factors in determining the companies between which relationships would develop and how they would develop.

A number of more specific issues also emerged from this project. For example, it appeared necessary for individuals to learn the 'language' of their counterparts; inter-personal interaction affected the extent and nature of the knowledge that was embedded in the relationship and the level of the risk that participants felt. It was clear that the personal attitudes and experiences of individuals could facilitate the development of effective business relationships but could also present severe impediments to that development. The role of relationships in addressing various types of problem (technical, operational, logistical and even financial) for the companies also emerged from the empirical data.

The importance of the inter-personal exchange and atmosphere for how business relationships develop led us to further studies of what we now call the 'actor dimension' in business relationships. For example, a number of studies explored the role of trust-building and commitment in the development of a business relationship and the effects on relationships and companies of knowledge exchange (Huemer 1998). The first IMP project introduced the importance of actors' idiosyncrasies in determining the kind of relationships that would develop between companies (Turnbull 1979; Hallén 1986; Wilson and Mummalaneni 1986). This was followed by other studies that showed the wide discrepancy between the extent and rate of development of relationships between a single actor and its counterparts. Together, these early studies raised the question of the interplay between the actor dimension and the matching of the resources and activities of different companies.

The second major IMP project explored the set of relationships that a business develops with customers, suppliers and other parties and the role that these relationships serve for the business itself. This study devoted considerable attention to the importance of third parties for the formation of a relationship between customer and supplier. One of the main aims of the project was to look at the interdependencies between combinations of relationships because there had been some indications of the significance of these in earlier research.

The main finding of the second IMP project was that important interdependencies between relationships exist in a number of dimensions. On a theoretical level, an important outcome of the project was the development of the ARA framework (Håkansson and Johanson 1992; Håkansson and Snehota 1995). This enabled us to distinguish between three different types of interdependencies, between activities, resources and actors in a single relationship and across relationships. The study used this framework to capture and describe the variations in the content of relationships and the interdependencies between companies.

The interdependencies found in and between business relationships lead to a vision of the single business as a node in a network-like structure of interdependent business relationships. The research demonstrated that the relationships that companies develop with others are important for the role that a company can play in the business landscape. The second IMP project has shown that the set of relationships that a company develops with specific counterparts connects it to different combinations of resources and activities outside the company. But the research also showed that the relationships of a company are not determined by pre-existing resources and activities but are the outcome of the interactions and mutual orientation between actors, both as individuals and companies.

The second IMP project made it clear that we cannot explain how a business relationship develops by examining a single relationship; we must consider how that relationship is connected to other relationships. Both parties to a particular relationship are also embedded in relationships with third parties and through them to a larger web of other actors. This 'embeddedness' adds another significant aspect of the actor dimension: An actor's acting is affected by the specific counterparts with which it is associated. Individual actors may seek to avoid or to develop their own dependence on a particular counterpart as well as avoiding or developing the counterpart's dependence on them. The interactive manipulation of dependence is a major element of choice for the individual or collective business actor and has profound implications for the actor's own activities and resources and the connections between them and the activities and resources of others.

An important conclusion based on the findings of the second IMP project is that the external resources and activities to which an actor is connected through other actors tends to be as significant in determining the *identity* of that actor as its 'own' internal activities and resources. The importance of externally connected actors, activities and resources means that an actor's interactions with any specific counterpart are always 'joint'. This interaction not only involves the actors themselves but also those to which they are connected.

Follow-up studies to the second IMP Project have explored particular aspects of actors' interaction and provided further insights into the actor dimension in business networks. For example, these have been concerned with how actors frame their context and form 'pictures' of other actors and the network that surrounds them; with the issue of the intelligibility of actors in interaction and the process of learning in interaction (Dahlquist 1998; Håkansson *et al.* 1999; Henneberg *et al.* 2006; Ramos and Ford 2009).

The findings on actors in business relationships from a number of studies suggest that while actors play an important role in interactive business relationships their individuality and discretion is constrained. It seems that business actors are as much a product of their interactions as they are the directors of them.

The results from the first two IMP studies and of the complementary studies that followed indicated the need to develop the idea of the actor further: The conventional notion of the more or less independent, active and complete actor certainly cannot be taken as a given in the interactive environment. Instead, the idea emerges of the actor as someone or something that develops an identity within a complicated pattern of evolutionary development. But even more importantly, the actor develops its combination of activities and resources interactively with the activities and resources of other actors.

The Idea of the Business Actor

A Traditional View

One of the reasons why it is challenging to examine actors from an interaction perspective is that the concepts of actors and agency in the social sciences have deep roots and are built on a long and respectable tradition of analysis.[2] Most of the research on economic organization and business builds on a tradition that takes an actor-centred perspective. The primary unit of analysis in this perspective is the actor, mostly in the shape of formal organizations (companies) or individuals acting on behalf of firms. The aim is to achieve some understanding of the actor in order to explain the ways in which actors act. Formal organizations are taken as the starting point because they are generally considered to be the dominant entities in economic and business activity. Actors are analysed in management research with the aim of explaining their actions and, most often, to provide some implicit or explicit normative guidance to the actors. The supposition is that how actors behave can be explained from their features and attributes. The assumption is that if we understand actors, we understand their acting.

This traditional approach implies that questions of who or what are the actors in business are not relevant. Firms and individuals as actors are taken as given and it is self-evident what a firm or an individual is. This starting point involves two broad but very important assumptions:

- The actor is a self-contained entity that is autonomous and independent with respect to others and to its environment. In other words, it is assumed that an actor has a clear form and specific boundaries. It follows that an actor is what it has and owns: the sum of its properties, attributes and capabilities. The boundaries of the firm are defined by what it controls through ownership and this definition provides a clearly delimited entity. A firm ends where its ownership (or, sometimes, its contracts) ends.
- Actors are autonomous in how they choose to act and how they act determines the outcomes for them. That is, the outcomes for an actor can, more or less unequivocally, be related to

---

[2]It is a strong and deeply rooted tradition in social sciences to define an 'action' as a practical conclusion drawn from intentions and beliefs, thus relating action to rationality. Apparently this way of defining action can be found, in particular, in the writings of Max Weber but the roots can be traced much further back. An extensive overview of the roots of the concept of action can be found in Davidson (1980).

their behaviours. Following in this tradition, firms and individuals qualify as actors because it is assumed that they can, and should, behave purposefully. This implies that firms and individuals can autonomously formulate goals and devise ways to achieve them in a particular context. In other words, actors are supposed to be capable of anticipating the consequences and outcomes of their actions.

This conceptualization of the actor has been termed 'economic man' in economic theory and 'administrative man' in the organizational or behavioural theory of the firm (March and Simon 1958; Cyert and March 1963; March 1988). The main difference between economic and administrative man is that administrative man has some limitations in his rationality and abilities, that is, in what he knows of alternatives and consequences and in what goals he has. In contrast, economic man is rational and acts accordingly, that is, he can optimize his behaviour.

An Initial View from the Perspective of Interaction

A view of the business actor from the perspective of interaction yields a picture that is strikingly different from that outlined above. An interaction perspective on the actor does not take its starting point as the actor itself, but those with which the actor interacts. This amounts to approaching actors from their acting *in interaction*.[3]

Considering actors from the perspective of interaction has some consequences for the conceptualization of the actor. At the most basic level, it means that we can envisage an actor without having necessarily to ascribe rational or purposeful behaviour to it. An actor acquires an identity in interaction with others because its behaviour, regardless of the motives or underlying reasons for it, is a matter of concern to or affects another. The particular identity of the actor is defined by that interaction with another. Even routine or ritual behaviour by an actor can matter to another actor because it forms interactions that have tangible outcomes for both the other and the actor. Even when there is clear intent on the part of the actor, the outcomes of its behaviour depend on how that behaviour is interpreted by the counterpart and by the reactions it produces. What makes an entity an actor is that its acting is of interest to others. How the actor's behaviour concerns others depends on those others, on their preoccupations and on their view of the context of the behaviour, rather than on the behaviour itself or the intent behind it. Thus an interactive view of the business actor infers that each actor exists as a different entity with a different identity in each specific interaction context.

---

[3] Approaching actors from the point of view of their behaviour in interaction has consequences for the concept of actors. Proponents of 'social interactionism' (Blumer 1969) take the position that the self is the result of interaction and therefore the individual actor's behaviour can only be understood on the basis of reciprocal acts and their interpretation. Among those proponents, Goffman argued that 'the proper study of interaction is not the individual and his psychology, but rather the syntactical relations among the acts of different persons mutually present to one another' (Goffman 1967:2). If the point of departure is the interaction, the identity of an actor has to be conceived as a variable rather than taking it as given. From this perspective, identity is not a structural entity but is continuously changing because, even if the actor does not undertake any transformation, the interaction itself changes. Goffman expressed this idea that what we are trying to understand is 'not, then, men and their moments. Rather moments and their men' (Goffman 1967:3).

In an interactive view of the actor, a first issue to address is who becomes an actor in the interacted environment. The interactive role of the actor can be attributed to individuals or to various more or less complex collective entities and organizations. The main reason for this variety is because it is in the eyes of the beholder that someone becomes an actor. This means that the form and role of an actor is something that is context-specific. In each of these contexts, the behaviour of the specific actor interacts with that of a counterpart. This leads to effects for both of them and to the sequential evolution of their behaviours. Thus the identity (and the entity) of actors is problematic. In the same way as for activities and resources, the entity of an actor cannot be taken for granted in an interactive world.

Defining actors in terms of their impact on others also has consequences for the assumption of the autonomy of actors. A view of actors from the interaction perspective means that the identity of an actor cannot be clearly separated from the identity of those with which it interacts. Actors are not self-contained nor are they independent: Each counterpart views a particular actor from their own perspective and from their interpretation of its behaviour and intent. In principle, an actor is free to choose how to behave. But the outcomes of an actor's behaviour arise from the way that it interacts with the behaviour of particular counterparts; they arise from the chain of reactions of the parties regardless of the intent of the two interacting parties (Thibaut and Kelly 1959). The outcomes can thus never be fully within the control of the actor. The actor's anticipation of the effects of interaction is therefore limited and its autonomy to act and react becomes restricted. Similarly, no actor can be self-sufficient because its behaviour is built on the behaviours of others. The outcomes for an actor of its behaviour depend on how that behaviour is interpreted by others and by how those others react to it.

The roles that are attributed to an actor depend on with whom it interacts. But actors are *selectively* attached to others: Each actor develops more or less strong bonds to a relatively limited number of specific others, perhaps as customer, supplier or development partner. These bonds consist of mutual orientation, preferences and commitment. They involve matching some of the actor's resources and activities to those of others. Through this bonding, the actor acquires some, but never a complete, knowledge of the resources, activities and intent of its counterparts. The bonds between actors are not the result of unilateral action but of interaction over time. This interaction also affects the resources and activities of counterparts and their knowledge of the actor.

The bonds between actors mean that they and their resources and activities become embedded in each other. This embeddedness and the interdependencies that arise from it contribute to the uniqueness of each actor and each of its relationships. In other words, how and to whom an actor becomes related have important consequences for how it is seen, how it can behave, what it can accomplish and how it can and will develop.

The interactive perspective leads to a view of the business actor as defined and formed through interaction, rather than having a fixed or interaction-free existence. This conclusion is the same as that which we reached for activities and resources in Chapters 5 and 6. From the interaction perspective, actors are in many ways special but they remain only one of the three layers of interaction alongside resources and activities. Actors interact with each other and interact with both activities and resources. Actors are at least as much the product of the interaction that takes place in business relationships as they are subjects that interact. With whom an actor interacts and how it interacts shapes what it can and cannot do, how it is constituted and ultimately, who or what it is. This situation is commonly seen in business today.

Companies are continuously evolving into myriad forms: Some design products or services; others produce or deliver them; some do both; some do neither. Some provide only services; some provide products and services; some advise others how to do things for themselves. Some companies sell to end consumers; some sell via distributors. Some distributors control or direct manufacturers; others do neither. We would conventionally attribute each of these situations to the intent of a single company or even the intent of a single manager. But each situation involves the respective intents and the enactment of a number of connected companies and individuals. The evolving outcomes for each company arises from the continuing interactions between those companies and individuals. Thus, every outsourcing involves a simultaneous insourcing!

The actor we have started to outline is different from both economic man and administrative man. The 'interacted actor' is not characterized by being rational or by limitations on its rationality. Instead the 'interacted actor' is characterized by its acting in interaction and how it is seen and enacted by some very specific counterparts. The small group of directly related counterparts see the actor as possessing some very particular capacity and knowledge that is useful to them. The actor in this 'small world' is characterized by its specific capacity and competence to combine activities, resources and actors. But the value of this knowledge and competence depends, of course, on its economic effects on the activities, the use of resources and the relationships to other actors of these specific counterparts. The actor in relation to these counterparts is effectively locked into a narrow environment that has clear boundaries in network space, but which can be developed extensively in network time.

The small world of every actor relates to a number of small worlds of other actors with which it is connected. These connections dramatically expand the surrounding space in which the actor exists. But the actor is not nearly as knowledgeable and influential in this wider space. There, the actor is just one amongst many and its friends are extremely important to it as they mediate the effects of the wide world!

In other words, the dimensions of time and space are vitally important for the single actor and we now discuss them in more detail.

Distinctive Features of Actors in Interaction

Actors considered from the perspective of business interaction appear to be a 'variable entity'. Thus it is not easy to identify common traits that characterize all kinds of actor or to identify types or groups that are homogeneous. But there are two features that appear to characterize all kinds of actor (individuals, companies and other collective entities) in business networks.

The first feature that is common to all actors is that their existence and characteristics depend on others, not in some generic sense but on very specific others. This dependence in turn, has two aspects: An actor exists only because it is of concern and interest to some other actor with which it interacts; every actor builds on and in some way can make use of what specific others do. Any actor is therefore a product of interactions with a specific variety of others and its interaction with them imprints particular characteristics on the actor.

The second feature that is common to all actors is that they all have both partial but deep knowledge and competence as a basis for their interaction. Each actor has specific knowledge about some activities, resources and actors. But they can never fully understand their resource and activity interdependences nor can they ever anticipate the behaviour of all other actors. These limitations exist because all of their counterparts are related to other actors that are more or less unknown to them. But each actor knows more than anyone else about its own specific relationships and interactions. This knowledge of relationships and actors, activities and resources arises from elaboration of previous experiences of interaction. Existing knowledge and insight is constantly changed through interaction with others during which new problems, opportunities and solutions may be discovered. But because this knowledge and competence develops and changes through interaction with others it can never be complete and there is always the potential for development.

Every actor appears to be dependent on a specific web of actors and exists as a consequence of interaction with these actors. Actors are the outcome of the history of their interactions within this specific web as much as they are a force that drives that interaction. All actors have a specific identity for specific others because they can be seen by these others as a distinct and meaningful entity to which they can relate. This specificity in both the counterparts and content of their interaction mean that an actor's identity is always specific in time and space. We referred to these two aspects in Chapter 3 as the *jointness* and *co-evolution* of actors. We now explore these two concepts in more detail.

Actors in Space: Jointness

The concept of jointness places others firmly into the identity of the actor. These others are part of the identity attributed to an actor in an interacted environment by association (an actor is always seen in relation to those it interacts with) and by usage (an actor always makes use of the resources of others in order to operate). Thus, actors combine and configure their resources and activities based on those of other actors. Hence the business landscape consists of a large variety of *overlapping* actors each with boundaries that are not clearly defined. In some situations, we may consider a company as an actor. In others, the actor may be a department or a single person from a company. A single individual may be the actor with respect to a particular resource or activity that forms part of more than one company, as in the case of a dyadic relationship or a supply chain. Thus, there are many more actors than the formal economic or legal entities.

Jointness is a way of characterizing a specific relationship between any two actors in relation to all others. Jointness is a measure of the spatial extension of an actor across the network via its relationships with others. Network space is multidimensional. Jointness involves closeness between actors across geographical space but also includes links between the respective knowledge, technologies, capital investments and cultures of the two actors.

Actors relate to each other selectively. When we consider companies as actors within business relationships, there is a clear and obvious logic in the ways that companies relate their resources and activities to each other. Companies form relationships and interact selectively precisely because they are different and because they can complement each other. Through interaction, they find out who they can complement and how. Companies cannot carry out business without making extensive use of resources that are held by others and activities in which others engage.

In Chapter 5, we suggested that a relationship with another company is itself a resource. This resource is valuable to each of the actors in their interactions with third parties, in which they take part *jointly*.

The actual set of counterparts with which a company develops relationships depends on factors other than their respective resources and activities. Some relationships appear to be truly accidental and develop in an apparently casual way. For example, some of the customer and supplier relationships of a company may have started because of the failure of another counterpart. Others may have developed because of proximity, personal contact, supposed mutual understanding or similar 'soft' actor-specific reasons. When we try to answer the question of why particular companies develop relationships with some counterparts and not with others, the answer is likely to be twofold.

A relationship does not develop because a supplier has specific resources or activities or because it can provide a better product, service, delivery or price. It does not develop because a customer is large, rich or trustworthy. A relationship develops because the counterparts believe that it can help them address one or more specific problems. These problems may be technical, financial or relating to other relationships of the counterparts. But they are specific to the actor and to the relationship. Thus for example, a supplier may have a single high-volume relationship that helps to reduce its cash-flow problem. It may have other relationships that are small but generate useful profits and still others that provide it with learning or access to third parties.

A relationship develops if the two actors believe and expect that they can 'live' and develop together. 'Use' and 'value' are never objective descriptions and the impact of problems and beliefs is often not made explicit. The views of an actor depends on its previous experience, its other relationships and its picture of the network. There are often complex patterns of interactions both within and between companies that mediate and negotiate the perceptions and interpretations of mutual convenience and expectations.

Bonds arise between actors (companies, individuals or others) because each has to relate to its surroundings in a way that has meaning for its own activities and resources and those of its counterparts. The meaning to them of their interacting resources and activities leads to mutual commitment and prioritizing. The development of bonds between any two actors also depends on the continuing bonds between each of them and others.

The bonds between actors reflect how they see and know each other, but they also impact on how they see and interpret the wider context and the specific situations in which they find themselves. Actor bonds play an important part in how the actors interact and with whom they interact. Actor bonds impinge on an actor's knowledge and capabilities. An actor's knowledge and intent about combining activities, resources and actors are directly related to its specific counterparts and the bonds it has with them. Thus, the knowledge of an actor is a construction that is very much marked by a particular set of counterparts that comprise its own small world.

The bonds of an actor impact on the actor's ability to act and the way it acts. Actors take an active part in forming bonds but they are themselves formed by their bonds. Consequently, if we wish to explain what is happening to companies in the network, we cannot separate each individual company from the web of actors of which it forms part. Any actor is a node that relates specific others in such a way that they become worthwhile collectively. Thus any business actor has an internal organizing process through which its business relationships are systematically combined with its internal resources and activities. Any relationship between two actors connects the 'small worlds' of the two actors into something useful. This useful relationship in turn is a resource that relates to other resources including other relationships in other small worlds. The business network involves many inter-company organizing processes involving actors and their resources and activities that are connected in different ways to the internal processes within individual actors.

A company or an individual makes use of others by accessing some of their resources, activities and actors in order to address particular problems. All actors involve others in their problems. The characteristics of its counterparts and the problems that it addresses for them are always an important aspect of an actor's identity. The importance of counterparts is not only for what they are, but for what they can do and what they may become. When actors interact they are engaging in a broad sense in the organization of a web of actors, constellation of resources and pattern of activities. This organizing function is never within the complete control of a single actor. Instead, the evolution of the network is the outcome of all actors' interactions. Each of them contributes to connecting diverse elements of the network into a larger but constantly changing and multiple-functioning totality. Organizing in the network is therefore jointly enacted rather than planned or contrived. The organizing cannot be to an *a priori* design because no single actor, or even all of them together, has all the design details. Each actor has its own detailed picture of a small part of the total web, but only a sketch of the rest of it. The accuracy of each actor's picture is constantly challenged by others who have partly complementary and partly conflicting pictures. Interaction involves a constant discussion of these pictures and it is the interaction that is the organizing force.

The jointness of actors creates some particular problems that are important for both researchers and for actors themselves: First, the identity of any actor is made up of the diverging attributions of several different counterparts since the actor is simultaneously engaged in interaction with several others. Thus each actor acquires, and has to maintain, a *multifaceted identity*. Each actor is unique in the space dimension. But each actor is differently unique in relation to specific counterparts. All of an actor's counterparts have different pictures of it and each is more or less true or relevant to that counterpart. Each is based on that counterpart's interaction and relates to the problems it wishes to address and the role that it seeks for the actor. This multifaceted identity is both a problem and an opportunity for a single actor. It impinges directly on the actor's resource, activity and relationship investments and it is likely to be constantly discussed and questioned both internally and in interaction with others.

Secondly, it may be that only a single individual from one company is involved in interaction with a counterpart company at a particular time. This individual may be viewed by the counterpart or by the individual (or by the researcher) as acting in his own interests, as a departmental representative, or as an agent of the whole company. This is both a problem and an opportunity for companies. The 'personification' of interaction can facilitate bonding with a counterpart. But it can also make a relationship vulnerable to the departure of that individual. It can lessen the company's control over its approach to interaction or even lead to 'side-changing' through which an individual acquires the view of a relationship that is held by a counterpart. This latter problem is common amongst sales or service staff whose working time is spent mostly on the site of a single counterpart.

Thirdly, jointness with a counterpart may produce benefits, but it can also lead to problems in relation to particular others. Interacting with some actors, or forming relationships and bonds with them, precludes interaction or bond formation with others. There are two main reasons for this: An actor can handle only a limited number of interactive relationships that require its attention and draw on its resources and capabilities, so a new relationship may be a threat to existing ones. The bonds that develop between two actors represent an asset or a resource that can form the basis for the actors to achieve their particular ambitions but this asset may not be able to be combined with other assets and this limits what an actor can achieve with others.

Actors in Time: Co-evolution

Business networks may appear to be stable in the ways that actors relate to each other, carry out their activities and combine resources. But the network is constantly evolving through interaction, even though that evolution can be difficult to register. Change and development in specific relationships and in the network as a whole becomes apparent in any empirical study that is not simply a snapshot at a single point in time. Any actor comes into existence and continues to live in a context comprising other specific actors. An actor has to interact with specific others in order to acquire an identity and a role, to create an impact and to generate valuable outcomes for others and for itself. Looking at a particular company as an actor will reveal that its history has been built by addressing the evolving problems of specific others and using their resources and activities to address its own problems. Businesses start and develop over time using and serving others and relating their own and the counterparts' resources and activities to each other. Thus, in order to continue to exercise the role of an actor it has to co-evolve with others. Co-evolution is of central importance for any actor.

Co-evolution involves a business in relating to only a limited number of companies and excluding others that might have been involved or could be involved in the future. Who the others are at any given moment is crucial for development but is also a result of past interactions. Actor-related factors such as closeness, intelligibility, perceived problems, liking and despair all play a role in how the interactions have developed and in how an actor is situated in relation to others. Co-evolution is manifest in the small world of direct relationships that makes actors into what they are.

Each small world impacts an actor's horizon and determines what it sees and ignores of the possibilities and constraints of the wide web of actors. Interacting within this specific set of actors marks the actors and the form they take as they react and adjust. Actors are never entirely stable because their relative small worlds diverge and always need adjustments to be connected. Instead, they continuously change their forms and characteristics as a consequence of the involvement of others and interactions with them.

Co-evolution of actors results from history, from the future and the connections between the past and the future. If we visualize an actor's identity as an on-going construction site where a set of counterparts are involved in the construction, we can see that the construction site has evolved through history but is also affected by expectations of the future. Some of the features of the site have evolved through earlier interactions with counterparts. In these interactions, the interdependencies between activities and heterogeneity of resources have been considered and exploited. The actors have learned from and taught each other. This process has taken place across the borders of the actors and they will have taken advantage of possibilities to co-evolve technically and commercially. Developing relationships have played a key role in this process.

But these relationships have not prevented each company from having its own ideas about the future.

The complexity of the network makes it impossible for the actors to anticipate the future in any complete sense. Their knowledge and understanding of how the web of actors around them will develop can only be partial and with regard to their small worlds. All actors have a narrow view of the future. But these views and expectations of the future can be shared and negotiated between important counterparts. Through this process, the companies at least partly construct the future in the ways that they work together and co-evolve. The jointness of views and expectations is not limited to dyads of actors. It is common for ideas of how business should be conducted and how it should change (or more commonly not change!) to stretch across webs of actors. These common views often take the form of codes of practice, tacit or explicit 'constitutions' that may lead to attempts to restrict the operations of deviant actors by joint action.

But actors always face uncertainty about the future and have to live with a certain amount of ambiguity. No amount of mutual learning can dissolve all of these uncertainties and therefore some trust is essential for the creation of commitment, relationship development and uncertainty reduction. Mutual perceptions and knowledge are important in forming trust between actors but they are not the most important factor: Interaction is at the heart of trust. Interaction has tangible consequences for organizing the web of actors. Thus, trust between actors is enacted and arises as consequence of actors' behaviour. Acting forms trust because it offers clues to the further behaviour of counterparts and impacts on the way that an actor interprets its situation. What happens between actors affects the actors themselves and other third parties. Therefore it is interaction that actually produces the organizing effect in business relationships combining developments in the past with expectations of the future.

Co-evolution has its own variety: Businesses and their agents appear to adopt different approaches, logics or languages when framing, interpreting, forming intent and reacting in co-evolution. Within the margins of uncertainty, they construct different narratives based on an incomplete set of clues. These narratives reflect the specific logics and languages that are more or less clearly understandable to others and they orient behaviours. How these narratives are constructed and the extent to which they are shared and mutually understood can facilitate or hinder 'joint action'. To follow a particular narrative amounts to focusing on specific problems and outcomes over others. Solutions negotiated between actors tend to reflect this focusing. Three kinds of logic appear to be frequently applied by actors in business networks as they construct the narratives that orient their behaviours:[4]

- *Instrumental or technical logic* focuses on solutions in order to achieve the desired performance. It is concerned with how physical resources and specific activities can be combined and linked to achieve desired outcomes. This logic appears in larger systems, such as technologies or

---

[4]The idea of different logics applied to business organization has its origin in Thompson (1967), which discussed the notion of instrumental versus economic rationality and how that impacts on business organizations. The institutional logic in orienting behaviours and organizational solutions is proposed by the institutionalist school in organizational behaviour (e.g. Mayer and Rowan 1977; DiMaggio and Powell 1983).

large physical systems, but also in trouble-shooting as problems arise in continuing business relationships.

- *Economic or business logic* is primarily concerned with economic efficiency and focuses on the economic outcomes of various solutions to particular problems. It is concerned with cost–benefit analysis. It relates to the collective wisdom within the specific network about the main cost and revenue drivers, and who will bear the cost and gain the benefits.
- *Institutional logic* focuses on compliance with shared rules and norms that often can take the form of legal boundaries. It tends to identify problems and find solutions that are norms. It is likely to come into play when actors are concerned with problems that are difficult to assess in their instrumental or economic dimensions. There is both an actor-specific and a collective picture of what these rules or norms should look like.

A problem can be raised by any of the three logics and lead to solutions within the same logic or by adopting another. Interaction between business actors always includes dimensions and consequences for all of them but it is common that it is initiated by one of them. For example, interaction in a relationship with a customer may be triggered by an institutional logic: New health and safety regulations for the use of cement require it to be packed in 25 kg bags instead of the current 50 kg bags. All companies have to comply, so the supplier has to offer 25 kg bags. This may be opposed by economic logic: Twice as many bags will have to be used and costs will rise. Or it may be opposed by instrumental logic: We will need to fill twice as many bags on the same line; it is impossible. The solution negotiated may follow economic or instrumental logic: To reduce costs, the products or processes must be redesigned.

The identification of the three logics suggests that there is a pattern to the changes in the nature and features of actors. But it also suggests that the logics can produce conflicting ideas about solutions that are confronted as actors interact. The switching between logics is one of the driving forces of interaction and, consequently, changes in how the actors organize by combining resources, configuring activities and connecting actors. The way that an actor lives makes it impossible to consider it as something that is fixed or as a mission that is accomplished. Instead, each actor continuously takes on new features and forms. New companies are born and become important actors, others change shape and dissolve, only to reappear in other forms as people and resources become absorbed by other companies. No company in a business network is immune from this continuous metamorphosis.

Ducati Case Study

We can illustrate the importance of time and space in business relationships for a single actor by a case study of the Italian motorcycle producer Ducati (Bocconcelli and Håkansson 2008).

The company was founded in 1926 under the name Radio Patents Ducati with the purpose of producing components for the rapidly expanding radio industry, based on a patent held by the engineer Ducati. Ducati's products enjoyed worldwide success and the company expanded rapidly, opening branches in London, Paris, New York, Sydney and Caracas in the 1930s. The company became one of the most important suppliers in the radio industry at that time. In 1946, the company introduced a small auxiliary engine, called 'Cucciolo', that could be attached to a normal bicycle but it was not much of a success. A year later, the company developed a special frame on which to install the engine and it became a motorcycle producer. This was the moment when the company was introduced to the mechanical industry. In the years between 1950 and 1970, Ducati gradually became an important actor in the high-performance sports motorcycle industry and the production of radio components ended completely. Ducati became known for its particular design of engine, 'desmodromic'. The business encountered some difficulties towards the end of the 1970s and in 1983 it was acquired by another large Italian motorcycle producer, Cagiva. A few years later it introduced its legendary 'Monster' model of motorcycle. Despite the global success of the model, the company was in financial crisis and in 1996 it was bought by an American investment company with the aim of turning it round.

Let us now look more carefully at this turnaround and relate it to the idea of jointness in time and space: When Ducati was acquired by the new owner, its performance in terms of productivity and profitability was so bad that in order to survive it had to make a sharp turnaround and dramatically reduce its costs. However, the economic structure of the company was such that this could not be achieved through internal changes. Over the years, the company's operations had become very specialized and accounted for only 20 % of the product costs. 80 % of the total cost of the motorcycle were accounted for by materials and components purchased from some 380 suppliers. The only possible solution to the performance problems of the company (apart from some marketing changes, to which we will return) involved its suppliers. But in order to achieve this change, the company had to change its internal operations and structure them in such a way that they could be more effectively linked to its suppliers in both time and space, as illustrated in Figures 7.1 and 7.2.

Over time, Ducati had to change its product development, its design and control of production, and its logistical flows. All these processes were adapted and integrated into the corresponding

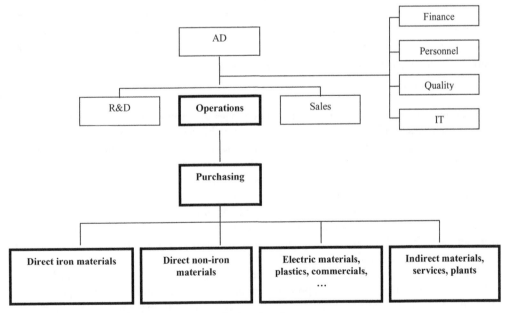

Figure 7.1 Ducati purchasing organization, before the change.

Source: Bocconcelli and Håkansson 2008

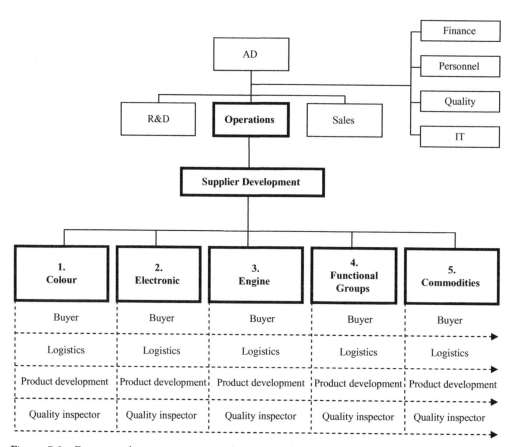

Figure 7.2 Ducati purchasing organization, after the change.

Source: Bocconcelli and Håkansson 2008

processes amongst its key suppliers. Over time, changes in activities and resources were able to build on each other and in successive stages it was possible to utilize resources more effectively. Ducati and its suppliers had to change in order to achieve these improvements. They had to learn to work together. They had to become involved in joint development processes and divulge detailed information about their own operations. Their joint ambition was to make all activities more time-dependent and together to build up a much more integrated network. Much of what happened could not have been known by the company or its suppliers beforehand. Most of the solutions adopted in Ducati's production and logistics came into effect interactively with changes in its suppliers. Not all of the existing suppliers were interested in taking part in this process. Partly because of this, but also because of the increased investment involved in the developing relationships with suppliers, the number of suppliers had to be reduced from 380 to 170.

   The activities of Ducati and its suppliers were also coordinated from the space perspective: 140 of the 170 suppliers were located in Italy, 40 of them in the Bologna region. An interesting illustration of the space dimension is that a group of suppliers was designated as the 'end product colour group' (see Figure 7.2). This group was not defined in a conventional way – specialized on buying paint – but its members were all involved in the painting process. The colour of a bike involved inputs from a number of suppliers and colour was a significant element in consumer choice. Previously, if a consumer decided to change the colour that he wanted after placing an order, he would have to wait an extra 60 days to get his bike. Following the reorientation of suppliers around colour, this change could be achieved in only five days.

The company had to change its internal organization in order to achieve this change in its supplier relationships. A significant indicator of this change, which can be seen in Figure 7.2, was to rename the Purchasing department as the Supplier Development department, indicating the difference in the work that it had to do. The departmental personnel were allocated into groups that included technicians and logistics experts. These groups were designed in relation to the particular elements of finished bikes, such as colour, rather than to general types of components. Following this reorientation, suppliers adapted to the same approach and created similar groups.

The results of the changes have been significant. One unsurprising change is that the suppliers' share of the total costs of Ducati increased further from 80 % to 92 %. Its production capacity increased from 12 000 to 40 000 motorcycles per year. Through the active use of suppliers, this increase could take place without any increase in the number of employees and it also made the company highly profitable. All of the company suppliers, but in particular the 36 major ones that account for around 80 % of the total volume of purchases, have been instrumental in the improvement in the company's performance. Further, it has been possible to drastically reduce delivery times, from weeks to days. Without the involvement of the suppliers, the operation would have been impossible. Indeed it is difficult to separate the internal and external changes because the activities of Ducati and its suppliers have become more or less seamlessly coupled. It is clear that the changes have been made possible by explicitly recognizing the company's jointness with others, through which the customer and the suppliers have made a distinct choice in their long-term priorities toward each other, making the boundaries between them rather arbitrary.

Ducati is a familiar and respected name among motor-sport enthusiasts in many countries, known for its high-performance motorcycles. Many of its customers belong to Ducati Clubs and are in touch with the company through Ducati stores in most major countries around the world. This development was also a change through which customers became more integrated into the company. The company has been transformed into what an executive calls 'an entertainment company offering a complete motoring experience'. Leaving aside the rather extravagant expression, these changes meant that between 1997 and 2004 the sales from complementary items (such as accessories and equipment) increased from 9 % to 19 % of total turnover.

Internal organization, external relationships and management methods have all undergone substantial changes in Ducati and its partners have played an increasingly important role. Some of the main current suppliers of the company have supplied it for several decades, in particular, the local suppliers of mechanical parts such as engine components, brakes and frame components. These suppliers have had to co-evolve with Ducati and in turn this has affected their way of doing business with other customers. The features in their evolved relationships with Ducati have had to be embedded into their total structure. Their concerns over this effect were one reason why some suppliers refused to take part in the venture.

Co-evolution makes a company (and pairs of companies) into unique actors in the way that they are configured internally and externally. This uniqueness is perhaps more visible in the Ducati case, but similar uniqueness of co-evolution can be found in other cases. The Ducati case is certainly special in that the role of suppliers is magnified, but it is not a one-off and many companies are in situations that resemble Ducati's.

Analysing Interacting Actors

We have argued that the identity of an actor is constructed by several others and that each of these others tends to construct an actor's identity from its own perspective. As a consequence, every actor is multifaceted and each of its faces changes more or less continuously. When an actor acts or tries to act, it is never possible for it to anticipate the outcomes of what it does, even if it believes that it can. This is because the outcomes of action are always mediated by the reactions of others to it. What an actor can do or accomplish becomes the outcome of the interaction, action and reaction, move and countermove.

The way that actors become related to each other is partly an effect of their resources and activities and partly dependent on how they see each other, on their reciprocal perceptions and interpretations. The bonds between actors reflect their perceptions and expectations of the use that can be made of resources, activities and the counterpart actors. The counterparts with which actors interact determine what they know, how they see others, and how they act and react. Actors become experts on their own small worlds.

The existence of these small worlds, each with their resident 'experts' stems from the complexities of perceptions, learning and making sense of others and their behaviour. This raises the question of the role of cognitive factors. Because the world is constructed by the 'experts', there is an interesting blending of learning and teaching that occurs. This blending involves mixing different motives and interpretations with the action of actors and the ways that their behaviours match or interfere. The bonds that develop between actors have a key role in this process because they organize the web of existing relationships, selectively connecting the actors and facilitating their development and the ways that they combine resources and design activities. By this means, actors confer on the network structure of the business landscape.

There is no well-developed framework for analysing actors and acting from the interaction perspective. One possible starting point is to use a classical model of action (see Figure 7.3) that identifies three broad variables involved in acting: the cognitive representation of the context (perceptions), the actual acts (behaviours) and the intended and expected results. These variables have been used to analyse the acting of actors in most of the social sciences. From the interaction perspective, the variables and how they appear to relate to each other is of interest.

Perceptions

Perception and interpretation of the context is usually seen as the basis from which actors act and are therefore often used as the starting point for analysis. These variables are assumed to underlie intended outcomes and to translate into particular behaviours to achieve these outcomes. In the interacted environment, perceptions have two very different aspects: First, the actor in its 'small

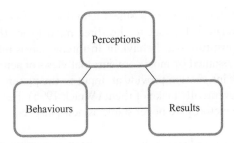

Figure 7.3 A model of action.

world' is strongly influenced by its normative perceptions or network pictures of how the small world should be, based on the way that the actor has to operate in order to survive. Thus, each actor acts and perceives the context from this point of view. Secondly, the actor's perception of how its particular small world is connected to all the other small worlds is much more diffuse and full of ambiguity. The actor has a less than complete picture, often consisting only of fragments, outlines, uncertainties or prejudices. These provide no real guidance, but often form the basis for extrapolations, hopes, dreams or wishes.

Both perceptions and interpretations are derived from past experience. The actors in each small world often share experience but this is not at all the case outside this world. Even within a small world and even after interaction over time, there will be tensions generated by diversity in the perceptions of different individual and organizational actors. But diversity in the pictures held by actors can also be productive as it keeps open paths of possible future development. In contrast, although homogeneity in views of the world is often strived for, it can be counterproductive as it may lead to a one-dimensional or static view of the world.

Behaviours

It is difficult in an interacted environment to differentiate between an actor and what it does. It is an actor's actual behaviour in interaction that is interpreted by the counterpart. Hence that behaviour forms part of the chain of interaction between any two counterparts. The actual behaviours are not necessarily triggered by clear intent or purpose. There are two possible reasons for this: First, an actor's behaviour in relation to others is often routinized, subject to norms of behaviour or simply a knee-jerk reaction to previous interaction. Routines are cost efficient and provide a solution to the problem of capacity for actors engaged in multiple interactions. Secondly, behaviour in business interaction is complex and multidimensional. It includes numerous actions concerning the flow of products or services, information and finance between the actors. It may involve technical changes, proposals, price changes, deliveries and changes in delivery systems. It is often impossible to overview this complexity and a corporate actor may act *inconsistently* based on the logic of different individuals or over time (Ford *et al.* 1986). For example, we have researched a situation where more than 200 people from one company interacted with those in another or where there no coordination is possible between different meetings taking place on the same day between different individuals concerning the same matters.

Therefore much of the behaviour of the business actor does not follow a finely detailed picture and it is often easier to relate behaviour to the three main logics that we identified earlier: technical, economic and institutional. Behaviour in interaction is related much more loosely to interpretations than is assumed by most conventional views of actors. Also, the actions and reactions that form part of interaction provide an input to the pictures of the actors and to the interpretations that they eventually make of them (Weick 1995). Because behaviours generate changes in pictures, those pictures are never stable as new perspectives are constantly acquired through interaction.

The intelligibility of an actor's behaviour to a counterpart is important. It plays an important role in the pictures and interpretations of those counterparts and influences their behaviour over time. This doesn't mean that it is never worthwhile for an actor to confuse a counterpart. For example, it may choose to behave inconsistently so that a counterpart cannot take it for granted (Ford *et al.* 1986).

Results

Given the problems with analysing behaviour in an interacted environment, it is obvious that there will be problems in correlating particular acts and results. But interaction is a problem-solving process and results or outcomes are central to it. The importance of results forces actors to constantly reassess their perceptions of counterparts and to try to find new and better combinations of activities, resources and counterparts.

There are important time and space dimensions to the outcomes of interaction: Any result is always specific to a particular position in network space and time. But there can be no complete consensus between the involved actors about what time or what space is taken for the purposes of assessing outcomes. Here again we come up against the existence of small worlds. In each small world, the 'experts' have very clear and specified results on which they are focussed. Each of them has its own preferences that only partly overlap. This is why there are always several different and often contrasting perceptions of consequences for different counterparts. Also, the results of interaction vary over time in the sense that they change or are seen to be different depending on the time horizons or evaluations of the actors. Thus business interaction often requires either or both counterparts to incur short-term costs for long-term benefits.

There is also variety in the effects of interaction. It has consequences not only in 'hard' dimensions, such as revenues, costs and profits, but also in 'soft' dimensions, such as the feelings of an actor about a relationship and the counterpart. The complexity of results in space and time means that actors have to focus on just some of the possible consequences. The choice of focus is partly due to the situation but may also depend on what is identified within the interaction. Interaction can be a creator of its own joint narrative that is constructed and connects clues and observed and experienced facts and relates these to outcomes. Consistency in focus on particular results among the interacting parties has an important short-term effect on the pattern of interaction, as in the Ducati case study. But it is also inevitable that there will simultaneously be some divergent focuses that arise in the interaction between two or more actors.

Looking at how actors act in interaction, there is an interesting interplay between the three variables: perceptions, behaviour and results. The three variables can work in a hierarchical way, from perceptions to behaviour to results, in the small world of each actor. Each actor has to believe that they are producing something valuable in that small world. They also have a picture that describes how that world works, at least as far as they are concerned, involving how perceived changes lead to behaviour that affects results. However, as soon as we move issues regarding this small world to other small worlds, then this order is completely broken up. All types of connection between the three are now possible in any order. All are important and they all illustrate important facets of the actor. It also becomes apparent that there are different actors in this wider world that have different styles of action that are based on different beliefs about how the three variables interact.

Challenges in Conceptualizing Actors

The emerging picture of the interacted actor leads to an interesting duality. It seems to be necessary to differentiate between the actor within the small world and the one within the larger interacted environment. The actor is perhaps a Dr Jekyll and Mr Hyde, but with an interesting difference. Rather than having just one of these identities at a particular time, the business actor has different 'personalities' at the same time. The actor will be acting in its small world at the same time that it is on the periphery of a number of the small worlds of many others.

The actor in its small world is knowledgeable and competent or at least some of the others around it will see it that way and listen to what it suggests. This position is effectively a requirement for an actor in order to be considered relevant by others, that is, as someone with which it is worth having a relationship. However, when this small world is extended elsewhere in the network, it encounters the small worlds of connected actors. Then the business actor is much more uncertain, ambiguous and marginalized. The actor knows few others in this world and there is likely to be constant discussion and conflict about how these small worlds can relate to each other. The actor is just one voice among many. Others may listen to the actor but they can also turn elsewhere. One issue constantly discussed in the interactions between the actor and its counterparts is likely to be where the boundary between the small world and the larger one should be drawn. The reason for this discussion is that activities and resources can be combined in different ways but there is always likely to be significant friction in these changes. The actor has no possibility of including all these in its business model. The actor can only hope that others will include its business model in their way of constructing their business models.

We started this chapter by questioning some common views in management literature because our various empirical studies highlighted features of the business actor and acting that did not fit with these. The Jekyll-and-Hyde view of business acting emerged in our empirical studies in which actors did not appear to be autonomous and that their acting was not one-sided, rational and purposeful. But at the same time, we also found in those empirical studies that companies did seek to behave purposefully. On the one hand, no actor is self-sufficient; every actor, individual or company, relies on others to such an extent that these others become part of the actor. But on the other hand, we could see companies act in a very self-conscious way, more or less forcing others to adapt to their will. We also saw many examples in which cognitive elaboration by actors of their context followed from action. We have also observed that the outcomes of interaction stem from interlocking behaviours and are very often different from the expectations of either of the actors involved. In other words, we could see self-conscious actors changed by the reactions of others.

A systematic conceptual framework of the interacted business actor is yet to be developed. Our attempt here is to understand some of the duality between the self-centred actor in a world of individually important others and the marginalized actor in the outside-looking-in perspective of the wider world. We do this by reviewing some propositions that seem to us to capture the essence of common approaches to the study of business and management in order to make clearer the ways in which they have to be questioned and the situations in which they are still useful.

Hopefully the propositions that we suggest are more than 'straw men'. They are certainly not representative of all streams of research. There are other researchers that lament the shortcomings of the mainstream framework for explaining business phenomena and share our views to some extent. However, these propositions appear to us to represent important dimensions of the business actor that become evident when analysed from the interaction perspective. We see them as useful points for discussion that could be included in the alternative but complementary conceptualization of actors that we feel is needed. We have formulated these propositions with reference to companies but they apply also to other forms of collective actors.

Important Features of an Actor

Initial Proposition 1

The attributes and features of a company that can be objectively established, such as its resource base and skills, explain what a company can and cannot achieve, its role and its economic value.

This proposition captures the way that an actor acts and is seen by its counterparts within its small world. The way that a company tries to link activities and tie resources determines its economic value for important counterparts. However, there are two important caveats that need to be raised to this proposition.

First, 'important others' are missing from this proposition. No business actor is equally valuable to all others and it is by identifying important others that the actor may define relevant activities and resources and can become an 'expert'. An actor's ability to focus on a limited number of counterpart problems and potential solutions can produce something that is valuable for those counterparts.

Secondly, the business actor diverges from this proposition when we consider the actor and the wider world. The actor's small world of significant relationships has a particular order and logic. But away from that world, the network is made up of numerous interconnected but distant relationships. These connected relationships or small worlds are partly, but never completely, adapted to particular others. There is always uncertainty in how they combine and relate to each other. In this wider world, the actor is far from having a fixed, clear and distinctive identity. It is but one among many other actors and subject to the possibility of large and dramatic change from elsewhere in the network.

These caveats lead to the revised proposition.

Revised Proposition 1

The role of a company, what it can achieve and, thus, its economic value is determined by how it relates to specific other companies, both directly in its immediate context and indirectly with those that are more distant and also by how it is seen by these others to match their operations, ambitions, beliefs, behaviours and problems.

Identity of an Actor

Initial Proposition 2

The identity of a company is comprised of the central, enduring and distinctive features that characterize its organization. Consistency in its projected identity is of value to other companies. Developing clarity in its mission and vision helps a company to focus internally on a desired direction and to communicate what it stands for to others.

This proposition, common in management studies, is similar to the previous one: Both refer to absolute and unvarying characteristics, but this one is more concerned with the self-perceptions of the company's members. This proposition is less concerned with the 'projected identity' or image that others have of a company and more with how that projected image should be managed. A clear sense of mission and vision is said to lead to distinctiveness for the company and to build the idea of trustworthiness and reliability in its focus. This proposition is also based on the idea that the identity of a company can be changed from within the organization, more or less at will. Again, this proposition relates somewhat to the situation of an actor in relation to its small world. It is an important node for a few important others and this means that it can have a relatively consistent identity, be self-aware and even manage its identity.

However, there are again some important caveats that need to be raised. First, rather than a single, self-determined identity, an actor in an interacted environment will be seen differently by different business counterparts even in its small world. For example, a single supplier is likely to be seen quite differently by different potential customers.

Secondly, the proposition does not address how the identity of a company changes and evolves despite the efforts of that company to keep it constant. However, the evolution of company identity in the 'eye of the beholder' is documented in numerous company case studies. This leads to the paradox that the features and attributes of the others that interact with a company are an important factor in the identity of that company.

Rather than corporate identity being the outcome of the company's own strategy, the identities of counterparts within the small world are attributed and constructed jointly in interaction. This process of attributing identity becomes much less controllable and much more accidental as the distance between counterparts increases. This process reflects not only the perceptual mechanisms of the actors but also the matching of their attributes and expectations. Identity, in the eyes of others, is based on a selection of clues about resources, activities, skills and expected attitudes and behaviours. There are no universal dimensions along which to characterize what an actor represents to other actors. Rarely if ever, can the identity of a company be expressed solely in terms of the features of a formal legal entity with its associated clear boundaries. Attributions may be based on the other actors with which the actor is associated, the resources that it can mobilize and the activities it can execute.

These caveats lead to the revised proposition.

Revised Proposition 2

The identity and attributes of an actor are the outcome of the way that it is viewed by each of its counterparts. An actor's identity is always multifaceted because any actor is involved in multiple interactions. The identity attributed to it in each interaction is but one facet of what an actor represents in the web of actors to which it is connected. The varying perceived identities of an actor explain the behaviours of different companies towards it and are factors in its evolution.

Success of an Actor

Initial Proposition 3

The success of the company depends on the economic efficiency of its 'business model' which is and should be the result of intentional and conscious design.

This proposition represents a rather static view of a company and of the context in which it acts. It seems to suggest that elaborating an effective business model is, to a large extent, an analytical and intellectual exercise that can be accomplished and kept for some time. Such a view has some purpose and validity in the small world of the interactive actor. Within the limits of a specified set of activities, resources and actors it is possible to carry out analysis and manage strategy in a conscious and deliberate way. It is possible for the actor, in interaction with a few others, to develop an efficient solution given that everything else is not incorporated.

However, these limits on scope are ultimately unrealistic. In practice, the strategic analysis would have to be repeated again and again with different resource, activity and counterpart parameters. These variations can often be handled by minor adaptations but in some situations the changes are so large that the small world and the company's way of living within it break apart and the actor suddenly meets a totally different world! Minor changes can often be referred to simply as a response to 'change in the environment'. But this tends to neglect the role of specific others.

Business actors are not born fully formed, nor do they develop in a linear way. They are born into an already existing web of actors and draw on resources and activities from those that exist at that time. But in order to acquire an identity, their presence and existence needs to be acknowledged by other actors in their close neighbourhood, their small world. Any actor draws on the behaviours of other actors that collectively provide the organization of the actor web and impact on the resource constellation and activity patterns in which the firm has to enact a position. The actor acquires attributes and identity depending on the actors with which it interacts. In a broad sense, the actor incorporates some of these others' attributes. Actors teach and learn with others and develop their respective capabilities.

This discussion leads to the revised proposition.

Revised Proposition 3

An actor's attributes and identity in each of its business relationships is continuously changing. Actors do not evolve autonomously; they co-evolve with specific others. Each actor is unique and each has unique requirements for success. Success for a business actor is time dependent, relationship specific and determined by the way that the actor co-evolves with others.

The Actor and Business Relationships

Initial Proposition 4

The relationships that a company develops with others are assets. Building and strengthening these relationship assets permits the company to increase its control over its context.

This proposition acknowledges the value of relationships with others. This acknowledgement has become common in management thinking within the ideas of 'relationship marketing' and 'supplier management'. The proposition holds at least partially in the small world of the interacting company in which the company is more or less defined by its small set of important business relationships.

However, the proposition assumes that a relationship can be controlled unilaterally. Studies of asymmetrical relationships have demonstrated that apparently weak counterparts can have a major influence over larger companies in specific areas such as technological or logistical policy and cannot be unilaterally controlled. There are also studies that show that companies are often able to do business and work together while having different views and even disliking each other. Business relationships are not based on liking each other, but are more about mutual usefulness. The bonds that develop between actors are based on this mutual usefulness, reliability and trust. But bonds are not necessarily productive and can lead to failure in particular interaction episodes and in the companies as a whole. Bonds, mutual orientation, commitment and preference can be a liability and burden. They are often demanding, costly and uncontrollable. If they are unbalanced, then bonds lose much of their effective value for the parties. Strong bonds entail intense interaction and bonds with some counterparts may preclude the development of productive bonds with others. Similarly, compliant counterparts are an asset but so are those that are difficult and confrontational. Confrontational counterparts may be important in productively shaping the features and the identity of an actor.

This discussion leads to a revised proposition.

Revised Proposition 4

Every actor is uniquely associated and forms bonds with a limited number of others. These bonds enable an actor but, at the same time, limit what the actor can achieve.

Actions and the Actor's Knowledge

Initial Proposition 5

Purposeful business action requires extensive knowledge and information about the business situation. Action in business depends on careful analysis and successful businesses demonstrate sound analysis.

This conviction is common in business and is also rooted in the idea of the independence of the individual company. The proposition relates quite well to the situation of the actor in the small world in which it has an extensive knowledge of its surroundings. The actor behaves and develops in its relationships in the small world on the basis of this knowledge. However, even in this narrow context, the actor's development is also dependent on the knowledge and experience of its relationship counterparts.

When we think of relating this small world to others, then it is apparent that the proposition overlooks that much of the action in business consists of reacting to demands from others. As we have noted, acting in these combined worlds is much more based on loose assumptions and hope. In order to have a view of all these combinations, the actor usually simplifies and relies on the explanations and knowledge of others. Classical examples of this reliance occur in the case of distributors and lead suppliers, both of which trade on their knowledge of other small worlds. Companies in this broader situation can rarely behave with any reasonable certainty of outcome. This is even the case in purely technical matters and much more so for involvement with other actors and their activities. The behaviour of any actor in this broad context involves a complex set of resource interfaces and activity interdependencies beyond the horizon of the actor. It also depends on interactions between actors that are far from the actor. This uncertainty is reinforced because of the constant motion of the interacted environment.

This leads us to a revision of Proposition 5.

Revised Proposition 5

The actions and reactions of business actors in interaction are based on partial knowledge and on interpretations of the counterpart actors on which actors construct their expectations.

Role of Outcomes

Initial Proposition 6

The anticipation of outcomes of interest guides an effective actor in business.

This common and seemingly obvious assumption has some validity in an actor's small world. Here an actor has some ability to anticipate how changes will affect the outcomes for different actors and also how the actors will react to the changes. But as soon as other worlds are affected by or involved in these changes then the outcomes of any activity are more or less impossible to predict. Most actors are likely to be aware of this and so their behaviour must be based on something else.

In this situation, norm-based behaviour may be a rational and effective behavioural strategy in pursuit of the actor's desired outcomes.[5] Behaviour that follows routines, rules and norms produces tangible outcomes both for the actor itself and for others. Norm-based or routinized, consistent behaviour is likely to develop bonds between actors and reinforce stability and hence accounts for many interaction outcomes. The outcomes for business actors do not necessarily depend on behaviour that is guided by anticipation of the outcome of an action. In other words, tangible outcomes do not strictly require instrumental motives and intent on the part of the single actor.

This leads us to the revised proposition.

Revised Proposition 6

The ways that actors interact and become mutually and selectively associated with each other has substantial consequences for those actors, for the actor web and also for the relevant resource constellations and activity patterns.

Conclusion

The importance of others makes each business actor relative, varied and unique. These characteristics affect the ways that an actor acts. In its own small world, the actor is a central node and important. In this small world, the actor can base its operations on its knowledge and capabilities. It can approach rational or deliberate action and can try to develop in a planned way. It is likely to know the main problems of its counterparts as well as their abilities and therefore can

---

[5]This apparent paradox of routine-based behaviour being rational has been raised as an issue in other contexts. In marketing, it was first raised by Katona (1953) in studies of consumer behaviour, claiming the rationality of routine-based choice behaviour. It has been raised and discussed in organization theory by March (1988) and it has also been a recurrent theme in Austrian economics (e.g. Hayek 1967).

anticipate their reactions. Through limiting its 'task environment' to specific activities, resources and counterparts, it can handle its interactions. However, as soon as the actor has to connect this small world to the other small worlds that exist around it, then the situation becomes quite different. Now the actor is not at all the dominant player, nor the only one with particularly interesting capabilities or knowledge. Instead it is on the periphery, one among several others, and it is only through relating to some of these others that the actor can influence developments.

From a research point of view, it seems clear that it is difficult to construct one model of the business actor that applies at the same time in these two situations. Instead we have suggested that it is useful to distinguish between the actor in relation to its 'small world' and the actor in relation to the broader network. In the small world, the actor and its counterparts often have a joint picture of important problems and opportunities. Interaction in these situations becomes very much dominated by continuous rationalization in the way that activities are handled and resources are combined. In this situation, the actor is likely to be seen by important counterparts as competent.

But uncertainty and ambiguity increase substantially for the actor as soon as we get out of this small world. The role and position of the actor changes and the task facing it becomes formidable. If it were to act rationally, it would have to be able to combine resources and adjust resource interfaces in relation to a large number of activities and resources controlled by a large number of other actors and relate to all of the continuing changes in existing and potential business relationships. Somewhat paradoxically, companies may aim to achieve this control, but these attempts hold the seeds of their own destruction (Ford *et al.* 2007). It is impossible to handle all of these problems and control the network.

Instead, the actor has to operate quite differently in this wider world. It has to realize that it has a marginal role and that its only chance is to relate to others. It has to work with and rely on these others on the basis of how they interpret what is going on and how they react and change. This reality is also the reason why each actor has to construct its own small and more understandable world: to make some very clear limitations in space for itself to enable it to take advantage of changes over time (co-evolution). Each actor in relation to the larger network world takes only a limited part and acts through others. It is likely to limit its interest to those dimensions that are crucial for its small world and for those important counterparts that it works with. An actor's interactions with its important counterparts enable it to learn how those counterparts view and handle changes that emanate from the wider network so that it may be able to adapt to those changes. These counterparts may misinterpret the changes and using counterparts as filters is not without its problems but there is no alternative: The larger world is just too complex and too varied to ever understand. Every actor draws on the wider world through those it interacts with in its small world.

Looked at from the interaction perspective, the role of actors is special. Interacting with others multiplies the actor's capacity to act but also imposes limits on what it can do. Interaction means that the actor is always exposed to contrasting demands for change and to resist change. Actors generate change but cannot control it. They are the force that generates the organizing of economic activity but, taken singularly, no actor is the dominant organizer. By mediating different demands in interaction, actors become a viable and variable entity.

The concept of the business actor and its role has consequences for how much we can explain of how the business landscape develops, and how businesses and interaction in business relationships can be managed.

Business Networks as an Analytical Tool

We have now described and analysed some of the empirical background to our ideas on business networks and have also discussed the effects of an interactive environment on three basic elements of business: resources, activities and actors.

In this third part of the book, we want to see what an interactive environment means for some of the areas where economic models have been used. The first of these areas is management and we devote two chapters to the managerial consequences of business relationships and networks. In Chapter 8, we describe how the existence of business relationships has been integrated into economic models that build on the market model. The current starting point in these models is that business relationships are seen as a kind of market failure or as a special case that only appears in certain specific situations. In Chapter 9, we try to take the opposite starting point: We start out from the assumption that business relationships are the norm and try to see the consequences of this assumption for the way that managerial problems are formulated and for the kind of solutions that are possible.

In Chapter 10 we examine the use of the network model for explaining the evolution of business. In Chapter 11, we explore the use of the network model in analysing industrial policy.

Finally, in Chapter 12, we consider what it means to live in the rainforest in terms of an interactive business landscape.

MANAGEMENT AND BUSINESS RELATIONSHIPS

8

The existence and importance of business relationships have been generally accepted by the business research community. The question then becomes how the idea of a network of relationships can be included in a general theory of business. There are two alternative approaches to this: One is to try to integrate the idea of relationships into the existing theory and the other is to take relationships as a starting point for a new theory. In this chapter, we describe the efforts that have been undertaken in the first of these approaches.

The basic starting point for most management thinking is the idea of the market. But in principle, the idea of the market excludes business relationships, so this starting point forces researchers to treat business relationships as a special case within an environment characterized by market-like features. In this chapter, we describe how this approach has been followed in four fields of study: strategy, marketing, purchasing and accounting. Following from this analysis, the chapter concludes with an assessment of how realistic and fruitful this approach has been.

Introduction

Relationships among companies play an important role in business. This empirical observation is not unique to IMP research but has also been made by scholars building on quite different assumptions (for example, Jarillo 1988; Porter 1990; Achrol and Kotler 1999; Krugman 1991; Castells 1996; Nohria and Eccles 1991; Gulati *et al.* 2000). The common message from these findings is that relationships between firms are a phenomenon of increasing significance and that the accompanying network-like features of the business landscape have considerable consequences for business.

However, these researchers build on frameworks where interaction is assumed to have a very specific role. In most cases, they are based on assumptions close to the mainstream view of the market. These characteristics in turn impact on views of the practice of management within and between firms. The implications for management of this approach are quite different from those that follow from a framework explicitly developed to deal with business interaction.

The aim of this chapter is to examine the nature of management practice as it appears in the predominant management literature. Because management is a broad field, it has attracted the interest of scholars from many research areas. Management has been examined from many different angles and it is obviously impossible to do justice to all these different accounts in one chapter. Therefore, our ambition is not to make a complete review of the rich bulk of management studies. Instead, our objective is to explore some of the underlying assumptions in the mainstream management literature with a particular emphasis on how interaction and the relatedness of companies are dealt with.

Inevitably, we stereotype some ideas of management when we label them as 'mainstream'. Stereotyping a rich and varied field of study such as management is unfair, especially to those who consider themselves to be renewing it. But, as claimed by Marglin (2008:5) 'the mainstream, in my view, is so dominant that the other streams have become mere trickles.' This dominance is apparent whether 'we focus on what is taught in the typical principles course, or in the entire undergraduate curriculum, or even in the content of graduate theory courses, I think there is a consensus . . .' (Marglin 2008:6). This consensus is the heritage from neo-classical economics: The idea of the market which is basically atomistic and, therefore, 'unstrained by past relationships' (Gudeman 2001:94).

When Management Theory is Coloured by the Idea of a Market

Management literature has a wide spread: It stretches all the way from theoretical models and concepts to anecdotes and 'war stories'. The practice of management involves issues that range from how to handle a company's everyday life to how to address long-term strategic issues and from what can be planned to how to cope with the exceptional. The sources that have inspired management literature are also widespread, including politics, economics, sociology, anthropology, administrative sciences and psychology. Most of these sources have contributed with insights on how to handle the internal problems and opportunities of companies and organizations, but increasingly management studies have come to focus on how to manage companies' external relations. In this respect, the management literature encompasses scholars relying on the rational views expressed by, for example Ansoff (1965), Hamel and Pralahad (1985), Porter (1990), Grant (1998) and Barney (2002) and scholars inspired by the assumption of bounded rationality articulated by authors such as Mintzberg (1987, 1993) Lindblom (1959), Carlson (1975), March (1988) and Weick (1979).

However, under this rich diversity of management ideas there is a common denominator, regardless of whether they rest on the perspective of a rational or boundedly rational actor: When it comes to examining how companies relate to each other, mainstream management studies have embedded the neo-classical model of how a market is constituted: A system in which the autonomy of firms represents normality and interconnections between firms are the exception (Pelikan 1988).

There is a very robust explanation of why the neo-classical assumption about a market populated by independent companies constitutes normality: From the starting point that single units of business (firms) are clearly delimited from each other and capable of independent choice and action, it is fairly easy to make an aggregation of what is happening from a 'micro-level' to a 'macro-level'. This assumption suits the work of mainstream management scholars: By holding on to the idea of company independency, the practice of management can easily be boiled down to a set of issues for the individual company.

The idea that a market populated by independent actors constitutes normality also has some severe consequences. But these consequences are not readily apparent because the idea of the constitution and functioning of a market is so strongly embedded in western thinking. Both society in general and the research community in particular often fail to register that words such as 'demand', 'market' and 'competition' denote theoretical constructs rather than empirical findings (Gudeman 2001; Marglin 2008). Therefore, a relevant question in relation to studies of markets and market features is whether 'one describe[s] what markets are really like or a present model of them?' (Gudeman 2001:94).

In the next section, we discuss some aspects of the nature and task of managing. We continue by pinpointing the basic assumptions behind mainstream management literature and then explore what consequences these may have for the way that interconnections are dealt with.

The Nature and Task of Managing in Markets

Broadly expressed, the task of management in business is to ensure the functioning and development of a business organization within a world of other businesses and other organizations. These tasks involve the control and coordination of activities and resources to ensure the continuous functioning of the company and the designing of resources in order to develop that business. The function of a business, consistent with the perspective of economics, is assumed to be the production and sale of goods or services. The essence of management, as presented in the literature on general management, is to make decisions about the functioning and development of the business. These decisions are about choices between existing alternatives to achieve some desired, a priori, internally formulated goals. For example, in relation to an end market, the main decisions of management are assumed to centre on the choices of customers to target, the features of what should be offered to them and how to make those offerings available (Kotler 1967).

The very notion of management hinges on the ability to distinguish between those factors and settings that can be influenced or controlled by a particular actor and those that are out of its control. One of the common assumptions is that the factors that can be controlled are those that are *inside* the company while the uncontrollable factors reside *outside* the ownership border of the firm. This view assumes a clear boundary between the company and its environment: Whatever is outside the ownership and contractual control of the firm is, by definition, in the uncontrollable market. Firms are composed of resources that are owned or contractually controlled. The boundaries of the company are clear and distinct within this perspective and they provide the basis for how the company should relate to others.

The view of the market in mainstream management literature is fairly close to the way it is sketched in the neo-classic economic model of the world. The market is seen as an impersonal entity: 'Market designates anonymous, short-term exchanges' (Gudeman 2001:1). The market demand for a product is the aggregate of what individual actors demand (Polyani 1944). Thus, it is not the demand of the individual customer that orientates the company's decisions on the selling side, but the aggregate demand of a collective of potential customers. In the same way, the supply side of a company is represented by input markets in terms of sets of similar and therefore comparable products and services made available by different vendors. The company can select the most appropriate offerings for purchase from these supply markets (van Weele 2002; Wilk 1996). The assessment of the condition of the firm and the generalized market environments are assumed to be critical for efficient and effective decisions on the two sides of the company. Whether the outcome of these decisions is in line with expectations or not is assumed to depend on how effectively current conditions have been assessed and future states foreseen. The general notion is that the more realistic and systematic the assessment of the present situation and the more reliable the projections made by managers, the more effective are the outcomes for the business.

We claimed at the beginning of this chapter that the importance of business relationships is recognized in the management literature. But as we have shown above, mainstream management tends to consider business relationships from the perspective of the market. Therefore interaction is a phenomenon that is more or less overlooked in the management literature. The general view is that business takes place in a market characterized by 'far-distant' exchange (Gudeman 2001:1). However, as the same author proclaims, business is not only about this type of transaction: It also involves 'up-close' interaction. It is this 'up-close' interaction that leads to long-term business relationships. Because the market and its 'far-distant' exchange dominates the management literature, 'up-close' interaction and long-term business relationships are seen as an exception.

Relationships Observed from a Market-Based Management Perspective

The assumption in the mainstream management literature that markets characterized by independence represent normality and that business relationships are the exception determines what management issues are important. In this section, we consider issues that are identified in the mainstream management literature as critical for the operation and development of a company, based on these assumptions.

The most fundamental issue that management literature brings to the fore is how the company should relate in a general sense to the environment in which it operates. In other words, what its 'strategy' should be. This task concerns how to develop and sustain an effective match between the company and the market environment and respond to changes in that environment. Two specific issues are part of this broad strategic problem but are so important that they have received particular attention: how a company should relate to the customer in terms of marketing and sales management; how to buy from the market in terms of purchasing management. A further crucial issue for management involves the question of how the company should organize its activities and resources in relation to its purchasing and marketing tasks and within the context of its overall strategy. The significance of these issues is reflected in the preoccupations of practising managers, in the ways in which business schools structure the areas of their staff and in how management periodicals normally specialize in one of these areas.

We now address business strategy, marketing management and purchasing management in a general way. When it comes to the organizational issues, we focus on a specific aspect: the economic accounting system. In all four areas, the roles of interaction and relationships have increasingly been acknowledged within the predominant management paradigm.

Business Strategy and Business Relationships

The importance of overall business strategy for the performance of companies has become widely emphasized in the management literature in recent decades. Business strategy is now a distinct area of management practice and a major discipline in the study of management. The concept of 'strategy' can be traced back to ancient Greece where it was used as a term in military command. When strategy was applied to business management it was considered mainly as 'a way to control market forces' (Ghemawat 2002:37). Formal strategic thinking was recommended after World War II as a means of active management because 'management is not just passive adaptive behaviour; it means taking action to make the desired results come to pass' (Drucker 1954:11). Drucker's claim was that economic theory treats markets as impersonal forces beyond the control of individual entrepreneurs and organizations. In reality, however, management has a responsibility for 'attempting to shape the economic environment, for planning, initiating, and carrying through changes in that economic environment, for constantly pushing back the limitations of economic circumstances on the enterprise's freedom of action'. It was this insight that became the rationale for business strategy, so that, 'by consciously using formal planning, a company could exert some positive control over market forces' (Ghemawat 2002:39).

Strategy has kept much of its military flavour when applied to business management. The relationship between a company and others has mostly been seen and described as a battle in which the aim is to conquer, defeat and destroy. This perspective on strategy goes hand-in-hand with the jungle metaphor that we discussed in Chapter 1.

Even when the military connotations of strategy are toned down, the issue of strategy development is primarily based on the idea of competition (Porter 1980). This perspective on strategy still dominates mainstream literature: For example, Barney (2002) claims that strategy is 'a firm's theory about how to compete successfully'. This means that business and corporate strategy is today almost synonymous with competitive strategy. This is illustrated by the following quote answering the question 'what is corporate strategy?'

> The most widespread view is that improving the competitive strategies of the operating units is the essence of corporate strategy.
>
> *Raynor 2007:1*

Generally, therefore, the centre of attention in the strategy literature appears to be the interplay between a single company and its competitors. This orientation may be explained in terms of the central assumption in neo-classical economics that resources are fixed and scarce (Wilk 1996). Hence, almost all strategy frameworks compare a company with its competitors in terms of its costs or the resources that it controls. The key concept in strategic thinking is 'competitive advantage'; that is, how to perform better than competitors. A company can gain competitive advantage either by controlling more adequate resources or by using its resources more effectively than its competitors.

Following this view, the conclusion is that 'strategy is about winning' (Grant 1998:3). To become a winner, however it is not enough to defeat competitors. If competition is paramount then a rather clear boundary between the company and others is inferred and this external market environment is seen as mostly hostile and threatening. Therefore, in the efforts of companies to 'tame market forces', suppliers and customers also become targets. For example, in the well-known Five Forces model (Porter 1980), both customers and suppliers are perceived to represent potential threats to the success of a firm. Therefore, it is considered important to gain power in relation to customers and vendors by making these firms dependent and at the same time staying independent from them. This view provides a particular perspective on the relationship between 'winning' and strategy. According to mainstream thinking, business is a zero-sum game implying that someone else has to lose and that rivalry is a significant ingredient in buyer–seller relationships.

Thus, even when it comes to relations with actual business partners, it is the separation of the company from the outside world that is emphasized. This focus on the demarcation line between the company and its environment implies that the company's *position* relative to others in the markets within which it competes is crucial to business strategy.

A firm's position consists of the products or services it provides, the market segments it sells to, and the degree to which it is isolated from direct competition. In general, the best positions involve supplying very uniquely valuable products to price insensitive suppliers, whereas poor positions involve being one of many firms supplying marginally valuable products to very well informed, price sensitive buyers.

> *Rumelt, R., 1988. The evaluation of business strategy. In J. Quinn, H. Mintzberg and R. James, eds. The Strategy Process. Englewood Cliffs (NJ): Prentice-Hall.*

When it comes to strategic manoeuvring and attempts to change this position, mainstream management takes the starting point that Drucker (1954) identified as the 'enterprise's freedom of action'. For example, Reve (1990) discusses the firm's position in terms of a 'nexus of internal and external contracts'. For its strategic action, the company relies on two frameworks: a theory of the firm and a theory of competitive positioning. This view focuses on the individual business actor. Its position is derived more in relation to its competitors than to those involved in business transactions. Positional changes are primarily attributed to the actions of the individual company.

A Business Strategy Perspective on Interaction

The observation of close interaction and relationships has not been interpreted by mainstream strategy as a general pattern of how companies relate to each other in the business landscape. In the words of Gudeman (2001), the 'far-distant' exchange dominates the literature more than 'up-close' interaction. The first conclusion from this is that long-term and close business relationships are most often portrayed as exceptions rather than normality.

A second conclusion is that the strategy literature recognizes business relationships as another type of resource that the company can use in its strategic game. Increasingly, the opportunity to mobilize others as 'partners' has become an emergent issue in the strategy literature. Strategic alliances and the emphasis on mergers and acquisitions are obvious reflections of this development. The impact of these examples of business relationships has been conceptualized by two game-theory strategists. Brandenburger and Nalebuff (1996) launched the idea of 'complementors' as crucial components in the process of value creation. These complementors represent other firms from which customers buy complementary products and services or to which suppliers sell complementary resources. The recognition of complementors acknowledges the inability of a single company to control all the resources that are significant for its operations. The crucial role of complementors is significant also in the evolving literature on value networks (e.g. Christensen 1997; Stabell and Fjeldstad 1998; Norman and Ramirez 1993; Allee 2003). Recognition of the role of business relationships also adds to the idea of strategy in another way, as it indicates that an important strategic issue for a company becomes the choice of counterparts, the operation of relationships and the differentiation between them.

Thirdly, a particular stream of research within the broad area of strategic management is directed towards what can be identified as 'relational strategy' where the importance of business relationships is emphasized. The idea that a firm's critical resources may span the boundaries of firms and be embedded in inter-firm resources and routines is advocated by, for example, Dyer and Singh (1998). Similarly, Sanchez and Heene (1997) argue that the resources that a firm uses reside both within the firm (firm-specific resources) and in other organizations (firm-addressable resources). Gulati (1998) and Gulati *et al.* (2000) claim that a firm's network of business partners should be considered as an inimitable resource itself and as a means by which to access others' inimitable resources.

Thus the relational view advocates the idea that a core aspect of strategy is the ability to build and maintain relationships with others. However, even when these conditions are at hand there are certain disparities in relation to the view articulated in this book. For example, Sanchez and Heene (1997:303) claim that the focus of strategic management should be on 'how firms may improve their performance in competitive interactions with other firms'. Inter-organizational researchers in general (e.g. Haugland and Reve 1994; Heide 1994; Powell 1990; Williamson 1991) increasingly suggest that business relationships should be seen as a governance mode complementary to markets and hierarchies. Within this acknowledgement, however, transaction-cost advocates tend to place more emphasis on potential problems with relationships than on the benefits that they may provide. Thus, transaction-cost analysis focuses on the risks of opportunistic behaviour and the subsequent need for safeguarding.

Marketing Management and Business Relationships

Marketing as a management issue is similar to business strategy in resting heavily on the neo-classical theory's understanding of the market. However, as shown by Gadde and Ford (2008) the early marketing and distribution literature was built on quite different assumptions and has in fact been an important source of inspiration for the industrial network approach.

The pioneers in marketing literature relied on a holistic view of business activity. For example, Sparling (1906) defined marketing as 'the commercial processes . . . concerned with the distribution of raw materials of production and finished output of the factory' (quoted in Gripsrud 2004:192). It is worth noting also that marketing in 1906 was deemed to cover the whole supply chain in today's terminology; it did not start at the point of a single manufacturer.

The activities of concern were identified as 'functions' of marketing and distribution. Clark (1923) systematized these functions into a coherent scheme and this framework has long dominated the view of distribution; it is considered the concept that contributed most to the development of marketing as a science (Hunt and Goolsby 1988).

The great representative of the functionalist view of marketing is Wroe Alderson, who continued the holistic line of thinking when arguing that the primary function of marketing and distribution is to connect the 'technology of production' with the 'technology of use', since what is transacted in the business landscape 'appears at very different settings at these two levels' (Alderson 1965:12). Alderson goes on to say that these connecting efforts are based on 'a system of action of which individual firms are elements' and the activities of one of these firms are 'supplementing the activities of other firms'. These conditions require coordinated action across the ownership borders of firms since the productivity of the operations rest in 'making the flow of goods semiautomatic even though the successive [business] units are autonomous'. Furthermore, he declares that there is a growing understanding that these 'coalitions' between firms represent essential cooperation for getting a job done and not necessarily monopolistic collusion that impose restrictions on the market. These coalitions tend to take different forms but have to be 'sufficiently integrated to permit the system to operate as a whole' and these conditions imply that firms must 'think of themselves as being highly interdependent' (Alderson 1957).

Alderson criticized mainstream economic theory in several respects. Firstly, he found it problematic that 'economic analysis of the factors in price equilibrium generally rests on the assumption that exchange transactions are free of cost (Alderson 1954:8). Secondly, when it comes to the view of resources, Alderson criticized traditional models of the market for ignoring one of the most crucial features of resources when claiming that 'real' markets are imperfect. Therefore in opposition to the economists' view of a homogeneous market, he presented a model of 'a perfectly heterogeneous market' because what is finally delivered to a customer is 'a relatively refined and specialized article shaped to a type of need fitted to the specific requirements of the individual customer who buys it' (Alderson 1965:29). Thirdly, he claimed that the cooperative aspects between companies had not been considered to the extent they deserved, despite the fact that 'cooperation is as prevalent in economic activity as competition' (Alderson 1965:239). He continued:

> The cooperative aspect of economic behaviour has been relatively neglected. Economists speak of competitive theory, of pure and perfect competition. There is no corresponding development of cooperative theory, no concepts of pure and perfect cooperation.

Acknowledging the fact that there is a general recognition of the importance of team work and the value of coordinative action, Alderson concluded that 'marketing cries out for a theory of cooperation to match the theory of competition'.

Unfortunately the Aldersonian view of marketing has not achieved the impact it deserves. Inspiration from neo-classical economics shifted attention away from the previous building blocks derived from institutional economics. Evolving frames of reference slowly moved distribution research 'from a system-wide perspective to a focus on how the channel captain should behave to secure an efficient distribution of his products' (Gripsrud 2004:195). Increasingly the view adopted had a strong manufacturer orientation since marketing channels were seen 'through the eyes of marketing management in production firms' and dealt with 'the route taken by a product as it moves from the producer to the user' (Rosenbloom 1995).

The basic conceptualizations of today's marketing management perspective were developed about 50 years ago. The view of marketing as a mixture of activities was first coined by Neil Borden in the early 1950s. He characterized a marketing manager as 'a mixer of ingredients, one who is constantly engaged in fashioning creatively a mix of marketing procedures and policies in his efforts to produce a profitable enterprise' (Borden 1964). Originally Borden's marketing mix was made up of 12 factors. Later on, however, McCarthy reduced the number of marketing activities to 'the four Ps' (McCarthy 1960).[1] The four Ps (product, price, promotion and place) provided a pedagogical instrument for teaching and education and were used for example in the first edition of the textbook by Philip Kotler (1967). Since that time, an overwhelming majority of the books in marketing management have been organized in accordance with the marketing mix and its ingredients. And so the 'four Ps of the marketing mix became an indisputable paradigm in marketing research, the validity of which was taken for granted' (Grönroos 1997:332). Another distinct feature of this literature is the strong reliance on strategic planning, typically illustrated by the working procedure: analysis, planning, implementation and control.

Mainstream marketing management thinking has clear connections to the concept of demand in the neo-classical economic model. A company is supposed to compete with others in relation to a more-or-less given overall demand. The marketing-mix problem is to design and combine the four major marketing instruments[2] and to allocate resources between them in the most adequate way. Theoretically, markets are treated as response curves related to the input of the four means. Further, it is assumed that specific sets of response curves can be identified through systematic market research. Hence, on this basis it should be possible to design the optimal marketing mix to be directed to various segments of the market. According to this view, the competitors of a company are defined in terms of the degree of similarity of the products they offer (for which there is a generic demand). Finally, it is implicit in the idea of a marketing mix that these competitors each manipulate a similar mix and the basis on which they compete is assumed to be similar. A clear example of this grouping of competitors can be found in the Five Forces model (Porter 1980).

When it comes to research, the transaction-cost approach is probably the most commonly adopted model in marketing studies today (Gripsrud 2004). According to this model, marketing is involved as one of the mechanisms for cost-efficient governance of transactions with customers. One of the assumptions of the theory is that the market will not function in an optimal way in all situations. When these conditions, identified as 'market failures', are at hand, other governance modes are required, such as the integration of transactions within the company (hierarchical governance) and the formation of business relationships (e.g. Rindfleisch and Heide 1997).

---

[1] Similar thoughts with a somewhat broader perspective on marketing were launched in Scandinavia (Rasmussen 1955; Mickwitz 1959).

[2] It is implicit in the marketing mix model that a producer is able to choose *its* distributors in accordance with *its* requirements and that goods pass unmodified to the market through *its* channel.

A Marketing Perspective on Interaction

Mainstream marketing developed from the holistic perspective applied in the early literature towards a narrower view focussing on the managerial issues of the supplier and the efficient handling of single transactions. Unfortunately, this change also implies that some highly relevant issues in today's marketing context have not received the attention that they deserve. One of these issues is the role of business relationships. Because these relationships do not conform to basic assumptions about markets and their functioning, business relationships have only become emphasized in recently evolving areas within the general marketing field. Examples include, among others, service marketing (e.g. Grönroos 1984; Gummesson 1979), business to business marketing (e.g. Hutt and Speh 2007; Fill and Fill 2005) and supply chain management (Christopher 2005).

However, mainstream marketing also acknowledges the increasing role of business relationships. For example, Fredrick Webster has claimed that there has been 'a shift from a transaction to a relationship focus . . . with an emphasis on long-term customer relationships' (Webster 1992:10). In a similar vein, Philip Kotler argues that 'marketing is poised for revolutionary changes in its organizational context as well as in its relationships with customers' (Achrol and Kotler 1999:146). The main ingredient in this revolution is supposed to be the 'networked organization' which is 'an interdependent coalition of task- or skill-specialized economic entities that operates without hierarchical control, but is embedded by dense lateral connections' (Achrol and Kotler 1999:148).

Despite these proclamations, interaction and business relationships still have a limited influence in mainstream marketing. Marketing management scholars have primarily handled business relationships in the same way as business strategists. An obvious reason for this is the strong adherence to the supplier-orientated, marketing-mix perspective. The four Ps of the marketing mix have been characterized as 'the holy quadruple . . . of the marketing faith . . . written in tablets of stone' (Kent 1986:146). The strength of this allegiance to a supplier focus has meant that relationships have been incorporated into marketing thinking as just another means to be used by a marketer at his discretion and as a complement to the traditional marketing means and within marketing's particular assumptions about business reality. For example, the networks discussed by Achrol and Kotler have other characteristics than those analysed in this book. The main feature of the significant changes observed by Achrol and Kotler is 'the emergence of large-scaled *managed* networks' (Achrol and Kotler 1999:147).

The significance of business relationships in marketing is emphasized in the rapidly evolving research field of 'relationship marketing' (for overviews see, for example, Sheth and Parvatiyar 1995; Möller and Halinen 2000). Here, business relationships are primarily considered as mechanisms through which influence can be exercised on customers. In this way relationships add to the instruments available on the marketing side and thus become another technique for marketers. Concepts and models developed within relationship marketing have been applied particularly to the marketing of services. This is because service elements such as installation, technical advice, logistics and information provision have become increasingly important dimensions of suppliers' offerings (Grönroos 1997). These conditions imply a move away from a transaction orientation towards greater attention to relationship building. This conclusion is clearly in line with the thinking presented in this book. More surprising, however, is that the implication for managing services still seems to be rooted in the features of competition. In this respect it is argued that 'relationship marketing demands a deeper understanding of how to manage service competition than what is required of firms pursuing a transaction-type strategy' (Grönroos 1997:322). The technique orientation of the relationship marketing approach is further accentuated by the huge amount of software that has been developed for customer relationship management (CRM); see, for example, Rigby et al. (2002) and Bligh et al. (2004).

Interaction is not a big issue in the relationship marketing literature. Grönroos coined the concept of 'the interactive marketing function' which has an obvious supplier flavour since it 'covers the marketing impact on the customer during the consumption and usage process' (Grönroos 1997:326). There is also an expanding stream of research in marketing labelled 'interactive marketing'. However, there is no similarity to the interactive view presented in this book. Instead, interactive marketing is viewed as a new tool for marketing that has been made available through developments of electronic information exchange, such as the internet and other web-based techniques. For example the *Journal of Interactive Marketing* (formerly the *Journal of Direct Marketing*) describes its aim to be 'a thought leader and catalyst for shaping ideas and issues associated with electronic, interactive, and direct marketing environments'.

Purchasing Management and Business Relationships

Purchasing and the supply side of companies is probably the management arena that has been most influenced by the notion of markets. Historically, the recommendations in the purchasing literature were centred on efforts to actively create market-like conditions. The main prescription was that customers should avoid becoming dependent on individual suppliers. By having a number of alternative vendors, the buying firm was said to be able to: Reduce uncertainty in single transactions; avoid becoming 'locked in' to the technical solution of a particular supplier; and encourage competition between different vendors, primarily in terms of price pressure. The main message was that suppliers should be 'played off' against one another in order to promote efficient procurement. Applying this strategy leads to what has been identified as 'arm's-length' relationships between business partners. These relationships are inexpensive to operate, because they require little investment. They impose limited dependence and make it possible for the buying company to switch supplier when better conditions are offered elsewhere.

According to this view, potential suppliers are considered as more or less efficient providers of identical input. Through this process of standardization, the benefits of the offerings from different suppliers are considered equal and consequently the lowest price determines vendor selection. The lowest price is supposed to be achieved through well-developed purchasing procedures involving systematic routines for making enquiries, handling tenders and principles for negotiation. Westing et al. (1969) is a representative example of mainstream purchasing management at a time when rational decision-making on the basis of competitive bidding was central to purchasing efficiency.

The rationality of these decision processes is concerned with single transactions. Several models of the buying behaviour of firms and what affected this behaviour were developed (e.g. Robinson et al. 1967; Webster and Wind 1972; Sheth 1973). In these models, the process of arriving at a decision concerning a particular acquisition is divided into a number of phases from 'recognition of need' to 'specification of item', 'location of potential suppliers', 'evaluation procedure' and 'vendor selection'. Some models of organizational buying behaviour seem to have been developed mainly as tools for the selling firm (e.g. Sheth 1973). These models reinforce the perception that the marketing function in one firm and the purchasing function in another are to be seen as antagonistic counterparts involved in a zero-sum contest.

The transaction-oriented perspective on purchasing peaked at a time when the supply side of companies was not considered strategic. The reason for this standpoint was that all important resources were supposed to be kept inside the company and thus within ownership control. Therefore purchasing was perceived as quite a passive function and characterized as reactive rather than proactive (Ammer 1969). For example, Ansoff (1965) described purchasing as an administrative and clerical function rather than a strategic one. Over time, these conditions changed considerably. Increasing reliance on outsourcing and suppliers' resources made the supply side strategic both in terms of the monetary value that it handles and the other resources that are made available through suppliers (see e.g. Farmer 1981; Spekman 1988; Mol 2003; Leenders *et al.* 2006). These changes influenced mainstream purchasing management and we can emphasize three aspects of this reorientation: a supplementary view of purchasing efficiency; a call for differentiation of purchasing procedures depending on what is purchased; and a modified view of the role of suppliers.

The 'classical' view of purchasing efficiency builds on the assumption that overall performance is maximized when each individual purchase transaction is conducted as efficiently as possible. In reality, however, very few transactions are isolated. A single transaction for a buying firm is actually part of a series of transaction over time, often with the same supplier. Also, at a specific point in time, each single transaction is related to other transactions that are undertaken simultaneously. This situation has meant that the focus on lowest price per purchase has been supplemented by an approach that brings in the indirect financial effects of variation in purchasing behaviour. In this respect, various interpretations of the 'total cost of ownership' have come to the forefront in the view of purchasing efficiency (Ellram 1995; Ferrin and Plank 2002). Applying this perspective also requires changes in the view of supplier relationships, to which we refer shortly.

The second aspect of the re-orientation of mainstream purchasing management has been a call for the differentiation of procurement behaviour depending on the supply context and the purchasing situation. The main contribution in this respect emanates from the transaction-cost model mentioned in previous sections and developed by Kraljic (1982). In the Kraljic matrix, the appropriate behaviour for various types of procurement situation is determined by the characteristics of the type of purchase. There are two dimensions in the Kraljic scheme, each of which may be characterized as high or low. One of the dimensions is the *importance of the purchase* for the customer, measured against criteria such as profit impact, costs of materials, total cost, volume purchased, etc. The other dimension is the *supply risk*, involving market criteria such as short-term and long-term availability, the number of potential suppliers and the structure of supply markets. In this way, four procurement situations are identified and each is recommended to be handled in a particular way in terms of purchasing behaviour and the nature of the supplier relationship that is required.

One of the cells in the Kraljic matrix (high supply risk–high importance to the customer) suggests a closer relationship with suppliers than is suggested in the 'classical' view. Furthermore, the shift away from a transactional perspective towards a total cost approach also requires increasing involvement with suppliers as does the increasing efforts of customers to use their suppliers to improve the 'marketability' of their own offerings. Increasingly therefore, the benefits of close relationships have been advocated (e.g., by Carlisle and Parker 1989; Lamming 1993; Nishiguchi 1994; Ellram and Edis 1996). In a more recent paper, Goffin *et al.* (2006) argue that, among other things, 'close relationships with selected suppliers can enable manufacturers to reduce costs, improve quality and enhance new product development'.

However, close relationships are resource intensive and so a customer cannot handle too many of them. Therefore, the supplier base of a company must be characterized by diversity in terms of the level of involvement with vendors. With some suppliers, the customer is closely connected, while others are treated in a more arm's-length fashion. The advantages of such a differentiated supply base have been explained by Dyer *et al.* (1998) and Bensaou (1999).

The focus on relationships with suppliers expands the unit of analysis from the single company to include what is outside the boundaries of the company. A further extension of this scope is to involve the customers of the customer and the suppliers of the supplier in this analysis. These considerations have been at the top of the business agenda under the label supply chain management (SCM); see, for example, Christopher (2005) and Lambert and Cooper (2000). The increasing attention on SCM also redirected mainstream purchasing management towards an enhanced process orientation.[3] This shift also affected the titles of textbooks in the area. Most of these are now entitled something like 'Purchasing and Supply Chain Management'; two significant examples are van Weele (2002) and Leenders *et al.* (2006).

In one respect, however, the view of the market as the key to efficient purchasing is unchanged. The idea that purchasing should be directed towards creating market-like features is embedded into the legislation of many western societies. The rules of competition defined by EU and US antitrust legislation are some of the most renowned in this respect. This legislation includes, for example, rules for public purchasing on the number of suppliers that must be asked for tenders and the frequency of re-bidding when it comes to more continuous purchases. The intention with these principles is to reinforce market conditions with alternative suppliers competing on price, specification conformity and delivery. However, within this market-based approach, it is often difficult to assess how successful a company has been in achieving the lowest possible costs in its purchases and it is also difficult to judge how well its buyers have performed or to monitor the integrity of its purchasing decisions.

A Purchasing Perspective on Interaction

When business relationships are observed from the classical purchasing management perspective, they are treated as a severe problem. The formation of relationships is a threat to the conditions of competitive markets in which there are sufficient independent players that no one can exercise economic power over others (Marglin 2008).

It becomes more difficult to evaluate the potential contributions of alternative suppliers when a customer is involved in a relationship with a supplier with its associated relationship-specific investments. Similarly, assessing the value of a relationship with a specific supplier

---

[3]Some of the academic literature and some government bodies have advocated a more widespread building of relationships between customers and suppliers into 'partnerships', within which a higher level of trust between the two companies is said to provide benefits to both parties.

and its 'non-product' benefits is difficult to align with the idea of market choice between suppliers for a straightforwardly definable commodity. Moreover, interaction is not an issue in classical purchasing management. Interaction would lead to unwanted dependence and, according to legislation, too much customer–supplier interaction is prohibited and therefore 'the term partnership gives lawyers discomfort' (Leenders *et al.* 2006).

Recent developments in purchasing and supply management acknowledge the importance of business relationships. In many cases, however, this is done with considerable reservations. For example, one of today's mainstream purchasing-management books is somewhat hesitant and includes a section on the 'myth of partnership'. According to one author, it is recognized that 'many large international manufacturers have spent a lot of time and money in the development of supplier-partnership programmes' (van Weele 2002:164). The results, however, are not encouraging since 'mutual trust between supplier and contractor are still out of reach' and empirical evidence points to broken promises, abuse of trust and conflicts. Therefore, it is concluded that 'the road to partnerships is long and difficult'. The reader might wonder if these outcomes are contingent on the recommendations for 'getting better results from suppliers' presented some pages earlier in the book. The first steps in this procedure are clearly indications of efforts to strongly manage suppliers rather than to interact with them. What is recommended by the author is 'contract review' and 'competitive bidding amongst current and new suppliers' (van Weele 2002:162).

We have not used the quotations above to criticize the specific author but to illustrate the general direction in today's mainstream purchasing management. The conclusion is that even when the importance of suppliers and their potential contributions are acknowledged, the focus is still almost completely one sided, on the customer company. Rather than applying an interactive view of the role of suppliers and supplier relationships recommendations are centred on the customer's selection of suppliers and on the active managing of them from the perspective of the customer.

Supply chain management thinking extended the unit of analysis on the supply side. For example, the objective of SCM is the 'linkage and coordination between processes of other entities in the pipe-line, i.e. suppliers and customers, and the organization itself' (Christopher 1992:14). However, it is still the competitive aspect that is considered the driving force and the outcome of the reorientation since it is claimed that 'real competition is not company against company, but rather supply chain against supply chain' (Christopher 1992:17). From the previous chapters in this book, it should be obvious that we do not share this view. Rather than focussing on the competitive aspect, we would emphasize efforts to improve performance as the driving force. Moreover, there is not only competition between the different supply chains. As shown in Chapter 6, the efficiency and effectiveness of a specific supply chain is in fact strongly contingent on how it is related to other supply chains.

Management Accounting and Business Relationships

That there is a close connection between the design of the organization and the characteristics of its environment has been discussed in organizational research since the 1960s. The extent of uncertainty and the degree of dynamism or heterogeneity in the environment have been found to be closely related to how an organization is structured and controlled (Evan 1966;

Lawrence and Lorsch 1967; Thompson 1967; Pugh *et al.* 1968). Over the years, this research has expanded and developed into a number of different approaches such as the institutional (DiMaggio and Powell 1983), the ecological (Aldrich 1979) and the social network (Burt 1992; Powell *et al.* 1996). Inter-organizational issues have been more or less accentuated in all these approaches. This research has been an important input into our studies and has influenced our way of approaching interaction. It has also informed the way that organizational issues are seen within companies. However, it has had less effect when it has been combined with economic models, such as when management accounting is analysed.

The field of management accounting is a good example of the problems of integrating organizational aspects into the economic area. Accounting is interesting as it is supposed to cover the whole company and its relationship with the environment and also to be able to identify the factors that influence the development of the company. It is in the company's information system where business activities are translated into financial dimensions: It is the place where organizational and economic models meet. Here the economic model that makes a clear distinction between hierarchies and markets still dominates. The reason is simple: Accounting has to be in congruence with the legal system and the legal system is highly influenced by a single company view and by the market model.

One key issue in all accounting is the need for distinct boundaries: Who has to pay for what and who has the right to sell what are key issues. One of the goals of accounting is to describe what happens at the company's interface with others and to determine the economic state of a company at a particular point in time, based on that boundary. The first issue to form part of this task is usually to measure the 'flow' of the business: To measure in economic terms the outcome of what has happened at this interface during a particular period of time. The second is to measure the company's 'stock' in terms of, for example, liquidity or solidity at a certain point in time. Consequently, there is a need to establish a clear boundary line and this is very much in accord with the distinction between the hierarchy within the firm and the market that characterizes the environment in the market model.

Accounting is concerned with describing and assessing the current position of the company as well as its past performance in order to exercise management control. Thus, for example, it includes estimates of the overall financial performance of operating units and of the company as a whole in order to determine costs and revenues. Accounting includes the more readily identifiable or attributable costs incurred by the company in its purchasing and marketing activities.

Within the company, accounting has traditionally analysed costs at the level of each of the operating units, and for each process and product within them. On the customer side, accounting has been concerned with analysing the revenue achieved from particular products, from particular geographical areas and, in some cases, from specific customers. It has also been concerned with the costs of making overall transactions and sometimes with the costs of specific major transactions or of dealing with specific customers. This issue in accounting inevitably involves a complex process of allocating indirect costs between these areas.

Management accounting attempts to translate business activities into financial terms. It values resources in absolute (market) terms and looks at the achievement of targeted return on investment in those resources over time. Many customer relationship management (CRM) systems make it possible to record the volume of sales to each customer and, sometimes, the actual price achieved.

Two key issues in existing accounting are the valuation of 'transactions' and 'assets'. Transactions are especially important when calculating the flow while the valuation of assets is central for all stock estimates. Single transactions with customers and suppliers are important ingredients in the estimation of costs and revenues. Prices received are assumed to describe revenues and prices paid to describe costs. Assets are generally valued in accordance with what they could be sold for to someone else. All these valuations are perfectly in accordance with a market view of the company.

An Accounting Perspective on Interaction

Into this world of 'clean' transactions and assets the observation of business relationships has been introduced (for an overview, see Håkansson *et al.* 2009a). It has been introduced both by the application of theoretical models emphasizing relationships and also through the development of special methods and techniques to be used by companies. Companies have developed a broad range of special accounting techniques, methods and control mechanisms that have been developed for handling accounting problems related to business relationships. Examples are open-book accounting, target costing, value chain accounting, quality plans, programmes of innovation, alliance boards, joint task groups, tournament procedures, supplier certifications, non-financial measures and risk-reward schemes (Mouritsen *et al.* 2001; Langfield-Smith and Smith 2003; Dekker 2003, 2004; Seal *et al.* 1999). All these methods are directed towards linking internal activities and resources of the company to those belonging to customers or suppliers or other collaborative partners. What is even more important is that many of these methods concern what can be achieved through having business relationships: They are more directed towards how the firm can benefit from its relationships than with the problems of having those business relationships.

A number of theoretical tools have been used when analysing the use of these methods, such as transaction-cost economics; agency theory; resource-based models and actor–network theory. All of these except actor–network theory are firmly based in the market model. The most widely used of them has been the transaction-cost economics approach (e.g. Ittner *et al.* 1999; Jones 1999; Roodhooft and Warlop 1999; Seal *et al.* 1999; Widener and Selto 1999; Anderson *et al.* 2000; Van der Meer-Kooistra and Vosselman 2000; Speklé 2001; Langfield-Smith and Smith 2003; Cooper and Slagmulder 2004; Dekker 2004; Sartorius and Kirsten 2005; Emsley and Kidon 2007). A typical issue in many of these publications is to relate accounting issues to the three governance forms: market, hierarchy and bilateral governance.

The central theme in transaction-cost economics is that the performance of the different governance forms is dependent on specific situational variables. The situational variables can be related to the transaction (frequency, asset specificity), to the transacting parties (information asymmetry, reputation) and to the transaction environment (uncertainty, market risks) (Meer-Kooistra and Vosselman 2000). Of these three variable groups, the most studied are the transaction-specific ones. The degree of asset specificity, transaction uncertainty and frequency are central in almost all studies.

In overview, the transaction-cost approach can be summarized as being concerned with the role that accounting can have in identifying transaction characteristics in order to choose the right governance form and in shaping the three governance forms, of which market and hierarchy have also been covered in traditional accounting, and the new types of accounting tool that are necessary to support bilateral governance (Håkansson and Lind 2007).

Business relationships are again analysed as an alternative way for a single company to handle counterparts in particular situations. One interesting consequence of this is that because the analysis is static, the situation in itself is not affected by the development of the relationship. A particular situation is supposed to suit a particular governance solution.

The consequences of the existence of business relationships for how transactions and assets are valued have not been a major concern in the transaction-cost approach. This is surprising as transactions certainly have a different role within a relationship compared with single market exchange, and business relationships affect other assets and are assets themselves.

Conclusion

The fields of management that we have discussed, strategy, marketing, purchasing and accounting, have each registered that interdependencies between companies and the development of relationships are important features of the contemporary business world. Except in the traditional purchasing literature, interaction and relationships are also treated either as an economically useful mechanism or as a resource. However, what these schools also have in common is that they have tried to integrate close interaction and relationships with the traditional market view in which companies are basically seen to be independent of each other. Thus, they view relationships as an exception to the norm. The most important consequence for management of this starting point is that business relationships are a type of mechanism or resource that can be useful in some particular situations if they are managed in the right way by an individual firm. There are some important benefits in integrating relationships in this way:

- There is no need to change the models based on the market view that have been used for a long time. Relationships are given a special place as something that is useful for a single firm in specific situations. From an analytical point of view, we have just to identify these special situations and then apply business relationships in order to create positive economic effects on isolated parts of the company.
- It is in accordance with the single company view that fits neatly with the western culture of individuality and the idea of the heroic manager achieving success solely through the brilliance of personal strategy and leadership. The world is seen from the perspective of a single company and its activities, which includes the possibility of creating more or less extensive relationships with some of its counterparts. These relationships are an alternative that can be used when seen to be useful or necessary by the managers.
- The issues around relationships can be handled in isolation from other issues such as investments in facilities or the design of overall strategies or organizational routines.

The consequences of this approach are that the issue of relationships and how they should be handled are marginalized or made to appear as a rather mundane day-to-day issue. In this way, the management literature has adopted interaction or relationships as techniques at their discretion when the circumstances are appropriate. This is a rather 'comfortable' way, especially for researchers and consultants, to deal with this ingredient in the empirical world. It preserves the idea of individual autonomy, independent strategizing and the easily identifiable company in relation to its markets. It may not be as convenient for managers as they have to live with some of the problems that we discuss in Chapter 9. But first we summarize how this 'comfortable' way is applied to our four fields.

Strategy management has assumed that a company can use its business relationships in order to create specific advantages in the market, without effects on other parts of the company. Thus, a business relationship is regarded as a one-sided resource that the company can control. For example, a business relationship can be employed without it having any effect on the boundaries of the company, on the activities it performs, or the resources it uses. Thus, in the mainstream strategy literature, business relationships can be used with an almost surgical precision: The only thing that is influenced by the relationship is the position of the company in relation to some specific counterpart in the market.

Marketing management has taken the view that a business relationship can be chosen and managed by the marketer. Thus, what happens in the business relationship is assumed to be a process of action by one marketing party towards the passive customer. When marketing management is based on the transaction-cost model, business relationships are assumed to constitute another form of governance, a special case within the overall market form. From this perspective, relationships are considered to involve relationship-specific investments by either or both parties. Hence, when marketing management ideas are based on a transaction-cost approach, business relationships are a means that have effects on both of the involved parties. However, management ideas based on the marketing mix and transaction-cost approaches have in common the idea of what business relationships and other marketing means are used for: To be part of the way that an easily identifiable or generic product or service is 'marketed' to customers by competing suppliers. Thus, in a way that is similar to strategy management, marketing management assumes that what is produced and marketed is unaffected by the development and use of business relationships. Therefore business relationships can easily be used as a marketing tool.

Purchasing management has considered business relationships to be largely negative. The idea of price negotiation for a definable commodity is an important basis for purchasing. Business relationships are considered as something that limits this. Traditional purchasing management considers itself to be a zero-sum game, or takes an adversarial approach to the dealings between supplier and customer. In purchasing management based on transaction-cost theory, business relations are considered to have positive effects in purchasing situations that are characterized by restrictions in the market. Also in this management literature, business relationships are considered as a managerial purchasing tool: Their effects are solely on the way that the company handles a particular purchasing situation, not on the purchasing company's entire activities and resources.

Management accounting has mostly been concerned with business relationships as a problem. A relationship has to be analysed and valued in some way that is unaffected by the relative value of other resources and activities. But here it is interesting to note that companies themselves have developed a number of techniques and methods to try to analyse the benefit from relationships or the consequences of relationships (Håkansson and Lind 2004).

An obvious question to ask at this point is: Is this really enough? Is it so easy to incorporate these business relationships into the market view? Doesn't the existence of business relationships lead to some 'special case' of management that applies in some 'not-quite-market' situation? We have seen how relationships have been viewed by a number of disciplines or functional areas as just some special case which requires only minor modifications to their mainstream approach. Thus, the special case could be handled by some complementary analysis and slight modifications to the *normal* management situation of independent action and market response.

But there is an alternative. It could be that the observations of interaction and relationships actually indicate that we are faced with a business landscape which has very little in common with how it is depicted in the model world of a market: That it is a different business world. The logic of this view is that a world of interdependent actors precludes the existence of markets and independent companies within that world.

In the next chapter, we make a first and very modest attempt to make this reformulation of the key issues in management by considering management as the process through which an actor attempts to cope with the interactive context.

MANAGING IN THE BUSINESS NETWORK

In this chapter, we consider the second alternative identified in Chapter 8. We start out from a basic assumption that business relationships are the norm and try to re-formulate managerial problems from this assumption. Thus, our starting point is to take the relationship as our unit of analysis.

We start by examining the approach to business management that has been taken in IMP studies over the years. We then revisit the model of the process of business interaction presented in Chapter 3. We try to bring together some of the ideas that we have presented on the nature of the three layers of interaction (resources, activities and actors) to develop a structure of the process of managing in business networks.

Introduction

The business landscape that we have described in this book is rather different from the conventional view that underlies many of the ideas of management presented in the previous chapter. An interactive perspective asserts that it can never be possible for an individual manager to manage a company, a non-profit organization, a product or a business relationship in isolation because none of these things has an independent existence. Instead, an interactive perspective views each company as embedded in a network of interdependencies and relationships with others. The existence of this network means that managerial action is not independently arrived at nor are its effects determined by that action alone. Instead, individual managerial action is affected by the interaction that has taken place with counterparts and is a contribution to the subsequent effects of that continuing interaction process.

Management has to be seen differently if we replace the conventional assumption of independence with the assumption of interdependency. Management is still important in at least two ways: First, the manager is not consigned to be a passive creature existing only at the whim of others. Each managerial actor in the network has the ability and the intent to act. There is a lot of management taking place and it all has effects, even if they are not the ones expected by the acting manager. Secondly, management is still important because interdependencies, relationships and networks can be influenced. Business actors still need to try to understand what is going on and to act and react in an appropriate way. There is both the room and the need for management.

Because management in a single company is intimately related to the interaction between that company and specific others, we cannot make sense of the process of management in a single company by considering what happens in that company alone. Management in a single company can only be understood by looking at what happens in its unique interactions with others. The uniqueness of interaction means that it always has to be considered from the perspective of the position in which it takes place in network space and the time at which it occurs in a continuing and evolutionary process. The importance of these two situational variables tends to drive out the chance of being able to make easy generalizations about the behaviour of individual actors, actors connected through dyadic relationships, or across the network as a whole. Thus the view of the business landscape that arises from an interactive perspective is starkly different from the underlying assumptions of mainstream management theory.

But interdependent companies still need to address their problems and opportunities; they need to do some kind of management. This leads us to the central question of this chapter: If managers can handle neither problems nor opportunities by themselves, how can we make sense of the process of management in an interactive business landscape?

The first aim of this chapter is to examine how management issues can be formulated in an interactive world. We do this by building on some of the ideas of business that have emerged from our empirical and conceptual work over the past 30 years.[1] We then try to draw these ideas together, using the descriptive model of business interaction that we presented in Chapter 3 to provide a tentative structure to explain how managers manage in business networks.

What then are the main problems in trying to combine the empirical observations of an interactive business landscape with the contemporary view of management outlined in Chapter 8? In the interactive world, multiple sequential 'outcomes' emerge through interaction between multiple parties. These outcomes involve complex combinations of activities, resources and actors. Most of these combinations are outside the knowledge of any one actor, and far beyond its ability to 'manage' them. Hence, we must doubt that it is possible to realistically attribute causality between specific managerial action and its apparent results. Similarly, when interaction between actors is unique in time and space, it is difficult to generalize about the behaviour of an actor across the range of its interactions. In an interactive world, it is difficult to establish the boundaries of a specific actor or to demarcate those areas that are within or outside its control and in which it can act. The idea of a networked world raises questions about the basic notion of management. Therefore, our starting point for this analysis is as follows: What view of the process of managing do we arrive at if we *start* from assumptions of interaction and interdependence?

This chapter does not attempt to provide a definitive or comprehensive answer to this question. Instead, our ambition is to trace the idea of management that arises from our empirical and conceptual research. By doing this, we hope to bring together some of the scattered findings and in this way present the research problems that we face for the future. It also means that we are

---

[1]Within the IMP group, Wilkinson (2008), Möller and Rajala (2007) and Anderson and Narus (2004) have also attempted to do this.

more concerned with the problems involved in finding alternative ways to formulate managerial problems than with trying to bring forward normative managerial formulae for an interactive business landscape.

The Relationship as a Unit of Analysis

A severe challenge immediately arises when management is approached from an interactive perspective. If business is not about what goes on within a company but about what happens between companies, then how can a company be managed? Our initial approach to this challenge was formulated in the first IMP study, as follows:

> The focus of the study is on relationships between buying and selling firms in industrial markets. This means that it is not selling or purchasing firms that are our research objects but the relationships between them. Our population in other words consists not of persons, products, firms or markets but of relationships between firms.
>
> *Håkansson 1982:32*

Thus, instead of taking the individual firm and its management as a starting point, the first IMP study was conceptually and methodologically based on a very particular idea of business. At the core of this idea is the business relationship and how those involved in it are connected to it, how they affect it and are affected by it. This idea is summarized in Box 9.1 using the concepts developed in the first IMP book.

The idea that interaction is a property of relationships rather than of any participating actor means that we can only make sense of what happens in and to a business actor within the context of interaction and in terms of its association with specific others. Within this interpretation, each actor is a dependent part of a wider structure and it exists as an adjunct to the process of interaction. Managing an actor has to start from the observation that *a company is not an independent actor*.

Box 9.1   IMP Concepts

A relationship has a separate existence beyond that of the companies or individuals involved in it. This relationship provides the particular context within which specific episodes of interaction between the companies and individuals take place.

All interaction episodes are influenced by the individual or corporate memory of previous interactions held by those involved in it. All interaction episodes are influenced by actors' explicit or implicit assessment of the effects of the episode on future interaction and on the relationship as a whole.

All interaction is affected by the social, technological and physical capital that has been established in the relationship between companies.

Each relationship is unique.

The notion of interdependency requires a consideration of the range of established relationships and of how they can be developed by those involved in them, notwithstanding that their views of the direction that development should take will never completely coincide. The notion of interdependency also implies that it is unrealistic to imagine that a coherent picture of the business landscape or of any actor's position within it can ever be acquired. Each relationship is connected to others, which means that a different picture emerges as soon as a new relationship connection is considered. The network is also in constant motion, so any picture of it immediately becomes out of date.

The issues of complexity and interdependency were addressed in the first IMP research project by taking the dyad as the smallest unit of analysis. The idea of investigating a company 'in itself' was abandoned: Companies were approached in terms of examining a range of the relationships in which they were engaged, based on a taxonomy of different product technologies (materials, component parts and capital equipment) and process technologies (unit, mass and process production). This research approach infers that it is equally valid to suggest that companies are the outcomes of their relationships and their history of interaction, as they are of their own intentions. The findings from this research also provided indications of how the characteristics of business relationships and of the actors involved in them are influenced by the specific activity pattern and resource constellations in which they exist. Perhaps more importantly, it demonstrated that a business actor 'acts' only as part of the process of interaction within particular and defined arenas of specific relationships.

However, the experience of the first IMP study also underlined that the nature of business actors and business behaviour are not solely determined by the context in which they occur. The idea of interaction does not eliminate the idea of the free will of the single business actor. But our first study did make two distinctions that are important to the ideas of the business actor and business acting. It distinguished between a specific episode (acting in the short run) in a relationship and the relationship itself (acting in the long run). However, the problem of how to systematically isolate or to distinguish between episodes was not addressed. It also distinguished between three aspects of the behaviour of business actors: their approach to interaction *within* a single relationship; the variations in their approach *between* relationships; and their approach to interaction and relationships as a whole. The research attempted to mirror this distinction by interviewing those who appeared to have responsibility for the company's approach to multiple relationships and those who operated within particular relationships.

An important result of this research is the suggestion that the evolution of the relationship between two business actors is in a true sense accidental. What happens between business actors is not the result of either of their individual intents. It is an outcome of their interaction. Consequently the relationship is not the possession of either of the actors, nor is it theirs to manage. But the research did show that variations in the perceptions of the actors of the separate and common problems that they wished to address within the relationship influenced the evolution of the relationship and the respective and inevitably different perceptions that each would hold of it (Håkansson 1982:6, 1982:316). It is apparent from this early work that relationships are a key resource for carrying out business activities and a company is to a large extent defined by its relationships. A conclusion from this is that managerial action within this context becomes a process of working with others within existing and emerging relationships.

Thus, the idea of interacting companies within continuing and often long-term and complex relationships transfers the researcher's area of attention from individual actors and their individual acting to the interplay between specific actors, to the wider structure of relationships and interdependencies within which interaction takes place and to the process of interaction itself. The nature of each individual actor in the network can then be considered as one of many related outcomes of this structure and process as well as one of its architects. This view then enables us to refine the earlier question into the following research problem: How can we characterize the approaches that business actors may take to the process of interaction?

We have no coherent answer to this problem, but a number of different suggestions have been identified, on which we build this chapter. One of the first versions of the form that management takes in an interactive world was presented not under the title 'How do companies manage?' but 'How do companies interact?' (Ford *et al.* 1986).

How Do Companies Interact?

The first IMP study found that interaction involved much more than conversation or negotiation and could involve inputs from both parties of product, service, information, logistics, physical and intellectual assets, advice and finance, and lead to the development and adaptation of all of these. Thus, interaction is a process over time that has costs and benefits, although these may be difficult or impossible to identify in detail. Interaction is likely to involve conscious intent and unintentional effects. It is likely to include a number of persons from both companies and so it involves numerous intentions and interpretations. This complexity means that any attempt to understand the approaches that actors take to their interactions must start from the position that the parties in a relationship are likely to have a clear or common view of where they stand with each other and what are each others' intentions.

Each new interaction episode between actors can be interpreted as a series of 'questions' and 'answers'. Each episode poses questions about the direction and usefulness of the relationship (see Table 9.1) and about each actor's counterpart and themselves. Unfortunately for the actors involved, the meaning of each question and the answers that it provides are not apparent from the episode itself and a clearer view can only be obtained within the context of other episodes and of the relationship itself.

What Can You Do for Me?

This question is concerned with the issue of *capability*. But capability has a very particular characteristic in the business network that has important implications for the nature of business management. Business interaction is problem-driven and is based on the perceptions of each actor of their own resources and activities and those of their counterparts and how these can be

Table 9.1 Questions in interaction and the issues that they address.

Question	Central feature
What can you do for me?	Capability
How do you see me?	Jointness
What are you prepared to do for me compared to what you do for others?	Particularity
What variations are there in these 'what's and 'how's?	Inconsistency

used together to address their joint and separate problems. Thus, from both an analytical and a practical perspective, *capability is a property of a relationship*, rather than being something that belongs to individual actors.[2]

This is because it is only through interaction within a relationship that the heterogeneous resources of the two actors are activated and it is through interaction that interdependent activities are exploited and made productive. Thus it would be common to try to analyse the resources and activities that are nominally within the ownership or control of a single business actor. But in the network world, an actor's resources and activities and its ability to capitalize on them are activated by, dependent on and defined by their specific interactions with other actors, activities and resources, rather than being generalized properties of the actor itself.

How Do You See Me?

If capability is a characteristic of a relationship then the interacting actors are likely to develop their own view of the relationship and their own approach to developing and using their joint capability. Each actor's approach to a relationship is likely to be strongly influenced by their view of the approach that seems to be taken by their counterpart. The question, 'How do you see me?' is concerned with the way that each actor seeks to understand how the other is using it, how it handles the relationship and how it views their joint and separate costs and benefits that could arise over time. In other words, this question is concerned with the concept of *jointness* that we introduced in Chapters 3 and 7. Jointness involves investments and trade-offs for each actor over time. Jointness may develop through individual sacrifice or be reduced by self-seeking. Jointness may also involve the formal or informal acceptance of togetherness or bonds between the two actors with respect to third parties. Jointness is the outcome of the intentions and interpretations of both actors and of the interaction that takes place between them. Jointness is simultaneously a measure of the limitations of an individual business actor and its potential with another. But jointness is also concerned with what a counterpart is prepared to do.

What Are You Prepared to Do for Me?

The question 'What are you prepared to do for me compared to what you do for others?' is concerned with *particularity* in the way in which a certain actor approaches different counterparts. Particularity is one of the most significant differences between the view of the business landscape as the world of the market and as the world of the network. The particularity of an actor's approach to different interactions may partially be explained by the structure of the network. For example, this structure may lead to the actor interacting with a single large customer or supplier or public body or with each of many small suppliers or customers. Particularity is also influenced by the previous approaches of either of the parties to the interaction or the current problems that each tries to address. The existence of particularity means that apparently similar actors

---

[2]This is increasingly recognized in recent marketing literature that focuses on relationship processes, such as Ulaga and Eggert (2006), Tuli *et al.* (2007) and Palmatier (2008).

experience different interaction processes when facing the same counterpart and these different processes affect the evolution of the separate actors differently.

The question goes to the heart of what it means to be an interactive actor. It means that a single business actor has a different identity in each of its important relationships in terms of the intentions and approach of the actor and the interpretations and approach to it of the counterpart. It also means that what is good is relative: An actor is evaluated in each relationship by others and by itself against different and specific criteria that relate to existing structures and processes. Hence it is unlikely that an actor is able to take a uniform approach to its relationships and the 'performance' of that actor cannot realistically be judged in different relationships against a single set of criteria.

What Variations Are There in These Whats and Hows?

Multi-person interaction between actors is based on the intentions and interpretations of each person who is involved. These intentions and interpretations inevitably lead to *inconsistencies* within interaction between actors and within the assessments made of and by counterparts. Inconsistencies may also arise over time as the interaction develops and the actors evolve. Both of these types of inconsistency may arise from the interaction itself. They may be accidental or the result of conscious policy by either or both of the actors. Each business actor takes an identity in each relationship from the multiple simultaneous interactions between different individuals and subgroups within that relationship. Each actor has a different identity in its interactions with each counterpart and that identity will evolve over time. Hence the existence, form and characteristics of the business actor are sensitive to the inconsistencies in its interactions with others.

Summary

These questions taken together provide at least some insight into the nature of management. They reinforce the idea of the interacting actor as part of different relationships, each having different capabilities within themselves and as seen by others. The questions suggest that capabilities, jointness, particularity and inconsistency are the outcome of interaction as well as important inputs into it. They are the key aspects of simultaneous and sequential managerial activities by multiple actors and they simultaneously determine the identities of those multiple actors.

In summary, the way that we have so far structured the managerial process gives a picture of how important interaction processes are in shaping managerial activities. In order to understand the effects of management, we have to translate it to the interaction process within which it is transformed. One reason for this transformation is that a network structure puts every actor into a number of very paradoxical situations. These paradoxes were the starting point for a later article which deliberately dealt with how management could be practised in a network-like business landscape. Again, this was not written under the title 'How should companies manage' but 'How should companies interact' (Håkansson and Ford 2002).

> **Box 9.2 Network Paradoxes**
>
> 1. A network is both the source of life for a company and the cage that imprisons it.
> 2. A company is both the determinant and the outcome of its relationships and what happens in them.
> 3. The more a company achieves control, the less effective and innovative the network becomes.

How Should Companies Interact?

The idea of the business actor that has emerged from our research indicates that a company does not have a singular, clear-cut identity, physical or financial shape, collective purpose or individual attributes. Instead, a company's identity seems to be acquired through interaction with others: It is both multifaceted and malleable. A company has an evolving and specific identity for specific others because it is perceived by them as 'a distinct, intelligible entity' that they can relate to their own company's problems. In other words, companies are actors because the identity of an actor is attributed to them by those with whom they interact. But most companies consist of different units or departments and each of these may be identified by counterparts as a distinct actor with its own identity. The attribution of varying identities by others, the individual identity of subunits and the actor as a collection of activities and resources that are part of wider activity patterns and resource constellations all suggest that any demarcation of a company's 'boundaries' is more or less arbitrary. A business actor has no natural boundary, nor is it possible to separate areas of resources or activities that are absolutely within or outside its control.

The interactive actor whose identity is defined by others and whose approach to interaction can be expressed as a process of questioning and answering, learning and teaching is living a life within individual relationships and within numbers of connected relationships. This life is both interesting and complicated as it places the actor in a number of intricate paradoxes (summarized in Box 9.2) which become evident as soon as we ask the question, how should a company interact?

First Network Paradox

The first paradox centres on the role of relationships and on how they can be used by the actor. The paradox is formulated as follows:

> External relationships are at the heart of a company's survival and the basis of its growth and development. But a well-developed network of existing relationships also ties a company into its current ways of operating and restricts its ability to change. Thus, a network is both the source of life for a company and the cage that imprisons it.

This paradox describes how relationships involve both opportunities and constraints. A company can develop in a myriad ways through its relationships. In principle, the actor is free to pursue any of these ways. However, relationships are also a prison because the reactions of counterparts limit what the actor is actually able to do. An actor seeking to change some aspect of its operations or establish new relationships often has to seek the approval of existing counterparts or take its existing relationships along with it. The more developed an actor's relationships, the stronger its bonds with others and the greater are the actor's possibilities. But the more developed an actor's relationships, the greater are the constraining forces on that actor. In this way, relationships are both a blessing and a curse. As a saying goes among psychologists, 'relationships can drive you mad, but without them you die'.

This paradox has two further implications for the business actor: the web of actors in which an actor interacts is likely to evolve only slowly and innovation often occurs from outside its immediate set of relationships; the actor is likely to be more concerned with its interactions with *existing* counterparts than about how it should choose new ones (Wynstra 1998).

Second Network Paradox

This paradox has to do with how an actor may handle relationships. The paradox is formulated as follows:

> A company's relationships are the outcomes of its strategy and its actions. But the company is itself the outcome of those relationships and of what has happened in them. Thus it is possible to analyze a company's position in a network from the premise that the company determines its relationships and from the premise that it is determined by them. Both situations exist simultaneously and both premises are equally valid.

This paradox describes the double process that is typical of interaction within business relationships. Insight into the management of the business actor seems to lie in the interface between the actor and its relationships with others. It is easy to fall into a trap when analysing this interface by assuming that an actor pre-exists its relationships and that it develops those relationships on the basis of an explicit or implicit strategy. This approach may be appropriate when examining day-to-day interactions over the short term. However, even in the short term, we have to accept that a relationship is at least dyadic and take into account the role of counterparts in relationship evolution. In an interactive analysis, we view an actor as rather like a town located at a cross-roads: It is at least equally valid to suggest that the identity of the town is the outcome of those roads intersecting and of where those roads come from, as it is to suggest that the town was a self-created entity that then built its own roads. The view of the business actor as relationship-derived is likely to be appropriate if we wish to examine the interface between an actor and its more important relationships. This would force us to search for the identity of an actor as the outcome of its relationships or as the manifestation of both parties' intentions and their interactions. The second network paradox also argues for the need to interpret business development as a process of co-evolution over the long term and as an outcome of the evolution of its relationships with other actors and of the evolution of those actors in their other relationships. More importantly, the paradox also suggests that we would find it impossible to separate the identities of individual actors from each other. The absence of a separate identity has at least two outcomes for the business actor:

- Relationships develop a commonality of knowledge and understanding between the parties about each other and about the substance of their relationships and the ways that they can and should interact both within this relationship and in others (Håkansson and Johanson 1987, 1992). The knowledge, understanding, norms and values that they acquire are both a source of strength for the companies and an impediment to change.
- A company's characteristics and its resources are the outcome of its interactions and relationships and its future is dependent on what happens in those relationships (Håkansson and Lundgren 1997). Thus any strategy has to be formulated in interactive terms. No company has sufficient resources to completely satisfy the requirements of any customer and so it is dependent on the skills, resources, actions and intentions of suppliers, distributors, customers, and sometimes even competitors. Similarly, no company can exploit or develop its own resources except in conjunction with others. Interdependence between companies suggests that the strategy process has to be interactive, evolutionary and responsive and that it takes place somehow between companies.

Third Network Paradox

This paradox relates to the link that seems so often to exist between the idea of a relationship and the idea of control. The paradox is formulated as follows:

> Companies try to control the network that surrounds them and to manage their relationships to achieve their own aims. This ambition is one of the key forces in developing networks. The more that a company achieves this ambition of control, the less effective and innovative the network becomes.

Despite the limitations under which it operates, each actor in a network tries to control its relationships with others as far as it is able, in a direction that suits its own perceived requirements. It tries to influence the knowledge and understanding within other actors and relationships and also to influence the process of co-evolution that occurs between them for its own ends. This constant urge to control is both a key and a necessary force in the development of relationships and the network. However, the paradox is that the more that an actor succeeds in influencing the thinking or controlling the operations of those around it, the more that it and those around it are also likely to encounter difficulties.

This paradox centres on the fundamental issues of the connections between the position of an actor in the network, the effectiveness of that actor and the effectiveness of the network as a whole. Each of the relationships of an actor forms part of a larger structure. Each relationship provides contact between the counterparts and has a different role or function for each of them within the context of their other relationships. Each relationship also provides connections to other relationships in the network and the total network structure is dependent on how each is related to others. The economic effects on an actor of any one relationship are influenced by its connections to others. Knowledge and understanding are transmitted through these network connections and in this way they act as a channel of change for and to the actor. The network evolves through the interplay between initiative and interaction throughout the network. But the more that a single actor is able to exercise control over a network, the more that single actor becomes the sole source of wisdom and innovation in the network and the more likely it is that the network becomes fixed in its processes and unresponsive to wider changes. On the other hand, if the actors don't try to achieve this control then an important development force disappears and the network becomes less dynamic.

The control exercised by a collective of actors can also encounter this paradox: The connections between actors facilitate the development of common ideas between actors in the network of 'what everyone knows'. These ideas may coalesce into a 'network constitution' (Mouzas and Ford 2006) consisting of rules, laws, norms or cultural patterns that can strongly and negatively influence the common reactions of actors towards innovation or the actions of others from outside their immediate experience. In this way, the connections between relationships can act as an impediment to network change and development and limit the ability of any single actor to determine or change its position in the network. The complexity of the connections between relationships also makes it difficult for an actor to plot the wider effects of any interaction across the network.

The three paradoxes indicate that a network is in constant flux between the forces of stability and change. All of those involved in managing in an interactive business landscape together create the forces that keep the network structure alive and prospering. Each has its own perspective on the state of the network and ideas for its development. The state of the network at any one time and the way that it evolves are the outcome of all these ideas and interactions. The network is not owned or managed by any one of them. The network evolves in a similar way to the rainforest.

Managing and the Interacting Company

The questions that we have suggested that managers ask and the paradoxes of the world in which they must operate together indicate the impossibility of trying to formulate any simple or overall rules for how to manage. In spite of this, shareholders still exert pressure on company boards; employees and suppliers still need to be paid; and customers still need to be served: So managers still try to manage in the business network!

In this section, we try to analyse the process of managing in an interactive world and show how managing is influenced by the existence of relationship and network structures. To do this, we use the basic model of action described in Figure 7.3 and translate the three concepts that we identified into concepts that describe the way that managers relate to the interactive world (see Figure 9.1).

The first dimension in the model is the respective views of the world around them, or the 'network pictures' that are held by different actors. The way that these pictures are expressed and the similarities and differences between them have important effects on interaction between the actors.

The second dimension is the multiple and sequential 'outcomes' of interaction between actors. The outcome of interaction is different for actors at different points in network space and for those actors at different times. These outcomes form important managerial clues and influences for subsequent interaction between actors.

The final dimension refers to the efforts of individual managers to influence the content and direction of the interaction between them. We refer to these conscious efforts as 'networking'.

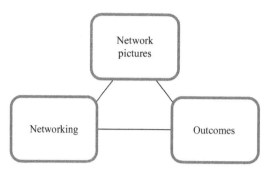

Figure 9.1   Analysing management in business networks.

Source: Ford *et al.* 2003:176

Network Pictures

A network view of the business landscape emphasizes the duality between a manager who is very knowledgeable about a specific combination of activities, resources and other actors (his small world) and the impossibility for the same manager of seeing or understanding all of the links that exist between all actors, activities and resources. Hence the typical manager appears to be quite knowledgeable and ignorant at the same time! The characteristics of a business network mean that a major issue for the business manager is how to live with those two very different situations and to try to take advantage of them in interacting with counterparts.

Each manager has their own subjective interpretation of the world around them and of the interactions taking place within it, whether or not they are involved in them. It is these subjective interpretations that provide each manager's particular *network picture*[3] of the process of the network and that form the basis for their networking. There is an interesting variation between even closely positioned managers: Despite being able to agree about the small world of their immediate operations, their pictures of the wider world are likely to vary hugely on the basis of their different experiences and perspective. These variations are reflected in their approach to interactions and their interpretations of the approaches of others.

Consequently no manager has a complete view of the network and each has to interact with others to try to learn from them or to convince them about their view. A wider view is not necessarily better from the perspective of an actor's economic performance. All pictures of the network are inevitably incomplete. Thus by using the views of others in the surrounding network, a manager may be better equipped to cope with that network than a manager that attempts, but inevitably fails, to construct a 'complete' picture. Using the views of others is of course the approach adopted by managers that work with retail distributors, overseas

---

[3] The term 'network picture' is here taken to refer to both a visual and a verbal representation of the network by a particular actor. The appropriateness of attributing a collective subjective interpretation or network picture to companies as opposed to individuals is complex. Ramos and Ford (2009) have investigated network pictures in a number of different situations and have examined the extent of commonality between individuals in the same company in different circumstances.

agents or key suppliers in order to capitalize on their knowledge of particular parts of the network.

There are two main ways that the subjective interpretations of managers are formed. One is through business experience, from which a manager progressively develops ideas of the network and how to interact within it. The other way in which pictures are formed is through metaphors or stereotypes, such as 'markets', 'clusters', 'alliances', 'industry', 'supply chain', 'distribution channel' and 'network'. However, these stereotypes inevitably involve simplifications of reality and are likely to restrict the views of managers of the importance of interaction that stretches across these arbitrary boundaries. All companies are managed on the basis of an ego-centric view of the network that is likely to see the company as the hub of 'its' network, 'its' supply chain or 'its' distribution channel. This may be a reasonable way of working in the small world that we discussed in Chapter 7. But an egocentric view of the larger network is inevitably unrealistic. Managers' network pictures are often expressed in terms of a moral philosophy of how they believe that the small world 'should' operate or what should be the 'blueprint' for its development, in line with their wishes.

Sometimes there may be a more or less commonly held view between many managers in a network of the form that interaction should take within it. These commonly held pictures may coalesce into formal or informal rules of interaction, some of which may be backed by the force of law. We have already noted that strong commonly held pictures by groups of managers may make them vulnerable to the entry of an intruder that either doesn't know or chooses to break the 'rules' of how a business should be run. A recent example of this rule-breaking occurred with the entry of low-cost airlines into the established airline network that was previously dominated by national flag-carriers operating under commonly held ways of doing business enforced by International Air Transport Authority (IATA). The network pictures of managers may also be based on a variety of different views of time in the network. Some pictures may be backward-looking and expressed in historical terms of what has happened in the network; others represent a more static view of how the network 'is' and yet others see the network as a process of development.

The dynamic aspect of network pictures means that managers should constantly question their own pictures and those of others around them. A significant consequence of network pictures for a manager is that future interaction depends more on how current interaction is interpreted by those involved in it rather than its 'objective' effects or the intentions of those actions. We noted in Chapter 3 that all interaction, whether personal, impersonal, physical or financial, involves communication and interpretation of its meanings by the interacting companies. Thus interaction has dual aspects for each company in terms of what it wants to happen in the interaction and how it wants the interaction to be interpreted.

The subjective interpretations of managers are not random but are a consequence of their wider experiences and previous actions and reactions. Managers consciously or unconsciously interpret and re-interpret the meanings of their own interactions and those of others elsewhere in the network – and constantly gossip about them! Their own subsequent interactions are based on these interpretations. A manager's interpretation of a counterpart's action is almost certainly different from the interpretation of the counterpart itself and both interpretations may be different from how the counterpart would like to be interpreted. A particular problem for a business manager is that there are also multiple and different interpretations of interaction by managers within the company itself, making it difficult to have a coordinated approach to counterparts (see, for example, Belbin 1993; Islei *et al.* 1991).

Network Outcomes

All the multidimensional and constantly evolving effects that appear to relate to interaction, economic, social and technical, are known as 'network outcomes'. An outcome that is apparently successful for a particular actor, activity or resource at a particular time may appear much less successful at a later date and vice versa. Similarly, an outcome that appears to be successful for one actor, activity or resource may so damage other activities, resources or actors that it has a severe effect on future interaction. In this way, multiple interaction outcomes appear and are reacted upon by all those involved and this means that they have an important role in shaping the interaction.

There is an interesting difference between the small world of a single actor and how it combines with all other small worlds. The outcomes within the small world are relatively easy for the actors in that small world to interpret. Often, the few actors that are involved agree with a focal actor about reasonable technical, economical and social outcomes. But the problem is that this small world is affected by and affects other small worlds. Then the outcomes become much more difficult to interpret.

Outcomes are central for initiating interaction: If they are seen as negative they create different reactions to try to counteract the outcome; positively perceived outcomes are likely to lead to supportive reactions. But individual managers apply their own economic logic to interpret outcomes, based on their individual network pictures. These interpretations determine how different outcomes are translated into interaction behaviour by different managers and how these behaviours are explained to others. This process of interaction and interpretation is likely to involve considerable experimentation that relates to the questioning that we have already discussed. The interaction that follows from the question 'What can you do for me?' may be followed by the question 'What do you say about this?' The replies can sometimes be very quick and firm while in other situations they may be more vague and slow. The outcomes from experimentation are a useful way of learning for managers about a counterpart's view of a particular relationship. Experimenting with inconsistencies at different times may also be a useful way for a manager to find out more about the perspective of a particular counterpart. Inconsistency in approach by using different members of staff who have different views or personal styles is also a common means of experimentation in interaction.

The importance of time and space in examining interaction outcomes leads to a reappraisal of the idea of managing in networks. Different relationships, activities, resources and actors are interconnected and are involved in a seamless flow of interaction over time. This means that it is effectively impossible to attribute a particular outcome to the actions of a particular manager. But, this also means that it is impossible to claim the opposite; that something is not an outcome of the actions of a particular manager! A business leader can often claim that a company is 'successful' because of the leader's decisions especially over a short period of time. However, apparent successes or failures in an interactive world are actually transitory phenomena that are the subject of multiple causes and are simply more or less arbitrary points in a moving landscape of interaction. Thus, the relationship between outcomes and managers is very much a question of creating 'stories' or 'who is writing the notes'!

Networking

Interaction is a constant process of action and reaction involving activities, actors and resources. Interaction is substantive. It is the process through which individual resources, activities and actors confront each other and through which they are modified and take their form. Interaction and its outcomes may be unplanned and unintentional. But interaction is also the process through which managers seek to achieve their aims. We refer to conscious attempts to affect interaction as *networking*.

Networking is therefore at the core of management in the business landscape. Networking in a simple dyad is based on the intentions of the management of each actor as they initiate and respond, respond and initiate, and so on. Managers choose what to do in their interaction and attach meanings to what is done. The ideas of managers are translated into substantive networking that may include the delivery of a product or service, payment, changes to activities, investments in resources, assignment of personnel, as well as orders, requests, instructions and verbal or other forms of communication. Of course the meaning attached to any networking by the manager is interpreted by a counterpart, whether deliberately or not. This interpretation then forms the basis of the counterpart's response, which is expressed through its networking. All companies are simultaneously networking intensively with some, and occasionally with many, counterparts and the totality of the interaction process in the network consists of all the intended, unintended and incidental juxtaposing of activities, actors and resources across the network. Views of this networking, then, form part of the evolving network pictures of each of the involved managers. A manager may attempt to network in the same way with more than one counterpart, for example by delivering an apparently identical offering to each one. But the outcome of that networking is always specific and dependent on the meanings ascribed to it by a particular counterpart and the specific interaction to which it leads.

Because interaction is a process over time, all networking is a response to a pre-existing situation. Thus any apparently initial action or initiative by a manager can usually be read as a reaction to a pre-existing situation. Networking is a continuing struggle within which the managers in the network seek to work with, against and in spite of others to achieve their aims and their desired changes to the pre-existing situation. Networking involves a manager in analysing and responding to the actions of specific others in specific situations and anticipating the possible reactions of specific others to its own actions. The existence of a structure of interdependencies and relationships in the network means that the incidence of this 'responsive networking' is likely to outweigh the incidence of a supposedly original 'managerial initiative'.

The three dimensions of managing that have been identified above: network pictures, network outcomes and networking are all interconnected. Thus, a manager's network picture forms the basis for networking that leads to specific outcomes. However, the network picture also influences the way that the manager interprets the outcomes of networking. Similarly, we have emphasized that all networking is a response to a pre-existing situation or the outcome of previous interactions. These outcomes influence the manager's network picture and networking. Finally, a

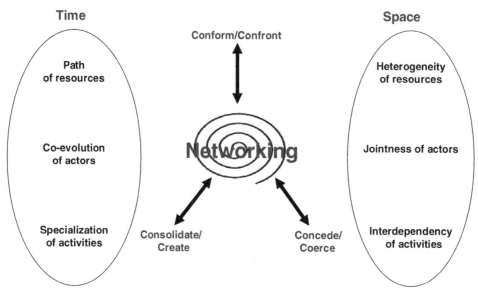

Figure 9.2   A model of business networking.

manager's individual networking influences the outcome of the interaction within a relationship and leads to a modification of the manager's network picture.

Networking in Business Networks

We can now develop the idea of networking further by examining some basic patterns that seem to comprise the essence of management in the network world. We build on the idea of interaction and the descriptive model of interaction that we presented in Chapter 3; the work on how actors interact in Chapter 7; and the network paradoxes and the dimensions of managing in networks already introduced in this chapter. We combine all this with three patterns in networking (see Figure 9.2):

- the behaviour in existing relationships, which involves *confronting* and *conforming* towards business partners;
- the position of the company with regard to combinations of relationships, *consolidating* current relationships and *creating* new relationships or changing the pattern of existing ones;
- intentional behaviour that involves attempts to influence or *coerce* and to follow or *concede* to business partners.

Table 9.2 describes each of these networking options in their pairs.

Even if there is a contradiction in these word pairs, we see that each company is likely to be involved in all these patterns but in different ways at any point in time.

Table 9.2   Managerial options in networking.

Option	Purpose
CONFRONT	Seek specific changes within existing relationships.
CONFORM	Keep the status quo in specific aspects of existing relationships.
CREATE	Develop network position by building new relationships or altering the balance between existing relationships.
CONSOLIDATE	Maintain network position by developing involvement in existing relationships.
COERCE	Direct specific aspects of interaction in accordance with own intent.
CONCEDE	Follow the intents of others in specific aspects of interaction.

Existing Relationships: Confront or Conform?

The dominant situation in which managing takes place in business networks is within the existing business relationships between actors, within the small world. These relationships would include those between a company and its direct customers, its suppliers and those with which it cooperates in order to reach other companies or to develop particular activities, resources or the companies themselves. In existing relationships, a manager is involved in networking and may choose to *confront* (seek to change) some aspects of the relationship while choosing to *conform* to the evolving status quo in other aspects. Similarly, both sides in a relationship have to respond to the networking of the counterpart as it confronts some issues and conforms to others. These managerial choices are based on the managers' network pictures and on their experience of previous networking and its outcomes. These choices involve far more than simply agreeing or disagreeing with a counterpart. Both confronting and conforming have immediate implications for the interfaces between the resources and activities of the two companies and each choice contributes to the cumulative evolution of a relationship.

Figure 9.2 relates these choices to the unique position in time and space in which networking takes place. Confronting and conforming may take place between numbers of managers in the two interacting companies as they network on a day-to-day or month-to-month basis. This networking takes place within the overall position of the relationship in the network as defined in the model by the relative jointness of the two actors, the specific situation and heterogeneity of their resources and the interdependence of their activities. Many day-to-day managerial choices in a relationship are likely to centre on the current activities of the two actors. For example, managers may have to decide when and how to produce, deliver, pay or assign staff to a specific activity. Similarly managers at monthly or quarterly meetings between companies have to decide whether to confront issues such as stock or service levels, pricing or whether to conform to the existing patterns of interaction.

Of course conforming and confronting are aspects facing both parties in a dyad and each is equally concerned with its interpretations of and reactions to the actions of counterparts.

For example, it is common for both actors in a relationship to assess the benefits and costs of the absolute and relative interdependencies in particular relationships with major customers or suppliers. They will also try to judge what may be achieved immediately in a relationship through confrontation, what has to be accepted currently and what adaptations can be attempted at some point in the *recursive time* marked by scheduled meetings or reviews, particular projects or deliveries. But an equally important aspect of networking is the willingness to accept or conform to other issues, even when these are not ideal, such as quality (however defined), frequencies and routines. Both conforming and confronting involve intention and an actor is likely to have aspirations to confront some aspects of a specific interaction process at the same time as it wants to conform to some other aspects. A problem of managing for the business actor is that it is often tempting to focus too much on confrontation in order to demonstrate managerial machismo. But it may be much more important to demonstrate and communicate conformation. One reason for this is that much of conforming occurs through the undramatic, successive development of routines, which take place both within and between actors and which contribute to the development of their relationship.

As well as a unique position in space, interaction takes place at a particular point in time. Therefore short-term actions within a single dyadic relationship build on what has happened in that relationship previously. These actions also contribute to the overall evolution of the relationship through time. The model expresses this evolution in terms of the *path* followed by the resources involved in the relationship; the increasing or decreasing *specialization* of the activities towards a particular counterpart; and the *co-evolution* of the actors concerned. Thus an important aspect of management in business networks is the realization that short-term relationship actions to conform or confront are all part of the long-term evolution of a relationship. Each confrontation or conformation that relates to a particular transaction is thus simply a single episode in the continuing process of interaction. This connection between the short and long term means that both business researchers and managers seeking to analyse the dynamics of a relationship need to separate the 'waves' of day-to-day interaction from the 'tide' that is running within a relationship.

The ability to manage the connection between short-term tactics and long-term strategy is likely to require good financial information on both the costs and benefits of immediate choices. Perhaps more importantly, management in networks requires extensive information on the long-term capital and revenue issues surrounding relationships, viewed as the primary assets of a company. The value of sound financial information needs to be tempered by an awareness of the limitations of any attempts to model network outcomes!

It is clearly important for a single company to both conform and confront in its interactions. It has to design a large number of activities in such a way that they conform to the activities of important counterparts and it has to react to the attempts of others to confront aspects of their relationship. But it is also important for the manager to confront some aspects of the current interaction in order to achieve efficiency in activities and to create a development path for its resources.

The question of when to conform or to confront relates closely to the first network paradox: Each company needs others to achieve its own aims but has to find ways to accommodate the aims of the others on which it depends. Hence each company has to analyse, discuss and find ways of working with others that can accommodate both conforming and confronting. One common way is to form project groups with counterparts. These can provide a particular mix of confronting and conforming. Without managerial attention to the interplay between conforming and confronting, interaction can degenerate into a situation with periods of undramatic conformation interspersed by dramatic confrontations. If that occurs then many of the efforts expended by both companies during both phases are wasted.

Relationship Combinations: Consolidate or Create?

The second aspect of networking for a business actor concerns the interconnections between the different interaction processes in which it is engaged. All actors attempt to manage and vary their interactions and relationships. Here we use the terms *consolidate* and *create* to capture these attempts. They lead to a number of considerations for an actor. For example:

- How should an actor differentiate between its expectations of particular relationships?
- How should an actor determine its relative attention to existing and potential relationships and allocate resources between them?
- What is the interface between interaction in any one of the relationships of an actor and the actor's overall position and its other relationships in the network. How should the actor capitalize on this interface or attempt to change it?

These considerations tend to have a longer time horizon than the more short-term pattern of confrontation or conformation. Changes in network position are likely to be slow, costly and involve changes in a number of relationships, some of which may be unplanned and unanticipated.

There are reasons for a business actor to be at least as concerned with the resources of others as it is with its own. All managers face questions about resource investments and interplay between multiple counterparts and about how the heterogeneity of these resources is manifested in interaction with their own. Similarly, managers face questions about the long-term effects of the interdependence of the activities on others. They are also concerned with the implications of their jointness with specific counterparts on their interaction with others.

The usefulness and value of specific relationship assets are relative measures. Both are determined by the 'interactive investments' made by the two counterparts and by the connection between those relationship assets and other relationships. Similarly, the usefulness and value of specific relationship assets are not constant over time. These assets are affected by the long-term path followed by the heterogeneous resources invested in it, by the evolving specialization of the activities of the two parties and by the co-evolution of the actors themselves.

Hence managers face choices in their networking of when and how to *consolidate* their involvement in their existing interaction processes and when and how to *create* new interaction and relationships and exploit relationship investment in new ways.

Managers consolidate their company's existing relationships in a number of ways, all of which involve networking with counterparts: First, they may try to access their own or others existing resources more effectively. This may involve them in confronting in particular relationships, rationalizing between relationships or reducing overall resource investment. But it may also involve them in developing new resources or in connecting existing resources better to each other. Secondly, managers may seek to specialize their company's activities more closely to some of their existing relationships, for example by tailoring their service provision to the requirements of particular customers. Alternatively, consolidation on existing relationships may involve a manager in rationalizing and systematizing its company's relationships with several counterparts through standardization. Thirdly, managers may seek through networking to build the feeling of jointness in the relationships to important counterparts. Consolidation is a dynamic process and involves managers in continuously conforming and confronting different aspects of their company's relationships. Consolidation often increases the 'heaviness' of the resources and activities involved in a relationship. Consolidation may increase the intensity of interaction in a relationship and raise the interdependencies between the companies, as was exemplified by the Ducati case study in Chapter 7.

In contrast, creation is the process through which a manager attempts to build relationships with new counterparts or alter the balance between existing ones. In other words, creation involves a manager in trying to change its company's role or position in the network in relation to its portfolio of counterparts. Creation may involve alterations to the particular problems which existing relationships address. It may involve major investments to develop new activities and build new resources or to alter those in existing relationships. Creation may involve shifts in the co-evolution that has taken place between existing counterparts and lead to the development of new interdependencies with others. Creation may be quite radical and involve a manager in attempts to change the company's position in the wider network; for example, the company may start to sell directly to end users, rather than using intermediaries, or give responsibility to a single supplier to source a range of its requirements from companies with which it previously dealt directly.

Rather like the pattern to confront or conform, managers in most business situations have to work hard at both consolidating and creating. Each manager has to consolidate within the company's existing interaction processes and at the same time plan and create different ones. In some cases, for example in the automotive industry, it is almost possible to identify two co-existing but different networks, one dealing with the regular daily deliveries that centre on existing models and another that is concerned with long-term developments that may be delivered in 2–5 years time. These long-term developments probably require that relationships are developed and new resources are exploited. Thus, a future network of interconnected relationships is developed while the current one is utilized. Consolidation is crucial for successive economizing of the combined interaction processes in which a company is engaged. Creation is central to the development of successive changes of the combined interaction processes to create new combinations from which it is subsequently possible to economize.

Consolidating and creating are usually handled quite differently in companies. Consolidation is continuous and involves incremental change on a daily basis. Creation may be project-based and experimental. Creation takes time. The time from first contact to first order from a new customer may be measured in months or years. A similar time could be taken from first enquiry to first delivery. Throughout this time, both companies are likely to have been investing time and money. Both are likely to have a negative cash flow from their relationship for many months or years. It is likely that the time from first contact to the time when the benefits to the customer outweigh its costs or the time when the supplier makes a 'profit' in the relationship are measured in years. This situation is more extreme in industries, such as aerospace, in which it is common for a supplier to receive revenue from a customer only when that customer makes sales or even when it achieves profitability in its relationships with third parties. The extent of resource investment involved in developing particular relationships limits both the extent of the change that can be created and its range across multiple companies.

Consolidation and creation each involve a particular organizational form within a business actor and a particular pattern of interaction between companies. Each can cause conflict with the other. Thus, attempts to create new relationship patterns can adversely affect existing interaction processes. These adverse effects may occur because of the way that current counterparts interpret the moves of a company as well as because of the actual effects of a change on prevailing interaction. Similarly, existing interaction patterns and the investments of counterparts in them may limit the ability of a company to achieve change. An explanation for this is indicated by the second network paradox: Co-evolution between companies is a major determinant of the characteristics of the companies themselves and of the relationships with which they are familiar and which they have the skills to manage. Relationship building involves time, resources and skills. Hence, the relationships that an actor is able to establish are likely to be similar to the ones that it already has.

Approaches to Networking: Coerce or Concede?

The first two patterns of networking to confront or conform and to create or consolidate concern the substance of interaction: the activities and resources involved in it and the interdependencies and relationships between the companies. The third pattern of networking is more concerned with *how* interacting managers perceive each other and how those perceptions affect the way they interact. This third pattern concerns the managerial choices of whether and when to attempt to *coerce* a counterpart in a particular direction and when to *concede* to the counterpart's wishes.

When we discussed the third network paradox, we suggested that each actor in a network tries to control its relationships with others, as far as it is able, in a direction that suits its own perceived requirements. Thus, it is natural to expect that a manager would wish to coerce the counterparts' views of their interaction so that the relationship develops in the direction that the manager believes is 'best'.

But within any interaction there is a variation in the positions held by actors in the network; in their relationships; in the resources they hold or have access to; in their knowledge of particular aspects of the network and in their specific technical and commercial expertise. The network position of an actor puts limits on the extent that each company can or should try to coerce another. One obvious reason for a manager to concede to the wishes of a counterpart in at least some aspects of their interaction is because interaction has to provide benefits for both parties, at least in the long term.[4]

A second reason for a manager to limit attempts to follow a coercive approach towards its counterparts is because there are always likely to be companies that have much stronger positions in the network and who may coerce others to follow their logic. However, even the companies in the strongest physical or financial position face problems in exercising this power.

---

[4]The idea of conceding to the needs of a counterpart in at least some aspects of a business relationship is neatly exemplified in the Japanese saying that it is wrong to 'break the other man's rice bowl'.

This brings us to the third and most important limit on actors' attempts to coerce counterparts. Business interaction enables a company to capitalize on intellectual, relational and other resources and on the experience of a counterpart. Companies frequently concede to the advice, leadership or instruction of others, such as when a supplier produces a product to a customer's own design (known as 'make to print'); when a supplier makes choices for a customer in the design or implementation of the offering it supplies; or when a particular company exercises price or technological leadership in a particular area. Mutual concession to the expertise of others is an important aspect of the interdependencies that develop between companies. The specialization by interacting actors in particular resources and activities enables each to invest in complementary areas and to maximize the return on those investments in a number of their relationships.

In contrast, an attempt by a manager to influence or *coerce* a counterpart in a particular direction inevitably restricts the involvement of that counterpart in the decision that is taken. An attempt to coerce a counterpart infers that the influencer knows what should happen. But one manager is unlikely to have this expensively acquired wisdom in all aspects of a relationship. More generally, if a company exercises control over other companies across an area of the network then the controlling company becomes the only point at which new initiatives can arise. This situation is likely to restrict the evolution of that part of the network to the detriment of those involved, particularly in the case of the 'controlling company'.[5]

The choice of when to coerce or concede is similar to the previous two patterns: Managers are likely to be simultaneously coercing and conceding in each of their interactions. It is important for managers to focus on particular aspects of their interactions for which they wish to coerce or concede, to lead or follow, to teach or learn from counterparts. The balance between choosing to lead or follow is frequently made by individual managers on the basis of their understanding of relevant technologies or knowledge of other directly or indirectly connected relationships. Both conceding and coercing affect the evolution of resources and activities and capability and the actor's position on particular dimensions of the network. The approaches to coercing and conceding by different counterparts are important ingredients in the development of both their small worlds as well as how this relates to the larger network. The patterns of coercion or concession, teaching or learning, following or leading are subtle and complex, and the approach to them is likely to be different between managers in a single company at the same time. For example, the technical or operations staff may concede to the knowledge of a particular customer or supplier whilst marketing, sales or purchasing staff attempt to coerce the same counterparts in the directions that they think are appropriate.

The pattern of coercing and conceding is also likely to vary over time: It is common in the early stages of a company's life or when it is facing a new type of problem for there to be a considerable gap between its knowledge and that of the counterparts with which it works. This gap may involve particular knowledge or abilities or may relate to the overall abilities of the company.

---

[5] This phenomenon provides an explanation for the problems encountered by companies that have achieved a large measure of control over the network. Examples include the retailer Marks & Spencer, which exercised considerable control over a small number of large suppliers that worked to its designs and its mandated procedures. Similar situations have arisen in the past with IBM and Toyota.

In this situation, the company's counterparts are likely to be providing problem-solving abilities and leading the company to a solution. However, over time the situation can be reversed so that a company is able to coerce its counterparts in particular areas. This evolutionary process has been common in the relationships between large retailers and some of their suppliers.

Conclusion

This chapter started from the premise that management in a network-like business landscape is rather different from the view of the mainstream management literature. However, it has not provided a coherent idea of the nature of managing a company in a network-like business landscape. Instead, we have attempted to outline some features of a rather fuzzy view of management that has emerged from our research. Inevitably, we have been influenced by our own preconceptions that have been derived from the conventional views of the active independent manager and of business marketing and purchasing strategy.

Managing in the business network is a process of conscious intervention or 'networking' in business relationships. Networking builds on the basis provided by the interdependent activities and heterogeneous resources associated with 'joint' actors. The work and aims of business managers centre on the functioning of existing relationships and the evolution and interconnections between multiple relationships. These relationships include those in which the manager is closely or more distantly involved. Managing in the business network involves working with, against and through others. It involves being led by others as well as attempts to lead. Managing in the business network is not an individual activity.

What are the main differences between this view and the views described in Chapter 8? The conventional view of business strategy is actor-centred. It sees the world as composed of independent actors that are assumed to be in perpetual competition with each other and are led by managers that develop and implement their own strategies for that competition. A conclusion from our research is that such a complete actor-centric view is both unrealistic and damaging. An interactive view of the business actor starts from the position of interdependence and acknowledges that the borderline between a company and its counterparts is diffuse and problematic from the point of view of both analysis and management control. This borderline becomes more of an arena for building interfaces between companies in a network world, rather than the dividing line between separate coordinating mechanisms, as in the market approach. At this border, value creation develops and resources and activities interact and are developed. It is here changes take place and where the company's position is defined and redefined.

But there is of course an actor-centric dimension to managing in the business network. Networking involves a particular position of a company in the network and is the major way that it can be changed. A company's position is made up of its immediate relationships and the access they provide to other relationships, resources, actors and activities. Networking involves working in those existing relationships and creating new ones to develop a company's interface with many resources and activities in order to achieve what may be called a 'strategic' change in its position. But strategizing in the interactive world is not an individual activity. It is something that occurs within the manager's networking with others and is intimately connected to their networking and their strategizing.

The managerial process that leads to the development of strategy in the network takes place across companies. Strategizing for the single firm is concerned with assessing what is feasible within an existing network position. Managers try to anticipate the actions and reactions of others. Strategizing for a single firm is concerned with the direction of relationship evolution, to consolidate or create, and with initiatives seeking to change position within the relationship structure. But strategizing also has to be concerned with coping with the networking initiatives or confrontations of others. Strategizing in a single firm involves conceding to the leadership or teaching of others as well as attempting to coerce others in at least some of the aspects of their interaction. Strategizing takes place within a structure of interdependencies and involves exploitation of one's own interdependencies and those of others. Analysis of the outcomes of strategy and the basis for future strategy extend beyond the company itself. Strategic outcomes are manifested in the activity patterns, resource constellations and webs of actors in which all companies operate.

It is difficult as well as unwise for a company to consider itself as a single entity or a single centre in a situation where its different relationships are its most important arenas and the receptacle of joint capabilities. In the same way that a company has multiple 'identities' in the minds of multiple counterparts, so it has multiple positions in its interactions.

A 'full-faced environment' of interaction with a few significant counterparts cannot be handled from one centre within a company and certainly not if issues that arise at a company's boundary are simply seen as inconveniences by those inside it. The internal structure of a company has to mirror the network world and must have well developed internal processes connecting different relationships with each other and with important internal resources. That means that an important issue for the manager is how to communicate and cope with an emergent, complex environment that defies understanding within a multi-centred organization. Coping in networks is less a problem of internal organization and more a problem of relating the 'not-really-internal' to the 'not-really-external' and to the company's position among others in multiple relationships.

This view of the interacting company and of managing in networks also has important consequences for the notionally 'internal' coordination of a company. The normal situation in business interaction is that there are several overlapping, virtual centres within a company that correspond to important relationships. The interactions of these centres are likely to be mainly with counterparts in other companies, but they are also involved in internal bargaining with other centres for resource and activity allocation and development. These centres function quite differently depending on the particular situation and evolution in the specific relationship that each of them serve.

The idea of the interacting actor poses particular problems for the internal accounting of a company. The development of a business relationship has its own internal logic that does not necessarily fit within conventional accounting periods or, more importantly, fit within the operating and capital costing and revenue categorization of a company. For example, in situations where a new product is being developed between companies, then conventional accounting has to cope with questions of the relative contributions of the participants: Who is doing what and providing what? at what time? to whom? And, indeed, who is the customer, intermediary or supplier at any one time and over time? Answers to these questions have to be set against complex and perhaps ephemeral returns at different times from that product and relationship as well as other related products and relationships. More generally, current accounting has difficulty in coping with intangible relationship investments and, more critically, assessing relationship value. For these reasons, we are likely to see the development of more qualitative assessments of micro- and macro-position within a network, rather than with simpler views of market share, margin or operating profit.

This chapter represents a call for research into the difference between the world that managers, politicians and commentators imagine and the world in which they actually live. Our studies call for research into the ways in which managers structure situations for the purposes of their own analysis and into the connections between a company and the activity patterns, actor webs and resource constellations in which it operates. We also need to develop our understanding of the way that conforming and confronting interaction within specific relationships connects with the consolidation and creation processes of change and development of combinations of relationships. We need to learn much more about the connections between parallel interaction processes that involve different individuals in the same companies. We also need to learn more about the processes of co-evolution between companies and how companies lead, follow, coerce and concede with the network as a whole.

EVOLUTION OF THE BUSINESS LANDSCAPE

10

The aim of this chapter is to examine how an interactive perspective can shed light on the dynamics of the business landscape and particularly on how these dynamics may be analysed and researched. We begin the chapter by looking at the predominant ideas on the evolution of business that are found in business literature and we try to clarify the connection between these ideas and the prescriptions that are advanced in 'business recipes' about how business *should* be organized. This analysis leads us to question the mainstream idea of the dynamics of economic organization. In particular, we use examples to highlight reservations about the view that network-like organization is a *new* phenomenon. Instead, we argue that this type of organization has in fact been an intrinsic part of the business landscape throughout previous periods, such as when 'the invisible hand' (based on market exchange) and 'the visible hand' (hierarchical governance in the integrated modern business enterprise) are assumed to have been ruling. We use this network view to provide further insights into the evolutionary processes of business.

Introduction

In Chapter 1, we discussed the role of basic metaphors concerning life in the business landscape. We concluded that the view of this life and of the behaviour of those living in the landscape is very different if it is perceived in terms of a rainforest or a jungle. In Chapters 2–9, we have tried to provide an understanding of what happens in this landscape as interpreted from an industrial network perspective. One of the central conclusions from this analysis is that the business landscape is in constant evolution. Resource constellations become modified through the recombining of resources and changes in their interfaces. Activity patterns are reorganized as single activities are adjusted and the coordination mechanisms among them are altered. Also the webs of actors undergo major modifications owing to mergers, acquisitions, outsourcing, insourcing and changing business relationships. These dynamics present those involved in the business landscape with major challenges. Surviving in the evolving landscape requires an understanding of the nature of these dynamics and in this respect three issues become particularly important: the ways in which the landscape actually changes over time; what the changes mean for those living in the landscape and how they can behave in order to take advantage of the evolving conditions.

The aim of this chapter is to shed light on the dynamics of the business landscape and particularly on how this evolution may be analysed and researched. Business history has a lot to tell us about how the landscape changes over time. Following an initial discussion about time in the business landscape, we continue by presenting the predominant ideas about evolution of the business landscape in business history literature. In this exposé, we try to clarify the connection between these ideas and what the changes imply for those living in the landscape and for their behaviour. Companies have always been provided with prescriptions about what constitutes appropriate behaviour and how business should be organized. The contents of these recommendations have taken various directions during the evolution of business and here we relate to the literature about 'business recipes'. This analysis makes us question the mainstream perception of the dynamics of economic organization. In particular, we have reservations about the view that network-like organization is a new phenomenon that emerged in the late 1900s. On the basis of a re-interpretation of previously presented empirical examples, we conclude that this type of organizing has always been an intrinsic part of the business landscape. What is now identified as a network was also present throughout previous periods, both when 'the invisible hand' and the large hierarchies ('the visible hand') are assumed to have been ruling the behaviour of companies. The final part of the chapter is devoted to a network analysis of business evolution, where we relate to concepts and models discussed in previous chapters of this book.

The objective of this scrutiny is not to say that a view focusing on the network-like aspects of the business landscape provides a better or more valid framing of business evolution. What we suggest is that a network perspective offers an alternative interpretation of history and supports our main argument that various governance mechanisms and organizing forms always co-exist in the business landscape.

Time and the Business Landscape

We have emphasized in previous chapters that time is a main feature of the landscape of companies, relationships and networks. In particular, we have highlighted the crucial role of time in the processes of interaction, implying that what takes place between two actors in a specific episode is conditioned by their interactions in previous episodes and by their expectations about future interaction. We have also tried to show that patterns of activities; constellations of resources and the connections between actors are all firmly rooted in the past and in a continuing process of evolution.

Hence, activity patterns are constantly rearranged and modified in this evolutionary process to enable them to function according to the changing requirements of the actors involved. Resource constellations evolve through the recombining of resources and adjustments in their interfaces as outcomes of technical and other developments. Business actors themselves change in line with this evolution and as new firms are born and others disappear. Business relationships develop over time and these changes impact on the operations of the actors in the business landscape. Aspirations for resource control and other strategic objectives of actors evolve as well and this, in turn, impacts on the overall structure of the landscape over time. Actors continually interpret the outcomes of their own behaviour and the actions of others and these interpretations impact on their future conduct as actors learn from history.

The enormous complexity of business processes and structures means that there can never be a single universal understanding of the evolution of the business landscape. Therefore, various observers interpret the changes and their causes, directions and effects differently. Despite this diversity, it seems obvious that some images of the evolution get more widespread attention than others. They may represent shifts that are highly visible in terms of new companies and techniques or that are significant from an economic point of view and therefore they are described, analysed and documented. These images, whether they represent the most important dynamics of business or not, tend to become manifest as *the* account of history. It is these narratives that form perceptions of how the landscape is changing.

Business history narratives tend to portray the evolution of the landscape as the continuous development of ever-more efficient forms of economic organization. Hence, these narratives have an impact on what is perceived as appropriate behaviour and so they become manifest as 'business recipes' (Spender 1989).[1] Therefore, there is a strong interplay between these dominant interpretations of business evolution and the prevailing recipes for how business should be organized (Gadde and Araujo 2007). For example, there is currently widespread attention to a narrative that suggests that the business landscape has become increasingly like a network in recent decades. It is further assumed that this transformation imposes dramatically changed conditions for the functioning and managing of firms and thus calls for a new business recipe. The attention to the idea of network-like change is also reinforced by the tendency that we have pointed to in this book for those involved in the business landscape to see its continuing changes as more dramatic than ever before.

At a particular point in time, the predominant perspective on the business landscape and its current development rests on two pillars:

- observable changes of business behaviour; for example, the apparently increasing willingness by many companies to outsource activities that they previously carried out for themselves;
- simultaneous adjustment of the frames through which the business landscape is observed and interpreted. Some of the ingredients in the currently evolving recipe are that companies should rely more on suppliers and apply a 'network approach' within which outsourcing is an appropriate prescription.

The interplay between the two pillars illustrates a general phenomenon: when business reality seems to change then the 'lenses' through which reality is viewed are affected and we are likely to modify our framing of reality accordingly. Actual changes of reality and modifications in the view of this reality tend to go together and the effects of the two are difficult to separate. Changes in what actually takes place makes us reinterpret our frames ('I believe it when I see it'). Once we have revised our frames, we tend to observe new things and interpret 'old' things in new ways ('I see it when I believe it').

Our claim is that historical analysis of the development of the business landscape tends to exaggerate actual changes. The business landscape and the frames through which it is examined

---

[1]Fligstein expresses these prescriptions in terms of 'world views that define one firm's relationship with others, what appropriate behaviour is for firms and how those kinds of organizations ought to work' (Fligstein 1990:295). According to Whitley (1992:125), business recipes are particular ways of 'organizing, controlling, and directing business enterprises that become institutionalised as the dominant form of business organisation' at particular times and locations.

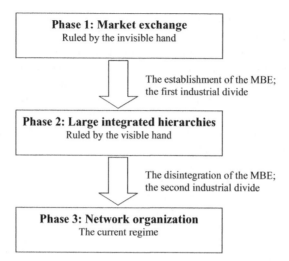

Figure 10.1   Evolution of the business landscape[2]

change together: Hindsight may make developments in the business landscape look more revolutionary than they actually were. Because of this, we tend to under-estimate the continuity that is an important underlying aspect of the evolution of the business landscape. On this basis, we question the stand-point that networks are new phenomena. In our view, they have always been an important feature of the reality out there. But they have been more or less hidden because of the particular lenses and business recipes that have been the dominant frameworks for observation and interpretation of reality.

Therefore we argue for reinterpretation of the evolution of the business landscape as it is described and analysed in mainstream narratives. In particular, we believe that the changes that have been defined as a transformation from 'self-regulating markets' (Biggart and Hamilton 1992:483) to the large hierarchy represented by the integrated modern business enterprise (Chandler 1977), and on to the current network form of economic organizing are more the outcome of a powerful narrative than an intrinsic characteristic of the business landscape.

The first step in our re-interpretation is to provide an account of the basic narrative of business evolution.

Narrative of the Evolution of Economic Organization

The mainstream narrative of the evolution of economic organization distinguishes between three phases characterized by different governance forms, separated by two main transformations as described in Figure 10.1.

This narrative of business evolution suggests that the two transformations occurred because they improved the conditions for exploitation of new opportunities provided through technical

---

[2]The idea of the 'industrial divide' was introduced by Piore and Sabel (1984).

development. The prevailing form of economic organization at any time is assumed to have been less appropriate for its task when new conditions emerged. For example, Miles and Snow (1992:53) are advocates of this view when they argue that new organizational forms 'arise to correct the principal deficiencies of the forms currently in use'. Hence, the large industrial enterprises, such as Ford and General Motors, are claimed to have evolved more than 100 years ago as a response to particular problems associated with market exchange and the 'invisible hand' regime of Adam Smith's days. Chandler (1977) provides a thorough explanation of the advantages accompanying the 'visible hand' of managerial coordination in the large hierarchical firm, the 'modern business enterprise' (MBE). Similarly, within the perspective of this same narrative, network organization is perceived to have emerged as a tool for solving some of the problems associated with the large hierarchies. Our presentation of the historical development according to the mainstream narrative focuses on some of the characteristics of the MBE: the reasons for its rise; its basic features and functioning; the problems related to this governance form; and, finally, its fall.

Rise of the Modern Business Enterprise

Economic organization following the Industrial Revolution in the late 18th century has been characterized as 'self-regulating markets based on firm autonomy' (Biggart and Hamilton 1992:483). The shift from this 'invisible hand' governance to the 'visible hand' regime of the large hierarchical enterprise is framed by Chandler's analysis of the development of some major US corporations (Chandler 1977, 1990). The MBE is portrayed as a result of 'the integration of the processes of mass production with those of mass distribution within a single firm' (Chandler 1977:285). The initial step in the creation of the MBE was investment in production facilities large enough to achieve scale and scope, because in capital-intensive industries high throughput is needed in order to maintain a minimum efficient scale. Exploiting the potential benefits from mass production required careful coordination of the flow through the processes of production in the factory. In fact, Chandler (1977) claimed that these 'economies of speed' were more crucial for manufacturing efficiency than economies of scale. Thus, the ability to integrate and coordinate the flow of materials through the plant was more important than the size of the factory and the subdivision of work within the plant. This coordination, in turn, demanded the constant attention of a managerial team or hierarchy.

The second step, which often occurred simultaneously, was the investment in product-specific marketing, distribution, and purchasing resources. Speculative mass production required product standardization, advertising and mass distribution. This was only made possible through a revolution in transportation and communication. Railways, steamships and streetcars dramatically changed the conditions for the physical transportation of goods and people. Moreover, the development of equipment for efficient information exchange such as the telegraph, telephone and postal services provided the means for coordination of the operations of the large hierarchies.

The economies of scale and scope that are potentially available are contingent on the physical characteristics of production facilities. The economies of scale and scope that in fact materialize are determined by actual throughput: They rely on organizational features and 'depend on knowledge, skill, experience, and teamwork – on the organized human capabilities essential to exploit the potential of technological progress' (Chandler 1990:25). Therefore, the MBE has been interpreted as an outcome of the combined effects of technological and organizational changes. For example, North (1981:169) claimed that organizational innovations of various types 'induced the technical change which in turn required further organizational innovation to realise the potential of the new technology'. Similarly, Englander (1988:352) argued that 'technological knowledge is acquired and diffused within changing institutional settings while at the same time technological change creates the opportunity and the necessity to change institutions'.[3]

Main Drivers Behind the Modern Business Enterprise

According to Piore and Sabel (1984), mass-production techniques put in place by the MBE replaced existing craft systems based on small firms employing skilled workers and general-purpose machinery. The financial impact of the shift to mass production was substantial. Ford's relentless pursuit of mass production and distribution to expand the market for cars by reducing prices enabled it to reach the majority of US consumers (Lamoreaux et al. 2003). The main determinant of cost reductions were savings in assembly and component manufacturing. According to Langlois and Robertson (1995), these greater savings were achieved by internalizing the production of components. The advantages of this shift were primarily related to the large-scale capabilities that could be developed in-house (e.g. in metal cutting), the larger lot-size production made possible through increased sales, and the previously mentioned economies of speed.

Another driving force was concerned with the opportunities for innovation. Firms in the existing craft system normally 'handled only a single economic function, dealt in a single product line and operated in one geographical area' (Chandler 1977:3). The activities of these small, personally owned and managed enterprises needed coordination and monitoring. According to Chandler, this coordination was governed by market and price mechanisms, while the argument of Piore and Sabel is that economic outcome in these industries depended on cooperation among firms. Irrespective of the merits of each argument, prevailing conditions severely restricted innovation. Piore and Sabel (1984:3) argued that unless the potential economies from innovation could be 'shared among firms and between capitalists and workers, those who stood to lose from change defended their interests by blocking it'.

Thus, conditions in the business landscape at the time were not conducive to innovation. The larger the number of firms that needed to be mobilized for a major change, the more difficult it was to promote innovation. For example, it was problematic for a potential innovator in the car industry to change the basic design of the vehicle because car assemblers relied on a huge cadre of unconnected suppliers. A further aspect of this complexity was that these suppliers were involved in other businesses which were perceived by them as more important. This was the case because early vehicles were 'put together from components developed for other purposes, such as bicycle wheels or from variations on known themes, such as wooden bodies' (Langlois and Robertson 1995:47). Piore and Sabel (1984:10) return to Adam Smith's analysis of the advantages of the 'partial pin-makers' concentration on a narrower range of tasks', which allowed them to perfect

_____

[3]These views are in line with our discussion about the interplay between physical and organizational resources.

their skills faster and waste less time switching operations than whole-pin makers. However, these same conditions have severe drawbacks as 'the more tasks were subdivided and connected in a precise sequence, the more difficult it became for the network as a whole to produce anything but pins'. Therefore, when firms in the automotive industry wanted to innovate and design cars from 'scratch', rather than assembling components that had been developed for other purposes, they 'found that their inspiration and needs outstripped the talents of their suppliers' (Langlois and Robertson 1995:46). The capabilities required for redesign of the car were not available in the current supplier network and had to be developed in-house.

Integration in the Hierarchy

Langlois and Robertson (1995) argue that systemic innovations, such as the development of the Model T Ford, sometimes force innovating firms to integrate forwards or backwards and become involved in tasks that they would actually have preferred to delegate to other companies. One explanation may be that suppliers literally cannot understand what the innovators want or they do not find the innovation commercially viable from their perspective. Therefore, in situations where many different elements of a system must be changed simultaneously, Langlois (2003) prescribes vertical integration and centralized ownership as a means to overcome the 'narrow vision and inadequate capabilities' of unconnected suppliers.

There are many examples related to the development of the large hierarchies that illustrate this claim, such as General Electric's integration with power-generating companies in order to make sure that 'power-generating capacity was planned to coincide with the distribution of lamps produced by the manufacturing process' (Piore and Sabel 1984:38). Similar benefits were achieved through vertical integration in the meat industry in the 1930s. A redesign of the arrangements for packing, shipping, and distribution of meat would make it possible to establish a 'high-throughput slaughterhouse' (Langlois 2003:361). Obtaining these benefits, however, called for huge investments in terms of refrigerated railcars and a nationwide network of properly equipped branch operations for storing and merchandising. The entrepreneurial innovator in this industry found it to be a better strategy to integrate into these complementary stages 'than to persuade the various asset owners to cooperate with him through the market' (Langlois 2003:363).

Langlois (2004) concludes that in the car industry, it was easier for Ford to mass manufacture parts than to try to teach techniques of mass production to its suppliers. In one respect, Ford could not actually teach its suppliers what it did not know yet itself. Mass production involved a lengthy process of learning by trial and error. In short, the greater and more complex the technical interdependencies in industrial production, the more vertical integration featured as the appropriate vehicle to change the whole arrangement.

Table 10.1 summarizes how the MBE configuration contributed to efficiency and innovation in the business landscape. It also shows the relationship features that developed in the MBE and considerably reduced the advantages of the integrated hierarchy over time.

The benefits of the large hierarchy when it came to innovation and restructuring of the industry configuration were obvious and over time 'industry after industry came under domination of giant firms using specialized equipment to turn out previously unimagined numbers of standard goods, at prices that local producers could not meet' (Piore and Sabel 1984:8). The success of the MBE

Table 10.1 The main drivers and consequences of integration in the hierarchical modern business enterprise.

Driver of change	Solution in the hierarchy	Relationship features
Efficiency: Cost reductions were required to increase sales.	Mass production replaced handicraft operations which enhanced economies of scale.	Massive standardization: • problems to customize • suppliers held at arm's length
Innovation: Problematic to reorganize activities since they were scattered among many firms.	Insourcing of design and production activities made it possible to modify both products and processes.	Arm's length relationships: • limited supplier interaction • problems with access to expanding supplier resources

thus established an ideal for economic organization and its ingredients became manifest as *the* business recipe of the time (Gadde and Araujo 2007).

Decline of the Modern Business Enterprise

Apparently, the dominance of the MBE recipe was not to last for ever; in the 1980s, the prescription became problematic. The crisis was particularly evident in the case of conglomerates, large businesses assembled through unrelated diversification, which became increasingly difficult to manage in the face of capital market scepticism towards this organizational form (Lamoreaux *et al.* 2003). Changing conditions obviously made particular features of the large corporation more or less obsolete, despite the fact that this organizational form as late as in the 1960s had looked 'inevitable and invincible' (Langlois 2003:370). Over time, however, the MBE appeared as an 'organizational structure increasingly misaligned with economic realities'. This apparent misalignment paved the way for enhanced attention to network-like structures. The integrated hierarchy was thus replaced by a new ideal type characterized as 'organizations that rely on long-term interdependent relations with external parties; and extensive efforts to leverage capabilities across a wide range of activities' (Powell 2001:68). It was no longer a fruitful approach for the single company to try to control all important resources through ownership. These conditions modified the narrative of the evolution of the business landscape to include the second transformation and paved the way for a new business recipe favouring prescriptions associated with network organization.

Critical Views of the Dominant Narrative

The dominant narrative of the evolution of economic organization as summarized above has been questioned in various writings. For example, Sabel and Zeitlin do not share the common view that the first industrial divide represented a transition from a world of decentralized handicraft production to a world of concentrated factories in which specialized machines turned out standard products. They criticize this 'epochal' perspective, claiming that in reality 'the epochs are less epochal and the choices less stark' than is commonly reported (Sabel and Zeitlin 1997:4).

Several sources support this conclusion and it seems obvious that the real impact of the large hierarchy was less pronounced than is suggested by the main narrative. Even if the MBE concept spread across industries, it has been questioned whether the 'Fordist' model actually became the dominant form of social and economic organization as popular belief suggests (Whitaker 1992:196). Langlois and Robertson (1995:146) share this opinion and argue that 'only some industries were affected by gigantism and that small firms continued to operate in many sectors of the economy'. Moreover, Perrow (1981:441) claims that 'vertical integration did not take place in all cases where Chandler's explanation predicted that it would'. Piore and Sabel (1984:20) conclude that 'the victory of mass production never proved so complete as its early triumphs suggested it would be'. On the contrary, they argue, 'some firms in almost all industries and almost all firms in some industries continued to apply craft principles of production'.

One possible reason for the strong adherence to the MBE narrative and its associated business recipe is that it fitted well into the metaphor of the business landscape as a jungle. Survival in this landscape builds on the power of the individual resident and this power has to be generated from inside because other dwellers in the jungle cannot be relied upon.

Similarly, some of the basic assumptions concerning the evolution of the current epoch have also been questioned. For example, Whitaker (1992:197) hesitated about the actual occurrence of the second transformation about 10 years after it is supposed to have started. He expressed 'significant difficulties with the notion that some such fundamental shift is occurring' arguing that these proclamations rely on speculation and hyperbole, and are based on selective examples such as the networks surrounding companies such as Toyota and Nike.

It seems relevant therefore to reconsider the features prescribed in the dominant narrative of the evolution of the business landscape. The main emphasis of our efforts in this respect is concerned with a reinterpretation of the era of the modern business enterprise – its rise, its main characteristics, and its fall.

Re-interpreting Business Evolution

Our alternative framing of business evolution builds on empirical evidence presented in some of the sources mentioned above, but also on an interesting case study from other literature. This case illustrates an entrepreneurial undertaking in the early 1800s when two brothers established a company called New England Ice.

Case Study: New England Ice

In 1805, William and Frederic Tudor from Boston in New England invested in a scheme to harvest and export ice from the frozen winter lakes in their region to, among other places, the West Indies (Weightman 2002; Utterback 1994). The business grew considerably and, in 1856, they shipped about 150 000 tons of ice to US ports, such as Philadelphia, Charleston, Savannah, New Orleans and San Francisco, and to the Caribbean islands, Havana, Rio de Janeiro, Madras, Bombay and Hong Kong. Locally, an equal quantity was being used in New England for 'meat processors, dairy farmers, restaurants and hospitals' (Utterback 1994:146). What 50 years previously had been thought of as 'totally worthless' had been turned into an indispensable commodity, which perfectly illustrates our propositions about the heterogeneity and value of resources. The prosperous achievement of the Tudor brothers could be interpreted as the outcome of creative and planned action by self-organized entrepreneurs like Ford and thus yet another example of a powerful stand-alone strong actor in the business landscape. A shift in perspective and framing, however, uncovers another story.

To achieve their success, the brothers had to find ships willing to accept this curious cargo. Normally, a shipper would simply buy space on a vessel to ship his goods. In this case, however, ships' captains who carried mixed cargoes were not willing to have melting ice in the hold, with the risk of damaging the rest of their shipments. The Tudors therefore were forced to buy their own vessel to get their business started. The initial trips to Martinique and St. Pierre were not very successful as neither local storage nor potential users had been prepared. These conditions changed when shipments to Havana began in 1807, since the Havana café owners were shown how to use ice for chilled drinks and ice cream.

Continued work on insulating the ice was successful and, after a few voyages, other ship-owners realized that the ice did not melt in the hold and the ships and the cargo appeared to be undamaged. The outcome was that ice became considered as a suitable material for ballast. Previously, most ships left Boston empty to go abroad to collect cargoes and needed ballast for stability on the outward journey. Thus for the ship owners, the shipping of ice for the Tudors at a very low price was a much better deal than the very expensive exercise of dredging stones out of the bay for ballast. The ice trade would have struggled to establish itself if ballast had not been a problem for Boston ship-owners (Weightman 2002:30). At the same time, the destinations to which the brothers wished to send the ice, such as India, caused Boston to open new trade routes by giving them income on long outward journeys. This led to the idea of bringing fresh tropical fruit back from the Caribbean to New England. The return trips from India also brought back jute which was the raw material for the New England mills to make sacks and ropes.

In 1815, the business had developed considerable expertise and involved large numbers of agents, suppliers, carpenters (for building ice houses and carrying structures in ships) and ice-house keepers. The Tudor company had developed leading-edge expertise in preserving ice in hot climates and during transportation. One example is that charcoal and sawdust were used for insulation. Before then, the sawdust from the forestry industry had no value and was dumped in the rivers where it caused pollution, blockages and even floods.

The ice-harvesting techniques were improved as well. The invention of a contraption based on a conventional plough enhanced productivity considerably. The new technology was easy to copy and attracted new entrants into the expanding ice business. By 1880, the Kennebec River in Maine had 36 ice companies and 53 ice houses with a holding capacity of over 1 million tons on just one very short stretch of the river. Yet at this time new technologies were being tested, although mostly in distant areas where access to ice was difficult or the cost was high.

Already at that time, however, the first signs of problems for the Tudors, as well as for 'natural' ice in general, had appeared. The American Civil War prevented access from Boston to the southern US ports. Ice suppliers from Maine managed to maintain access and increased their market share. At the same time, ice users in New Orleans became interested in mechanically produced ice and managed to smuggle in two French devices for use in hospitals. Meanwhile, the development of railways had led the meat-packing industry to relocate to Chicago, where the large suppliers moved the meat around using ice-chilled rail wagons. It was not long before their enterprises also wanted to test steam-driven artificial refrigeration units. The same tendencies could be observed in India. Unreliable supplies had led these customers to import ice machines in 1878 and US shipment of ice to India was dead by 1882.

Despite developments and improvements in mechanical and electrical refrigeration, the quantities of ice harvested in the US grew annually until the first decade of the 20th century. Between 1900 and 1920, large numbers of ice-producing plants were built and issues such as the level of pollution in the Hudson River speeded the process. After World War I, refrigeration began to replace ice and the natural ice industry was no more.

Why did the Tudor company and other suppliers of natural ice die? A conventional analyst's view would be to say that they misunderstood what business they were in and failed to see the powerful alternatives that over time were made available to ice users. Utterback (1994:155) suggests that the natural ice industry had created an entire system for harvesting, storage and distribution that was 'remarkably efficient'. He argues that because of the considerable investment involved, the whole industry was in some way 'impeded' from making industry-altering innovations. In the next section, we discuss our interpretations of the Tudor case as they appear from an industrial network perspective. Three main aspects of the case are identified and each of these are then further scrutinized with other empirical examples.

Network-like Features in the Evolution of Business

The ice business case study highlights how a new product and a new business was built on and affected existing networks of interdependencies. The business of the Tudor brothers developed through the exploitation of potential connections with other actors, their resources and activities. The business was subsequently affected by changes in the activity pattern and resource structure in the network and in technology developed by itself and others.

To get their business started in a sceptical and difficult business world, the Tudor brothers first had to connect with the business of sea transportation. By buying a ship and staffing it, they also had to work on what they would be bringing back to make the journey economic. Both these areas of ship-owning and international logistics were well established networks into which they had to enter in order to become established. Secondly, the provision of ballast for ships leaving Boston was another associated network linked to shipping. Tudor did not have to get closely involved, but needed to build adequate relationships to understand the economics and pricing mechanisms, which would give an idea of what they should charge others for resource combining between ice and the ships, as a replacement for conventional ballast. Thirdly, to harvest, store and transport the ice required complementary resources and activities. Tudor gained access to these by building relationships with those in apparently separate networks and thus linked to new business areas in a novel way. Throughout their career, the Tudors were to do this time and time again. They gained access to the technology of mechanical harvesting through a resource innovation developed by one of the ice suppliers. Moreover, they received help from a brother-in-law on how to store ice using ice houses, and hired and trained carpenters to build the ice houses and fit out the ships to take the unusual cargo.

It is important to realize that the Tudors did not build the network in which their company became involved. Nor could it be managed entirely from the perspective of the Tudor company. Tudor developed relationships with firms in networks that already existed and these connections allowed the business to operate. Through these relationships, the company gained access to

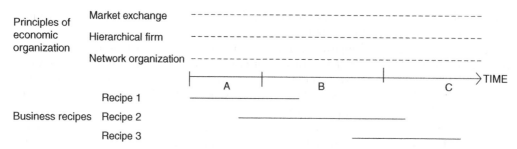

Figure 10.2 The influences of narratives on the perceived interplay between business recipes and economic organization.

resources, activities and business counterparts that would otherwise have been more difficult to approach.

The decline of the natural ice companies is explained by Utterback (1994) as being caused by their considerable investment and overly strong focus on current operations. But the simple fact that refrigeration technology replaced ice cutting does not explain why neither Tudor nor any of the other ice producers exploited the new ice-making technology. The ice-shippers had the global customer base and access to the international transport and logistics networks that were still needed for selling the ice, which was now produced in large industrial refrigeration plants and shipped. But the previously dominant ice-shippers lacked relationships to the networks that were central for mechanically produced ice. Again, we see the important connection between technological changes and organizational changes highlighted by business historians and the interplay between physical and organizational resources discussed in previous chapters. For Tudor to continue its business after the introduction of mechanically produced ice would have required changing many of the major existing relationships drastically and developing some entirely new ones.

The actions of the Tudor Ice Company during its life in the business landscape undeniably impacted on relationships in the network. For example, Tudor persuaded ship-owners to switch from refusing to carry ice to searching it out as a cargo in place of expensive ballast and suggesting destinations such as India. The consequences of these changes led to much wider effects in patterns of trade and commodity use which clearly illustrates the strong impact of networks in an era that has been characterized as 'the self-regulating market based on firm autonomy'.

Our re-interpretation of the evolution of the business landscape illuminates three issues deserving further examination. The first is that the dominant narrative suggests a strong interplay between one particular organizational form and a specific time period. In reality, however, various forms of economic organization do exist in parallel. Different organizational forms are applied simultaneously, some of which are market-based and some hierarchical, while others have network-like features. In Figure 10.2, this is indicated by the dotted lines related to the three principles for economic organization.

Secondly, the well-established fact that a particular organizational form (such as the integrated hierarchy) gains a stronger foothold in a certain time period is to a large extent explained by the impact of the business recipe of the time. These recipes are important features of the social dimension of the business landscape and tend to function as norms for business behaviour. These recipes tend to be given priority in specific time periods (illustrated by Recipes 1, 2 and 3 in periods A, B and C in Figure 10.2). Strong adherence to these recipes means that they influence the view of the principle of economic organization that dominates the respective period.

Thirdly, narrative and recipe together impact on what is perceived to be the most relevant unit of analysis in the business landscape (market, single firm, or network). The unit of analysis, in turn, determines the world views of the business landscape.

These three issues are discussed in the following sections.

Variety in Organizational Forms

We agree with Lamoreaux *et al.* (2003) when they claim that 'environments tolerate a variety of organizational forms', that wax and wane depending on specific socio-economic patterns. But this conclusion needs to be extended further and our claim is that the business landscape *requires* variety in this respect, since there is considerable variation in the business conditions for different firms at the same time. Therefore, organizational forms never exist in isolation but co-exist in various combinations making the established view of major step-wise transformations within the business landscape less relevant.

The variety of organizational forms at any one time is accompanied by heterogeneity within any of those arrangements. The MBE did not take a single form and was itself subject to evolution. For example, the ever-greater integration of the operations practised by Ford was only successful as long as demand for the Model T was strong. The underlying problems and inefficiencies of Ford's one-product, cost-reduction strategy became apparent in the 1920s when the platform production system employed by General Motors facilitated multiple models with minor differences in features. In this way, GM was able to satisfy different customer demands on the basis of Alfred Sloan's knowledge of the technologies of marketing, the development of market segmentation and not withstanding GM's intrinsically higher cost structure (Lamoreaux *et al.* 2003; Best 1990). Similarly, whilst Ford and General Motors were internalizing manufacturing activities between 1920 and 1940, Chrysler continued to rely on an extensive network of suppliers to obtain production efficiencies and cooperative relationships for product development (Schwartz 2000).

Altogether this means that at any time vertically integrated organizations were likely to require the existence of companies organized along quite different lines. For example, it is claimed that mass production and speciality systems 'always demanded the existence of firms organized along completely opposite principles' (Hollingsworth 1991:50). Business evolution therefore might be portrayed as parallel, combined patterns of change related to all three organizational forms that together alter the overall structure of the business landscape through processes where business recipes are central.

Social Context and Business Recipes

The dominant narrative of business evolution in general and of MBEs, in particular, appears to have had greater impact on business recipe prescriptions than on the actual occurrence of large hierarchies in the business landscape. But even if the 'real' MBEs were few, other firms were strongly affected by the general idea behind the large hierarchies. The vision of the MBE in terms of large-scale, ownership control of resources, and managerial coordination, determined the way in which most managers perceived the business world in which they were engaged. This apparently strong influence supports the assertion that managers' 'social construction of the world is as important as the "objective" character of the world' (Fligstein 1990:304). What hindered firms from becoming MBEs was the lack of financial resources required for massive integration.

Business recipes play important roles in the social construction of the world. Perrow (1981) questions whether managers were sufficiently aware of the actual effects of vertical integration; rather, they adopted this idea because recipes prescribed this medicine. Fligstein goes one step further, arguing that managers rely on business recipes because they 'rarely know what is economically efficient' (Fligstein 1990:302). Both these authors claim that the main interest of managers is to preserve their organizations and further their individual and collective interests and therefore they require ideas and models about what constitutes efficient action in this respect. One important aspect of these constructions of efficiency is what Fligstein defines as a 'conception of control', including strategies and structures that define the organizational fields of companies. Conceptions of control are historically determined and reflect the thinking of the particular time period and the problems that managers perceive. These conceptions tend to impose restrictions on company actions because managers 'tend to go with what has worked in the immediate past or with the conventional wisdom guiding their organizational fields' (Fligstein 1990:302).

Business recipes (as well as strategic thinking) have tended to focus on the ownership boundaries in the organizational fields. Boundaries provide firms with buffering and bridging functions (Thompson 1967): They both separate and join the firm to what is outside. The view of boundaries in the MBE recipe emphasized the buffering function, making the single corporation the relevant unit of analysis. This perspective seems to be a direct consequence of the jungle metaphor in the perception of life in the business landscape. When the business recipe needed reformulation, owing to the problems of MBEs, the bridging function came into focus. Outsourcing and close relationships directed attention to boundary-spanning issues. In this way, the unit of analysis changed from the single company to the position of the firm in its network context. There is thus a strong interplay between the social context in terms of, for example, established business recipes and the unit of analysis for examining the evolution of the business landscape.

Unit of Analysis

A defining feature of the narrative describing the MBE is that it is built around the behaviour of single companies that are assumed to be more or less complete in their knowledge and able to act independently. But the ice case study clearly shows that business evolution is a phenomenon that cannot be understood at the level of the company and cannot be explained by what happens within a single firm.

The 'modern' firm was not invented or created by Henry Ford. Like the other 200 car makers in the US at the beginning of the 20th century and like the Tudor brothers in the ice business, Ford's company connected itself to existing networks in order to get the business started. As described above, the main feature of these networks was a typical craft system. Car assemblers relied heavily on suppliers involved in other businesses and built their cars from frames, axles, springs, wheels, motors, radiators, steering gears and electrical systems designed for other purposes that were

> ### Box 10.1 Economic Organization in Birmingham Gun-making Factories
>
> The master gun-maker ... seldom possessed a factory or workshop ... Usually he owned merely a warehouse in the gun quarter and his function was to acquire semi-finished parts and to give these out to specialized craftsmen, who undertook the assembly and finishing of the gun. He purchased materials from barrel-makers, lock-makers, sight-stampers, trigger-makers, etc. All of these were independent manufacturers executing the orders of several master gun-makers. Once parts had been purchased from the 'material makers' ... the next task was to hand them out to a long succession of 'setters-up' each of whom performed a specific operation in connection with the assembly and finishing of the gun.
>
> Allen, G.C., 1929. *The Industrial Development of Birmingham and the Black Country.* London: Allen & Unwin.

all available and ready to install (Langlois and Robertson 1995). It is also possible to question whether the business landscape at the time when the car business was started can appropriately be described as one of self-regulating markets and autonomous firms. The owner-entrepreneur in the assembling firm was often in direct and close contact with both customers and suppliers. Moreover, much of the design came from small machine shops and the assembler had to rely on the capabilities of supplier firms skilled at producing precision components for bicycles and horse carriages. Similar conditions that can be characterized as network interdependencies prevailed in other industries, such as the gun-making factories in Birmingham in the 1860s (see Box 10.1).

These features of the arrangements in gun-making 150 years ago are not very different from what today is perceived to be a new form of economic organization in the business landscape. Dependence on the innovations and technical development of others is illustrated also by the conditions in the network of gun-makers and machinists in New England. This network created an innovation that formed the basis for all subsequent mass-production businesses, including the operations and subsequent success of MBEs. The stock of a gun at the US Springfield Armory was made on a bank of 14 specialist lathes that were designed, built and integrated into a production line. This system for manufacturing identical and replaceable parts eliminated hand-filing and fitting and the need for craft-skilled workers and fitters. The performance of each machine, tended by an operator, was measured by precision gauges set against formal specifications. Innovations in machine tools depended on actions crossing the borders of companies and were facilitated by relationships between users and suppliers described in the following way:

> The system was not centrally managed; it was self organizing. The makers and users of the specialist machines were independent firms, but they 'were anchored in a community of workers ... skilled in the development and use of the new technologies'.
>
> *Best 1990*

An alternative interpretation to that of highlighting the great innovators and entrepreneurs in various industries would thus be to argue that it was the resources already available in the networks they entered that paved the way for their success. This becomes obvious when the unit of analysis is shifted away from the single firm.

A single company perspective has also been applied to the current transformation of business, the de-integration of large hierarchies into more specialized companies dependent on the skills of their suppliers, customers and others. The basic assumption in most of these analyses is that both the establishment and dismantling of the hierarchical firms was planned and directed solely by the single manufacturing company and wholly due to the moves that were made by these companies. In the same way, many of today's successful businesses, for example, Toyota, Nike, IKEA and Dell, are assumed to have gained their strong positions from networks that they have built around them. But none of these businesses could have been started or achieved a strong position unless they had first connected to existing networks. In fact, the form, timing, and success of these businesses actually depended on the resources, motivations and actions of many other companies. These other companies were all evolving themselves and in their relationships. It was their possession or absence of particular skills and their problems and aspirations that led them to move in various directions. These movements sometimes restricted and opposed the ambitions of the MBE firms and today's network-like organizations. In other situations, the actions of these other companies allowed and encouraged, or even forced, changes to happen in those companies that became the large firms of the time. For example, if one company wants to outsource activities to others, it requires other companies to be able and willing to take on those activities or for companies to be formed to undertake them. The understanding of both integration and de-integration of hierarchies as well as the development of new businesses would thus benefit from being analysed in a network context and this is the theme of the next section.

Network View of Business Evolution

A network analysis of business evolution has its basis in the dynamics of activity patterns, resource constellations and webs of actors. Through the examination of the interplay among the processes in these dimensions, we are provided with an alternative interpretation of the changes in the business landscape from that which is offered through the single company perspective that is normally applied. In the following sections, we use concepts and models from previous chapters to analyse business evolution. We apply these tools to changes in the configuration of activities and combining of resources as they have been reported in descriptions of the MBE and its rise and fall. One reason for selecting the activity and resource dimensions for this analysis is that we dealt with the actor dimension in the discussion about the role of the unit of analysis above. The main reason, however, is that previous investigations have been so focused on the role of actors. Most analyses of the historical development of business have taken the starting point in the single firm. This means that the actor dimension has been highlighted in narratives and business recipes and has thereby framed the analysis. For example, the common understanding of the rise and benefits of the MBE points to ownership control of crucial resources, managerial coordination, and the large scale of internal operations as central ingredients of the recipe.

Our network interpretation of the evolution of the business landscape therefore takes its starting point in the activity and resource layers of the network. This approach highlights the bridging function of boundaries because activity links and resource ties cross the borders of firms. In such settings, boundary drawing becomes an interactive process involving more than establishing a distinction between the inside and outside of the firm (Araujo *et al.* 2003). We begin our exposé with an exploration of the role of resource combining and recombining in these processes, followed by an analysis of the historical changes in the activity configuration of the network. Finally, we highlight some consequences for the webs of actors.

Evolution of Resource Constellations

The established craft network provided certain benefits for the setting-up of the Ford Motor Company and other car assemblers. These new business enterprises were offered access to resources that they could share with already established firms and thus gain from similarities in resource exploitation. The pattern of activities in the craft networks they exploited were characterized by strong subdivision of tasks and this implied that resources were scattered amongst many firms. As previously pointed out, these conditions were not favourable to innovation in car design because the necessary modifications in resource combining and resource interfaces would require changes by many firms. This problem was accentuated by the fact that at that time car assemblers were not the most important customers of their suppliers. Hence it would have been difficult to make systematic changes to the car in cooperation with the current suppliers because their main attention was directed to other customers. As we described above, this was one of the fundamental reasons for innovative companies in various industries to integrate operations within their boundaries.

Internalizing operations within the boundaries of the firm provided new opportunities for resource combining and adjusting interfaces. Once the main part of the activity pattern and resource constellation became located in the large corporation, new conditions for creative resource combining appeared:

> Once the separate tasks were brought together under one roof and performed in proximity to one another, people were lead to perceive the productive processes in new ways and this changed perception was itself a source of innovation.
>
> *Piore 1992:440*

Integration within the hierarchy also provided opportunities for identifying economies of scale and similarities in manufacturing that would not have been apparent to decentralized parts suppliers. The same was true for the tools and machines that were necessary for the manufacturing of components. Ford and his engineers were forced to develop many of these devices themselves. The main reason for this was not that the technical advances were beyond the understanding of independent suppliers; rather, 'it was because only the men at Ford understood the uses to which the new machines would have been put' (Langlois and Robertson 1995:53).

The network interpretation of these conditions would be to say that when 'the separate tasks were brought together' new opportunities for recombining resources became apparent. The main explanation for this is that the heterogeneity of the resources could now be exploited to a much greater extent than when Ford and other car assemblers had to rely on supplier resources that primarily were used in relation to other types of customer. Moreover in the new in-house

Table 10.2   Network evolution from the perspective of the resource layer.

	From market exchange to internal resource combination	From internal to interactive resource combination
Opportunity for resource combining	Considerable: All important resources available in-house Limited by the capacity of the internal resources	Active involvement of other companies required Considerable, if business partners can be mobilized
Space effect	Better connection between 'produce' and 'use' Limited interaction with others Problems in exploiting heterogeneity	Substantial input from interaction Heterogeneity better exploited
Time effect	No co-evolution with other firms Paths generated within narrow scopes Control of recombination, only within the narrow path generated over time	Paths generated by access to other companies' technical development Recombination opportunities enhanced, but involvement of other companies required

arrangements of the MBE, the connection between the two aspects of a resource were reinforced since 'use' and 'produce' were now more closely linked than before.

The prescriptions of the MBE recipe proved to be powerful. The more successful a recipe appears, the stronger the foothold it will gain and the more its benefits are likely to be exploited through its own momentum. Langlois and Robertson argue that once vertical integration was initiated 'it was self-reinforcing in certain ways' (Langlois and Robertson 1995:53). We have pointed out some clear benefits of this force in terms of both cost advantages and systemic innovation. But the same momentum also had its disadvantages because it may have driven integration too far (Langlois and Robertson 1995:55–6). In particular, the authors raise this issue in relation to some of the later extensive integration into fields that were only loosely connected to car manufacturing (such as rubber, glass and railroads). They conclude that some of these undertakings were 'in fact "mistaken"', meaning that this integration had no particular efficiency rationale and existed only because Ford wanted to control important resources, and the profits of the Model T could stand it. Over time the effects of this ever-increasing integration was that Ford became an 'unwieldy monster' that was increasingly 'expensive, unmanageable, and horrendously unprofitable' (Drucker 1990). These problems could be expected from a network perspective because through these arrangements, Ford became involved in networks where the company had no previous connections and no particular competencies of its own. Moreover, the resource collection of the company expanded dramatically and the connections between the various sub-sets of this collection were not always evident. In the long run therefore, significant difficulties appeared when it came to recombining of these resources and modifying their interfaces. Table 10.2 summarizes the opportunities provided and the network effects realized when analysing the changes from market exchange to hierarchy and from hierarchy to network.

Within what can be defined as the core business of Ford and other MBEs, problems emerged as a result of over-reliance on this specific recipe. The strong adherence to cost efficiency and large-scale operations provided a limited breeding ground for variation and innovation in the manufacture and development of parts and components. According to Piore and Sabel, the mass-production machinery was so precise that no hand-finishing was necessary. The final assembly of the product required very little craft skill and the introduction of automatic machinery had made the worker into an adjunct to the machine. Whereas the worker had once defined the product, the worker was now defined by the product and the machine – 'whose purpose, far from translating human skill into action, was to make human involvement in the production of the good superfluous' (Piore and Sabel 1984:23). This combination of machine and man resulted in 'deskilling' of people (Langlois 2003). In our terms, we would argue that in MBE arrangements, the role of organizational resources was downplayed while the efficient utilization of physical resources was given priority. It is not surprising therefore that innovation and variety did not prosper in the established MBE. Langlois and Robertson illustrate this clearly in their observation of the modifications over time of Ford's Model T:

> All these improvements remained, however, within a single design paradigm. The radical change in product characteristics of the era of product development had given way to incremental product change and the focus began to shift to process innovation.
>
> *Langlois and Robertson 1995:51*

This observation supports the discussion in previous chapters about the role and impact of paths in constellations of resources. The successive recombining of resources and the modification of resource interfaces tend to result in path dependence in the constellation of resources. In activity patterns, the long-term ambitions of actors to adjust activities to each other in order to improve performance leads to what we identified as specialization in activity patterns. As concluded previously, these arrangements are beneficial for current operations but make it difficult to connect to other resource constellations. In this way, the MBE resource collection was locked within the boundaries of the firm, which made it difficult to relate to the evolving technical conditions in other resource constellations.

Throughout this book, we have claimed that the connection between interaction and the time dimension is a critical force in the evolution of the business landscape. The interaction between the MBE and its suppliers did not provide much stimulus for variety and innovation from the outside. The purchasing philosophy was based on short-term contracts and multiple sourcing, and car assemblers instituted policies that reduced the barriers to entry for potential suppliers (Helper 1987). This approach aimed to enhance competition amongst external suppliers and the MBE tried in this way to create markets outside its own boundary! Relationships with independent suppliers were governed in most cases by arm's-length relationships (Scherer 1991:218). Suppliers normally received detailed blue-prints of the components they were to supply and the interaction and knowledge sharing was limited with the bulk of small suppliers. On the other hand, the assembler was in more or less constant communication with its large suppliers. However, the exchange of information in these cases seems to have been related mainly to price and delivery issues and 'fine tuning the engineering effort', while only in 'very rare cases did suppliers and assemblers cooperate in the initial design of the project' (Scherer 1991:219). These conditions obviously lead to the type of standardized exchange between business partners that we described in Chapter 3. Consequently, creativity and innovation in the MBE gained little contribution from outside suppliers. According to Helper

(1987), interaction was not much more developed between car assemblers and their in-house suppliers.

These conditions caused severe problems when the technological frontier expanded dramatically during the second half of the 20th century. This expansion particularly concerned the greater inter-relatedness between formerly distinct fields of technology (Fai and Cantwell 1999:115). These technology developments provided substantial opportunities for recombining resources and modifying their interfaces. These changes required the combination and application of advances in many fields of specialized knowledge (Patel and Pavitt 1997). For the individual firm these conditions implied that the number of disciplines required for design, development, manufacturing and distribution escalated. Any company had to employ an ever-widening range of product, process and marketing technologies in their offerings and the costs of developing each subsequent generation of these technologies escalated.

The technological capabilities of a firm need to reflect the complex and multi-technology nature of their products and methods of production. These conditions placed increasing demands on the interplay between organizational and physical resources. For example, Loasby (1999:6) argued that 'there is no way that knowledge, especially "knowledge-how" that is required ... can all be collected in one centre, or understood by any cohesive group of people'. Consequently the company had to look outside its ownership boundary to identify specialized suppliers of equipment, and knowledge, whose resources were to be combined with its in-house research and development assets. The detailed characteristics of these resource constellations in today's business landscape have been described and analysed in previous chapters.

Changes in the Patterning of Activities

Both the rise and fall of the MBE recipe are excellent illustrations of reconfiguration of activity patterns. The establishment of the MBE was focused on efforts to increase the similarity of activities in order to gain from larger scale. Consequently, this patterning allowed limited diversity, which is nicely illustrated by Ford's slogan, 'you can choose whatever colour you want as long as it is black'. Full exploitation of the potential for economies of scale required standardization of the whole process of the operations inside and outside the MBE. Lampel and Mintzberg identify this period in American industry as the era when the 'logic of aggregation' ruled the game and required the following conditions:

> Standardization of taste that allowed for standardized design, standardization of design that allowed for mechanized mass production and a resulting standardization of products that allowed for mass distribution.
>
> *Lampel and Mintzberg 1996:21*

Thus the features of the physical resource constellation were shaped to provide benefits in terms of scale and similarity of activities, but there were obvious constraints with regard to variety and diversity. The MBE also coordinated serial interdependences among activities and its in-house activity structure was tightly sequential through the enhanced synchronization of the operations within the plant. This activity configuration of the MBE became a problem when new conditions evolved.

Technological developments provided opportunities for the recombining of resources and for changes in their interfaces, which in turn made activity reconfiguration possible. Mass production was no longer a prerequisite for economies of manufacturing in the new arrangements. Redesign of production facilities reduced set-up costs and thus the advantages of large scale. These compositions caused a shift from the logic of aggregation towards the logic of individualization (Lampel and Mintzberg 1996). Standardization and similarity could now be balanced with diversity and customization, and 'tailor-made' became a keyword in a wide variety of industries (Pine 1993). Now a supplier was able to provide customers with differentiated offerings at a reasonable cost and within a reasonable lead time. The MBE was not an appropriate resource collection for taking advantage of the new conditions in technical development, since its configuration of activities built on standardization and was rooted in a heavy physical resource constellation designed to reap the benefits of large scale. These features of the activity structure made it difficult to adjust to the upcoming situation. The emphasis on customization was supported also by technical developments in logistics and transportation. Distribution operations became increasingly effective because of the evolution of logistics facilities, equipment and techniques. The combined effect of changes in production and distribution made the build-to-order production arrangements discussed in previous chapters a feasible approach. To a large extent, these improvements were enabled through the progress of resources such as information systems and communication infrastructures. These developments are important in themselves because they improve both the speed and the accuracy of information flows, but their main effects are improvements in the control of materials flows.

Activity reconfiguration required changes in both physical and organizational resource set-ups. The previously mentioned developments in the infrastructure for distribution were supplemented with increasing involvement in business relationships with suppliers to which activities were outsourced. The arm's-length relationships promoted by the MBE were not sufficient for the reconfigured activity patterns. Previously in-house activities were strongly integrated within the large hierarchies, while the links to the activities and resources of suppliers were purposely weak. This was a deliberate choice by the MBE because these conditions left the company free to change counterparts and reduced the costs of handling relationships. In some way, however, the activities of the MBE had to be linked to those of its suppliers. Owing to the multiple arms'-length relationships prescribed by the dominant business recipes, the MBE had to protect its technical core from environmental disturbances in terms of variation of input and demand for output (Thompson 1967). For example, securing the input on the supply side required substantial inventories as buffers to compensate for long and varying lead times in production and distribution.

Outsourcing of activities to suppliers required modifications of the linkages among activities. The MBE had synchronized its internal activities to gain potential benefits from economies of speed. When some of the internal activities of the MBE were outsourced, it was necessary to retain this coordination – i.e. the internal activities of the outsourcing firm needed to be integrated with those of its suppliers. In turn, this required an updated business recipe since the prevailing one recommended as little dependence as possible on other firms.

The alternative business recipe launched to replace the MBE was based on experiences from the Japanese motor industry. Some of its ingredients directly related to the configuration of activities which is illustrated by the findings of a US research team at the time. The main conclusion of the team after a study visit to Japan was that 'it only takes 10 minutes inside an assembly plant' to become aware of the substantial differences compared with the activity configuration applied in the Western world:

> The visitor accustomed to the loading docks, the large storage areas and the large incoming inspection areas, typical of US plants, is likely to be taken aback by the stocking of Japanese assembly lines. Trucks from suppliers back up through large bay doors right to the assembly line; supplier personnel unload a few hours of parts, clean up the area and depart. There is no incoming inspection, no staging area, no expediting of material, just a seemingly continuous flow of material.
>
> *Hervey, R., 1982. Preliminary observation on manufacturer–supplier relations in the Japanese automotive industry.* The Joint US-Japan Automotive Study: Working Paper Series No. 5. Ann Arbor: University of Michigan, p.8.

The research team had discovered the just-in-time principle applied by some of the large car producers in Japan.[4] In these factories, the reliance on buffering of internal operations from those of suppliers was replaced by activity synchronization across the boundaries of firms. The configuration of the Japanese arrangements primarily focused on handling serial interdependencies in the activity pattern. In the terms we have introduced in this book, activities undertaken by different companies were consciously changed from being merely sequential to tightly sequential. By applying the new recipe and integrating operations with suppliers' activities, it became possible for the outsourcing firm to expand the scope of the economies of speed outside its own operations. The increasing integration of processes across the boundaries of firms made it possible to reduce buffers in the supply system. These changes made the processes more efficient and effective at the same time as costs could be reduced. This enhanced process orientation is one of the main features in the reconfiguring of activity patterns where the principles of postponement and build-to-order production are central characteristics. Just-in-time deliveries and the principle of modularity were instrumental in these change processes.[5]

The opportunities and potential effects of changes from one principle of economic organization to another as interpreted from an activity layer perspective are summarized in Table 10.3.

Consequences for the Web of Actors

The changes in activity patterns and resource constellations affected and were affected by changes in the web of actors. Enhanced reliance on outsourcing and suppliers impacted considerably on the roles and positions of actors. This becomes evident through an examination of the changes in large hierarchies. One example is the shifts in the proportion of in-house manufacturing

---

[4]From a historical perspective, it is interesting to note that Schwartz and Fish (1998) demonstrate how a similar system (hand-to-mouth inventories) operated in Detroit in the 1920s but without being elevated to a central feature of automobile production systems.

[5]Neither is the principle of modularity an entirely new phenomenon. It was applied even in the MBE (Starr 1965).

Table 10.3 Network evolution from the perspective of the activity layer.

	From market exchange to internal resource combination	From internal to interactive resource combination
Opportunity exploited	Cost reduction through economies of scale and enhanced coordination of internal activities	Cost reduction by exploiting scale in the operations of suppliers and coordination across company borders
Space effect	Avoidance of interdependence (particularly joint) Serial interdependence handled in-house Problems with variety and diversity	Lots of joint interdependencies Tight sequentiality to business partners Variety and diversity exploited through resource heterogeneity
Time effect	Specialization within own resource collection and activity pattern Improved opportunity for activity fine-tuning Problems with major reconfiguration	Specialization in jointly developed activity patterns increases opportunity for major restructuring Change requires others' involvement

and supplier deliveries at Ford Motor Company. In 1980, the costs of components and systems manufactured in-house accounted for 70 % of the total cost for producing a Ford car. Twenty years later, suppliers accounted for 70 % of total costs, while the proportion of in-house manufacturing had decreased to 30 % (Quinn 1999). Similar changes occurred for most car manufacturers, although many of them started from an in-house proportion lower than that of Ford. The outsourcing trend then spread to other industries.

Within a network perspective, we would note that these changes did not arise simply because MBEs chose to move to this form under their own initiative. As discussed in previous sections, many other factors were involved and many other changes occurred at the same time. One of these changes was led by retailers that had developed their use of the technologies of marketing to build their own brands. These retailers developed product and process technologies either alone or in conjunction with suppliers that were often smaller than themselves. These retailers specified design, process, materials and labour policies to suppliers. They developed logistics ahead of the standards of manufacturers and often took over this function from them. The de-integrated organizational form was, in some cases, pioneered by new entrants. Information technology companies grew in importance in the network: They provided the technology to enable 'manufacturing at a distance' and de-integration to take place efficiently. The emerging form and characteristics of other companies were vital. Important examples were the acquisition of relevant process technologies by producers in low-cost environments; the growth of contract manufacturers; and the development of innovative intermediaries that were able to bridge the geographical and cultural gap between these suppliers and new potential customers.

Influenced by the emerging business recipe to 'stick to the knitting', and the cost, range and interrelatedness of technologies, companies focused on the activities and capabilities which they assumed were central for the firm's identity and long-term survival. Hence they had to rely on others for the capabilities that they needed but could not control (Fai and Cantwell 1999;

Ford *et al.* 2003). The effect of these developments was that technology became increasingly specialized and professionalized. At the same time, new actors emerged in the network focusing on limited sub-sets of product or process technologies, and even on only the technologies for designing products or on process technologies to produce them. Other actors specialized in distribution operations that became increasingly efficient and effective owing to the development of specialized logistics companies' facilities, equipment and techniques. Information technology providers also contributed to the fragmentation of resource constellations and activity patterns. To a large extent, these improvements were enabled through the progress of information systems and communication infrastructures also developed by specialists.

Gaining the full benefits from suppliers in terms of resource access and activity coordination required significant involvement with suppliers. Once the nature of relationships changed, we can observe a momentum in relation to self-reinforcing benefits in the same way as when the MBE was established. When relationships became more cooperative, buying firms realized that suppliers could play an active role to support both rationalization and development efforts (Gadde and Håkansson 2001). For example, the development of a 'dominant design' (Utterback 1994) in the car industry and in other industries made it possible for an independent supplier serving a number of manufacturers to work at larger scale than even the biggest manufacturer could. Thus, when the business recipe was modified, the advantages of external scale outweighed those that could be achieved within the integrated MBEs.

The outcome of these changes is that the current web of actors in some respects resembles the features of the business landscape before the MBE: A huge cadre of specialized firms with capabilities and operations supplementing each other. The main difference is that the assemblers in the pre-MBE structure had to rely completely on what was available out there. In current activity configurations and resource constellations for manufacturing, distribution and product development, the basic design is made by the assembler and then outsourced to suppliers. However, what can be learned from history is that future changes of this basic design may be problematic. Today's assemblers rely on a cadre of specialized suppliers that are not only responsible for manufacturing components and systems: In many cases these suppliers have been made responsible also for technical development. Each of these suppliers normally serves different types of customer. These customers will have different views of potential adjustments and reconfigurations. Therefore, any attempt to change the features of what is outsourced will create tensions in relation to other customers. The opportunities for modifications are thus constrained by the capabilities and resources of suppliers and the conditions of other customers. Another problem with the present arrangements is that the 'use' and the 'produce' sides of a resource element are less well connected than within the hierarchy of the single firm. It should come as no surprise, therefore, that companies are now increasingly involved in 'insourcing' and 'back-sourcing' to solve these issues.

Conclusion

A view of the dynamics of business from a network perspective shows more or less continuous modifications in the balancing of activity patterns and resource constellations (Table 10.4).

Table 10.4 Network evolution balancing activity patterns and resource constellations.

Network layer	Types of balancing
Resource constellations	Internal vs external resources
	The interplay between physical and organizational resources
Activity patterns	Similarity vs diversity
	Integration vs de-integration
	Insourcing vs outsourcing

In activity patterns, this balancing is concerned with integration and de-integration and also with balancing similarity and diversity. In resource constellations, the issues are those of balancing internal and external resources and the continuous interplay between physical and organizational resources. On the basis of a network perspective, it can be disputed that industry has undergone the revolutionary transformations that popular beliefs tend to claim. The integrated MBE certainly dominated some industries. But it was never universal and it was subject to evolution alongside other production systems that continued to exist, both as complements and alternatives to mass production (Piore and Sabel 1984; Scranton 1997). Specialty and mass production arrangements were strongly interdependent because they complemented each other. In the same way it can be argued that the MBE recipe is still important in these contexts where large scale and ownership control are important.

In this chapter we have offered a network explanation of the development and decline of the MBE as a popular organizational form. We have tried to interpret the evolution of the business landscape in terms of changes in activity patterns and resource constellations. As illustrated in our discussions, these changes are associated with modifications to the web of actors. Our main conclusion is that governance mechanisms never exist in isolation but co-exist together in various combinations. However, in a specific time period, it seems evident that one type of governance mechanism becomes more dominant, since 'at any time actors tend to organize themselves, adopt rules of exchange, and utilize means of compliance that are typical of one governance mechanism more than another' (Lindbergh et al. 1991:32). In this sense, the characteristics of this governance mechanism evolve as an ideal. In the terminology adopted in this chapter, they form a business recipe that becomes the dominant framework.

Our discussion of business dynamics and business recipes has revealed that too strong an emphasis on one particular recipe may cause problems over time, because the 'tools of victory for one transformation may become liabilities at a later time' (Portz 1991:291) and 'core capabilities' can turn into 'core rigidities' (Leonard-Barton 1992). A further aspect of the current processes and structures in the business landscape is that the features of companies are far less fixed and pre-determined than in the case of the integrated MBE and its suppliers. Companies exist in a wide variety of forms with different combinations of internal and external resources depending on their individual problems and histories. A network view of business and its evolution emphasizes the interdependencies between companies. Companies may choose to exploit some specific interdependence between their own resources and those of others as a means of allowing them to invest in more productive resources. Some interdependencies may be forced upon them through those same patterns, and these network interdependencies are free of neither cost nor risk.

The final implication of our argument is that firms should be careful with uncritically applying prescriptions that are considered to be *the* prevailing business recipe. Our historical review indicates that these prescriptions are context specific. Therefore, firms should avoid searching for a 'single logic which will "work" in all circumstances' (Whitley 1992:123). The more varied the business conditions become, the more varied successful forms of business organization will have to be and the more difficult it will be to transfer techniques and strategies between contexts.

Networks and Industrial Policy

11

This chapter takes a wider perspective on the business landscape. Here we are concerned with two interconnected issues: The process of innovation in the network and the role of government and policy-makers in this process.

The chapter starts out with a discussion of how the basic characteristics of the business landscape are interpreted in economic models used in contemporary policy-making and contrasts these models with the interactive view presented in the previous chapters. Three important questions are addressed in the chapter that relate to policy-makers' ambitions to develop and use network-like structures in order to create industrial development and economic growth:

- How are networks defined? Despite the increasing attempts to create new and support established business networks, there is no consensus in the understanding of what a network actually is. If networks are defined from the perspective of traditional market thinking or from a new institutionalist perspective, they appear completely different from how they appear if they are defined from an empirically based interactive view.
- What is required in order to create and influence networks? Again there are very clear differences between policy recipes that start from a traditional market or a new institutionalist perspective and those that are empirically based.
- What effects do network forces create? That is, we consider the 'dark' and the 'light' sides of networks. Empirically observed networks do not have a self-regulating mechanism. There is no necessary reason for them to operate for the public good, however that may be defined. Therefore the non-democratic, non-transparent features of networks need to be thoroughly considered.

Network – One Word but Many Meanings

It is usually only if a dramatic change occurs that the interdependencies within the business landscape are highlighted for 'outsiders': For example, if a global company goes bust; if a bank defaults; if two large companies merge, or if there is an attempt to replace an established technology that has negative environmental effects. As long as businesses are operating as usual, the interdependencies that stretch across company, regional and national boundaries are most often hidden, at least from those who are not directly involved in them. It won't even be clear to those who are involved what interdependencies between resource combinations and activity links have been created over time and space.

Policy-makers have generally interpreted the idea of the network as having positive associations, especially in the areas of innovation and growth. In fact, the idea of the network as a route to stimulating business development and economic growth has become almost a common denominator in contemporary economic policy, irrespective of the geographical location, political perspective or industrial focus: health care, energy, environment, communications or military (Pavitt 2004; Eklund 2007). A main characteristic of empirically observed business networks that we have discussed in previous chapters, is that they evolve *across* time and space, that is, across both regional and national borders and outside of the time perspective of most politicians. Despite this, a main characteristic of policy oriented towards networks is that they aim to create effects *within* particular regional or national borders and often within limited time frames.

Thus, policy-makers' attempts to use and create and networks as tools for regional and national economic development raise at least three important questions: The first significant question is, what is a network? It is striking how many widely different economic phenomena are regarded by policy-makers and academics as 'networks'. For example, the term 'network' is commonly used to refer to companies and organizations located within a particular region or country; to formal agreements between companies and other organizations; to companies and organizations related to a particular technology or industry; and to the informal relationships between individuals around particular organizations, technologies, businesses or places.

There is however another, rather different way to use the network metaphor, which is represented by this book: A network consists of the tangible and intangible investments that comprise the connected relationships between more than two businesses. It is this interpretation of the term 'network' that we relate to the rainforest metaphor.

The wide range of connotations of the network idea has important consequences for policy-makers: For example, is the word network used to characterize competing relations between independent companies? If so, is it able to absorb innovations without the need to consider how related suppliers and customers are affected? Is the word network used to characterize the interdependencies that over time emerge among suppliers, sub-suppliers and complementary companies related to a particular end-product?

A second important question, which relates to the first, is what is needed to create or maintain a network? If networks are composed of social relations between people within a particular geographical area, representing a particular type of skills, then creating the network is rather simple and straightforward. In contrast, if the aim of the network is to create the kind of substantial, connected relationships that we have discussed in this book, then the task of how to develop and live with it is far from easy. In this interpretation of the idea of networks, their creation and development can be regarded as a question of endurance: A network develops through the process of constantly mobilizing and combining internal and external resources and activities. The development of policy principles requires consideration not only of what a network is, but also of the kinds of investment and mobilization that are required in order to develop new and support established business networks.

A third, critical question is, what kind of effects do networks create? The network ambitions expressed by policy-makers explicitly or implicitly rest on the assumption that networks are positive phenomena. However, networks produce negative as well as positive effects. Business networks are powerful and can stimulate efficiency improvements and innovation processes in particular directions. But network effects do not favour all the companies, organizations and areas involved in the network. Instead, network effects are more likely to favour those who have the ability to effectively mobilize their own and others' resources. The negative effects of the network from the perspective of public policy may be anti-democratic, non-transparent and manipulative. We refer to the potentially negative effects of networks in this chapter as 'the dark side' and our discussion of the policy implications of networks is in terms of empirically observed light and dark sides.

We start with a discussion of the different interpretations of what a network is and seek to answer the question, 'What basic assumptions about networks and their way of functioning characterizes contemporary policy?'

On What Principles Do Network Policies Rest?

A policy agenda may, for example, include the task of building new companies based on a break-through in science, or it may be concerned with revitalizing companies in a particular industry or geographical area. Irrespective of the agenda, the attempt to develop policy must rest on some principles.

These principles can be based on formal models or have their roots in empirical observations or the different experiences of participants or some mix of these. If the principles are based on traditional economic thinking, on a model of the world that assumes that markets tend towards some sort of stability between supply and demand, then the basic policy approach is concerned with how to reduce market imperfections. If the economic landscape is understood as a place where 'producers, buyers and sellers, in firms, households and markets have perfect knowledge of information' (Wilk 1996:62), policy-makers do not have to worry about how to organize the development and use of new economic resources and the creation of economic growth. As long as the market is active and the process of allocating scarce resources is not disturbed, new resources are automatically absorbed by the market and create growth, and a new equilibrium emerges.

But the principles of policy-makers may have been affected by the ideas of institutional economics, that 'when information is hard to come by there are many reasons for people to stick together and cooperate, even when they otherwise may do better on their own' (Wilk 1996:62). Thus, informal and formal organizations based on kinship, politics, business, research, and so on are assumed to be developed in order to reduce the transaction cost of gaining information.

Policy is often based on principles that are close to those expressed in traditional economic theory and institutional economics, but it is seldom influenced by empirical studies of business networks. Policy often follows the principles of traditional economic theory and aims to create an active market. For example, these policies may be concerned with reducing state or private monopolies and stimulating increased competition. They are often developed in respect of particular areas, such as the energy and communication sectors. Other policies are based on ideas

Table 11.1 Established principles for industrial policy.

Policy	Market theory	Economic institutionalism
Basic aim	Creating vivid markets in the business landscape as a whole	Creating network-like structures in parts of the landscape
Mechanisms	Reduce market imperfections Promote competition	Stimulate network building in a limited part of what is generally featured by market conditions

that are very close to the principles arising from economic institutionalism: policy activities that aim to create network-like structures for specific sectors or locations. Policies that aim to stimulate the development of networks among science and business, flourish among areas considered to be especially promising for the creation of high-tech innovations, possibly to transform economic resources. The main characteristics of the two approaches discussed are summarized in Table 11.1.

The OECD Committee for Scientific and Technology Policy has placed the 'promotion of stronger relationships between science and innovations systems' at the top of the policy agenda for the OECD countries. The ambition to create close, network-like relationships between science and business also permeates EU policy-making in activities with the aim of developing 'innovation networks'; a 'network in Europe for transnational technology transfer'; a 'network of regions'; 'networks of regions of excellence'; 'networks among players in innovation financing (e.g. venture capitalists and incubators)' and networks 'amongst industrial liaison offices in public research organizations to strengthen public–private links', and so on. Individual countries are also involved in activities that are aimed at creating 'network forces' which in turn are assumed to breed new resources and economic growth. Or, as is expressed in Japan's 'Science and Technology Basic Plan':

> More specifically, by utilizing a human resource network and systematic collaborative researches, the system fosters interaction between the original technological seeds of the public research organization and the business needs of regional companies to create a chain of technological innovations and new industries. Within such a system, regional development can lead to world-class technological innovations.

Fostering of networks among knowledge producers and economic actors is prioritized in planned and developing economies. For example, the Chinese Academy of Science, on behalf of the Chinese government, is being encouraged to create a 'modern science civilization and innovation culture in China', through the 'dissemination of scientific knowledge, spirit and methodology throughout society by adopting an open and networked means'.

These few examples of policy initiatives inspired by economic institutionalism and related models reveal that scholars (for example, Perez and Soete 1988; Freeman 1982; Nelson 1993; Leonard-Barton 1995; Malerba 2002; Krugman 1991; Porter 1990; Almeida and Kogut 1997; Saxenian 1994; Powell *et al.* 1996; and Lundvall 1988) have made space in economic thinking for subjects that traditionally only attracted the attention of anthropologically or empirically oriented researchers who were concerned with the role of interaction and relationships in economic exchange (Wilk 1996). However, the network schools inspired by institutional economics have in common that they see the interactive features of the business landscape as an exception to the rule of the market as depicted in traditional economic theory. What takes place within networks is treated as 'islands of relationships' in an otherwise atomistic ocean. Castells (1996:187) express this understanding as: 'Inside the networks, new possibilities are relentlessly created. Outside the networks, survival is increasingly difficult.' This development of network approaches based on stylized models instead of empirical experience has meant that, as Wilk (1996:62–3) puts it, 'economists are going ahead and reinventing anthropology on their own, without the benefit of careful fieldwork (see, for example, Douglas North's 1993 Nobel Prize lecture).'

One interesting legacy from traditional economic theory that has more or less consciously been embedded into the network approaches based on economic theory practised by policy-makers is the assumption that both 'markets' and 'networks' include some kind of basic, self-regulating mechanisms. The market model, as we underlined above, is based on the assumption that as long as it is not disturbed, the market is self-regulating, always tending towards equilibrium. However, these assumptions also colour network models and policy recipes inspired by economic institutionalism, such as innovation systems and cluster approaches. The network forces that are assumed to be created when knowledge producers, investors and business are brought together are considered to create benefits for all actors in all the contexts involved. This is despite the rather different rationalities of for example, the scientific world, investors, the business world and the general public. Thus, it is only the supply of information that is approached as 'sticky', while the use of the new resources developed through the combination of this 'sticky' information is approached in the same way as in the traditional market model – as motion in a smooth landscape.

With these assumptions, it is easy to understand the high expectations that policy-makers and others have of networks as creators of 'economic goodness and prosperity'. Networks are seen as structures where knowledge producers, governmental and non-governmental organizations, investors, and businesses co-operate and support each other to create new resources that contribute to prosperity for each involved actor and lead to general economic growth and increased societal well-being. Further, these interpretations of networks as entities that can be created based on a particular technology and in a particular space also fit with policy instruments which are developed to work within certain regional or national borders.

However, these assumptions are rather far away from the view of the content and functioning of networks that has been presented in the previous chapters in this book; that is, they are far from how networks appear from an empirically based interactive perspective. In this context, the economic anthropologist Sahlins (2004:ix–xiii) refers to the value of empirical studies of exchange which are not burdened with the pre-supposition of a 'self-regulating economic domain'. Sahlins suggests that studies that do not make the 'ethnographic category mistake' of filtering their empirical observations through the traditional economic theory's ideal have one thing in common: They highlight that economic processes take place in contexts characterized by 'relative rationalities'. Thus, they are concerned with an economic landscape where any economic process has a different meaning for each participant.

Thus, any discussion of the policy implications of networks has to be based on a definition of how the network phenomenon is understood: 'Are networks considered as exceptions in a business landscape that in general has the characteristics of a traditional market?' 'Is it possible to assume that those networks can be developed in order to solve some specific, information-transfer problems within the borders of particular regions or nations?' Or instead, 'Are networks a fundamental aspect of economic activity involving the tangible and intangible investments of multiple actors stretching over time and space?' This latter question provides a starting point that networks always involve interaction across time and space, and consequently across different rationalities. These networks are creative and forceful but also involve manipulation non-transparency. Furthermore, in contrast to traditional theory's understanding of a market, they are not equipped with any self-regulating mechanism.

If networks are based on interdependencies that stretch across both time and space and if they have both a light and a dark side, then what can policy do? This question is at the centre of our discussion of the policy implications of networks and, in particular, of how network forces can be stimulated and how they can be controlled. We start this discussion with a short example of what has been acknowledged, both within policy circles and among academic scholars, as a successful policy-created business network. The example is based on a study reported in Shih (2009)[1] and focuses on the emergence of a semiconductor business network in Taiwan; on how this development is interpreted and used by Taiwanese economic policy; and on how it appears from an empirically based interactive perspective.

Taiwanese Semiconductor Development – From Virgin Land to a Successful Business Network?

In Taiwan, as in any other country, policy-makers are surrounded by recipes on how to create prospering business networks, with Silicon Valley as one of the most popular role models: 'The idea that so much could grow in so short a time within such a small geographical area sent planning bodies from Albuquerque to Zimbabwe scrambling to grow the next Silicon Valley in their own backyard' (Sturgeon 2000:15). However, although some 'generic' features of Silicon Valley have been identified and copied (such as, access to cutting-edge science, venture capital and entrepreneurial start-up firms within close spatial proximity), there are few examples of economic policy creating prospering business networks. One of the few successful examples in which policy-makers really have managed to breed a business network based on science and high-tech knowledge is the one related to the Taiwanese semiconductor industry. However, when Shih (2009) approached the Taiwanese business network related to the supply and use of semiconductors from an empirical interactive perspective, a rather different picture from the policy interpretation was outlined. In this section, we take a brief look at how Taiwanese policy has interpreted and used the emergence of a Taiwanese semiconductor business network and discuss how this development process appears from an interactive perspective. We then outline the policy interpretation of the impressive development.

---

[1]The study is a part of a PhD project carried out by Tommy Shih. It includes a study of how Taiwanese policy-makers have interpreted the development of Taiwan's semiconductor business network as it appears from an empirical interactive perspective. The project also includes a study of how the 'semiconductor model' is applied to a new research-based area, biotechnology, in order to breed a new business network based on this knowledge.

Policy Perspective

In the early 1970s, the Taiwanese business landscape was dominated by small-scale agriculture and manufacturing businesses, together with a host of foreign companies associated with the mass production of mainly labour-intensive consumer goods, such as textiles and electronics. With both political and economic crises to deal with, the Taiwanese government saw an urgent need to create a shift in the traditional domestic business landscape towards a more technological advanced business base. Thus, a main task for economic policy became to find a technology that could help Taiwan to develop high-tech companies. At that time, integrated circuits had been in use for several years and their great potential in terms of low power consumption, rapid operations, reliability and low cost per function was already acknowledged. If Taiwan could develop an improved semiconductor design and production technology, this could be the 'technological upgrading' from which companies producing and using semiconductors could emerge.

However, there was a major obstacle: Taiwan was basically virgin land in terms of knowledge about semiconductors. The country had no domestic companies engaged in semiconductor production and its production of academic knowledge about semiconductor design, manufacturing and use was more or less non-existent. Thus, a common understanding among Taiwanese policymakers was that there was no established domestic knowledge producer, nor any established domestic company that could be expected to take the role as leader in the technologically and economically advanced task of developing semiconductor based businesses. From the economic policy perspective, there was simply no alternative to the creation of organizations that could act as an engine in the production and commercialization of semiconductor knowledge (see Box 11.1).

The first step in this process was taken by the Ministry of Economic Affairs and one of its first tasks was to merge three established research institutes (Union Industrial Research Laboratories, Mining Research and Service Organization, and Metal Industrial Research Industry) to form the Industrial Technology Research Institute (ITRI), with the aim of developing a Taiwanese semiconductor knowledge base. In 1974, ITRI established a research laboratory devoted this issue: the Electronic Research and Service Organization (ERSO). There was very restricted development of semiconductor knowledge within Taiwan: There existed only one small laboratory engaged in semiconductor technology, located near Chiao Tong University in Hsinchu. Hence

---

Box 11.1   The Creation of the Semiconductor Business in Taiwan

The semiconductor industry was a creation of government policies. To take a few examples, it was our government that identified semiconductor technology as Taiwan's chance to catch up with developed countries. There was no semiconductor industry when ITRI started its operations in the 1970s and basically everything was developed from nothing. It was the government that created ITRI which since then has been a very important part of the infrastructure to build up a semiconductor industry. The government also decided to set up a science park where the industry could be located.

Lee Chong Chou, STAG

the Technology Advisory Committee determined that the only realistic solution was to buy semiconductor technology from abroad.

However, although a substantial amount of money was invested in ITRI and ERSO, these organizations soon found that it was very expensive to license any cutting-edge solution. The only solution these organizations could afford was a technology (the 7.0 micron CMOS IC process) held by one of the world leaders in the area, the US company RCA. Although this technology was considered to be mature and on its way out of commercial use, it was licensed by the Taiwanese research organizations and, in 1977, the ERSO pilot plant started limited production of these integrated circuits. The CMOS circuits proved to be both energy efficient and robust. The first customer for the products was a producer of digital watches (an application for which energy efficiency was important) based in Hong Kong. In 1980, the Taiwanese government decided to create a science park in the Hsinchu area, where ITRI was located and ERSO became the first company there. ERSO's pilot plant together with some dozens of engineers was spun off as the United Microelectronics Company. As well as this major project, Taiwanese economic policy started to encourage employees of the research institute to establish spin-off projects and to start their own companies, something that was regarded as an important step in the enlargement of the Taiwanese semiconductor business network. Some of the companies that were spun off in the early 1980s were Taiwan's first integrated circuits design houses, Syntek Semiconductor Co. Ltd and Holtek Microelectronics. However, in the mid 1980s, Taiwan still had no large-scale producer of semiconductors.

In the early 1980s, Taiwanese policy experts advised ERSO to become involved in Very Large-Scale Integration (VLSI) technology, which the leading semiconductor companies in the US and Japan were already using. Compared to the CMOS, which ITRI and ERSO had improved from 7.0 to 4.5 microns, the capacity of the VLSI was about 1.0 micron. ERSO signed an agreement with two start-up organizations based in Silicon Valley and, in the mid 1980s, the Taiwanese research institutes had the capacity for the design and production of 1.0 micron semiconductors. The VSLI technology became the basis of the Taiwanese policy organization's ambitions to create a company engaged in semiconductor foundry work. In 1986, the first company engaged in large-scale production of advanced semiconductors was spun off, the Taiwanese Semiconductor and Manufacturing Company (TSMC), with Philips as co-owner. This company became the large producer of semiconductors that policy had long aimed for. It was followed by a number of start-up companies in the Hsinchu region, such as Destiny Technology Group, Realtek, Weltrend, Sunplus, ICSI and Eltron.

What's Missing?

The development of a business network related to the development, supply and use of semiconductors in Taiwan is without doubt remarkable. About 25 years after Taiwanese economic policy started to engage in the development of domestic knowledge production and commercialization of semiconductor technology, in the early 2000s, the country was ranked as the fourth largest producer of semiconductors in the world (in terms of revenue generated and production value), after the US, Japan and Korea. The Taiwan Semiconductor Industry Association estimated that 60 % of worldwide IC foundry, package and testing revenue and around 25 % of the worldwide design revenue was generated by Taiwanese semiconductor businesses.

It is easy to understand why the emergence of such a dynamic business network based on knowledge of the design, manufacturing and use of high-tech innovations has attracted so much attention. The widespread interpretation of what has happened, not only by Taiwanese policy-makers but also by academic scholars, is that the Taiwanese semiconductor business network is a text-book example of how research policy has successfully engaged in the production, transfer and commercialization of knowledge. Besides Silicon Valley, this is one of the success stories that has attracted most interest among social scientists trying to find the generic features of science-based businesses and economic growth. Taiwanese policy making towards the semiconductor business network serves as a major reference model for 'policy-driven development' of new, high-tech, knowledge-based business areas. Or, as it is expressed by the Taiwanese Ministry of Economic Affairs:

> In the coming decades, the biotechnology industry may very well be the major driving force behind Taiwan's economic development. We believe that with government policies driving the development of the industry, as well as the all-out promotion effects under the direction of the Ministry of Economic Affairs, the biotechnology industry will retrace the steps of its illustrious predecessors – the semiconductor industry and the information products industry.

But can the Taiwanese semiconductor business network really be regarded as the result of 'policies driving the development of the industry'? Were Taiwanese policy measures really undertaken in a virgin landscape or did they interact with some powerful forces in an already established semiconductor business network? Let us take a closer look at how the Taiwanese semiconductor development appears from an empirical interactive perspective.

Policy Measures and their Interaction with Established Activities

When the Ministry of Economic Affairs engaged in the development of a strategy to establish semiconductor businesses, the task of leading this work was given to a Taiwanese engineer working in the United States, at RCA Princeton. Through this recruitment, the door was opened to a rather special source of knowledge: Almost all the experts engaged in the Technology Advisory Committee were 'overseas', or US based, Chinese and Taiwanese engineers engaged in semiconductor development in academia or business. It was also these experienced semiconductor experts that started to develop ITRI and ERSO. (All these activities were located in the Hsinchu region, where Chiao Tong University had established Taiwan's first research laboratory engaged in semiconductor technology in 1964.) Thus, from the first day of activity in developing a domestic base of semiconductor technology, the Taiwanese engineers had major interaction with RCA, the world leader in this field.

When the ITRI was given the task of searching for a semiconductor technology to license from abroad, the most advanced integrated circuits were based on a 3.0 micron bandwidth. However, after approaching more than 20 US companies engaged in semiconductor development, it became clear that no foreign supplier was interested in licensing any cutting-edge technology to Taiwan. The only solution available was the mature 7.0 micron chips. However, one company's offer of this technology appeared much more interesting than the handful of others. RCA offered a 7.0 micron technology at a price that was twice as high as the second highest offer. But RCA also offered something more to the emerging Taiwanese research institute: A complete production technology, including process design, product specification and testing technology, and training for 35–40 Taiwanese engineers at RCA in the United States for about one year. When the agreement with RCA was completed, 37 Taiwanese engineers were sent out to different RCA plants and laboratories to learn more about the licensed technology. Meanwhile, the ERSO semiconductor laboratory established a pilot plant for semiconductor production.

The technology that was licensed to Taiwan was Complementary Metal Oxide Semiconductor (CMOS) technology, which was developed by RCA. The original bandwidth was 7.0 micron, but the technology was radically improved by ERSO. In the early 1980s, ERSO could provide CMOS of 4.5 micron and in the mid 1980s of 1.0 micron. The fact that Taiwan could not afford the most advanced technological solution, but had to go for the mature CMOS technology soon turned out to be an advantage. Although CMOS integrated circuits were a slower alternative to the more advanced solutions, they consumed less power. This meant that CMOS became an attractive solution for products where low power consumption was of greater importance than speed, for example in the watch industry. Because the CMOS technology was considered by the dominant US and Japanese semiconductor companies to be on its way out, it became a niche product which ERSO's spin-off, United Microelectronics Company, was one of the few able to supply. About two decades after ERSO started to engage in CMOS, this had become the predominant technology in integrated circuits through a combination of geometric downsizing, the development of its operating speed, energy efficiency and low manufacturing costs.

In the mid 1980s, Taiwan's involvement in semiconductor knowledge development and commercialization took a new direction, communicated by the new president of ITRI. The new president had three decades of experience in the US semiconductor industry, including time as head of global operations at Texas Instruments. This new direction was based on US companies' requirement for large-scale sub-suppliers of semiconductors. Hitherto, approximately 20 companies, the largest semiconductor companies in the world, had integrated the design and production of semiconductors. The growing use of semiconductors had increased the need for a large-scale supply of VLSI semiconductors, but none of the word's leading semiconductor companies was interested in undertaking the role of being both a sub-supplier and an end-product producer. For the Taiwanese research institutes ITRI and ERSO, however, this situation appeared to be an attractive opportunity. With its knowledge of VLSI technology, the Taiwanese research institutes could provide the design of 1.0 micron semiconductors, which at that time was considered to be very advanced. However, there were not yet any large-scale applications of the VLSI technology within reach.

The possibility of creating a large-scale VLSI semiconductor business, through governmental financial support combined with engagement from an international semiconductor user, appeared an attractive solution. Four world-leading semiconductor users (Texas Instruments, Intel, Philips and Matsushita) were also interested in the Taiwanese ambition to create an ITRI spin-off totally focused on a semiconductor foundry. Apart from Intel, all of these companies had a long tradition of production activities in Taiwan.[2] After negotiations, Philips remained and became the largest

---

[2]Philips was the pioneer foreign company to produce in Taiwan, in 1961, TV sets, audio equipment and related components. In 1962, Matsushita established a production facility in Taiwan, to be followed by, among others, RCA and Texas Instruments.

shareholder of the Taiwan Semiconductor Manufacturing Company (TSMC), established in 1986. Since the production facilities of Philips and most of the other foreign companies in Taiwan already included semiconductor assembly operations, it was but a short step to an involvement in a semiconductor foundry. Philips's involvement in TSMC was not only as a source of capital, but also as a large, skilled and demanding customer. Besides being its first customer, Philips also supported TSMC with a cross-licensing portfolio, product and process know-how and, not least, by adding legitimacy to the new production facility and its outputs. Until the end of the 1980s, TSMC had to rely on support from Philips in order to be able to produce advanced integrated circuits. However, at the end of the 1980s, both its customer base and its knowledge and experience of advanced semiconductors had grown so much that TSMC was able to design 0.8 micron integrated circuits without any technical support from Philips. In the early 1990s, a decade after the operations started, TSMC's annual sales surpassed US$1 billion and its production activities included the design and manufacturing of integrated circuit chips. A structure of related companies, many of them located in the Hsinchu Science Park, started to emerge around TSMC and its interaction with customers such as Intel and Texas Instruments.

From an empirical interactive perspective, the development of a business network related to the Taiwanese development, supply and use of semiconductors stands out as a remarkable journey. But the role of policy appears to be rather different from that which we outlined earlier. Certainly the Taiwanese policy organizations still appear skilled in their involvement in developing semiconductor technology. However, the skill that appears to have been most critical is the policy-makers' role as network actors: their ability, with the help of others and in relation to others across national borders, to create a space for Taiwanese organizations and companies in an international network related to the supply and use of semiconductors.

We use the experiences from the Taiwanese semiconductor development in a discussion of the role of policy in an interactive business world in the following sections. But first we consider some basic characteristics of business networks that policy aims to influence.

The Heaviness of Business Networks

The importance of others, in this case the importance of a pre-existing network developed in relation to the supply and use of semiconductors, is the main impression left by the Taiwanese semiconductor development journey. Strong interaction with and support from some global actors engaged in the development, production and use of semiconductors is a key feature of Taiwanese semiconductor development. However, this is not to say that Taiwanese policy measures were not important. They certainly were, but above all in terms of relating a domestic development to an already established global network involved in the development, supply and use of semiconductors.

This development journey also underlines two of the most critical features of business networks, one related to network structures and the other to network processes. Firstly, the Taiwanese semiconductor adventure illustrates the heaviness in terms of the related tangible and intangible investments over company and organizational boundaries that characterizes business networks. It was through relating to this heaviness, through mobilizing and recombining resources in

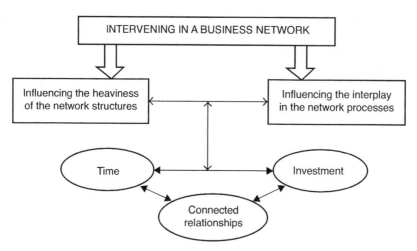

Figure 11.1 Intervening in business networks.

relation to the established semiconductor business network, that Taiwanese policy could both mobilize important technological solutions and interpret the large semiconductor users' need for sub-suppliers. All business networks have a structure that is based on the ways that resources are combined in specific constellations over company boundaries and this basic structure cannot be neglected by policy-makers.

Secondly, the Taiwanese semiconductor journey underlines the kind of interaction that is needed in order to influence or enlarge a network. The Taiwanese policy endeavours were a combination of measures carried out in relation to patterns of resource combinations, interrelated activities and interaction among actors that together constituted an international semiconductor network.

Thus, it takes something much more profound than bringing together some actors located in a particular place to interact socially with each other to influence a business network. Resources have to be developed and combined with related resources from other actors. Activities have to be designed and linked to related activities. These tasks are complicated because which resources and activities to use and where they are located in network space cannot be completely determined in advance. This implies that any actor that engages in the development of business networks as a policy maker or as an individual company is involved in processes of which they have an incomplete understanding. These fundamental aspects of the connection between policy and business networks can be further specified in three closely related aspects (see Figure 11.1).

Time

The criticality of time as a dimension in the emergence of a business network was clearly illustrated by the Taiwanese involvement in the development and commercialization of semi-conductor technology. When, in the mid 1980s, Philips decided to invest in TSMC, Philips had more than two decades of experience of producing electronic products in Taiwan. The policy-makers that were behind the design of TSMC had, in their turn, decades of experience working with US electronic companies in general and with semiconductors in particular and more than a decade of domestic development activities in relation to the US semiconductor business network. This time dependence is not unique to the Taiwanese semiconductor business network. Almost all companies which have actively developed their networks have worked with these issues over a long period of time; Toyota, Dell and IKEA are some of the best-known examples.

Time is important for several reasons: First, it takes time to develop new resources linked to connected resource combinations in suppliers and customers; to design activities related to the activity patterns on the supply and user sides and to involve related actors. Further, this issue is complicated by the fact that quite different types of companies, representing different types of resources and activities, have to be involved in order to cope with different development, production and use stages. Thus, the imperative for adaptations across organizational boundaries means that the emergence of business networks always will take time.

But time is also built into business networks. As the Taiwanese involvement in semiconductors illustrates, business networks are never solely based on new technological solutions, but on how these can be combined with the technology of yesteryear. It was not only the possibility of designing and delivering a robust and efficient type of semiconductor that was behind the establishment of TSMC, but also the ability to provide Philips and other big users of semiconductors with a production structure that increased the value of their established business activities. In order for any new technical solution to gain commercial use and to become embedded into a structure of producers and users, it has to be adapted to what already exists. In this way, business networks are conservative: They tend to preserve and protect existing investments. Both these aspects of time are important ingredients that have to be taken into account in attempts to influence the development of business networks. The importance of time has severe implications for policy-makers: first, a long-term commitment is necessary for any actor that wants to influence a network. Instead of expecting results within years, it seems to be more reasonable to expect an outcome within decades. Secondly, any actor that wants to influence a network has to relate to the historical processes that are built into contemporary development patterns. Development is likely to involve these being combined in new ways. For example, the Taiwanese policy-makers were involved with the CMOS semiconductor technology, which was generally thought by producers to be in decline because of its low capacity. But from the perspective of the users, including the watch industry, this technology was useful because of its low energy consumption.

Investments

Closely related to time is the need for investment in the design of activities and in the combinations of resources. Any business network consists of a number of activities and resources that have been systematically related to each other. These processes require substantial investment. As the Taiwanese semiconductor development illustrated, these investments are typically carried out stepwise over time, but once they are established they significantly affect the way that companies function in relation to each other. For example, the emergence of TSMC was the result of a series of stepwise investments; among others, in a new semiconductor production technology and in a large-scale production facility. However, once it had acquired this large-scale production facility, TSMC gradually took on the role of central sub-supplier and semiconductor developer, to which almost all of the largest semiconductor users became related.

The case above also illustrates that these investments can be carried out in many dimensions, from one company's education of another organization's staff, to the establishment of a production facility carried out in relation to a main customer. Investments in related activities and resources in well-established networks always covers a broad spectrum of dimensions; for example, administration, production technology, logistics, and so on. All these investments involve both physical and organizational resources. Any investment in adaptations to products, facilities and technological systems includes investment in the human resources that handle them. Together these resource investments form resource constellations that stretch over company boundaries. The total amount, as well as the dispersed nature, of these investments makes them difficult to manage or influence in any more substantial way. However, a network can be influenced by enhancing the type of investments that businesses are interested in but cannot afford to carry out by themselves. This was an approach taken by the Taiwanese policy-makers. Another way to influence investments in a network is to put the actors in the network under pressure, for example through legal regulation. However, both these types of approach to influencing a network require that the policy measures are backed up with some substantial resources.

Connected Relationships

The need for time and the dispersed type of investment patterns in business networks are an outcome of development processes that take place across company boundaries and consequently across spatial borders between regions, nations, cultures, industries and technologies. The spatial aspects of a network mean that companies engaged in the development of new resource combinations and the design of new activities invest *in relation to each other* in terms of adapted activities and resources and also in terms of knowledge about each other. Thus, interaction over time and space creates a number of imprints on the companies and the network. A crucial aspect of the development of business networks is that it is not enough that a policy organization and a company should develop a specific relationship, but that these relationships are connected to others in appropriate ways. For example, the Taiwanese policy-makers' co-investment with Philips resulted in a relationship with a leading, global semiconductor user. But this relationship also opened the door to other big customers. Thus, it is not relationships in themselves but the connections between relationships that provide opportunities to multiply the effects of individual investments.

If the investments made by different actors build on each other, as in the case of the US and Japanese adaptations which made possible the use of TSMC as a sub-supplier, then each actor gains greater benefit than if their investments had been made in competition with each other. Any actor that wants to influence a business network needs to consider how co-evolution can be fostered. One obvious aspect of this is that no relationship can be developed in isolation from other relationships. Thus the development of relationships can never be restricted to within specific spatial borders, but sets of relationships must systematically be connected to each other, between the 'small worlds' that we have referred to elsewhere in this book. But this does not mean that a joint master plan can be developed to encompass all of this relationship development. If there is such a master plan then the network disappears and is replaced by a form of hierarchy. In

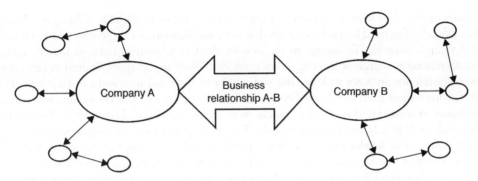

Figure 11.2   Connecting business relationships: a complex issue.

Chapter 9, we referred to the problems that arise for a single actor and for the network as a whole when a single actor attempts to control it as the third network paradox. It is through connections between pairs of relationships where each relationship is linked to others that developmental patterns emerge.

Taken together, these aspects of networks indicate the issues that face any actor that seeks to influence or 'create' a network: the economic heaviness of a network, its complexity, multidimensionality and interdependencies. These issues have some clear consequences for policy-makers.

The first consequence is that it is not easy to create business networks. It is in fact impossible for any individual actor (government included) to create a network by itself. The emergence of any business network is always the result of a number of companies' and organizations' interactions with each other (see Figure 11.2).

The issue of interactions as the driving force in network development is further complicated by the fact that these interactions have to involve different stages in development, supply and use of particular products or processes and consequently stretch over different technologies, industries, knowledge areas and space. However, as the Taiwanese semiconductor development has illustrated, this does not mean that it is impossible to affect a business network or support its emergence in a particular direction. But in order for policy measures to have any effect, they have to be tightly embedded into an already established and evolving supplier–user business network.

Another related consequence is that measures to create or influence business networks require endurance. It is only within a long time horizon and broadly defined purposes that the results of attempts at network development can be expected. The nature of network evolution involving extensive and diverse resource investments over time means that anyone who wants to be involved has to demonstrate that they are prepared to be engaged for a long period of time. The economic heaviness of business interaction only produces returns over the long term and this requires endurance from each participant. Further, the dynamics of the business network also require participants to be prepared to operate in a multidimensional context. Even if a single aim dominates a network for a period of time; for example to solve an environmental or narrow industrial issue, all networks all the time involve multiple, often competing aims and objectives for multiple participants. A business network is always used in different ways by different actors.

This may be excellent from a commercial perspective, but it makes the task of directing change rather difficult. The need for endurance also has some implications for those who seek to change and develop a network: To engage in the development of a business network may be easier than attempting to withdraw from it, unless economic losses are accepted. Indeed in one sense it is impossible for an actor to leave the wider network and still to remain in existence. But even leaving a more narrowly defined network for a business actor involves making its existing investment in human and material resources more or less worthless. The same is also true for policy-makers. It is only in retrospect that the Taiwanese policy measures appear as a successful contribution to the development of Taiwan's position in the semiconductor business network. It is easy to forget that for more than 15 years, the Taiwanese policy engagement was something that involved tremendous costs, but which did not result in any large-scale production and use of semiconductors.

Thus to engage in the development of a business network is to sign up for an endurance race and to engage in processes that stretch across spatial boundaries. However, policy measures can support network development if they relate to the pre-existing and evolving processes within a business network, especially to those within relationships across company and organizational borders. A critical issue is how to relate to continuing interaction and to the processes that can be facilitated or intensified. The interaction between companies and organizations that are related through their supply and use may be very light for historical reasons with legal, social or political roots. For example, the heritage from a centrally-planned political system, a top-down managerial culture, or a legal system oriented solely towards competition can hinder the development of decentralized interaction. In such situations, policy measures can be important for the support of interaction oriented towards the development and adaptation of physical and organizational resources.

However, and this is important, the fact that policy measures can develop network effects does not mean that network effects are entirely positive. As was underlined at the beginning of this chapter, the network also has a dark side; it can be non-transparent, non-democratic and manipulative. In the next section, we use another short empirical illustration to discuss the dark side that always accompanies the light side of networks. This network is also described as 'successful'. It involves relationships between scientists, investors and companies and results in a powerful mobilizing of resources directed towards a few influential actors.

What Is in the Shadow of a Successful Network?

Let us take a closer look at a network that is seen as a 'role model' in policy quarters and also among research financiers and business investors. (The following text is a short version of a case fully reported in Waluszewski 2006.)

An investment company, Woodheads AB, has been assigned the right of first refusal for commercialization of their research results by 45 researchers working at five Swedish universities. The foundation stone of Woodheads AB was the Populus Genomic programme, one of the most comprehensive tree genome programmes in the world. Woodheads was formed and is owned by researchers working at Umeå University (with Umeå Plant Science Centre as the lead department) and, in order of involvement, the Royal Institute of Technology, the Swedish

University of Agricultural Sciences in Umeå and Uppsala, Stockholm University and Uppsala University. The company is organized as a network; the researchers have their main work at their respective university, but the jointly owned company has first rights to exploit the research results for commercial purposes. The construction is completely in accordance with the Swedish system of regulations; through the 'teacher exemption', the researchers retain the copyright on their research results.

The world of research noted with great interest the work of mapping the genes of the tree *Populus trichocarpa*. When in 2005, the research network linked to Umeå Plant Science Center and Woodheads AB announced that they had found the gene that governs the tree's flowering, the news had great impact, with a publication in *Science* and an article about the project in *Nature Biotechnology*. The Woodheads researchers are also represented on bodies such as the government research committee, the Royal Academy of Sciences, the Swedish Research Council, the Swedish Natural Science Research Council, the Royal Swedish Academy of Agriculture and Forestry, and the Royal Swedish Academy of Engineering Sciences as well as a number of company boards. Since the company was set up, the 45 Woodheads researchers have also been successful in attracting research funding, or 'investments' as they are called in Woodheads' own terminology. The company reports investments of SEK 400 million over the last 10 years.

How then does Woodheads AB try to commercialize the results of the research to which it has access through its researcher network? Just as the researchers have assigned the first rights to Woodheads AB, this company has in its turn ascribed first rights to commercialization to the business world. The rights have been transferred to SweTree Technologies AB, which is a plant and forestry biotechnology company focusing on plant breeding for forestry companies and for industry based on wood fibres, such as pulp, paper and packaging companies. SweTree's vision is to become the leading supplier of a gene technology which regulates the growth of trees and the quality of wood. In this way SweTree hopes to be able to supply 'quality-improved' trees for areas that they believe can be particularly financially rewarding in terms of stronger or less energy-intensive wood as a raw material for the pulp and paper industry. SweTree's local manager in Umeå, Petter Gustafsson, who is also a Professor at the Department of Plant Physiology at Umeå University, is very optimistic about the practical applications:

> We can create trees with twice as much growth. In this way felling can be done in half the time that is currently required and the Swedish forestry industry has a real chance of countering the threat from the South American pulp and paper industry with its quick-growing eucalyptus.

The forestry industry's interest in SweTree was confirmed in May 2005 when SweTree acquired a new ownership structure. SweTree Technologies had already sold some licences to BASF Plant Science among others. But, in connection with a new share issue of SEK 50 million, three Swedish forestry companies, Holmen AB, Sveaskog AB and Bergvik Skog AB, joined as active part-owners of SweTree Technologies. The three Swedish forestry companies express great hopes that SweTree and the biotechnology proficiency of its researcher network will be able to increase the value of the raw forest material. Woodheads AB and its researchers on their part regard SweTree Technologies as the organization to which future commercialization will be referred: 'We estimate that SweTree Technologies in future will handle the majority of the "intellectual property" emanating from Nordic research in forest biotechnology of relevance to SweTree's business sphere.'

What then are the effects of the formation of the researcher and business network involving Woodheads AB and SweTree Technologies? Measured in terms of the number of patents produced, they are impressive. Before the construction of the network, the researchers at Umeå Plant Science Center did not possess a single patent. A decade later there are seven approved patents and approximately 70 more are under development. Thus, these developments can be regarded as concrete proof that it is possible to develop what so many policy operators at regional, national and trans-national levels have been wanting: Network-like organizations between university researchers and commercial operators. Seen from this perspective, it is scarcely surprising that Woodheads AB and SweTree Technologies have become a frequently told tale of success. For example, the Swedish Government Agency for Innovation Systems (Vinnova) draws attention to this network as a successful system of innovation, and as a positive model for how research can be used to create economic growth. Vinnova also encourages similar investments in related areas. The Swedish Research Council's chairman praises the construction in a column in the council's journal:

> I recently listened to Professor Ove Nilsson, head of SweTree Technologies, in Umeå. He gave a long list of examples of how patents and products have emanated from pure basic research. But more examples of this kind can be given. Even if it is difficult to make quantitative calculations of what an investment in research provides, one can use qualitative reasoning. And this convinces me at least that we need to invest in research in Sweden if we are going to keep up with international competition.

However, there have been some, rather weak, critical voices raised about the effects of the particular format of Woodheads/SweTree and the general idea of linking issues that were traditionally handled in more transparent organizations to non-transparent networks.

A first controversial issue concerns the gene technology itself, where the overriding question is whether it should be applied in a commercial situation at all. Environmental organizations such as Greenpeace, the Rainforest Action Network and the Union of Concerned Scientists do not wish to see any genetically modified tree species. The potential commercial users in business are also concerned at the strong reaction that genetically modified forestry provokes: 'Several forestry companies have expressly said that they do not want to have anything to do with genetically modified plants. Their environmental certification rules prohibit this.'

A second issue has been raised, including by researchers engaged in science studies (see e.g. Nowotny et al. 2005; Gibbons et al. 1994), in research environments that host research that constitutes the 'main investments' of private companies such as Woodheads/ SweTree. The issue concerns the compatibility between public universities' development of knowledge that is free to be used by anyone after it has been published and the creation of network structures which transform public knowledge into the property of private investors. A key issue is what happens when knowledge development financed with government or research funding is transformed into private intellectual property. One effect of these networks is that the economic use of research results is restricted to particular types of operators, those who can afford to invest in patents, as opposed to all the organizations and companies who can only make use of official publications and 'shareware'. A related question concerns how compatible these network structures are with the independence of research, when the same individual may be engaged simultaneously as a researcher in a university, a member of the board of research financiers and a representative of private investors.

A third topic is conspicuous by its absence. What the Umeå Plant Science Centre, Woodheads and the SweTree network has in common with so many other networks involving science and investors is that it has been successful in terms of raising money and creating patents. However, it is still a development company, which lives on its investors' money. It has a few pilot products, but it is far from relating to a substantial structure of business users. Thus, what is applauded as a success story is actually a network which has managed to organize the production of academic knowledge to include the supply of new economic resources. But it is still to be proved whether this network construction can also extend to the use of these resources.

The ambition to organize a network involving science and business underlines two important dimensions of networks: The first, which we also saw in the Taiwanese semiconductor example, is how difficult it is to establish networks that include the development of new knowledge, but also the use of that knowledge in a business setting. The second, which we discuss in the next section, is the non-democratic features of networks.

Light Side and Dark Side of Networks

Politicians, policy-makers and business want the light side of networks. One of the great benefits of a network is that its positive effects can be distributed among both directly and indirectly related actors, as was illustrated in the Taiwanese case study. For example, when a new end-product reaches customers, the benefits are distributed amongst related suppliers, sub-suppliers and complementary companies, across regional and national borders. Similarly, if some dominant companies commit themselves to involvement in innovation and efficiency improvements, it encourages related companies to join these endeavours. For example, several of the suppliers and sub-suppliers to IKEA underline that they would probably not still be in business, had they not been dragged into a tough and demanding development process.

However along with the light side, also comes the dark side of networks. The dark side has a number of aspects: The first of these relates to the power of pre-existing investments. Both of the cases that we have described illustrate the powerful effects of networks in giving direction to innovation and efficiency improvements. However, these effects tend to favour the main players in the existing structure of resource combinations and activity structures. Thus, network effects always tend to favour those who have the ability to mobilize resources, their own and those of others.

A second aspect of the dark side of the network appears when an end product faces a crisis. Then it is revealed that it is not only the benefits of the network but also its disadvantages that are distributed amongst interrelated firms across regions and countries. For example, when US consumers bought fewer cars from GM and Ford, the European media immediately highlighted the companies in European countries that are embedded in the associated business networks. A crisis in Detroit can have a major effect on a small component producer in northern Europe.

Last but by no means least, networks have a dark side in their relation to democracy, as our second case showed. There is no intrinsic fairness in a network. There is no reason to suppose that a network will provide the same opportunities for all those related to it; that it will operate in some 'common interest'; or that its direction, outcomes or benefits will be apparent to all. When some of the central actors in a network, such as the research leaders behind Umeå Plant

Science Centre and Woodheads, become involved in attempts to exploit particular knowledge resources in a commercial setting, it is difficult for more peripheral actors to mobilize support for development in a conflicting direction. An individual researcher, an environmentalist or a business actor operating under a different rationale may prefer to use plant biotechnology in a commercial setting in different ways. They face huge difficulties in carving out a space for alternative intentions so they are more or less forced to follow the dominant logic. A network can, as Hasselberg and Peterson (2006:358) underline, 'exercise an indirect influence over decision making which is almost invisible', i.e. it can function as a 'board in the shadows'. A strongly directed network can thus become a force which effectively destroys all other developments that conflict with its interests and those interests are not necessarily the same as those of the companies, organizations or societies within the network (Hasselberg and Peterson 2006:358–9).

The dark side of the network has some important consequences for economic policy: Networks are non-transparent, and support the main investments of the network and not local, regional or national interests. If a network is dominated by the investments of a few strong actors, then the network forces will protect their resource constellations and activity patterns. Thus, a first policy consequence is that there is no justification for leaving networks to themselves. In contrast, an important role for policy is to develop countervailing forces when the interests of the actors are seriously unbalanced. The influence of dominant actors' often needs to be restricted and the influence of weak actors needs to be supported. For example, a network that is characterized by minimal concern for environmental issues can be affected if actors that represent these types of resource constellations and activity patterns are supported.

However when considering attempts to influence a network, it is important to emphasize that a business network is not a smooth landscape and there is no homogeneity between different topic areas. This is illustrated in the next section when we try to summarize what policy-makers can do to improve innovation in a network setting.

What Can Policy-makers Do for Innovation?

Our discussions have suggested that there are at least three different aspects to all innovation journeys, which require quite different approaches from a policy point of view (see Figure 11.3).

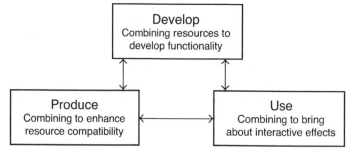

Figure 11.3   The interplay between development, production and use.

The first aspect is the need for development of new ideas and of new artefacts. Development can take place within established producer–user relationships and involve their respective R&D units, or it can take place in more distant settings: elsewhere in industry, in academia or in R&D institutes, and so on. There are a number of interesting possibilities for policy to influence both of these types of development process, as we discuss.

The second aspect of the innovation journey is the production of what has been developed. Anything new, whether it is an improvement to an established solution or a radically new science-based artefact, needs to be embedded in an efficient production setting. This in turn involves further development. The production setting is special because existing investments within suppliers and sub-suppliers have a strong impact on the design for producing something new, as we saw in the Taiwanese semiconductor case study. This aspect can also be influenced by policy, but it requires a different type of support from development.

The third aspect concerns how to develop the use of the new solution. As we discussed in the introduction to this chapter, this aspect has been rather overshadowed by the contemporary policy focus on how to achieve a transfer from knowledge development to a business setting. When a potential innovation is taken into a production setting, it is often described as having been 'commercialized', even though the long-term commercial use of the innovation has not been established. The Woodheads/SweTree case illustrated that a transfer of scientific-based knowledge to a business setting can be labelled as a success, even if the transfer only amounts to the establishment of a producer setting financed by venture capital, without any established user interface to give the new solution its long-term economic value. This does not necessarily mean that the question of use was absent when the new solution was developed and when it was embedded into a producer setting: A potential customer need has probably been defined. However, it is not until a direct interface has been established with some users that the benefits and drawbacks of relating the new investments to their place in a user setting will become apparent. The effect that the innovation has on its direct and indirect interfaces in the user setting determines its economic value.

Thus, in order for a new solution to become an innovation in widespread use, it has to survive in a developmental and producing context and also in use. This means that the innovation has to be adapted, in a number of ways that are often contradictory, and related to a number of established and new interfaces in each of these three settings.

In this section, we take a closer look at each of these sub-processes and their basic characteristics. It is important to remember that there is no simple and straightforward connection between the three settings: They are not made up of recognizable steps or stages, but are simply different empirical settings in which anything new has to survive in order to become an innovation. Secondly, these settings can be close to or distant from each other in network space. Development, production and use can take place among established business relationships, for example between a supplier and the development departments of its main customers. As we underlined in Part One, this is the most common way for innovations to occur in the business landscape. However, development, production and use can also take place in widely different settings, with little or no connection to each other before embarking on trials to convert a new solution into an innovation, as we illustrated in the SweTree/Woodheads case. The innovation journeys that include these different settings, especially where the new knowledge stems from scientific research are targeted as being of key interest for policy-makers. In order for anything new to become an innovation, it has succeed in each setting. If it fails in one of them, there will be no widespread use of something new: There will be no innovation.

Searching for New Functionality

The previous chapters have given many examples of the continuous search for new combinations of resources and successive changes of activities that take place within established relationships, within all the small worlds. These continuing processes provide policy with at least one main opportunity and one main difficulty. The difficulty is related to the way that these processes are hidden. We underlined in Chapter 8, that almost all company records are concerned with what is happening within companies. It is not easy for outsiders to gain an understanding of the kind of development efforts that go on within almost all kinds of producer–user interface, many of which are far away from being targeted as 'science-based' or 'high-tech'. However, policy has an important role in relation to the development of new ideas: It can intervene when the process appears to be lagging for whatever reason. First, policy can act as support when some of the actors lack resources compared to their counterparts that are involved in the development process. Secondly, policy can intervene in these processes if companies that dominate particular parts of a network contradict governmental policies on particular issues, for example in relation to overall economic policy, defence or environmental issues. Finally, policy can support companies that become vulnerable due to changes within some of their larger counterparts, involving mergers, relocations or financial problems. However, it is not easy to organize support for parts of established business networks, especially those that are under pressure, because the ownership and control of these companies are likely to stretch across geographical and political boundaries. Collective R&D programmes together with tax incentives for R&D investment are common approaches to the support of companies involved in development. The monitoring and maintenance of development processes within established business relationships is also an important – but often neglected – task for policy. Established business relationships are the main source of innovation in business networks. For this reason, it is probably more important for policy to consider how to support these development processes when compared with the search for potential innovation outside established business relationships, to which we now turn.

The search for innovation can have many origins: It can start with a particular resource which is tried in new combinations with others. But more commonly, it is the idea of a wholly or partially 'new' resource that is the starting point. The problem here is to turn the idea into concrete form and this usually involves production and testing facilities, which have to be found and assessed. Further, as soon as there is a prototype of the new resource then this has to be put into a context: All the expected and intended resource interfaces have to be examined. The functionality of the new resource is tested in the combining of all of these interfaces. This is obviously a creative process where many resource combinations are likely to be tried out and where restrictions and limitations become apparent. Regardless of whether a development project takes place in a business setting, an R&D institute or an academic environment, the functionality of a new process, product or component is at least partly unknown. Usually, a solution to the question of functionality is found by combining and recombining a large number of tangible and intangible resources. One very typical feature of this process is that it seldom achieves an optimum point or has a natural ending. Each ending is more or less an arbitrary freezing of a continuous process.

Thus, the main problem with this process is its openness. Almost anything is possible and the ways of combining and recombining resources are endless. This openness is important as it provides the opportunity for positive surprises. However, it is a problem from an economic perspective, as the process is costly; it has to be 'closed' or 'stabilized' in one way or another. Closing involves narrowing the solution on a number of dimensions and making the functionality more precise. Most innovators will have experienced a seemingly endless number of problems that arise during this process of closing the functionality. One common problem is that it is impossible to find a 'right time' for closing: The time is always arbitrary and the outcome is the best solution that the process has led to by the deadline.

The main problem with searching for and closing functionality is that this process is not fully anchored in any specific network. The new solutions may have been tried by many different actors *as a prototype,* but prototyping is far from really testing a solution in full relation to existing tangible and intangible resources. There is an obvious difference in this process when compared to development within established producer–user interfaces. When a new science or high-tech-based potential innovation has to be embedded into producer–user interfaces, its newness in relation to established solutions is not only obvious, but emphasized. This newness may not be welcomed by the existing network.

A general problem when developing and closing a new type of functionality is that some radical new feature can appear to be absolutely 'right' from the perspectives of the developer or policy-makers, but that same 'rightness' may create more problems than it solves in the network. The Taiwanese semiconductor development provides a good example of this phenomenon. It was not the most scientifically or technologically advanced solution that became embedded into a producer–user setting, but a mature product which created benefits on both sides of the interface. From a network point of view there are no reasons to extend this type of searching for new ideas: There are always too many of them. What are needed instead are serious efforts to try to anchor these ideas in a particular network.

Searching for Compatibility

A 'new' solution must also be embedded into a production structure. If it is a physical product then it has to be produced using particular inputs and a particular production process. If it is a service it has to be delivered using particular material and human resources. A main issue in both cases is the extent to which existing production facilities and processes can be used. This issue largely determines the cost of the new solution. The issue can be characterized as the search for compatible resources. In order to produce a wholly new solution or one that is an improvement on an established solution, it must be combined with other products and services, and production or logistic facilities. This will involve an already established network of production and delivery of material, components, software. The form of this existing network will have an important effect on the production and delivery of the new solution and on its design. The more that the new solution breaks with the pattern surrounding existing solutions, the more difficult it is to embed production of the new solution into that existing structure and the more expensive the new solution will be.

The main problem with this process is its dependence on other processes. A new solution has to be compatible with existing resources in order to be able to be produced economically, but it is never perfectly compatible. A key question then is, 'Will the new solution become more compatible with other resources over time?' In other words, 'Will others adapt their new resource investments to accommodate the new solution?' In this way, the production issue involves both the search for compatible resources and attempts to make the new solution so recognizable that the resource path followed by others can be adapted to it. In the Taiwanese semiconductor case, the new production facility became a central node in the evolving global production structure. Taiwanese policy played a significant role in this process. But the need to support companies in relation to wider production structures appears not to be an area that is prioritized by policy-makers.

Searching for Interactive Effects

The use of a new solution is, or should be, a central aspect of its development and production design. The idea of the use of a solution may emerge interactively between developers and users. However, the further away from producer–user interaction that the new solution has emerged, the greater are the potential surprises when the solution is exposed to user interfaces.

When a new solution is used, it encounters a number of interfaces with established resources in the use context. Some of these interfaces would probably have been identified, based on experience, when the new solution was developed and its functionality was designed. But other interfaces may not have been anticipated and some may be affected negatively. The resources that are directly involved are, in turn, related to other resources that are affected indirectly by the new solution. This can lead to a variety of positive and negative reactions. A solution that a user may find valuable in relation to the resources with which it is directly involved may be much less valuable when its indirect technological, economic or social effects are taken into account. The use of a radical new solution inevitably involves considerable uncertainty when a number of direct and indirect interfaces meet the solution for the first time. This may lead to a long process of trial and error before any reasonable use can be found for something radically new.

The use process is similar to the previous two processes. It is similar to the idea-generation process as it involves the same open combination with other resources. Further, potential users are likely to have quite different interests and these lead to the search for new resource combinations that were not considered during the development process. The use process also has similarities to the production process. Both involve the requirement for the solution to combine with a number of other tangible and intangible resources.

The use process is problematic for policy-makers to influence, but at the same time it is the most crucial one. Innovation boards or agencies often require that there must be one or several users involved in development projects. But this is usually not nearly enough: It is easy for a single, possibly an unusual, user to find reasons to take part in a development project. One way of involving users that has been tried is through government. But the government may not be a 'normal user' and there are many examples in which involving government has taken innovation away from civilian use. Governmental involvement has also been severely restricted by the limitations imposed by legislation on governmental purchasing.

An Iterative and Interactive Process

The differences within the three processes involved in innovation make it very unlikely for them to ever appear in a linear form that starts with development and ends in use. Instead, especially in the case of more radical situations, a solution has to go back and forth between the three processes: A preliminary version is developed, produced on a small scale and trialled. The experience from this process is then used to revise the development, which in turn is the starting point for a new production, which in turn is the starting point for a new use, and so forth. Thus, the development of something new means searching for new solutions, but so does the production of something new and the use of something new. The need to support the development of something new is well recognized by policy-makers. However, the need to develop production and use is seldom recognized on the policy agenda. If policy-makers seriously want to support the development, production and use of something new, then the developmental endeavours involved in production and use also have to be recognized and supported.

Conclusion

Any discussion of policy has to be based on an idea of the business landscape. Both policy-makers and researchers commonly view the business landscape as a 'network', but with some very different interpretations. Contemporary policy-making often rests on the assumption that the business landscape has the characteristics of a traditional market and that it is possible to develop network-like innovation systems within that market in order to solve some specific, regional or national knowledge development and transfer problems. The approach outlined in this book presents a view of a very different type of business landscape, where each interdependent company is embedded into a network structure where resource combinations and activity structures are developed and related to each other over time and space. If policy is to intervene in a business landscape having these characteristics, it has to deal with interaction between different actors with different rationalities, not only across company borders, but also across geographical and political borders.

The conclusion to this chapter is that there are strong reasons for policy-makers to be highly involved in a business landscape characterized by networks, in order to deal both with its light and dark sides. From a democratic point of view, policy has reason to act as a counterforce against the non-transparent, non-democratic and economically conservative features of business networks. However, policy can also use the positive features of business networks: The combining of resources and linking of activities that continuously take place within and across business relationships provide opportunities for policy initiatives and support. These initiatives may be undertaken in order to intensify particular processes of knowledge development or production or to improve or facilitate the use of new products or services.

This chapter has pointed to two important requirements for policy: its involvement has to have endurance. Particular network processes have to be followed and supported or hindered over time. Secondly, the engagement of policy has to be spatially dispersed. Particular network processes have to be followed, supported or hindered over space. Both these requirements are challenging to those who set the policy agenda, which is often based on an over-developed trust in their ability to create rapid network effects within narrow geographical and political borders.

Finally, this chapter has moved our discussion of the characteristics of the interacted business landscape away from a narrow focus on companies and individuals and into a wider network view that encompasses policy-makers, government agencies and academia. But our discussions within this chapter have emphasized that this wider perspective is still one of a network. All of those involved in the network are simply actors in it, all are interdependent with others and all of their activities and resources, and they themselves take their form and play out their role interactively with others. Each can influence the direction of the network, but none of the actors started the network, no one designed it, no one owns it, no one controls it. Nor is it limited to the geographical, cultural, industrial or intellectual boundaries of their imaginations.

LIVING IN THE BUSINESS RAINFOREST

12

The Rainforest Metaphor

We started this book by using the metaphor of the rainforest to highlight what seem to us to be the dominant characteristics of the business landscape. In this final chapter, we reflect on the rainforest metaphor and on the insights that it provides into the business landscape and also on some of the things that we have learned during the writing of this book. We then build on some of the ideas that we have developed in the book to suggest some of their implications for a variety of the inhabitants that populate what we refer here to as 'the business rainforest'.

It is important to state that we did not have the rainforest in mind when we started our research into what we then referred to as 'industrial marketing and purchasing' all those years ago. But the rainforest metaphor came to us during the research process and seems to us to neatly encapsulate much of the essence of the business landscape that we have been and are still groping towards.

The starting point of our research was the empirical observation of business relationships that existed between companies and stretched over time and space – and thus involved multiple transactions. This observation evoked the understanding that the millions of daily business transactions are somehow related to each other – which is intuitively appealing. It also evoked an interest in further, deeper investigations of the content and effects of this relatedness. Our research revealed that those involved in buying or selling appeared to have aims, expectations and above all problems that are unique to them and that go beyond what can be reached or solved by any single transaction or generalized as a 'market'. It showed that a business transaction involves costs of search and evaluation before it takes place, and re-evaluation and learning after it has taken place. Thus, each transaction affects both the other transactions of those involved and their internal operations. This relatedness implies that business transactions include adjustments and adaptations by those involved. They involve specific investments by both parties to a transaction. Achieving a return on these investments requires more than one transaction. Thus, making those investments involves expectations of future, as well as more immediate, benefits.

From these observations it was easy to embrace the continuity of business transactions and the interdependence within the relationships. A related observation was that for any business transaction to come to fruition requires that both participants are involved in transactions with others. Similarly, any transaction enables both participants to take part in other transactions with others, based upon it. Thus, for a single service to be provided to a customer requires that the supplier has bought materials and equipment from others and hires and transports staff to the customer. Following receipt of the service the customer can then supply its services or products to others and so on across the landscape. Thus the observation of the uniqueness and connectedness of each problem-solving process between businesses over time and space was already indicated in our initial observations of business relationships.

By taking the relationship as the unit of analysis for our early research, we *accidentally* set ourselves on a path that was to lead to the rainforest metaphor. It is only in retrospect that we are fully aware that our research has been concerned with the ways that the business landscape shapes each unique business actor. It is now clear that we have been looking at the interplay between the business landscape and the actor and our starting point has been in the business landscape rather than the actor. We may contrast this approach with that taken in the majority of academic studies and disciplines and, predictably, by managers, which we outlined in Chapter 8. The almost universal unit of analysis in business research is the company. To use an analogy: It is as if the company was a box and the researchers and managers are together in the box. They are concerned with what happens in the box because these happenings appear to be the most important contribution to the well-being of the 'box'. The view of the world for those in the box is from the inside, looking outwards. Almost inevitably, this view of the business world is expressed in terms of the problems, culture, activities and resources of the people who are in the box. Those in the box are likely to view management as a process of developing supposedly independent actions by the box towards the outside world and of reacting to what that generalized 'outside' can do to the box.

But our accidental path that started with the observation of business relationships led us to see each company as only a part of those relationships. This path led to the empirical observation that individual business relationships were multidimensionally *unique* in the resources and activities that are involved in them and in how they evolve in juxtaposition with those of others along a time continuum. It appeared that a small number of these unique relationships are individually of overwhelming importance for each actor. In fact they appeared to be so important that by describing them we could arrive at a very accurate view of the actors themselves. The relationships we observed were clearly inter-connected with others in a network form and so it appeared that what happened in any one relationship was but a single set of outcomes related to what was happening in many others.

It seems a simple truth that business involves actors in providing economically valuable outcomes for others. It is an equally simple truth that the provision of economically valuable outcomes for others has to relate in some way and at some time to the receipt of similar outcomes from others. It is also a simple truth that no actor can provide these outcomes for others alone, on the basis of its own activities and resources. Further, each actor effectively receives these outcomes 'on behalf of' others with which it interacts. But almost all of the business actors that we observed empirically depended on the resources and activities of others to a much greater extent than they depended on their own.

Expressed more simply, the accidental path of our research towards the network that surrounds business actors led us to the view that what happened outside a company and between it and others was more significant to that company than what happened inside it. We acquired the view empirically that business is something that takes place uniquely between identifiable actors. This empirical observation pointed us to the idea that the activities and resources that are notionally within an actor are not the outcome of processes within the actor but of their interaction with those of specific counterparts.

The rainforest metaphor emphasizes processes that take place within business interaction and interdependent relationships. It doesn't depend on explicit or implicit cooperation between business actors, but it does suggest the universal 'taking account' of others. Thus the rainforest metaphor posits a universal relatedness which we can trace across the business landscape. This relatedness affects what happens between all involved companies. It is the evolving outcome of interaction through which individual actors seek advantage with, through, against and alongside others.

The idea of interaction has permeated this book. But it is an idea that has been difficult for us to capture clearly. Interaction is a very general term that is used throughout the social sciences and in common speech. It is associated with coming together and with the benefits of getting to know others. Business interaction does involve what happens between individual actors but the key to business interaction is that it is not limited to what happens between people or to their conversations or negotiations. Substantive interaction is the process through which activities, resources and actors are confronted, sometimes brutally, sometimes destructively and sometimes creatively. When activities, actors and resources interact they are changed and ultimately transformed.

Interaction is a process of the rainforest. It is also a process of the business landscape and most profoundly it means that no actor exists alone or acts alone. Each actor is the outcome of previous interactions and its place is a result of a network of interactions. Each actor is in a stable but evolving state. At the simplest level, interaction may involve the connections that develop between a production schedule and a logistics schedule. At a more complex level, it involves the evolution of whole patterns of activities and constellations of resources.

The early part of this book was built on an analysis of the interaction between different activities and resources in Chapters 5 and 6. This analysis is close to much of our research experience. The most straightforward issue that comes from this analysis is the absence of a fixed or objective existence for either activities or resources. An interactive view of the business landscape suggests that the form, use and development of each resource and activity is not determined by a single actor or by the characteristics of the activity or resource itself, but by its interaction with others. This again relates to the rainforest metaphor. An interactive view of inanimate activities and resources is perhaps easy to cope with. Less easy to cope with is an interactive view of the business actor. How can an actor, safe inside its box be defined by others? Indeed we have admitted that our ideas on the interactive impermanence of the business actor are still undeveloped. In Chapter 7, we attempted to come to terms with the inherent contradictions of being a business actor: The rainforest metaphor points us towards the connections between individual plants and species. Each is an individual entity but each can only survive with others. The idea of jointness captures the contradictory existence of the business actor as an observable and accountable unit with mutually essential co-existence with others. Business actors and the managers within them are knowledgeable. They know their own activities and resources and those of their immediate counterparts, in their *small world*. But they are faced with a wider world on which they depend but of which they can know little. The small world of the business actor is the basis for its co-evolution alongside others.

Throughout this book, we have suggested that the network-like business landscape that we have observed is not a transitory phenomenon, but its particular form at any one time is impermanent and subject to interactive evolution. The business network is not a managerial innovation nor is it a business technique. The idea of the business network that we have expressed in this book is only valid if it is a description of the pervasive network form rather than simply of the *current* business network. The forms of interaction may change, the pattern of interdependencies may shift but there is interaction and there is a network (Johanson and Waluszewski 2007). It is perhaps inevitable that the idea of the business network would be appropriated by consultants and by policy-makers as a technique. But rather than a technique that can be applied by a single practitioner, all those that inhabit the business network are simply actors in that network and are not its initiator, owner or controller.

We can now look in slightly more detail at what it means to be a particular sort of actor in the network or to live in the rainforest. We do this with trepidation because, as we have said throughout this book; all actors are unique at a particular point in network space and time and there are no generalizable formulae for 'network success'.

Living in the Rainforest

We have described the business landscape as being formed through interaction in which resources, activities and actors are combined and transformed. Life for an actor in this landscape, whether for an individual, a company, a business unit, a government body or another organization, involves coping with the constant motion of the landscape in which all activities, resources and actors themselves change over time. Each business actor is involved with others in exploiting the heterogeneity of resources by combining them in new ways at the same time as they are linking their own and others' activities differently to exploit and develop interdependencies. Each business actor is also changing, partly because of the combined effects of shifts in resources and activities and partly because of the developing jointness between them and others. The result is that the landscape is in constant motion as actors co-evolve, resources move along particular paths and activities become successively more specialized in one or more directions. This is a multidimensional process in which there is no fixed point and in which it is interaction between elements that provides the major means of achieving change and stability.

Even if most actors are very knowledgeable about their own small world there is no one who understands the total structure of the network. The diversity, motion and pattern of interdependence of the landscape means that no individual can operate in it alone, none can achieve change alone or predict outcomes with any certainty. Each actor in the network has its own individualistic 'picture' of the network which forms the basis for its assessments, intents and approaches to others. This picture is based on its own experiences, its position in time and space within its relationships and its interdependencies with others.

The structure of the business network cannot be adequately described in terms of companies and their products. The structure is ephemeral and difficult to capture because it consists of the relationships and individuals that stretch between actors. But this unknowable, ephemeral structure is 'heavy' with the human, physical and financial investments that have been made in it. The heaviness simultaneously acts as a brake on change and at the same time provides the means for change. This situation was described by one manager as follows: 'If I get the network with me everything is possible but if I don't get the network with me nothing is possible.'

Interaction with others is the key means for those who live in the business rainforest to prosper and develop. The resources and activities of these 'others' are as important for a single actor as are its own. Similarly, the intents of these others are as important in determining the direction of an actor as are its own wishes. It is through combining resources and linking activities with each other that actors develop, create value for each other and address each other's problems. It is only through others that business actors can acquire their respective and collective identities and roles. It is through others that actors can live and prosper. It is through interaction with others that business actors learn, teach, serve, utilize and become appreciated.

In order to get a more detailed picture of what it is like to live in this business landscape, we now take some of the typical titles given to individual business actors and sketch out some aspects of the roles that may be associated with those titles. Five titles may be identified as useful starting points: the entrepreneur, the initiator of a new business; the Chief Executive Officer (CEO), the leader of a business unit or company; the accountant manager; the consumer; and the politician. The CEO and the accountant relate closely to the way that we have discussed the problems of managing in a business network and provide a summary of some of the main points of that discussion. The consumer and the politician are important elements both in specific interactions within the network and, at the same time, in a wider or more general role in shaping its overall form.

The Entrepreneur in the Business Rainforest

The emergence of a new business actor within a network can take many forms. At a mundane level, the entrepreneur may simply be an individual establishing a new business that attempts to operate on a similar basis to many that already exist. Perhaps the entrepreneur seeks to capitalize on his previous experience or existing relationships to achieve this and develop or gain access to similar activities and resources to those that already exist. In terms of the rainforest metaphor, this represents the arrival of a new example of species of plant that already exists in the rainforest. This entrepreneur faces similar problems to others around it and probably finds it necessary to adapt its resources and activities to be at least slightly different from those of others if it is to succeed in developing a viable position in the network. In fact, no single new entry to the existing business network is the same as those already existing: Whether by accident or design, the new entry develops at least some different features or relationships or is associated with different activity or resource structures and in this way contributes to the evolution of the network.

On another level, the entrepreneur may be someone who seeks to develop a new form of business. This may involve new technology, or the introduction of new resources or activities, either to particular parts of the network or to small worlds of actors. It may also involve altering the existing structure of relationships and interdependencies by removing (de-intermediarization) or adding (re-intermediarization) intermediaries to existing relationships. For example, the entrepreneur may seek to establish itself as an intermediary between particular actors and their customers or suppliers to achieve greater efficiency or effectiveness or to address particular problems that existed in the previous relationships. In contrast, the entrepreneur may seek to side-step existing relationships and interact directly with customers or suppliers. In terms of the rainforest metaphor, this sort of entrepreneurship is the business equivalent of the introduction of a new species.

An entrepreneur of this type inevitably disrupts some aspects of the existing network: its activity structure, resource constellations or the interdependencies between actors. Each actor that enters the network, like any newly-arrived species, faces a variety of different conditions, both favourable and unfavourable. The key to this is the characteristics of the existing relationships that surround it: On the one hand, the more that the new actor fits into the existing activity, resource structure and interaction patterns, the easier it is for it to become part of that existing structure. But, consequently, the less is the impact of the entrepreneur on the network. In order to add to or to transform this structure, the new company has to break with some aspects of the existing structure. Thus it is likely that those entrepreneurial actors whose approach involves the most development of activities and resources or that face the greatest difficulties in establishing themselves in the existing interaction pattern will have the greatest effect on the network. Thus each entrepreneur faces important choices about how different to be. Similarly each entrepreneur faces the same important issues about the stages of innovation, design, make and use that we considered in Chapter 11 in the particular case of technological innovation.

A typical feature of entrepreneurship is the length of time that is involved. Much of this time is spent in the development and production phases before the entrepreneurial venture is more widely apparent to those in the network. As we saw in Chapters 5 and 11, the development process for innovation is unlikely to be neatly sequential. Initial ideas usually have to be changed and modified, particularly in relation to the existing structure and process of interaction. Counterparts have to be won over to the changes in activities and resources that are needed and mobilized to investigate how they can link into the entrepreneurial actor. Those that may be damaged by the changes may have to be circumvented, excluded or bought off.

The existing actors in the business landscape usually have a confused attitude towards new ideas and new entrants. On the one hand, actors are constantly searching for ways to improve their own activities, use their own resources and develop their relationships with other actors. On the other hand, these actors have significant investments in existing ways of living in the network. They may be comfortable in their small worlds and keen to avoid change that may be costly or appear threatening and that may conflict with the rules, norms and 'network constitutions' under which they live. The longer that these accepted ways of operating have persisted, the more likely are incumbents to react against outsiders. But on the other hand, the more reactionary incumbents are, the longer is the time before they effectively respond to the entrepreneurial actor. Changes that improve conditions for incumbents without changing the status quo too much are always appreciated, but larger changes take a much longer time and require that a greater number of counterparts are mobilized. The ambition to create a revolution is seldom applauded in a business network.

Who is a successful entrepreneur in this kind of business landscape? One critical aspect is likely to be having experience and close contacts with the existing structure. Another is special knowledge around either activities or the resource structure. Many successful entrepreneurs are those that bring an existing activity and resource structure from one part of the network and apply it elsewhere.

In both of these cases, it is clear that there are rarely any 'new' actors. Most apparently new actors are the outcome of previous interactions, either directly within existing relationships or those that surround particular resource and activity combinations. The identification by a potential entrepreneur of a particular or even a common problem in the network is unlikely on its own to form the basis for the development of a new species, unless it can be associated with a viable interactive structure and process.

The CEO in the Business Rainforest

To act as the top manager (CEO) of a company in the business rainforest is to be part of a vast interlocking network of activities, resources and other actors that stretch within and across the boundaries of her own company and many others. Even the CEOs of the largest companies are just nodes in the network. None of them is at its centre and none of them controls it. To act as the CEO of a company means taking responsibility for at least some of the outcomes from a vast array of activities, actors and resources. However, only a few of these are within the CEO's direct control, knowledge or even within her sight. For better and for worse, to act as CEO means to be judged as if the things that happen to her company are within the CEO's capacity to order and as if the outcomes are the result of the CEO's decisions. Thus, to act as CEO of a company means to be assessed at arbitrary points in time for processes that started long before the CEO's arrival. And, it means to create good and bad outcomes for many different actors long after the CEO has gone. All aspects of what a CEO does, the resources she seeks to use, the counterparts with which she trades, the activities that take place around her are but transitory outcomes within an evolving process of interaction between limitless numbers of activities, actors and resources.

Throughout this book we have discussed interaction in time and space. Time is perhaps more important for the CEO than for all other actors: Specifically the times of the CEO's entry to and exit from a company are critical for her 'success' or 'failure. This is expressed in terms of the seemingly defining but in fact only transitory outcomes of interaction at those times. Space is equally of huge importance for the CEO personally: An interactive perspective on business highlights that a company is not 'good' or 'bad' because of what it has, what it does, or how it does it, but because of how it relates to other actors in the network space. Experience emphasizes the importance of the 'picture' that the CEO has of her own company and others within network time and space and outside her small world, as opposed to the CEO's abilities to manage operations or even to motivate others. Experience also suggests that many of the most significant battles fought by CEOs are those with others inside the 'box' of her own company, whose attitudes to change are similar to the attitudes to entrepreneurial change of those operating in long-established networks. These internal battles were neatly expressed to us by one chief executive as follows: 'The bastards are trying to sabotage my changes.' Other battles fought by CEOs are likely to be those with significant counterparts that have a different picture of the network in space and of who does what and who should do what, at what time, and these involve different views of costs and benefits for different actors over different time-scales.

Most companies are highly dependent on a relatively small proportion of important customers and suppliers. The CEO probably knows this small world rather well. Relationships with a company's major counterparts are likely to be intense and complex and at least partly visible to the CEO. Many companies also have a large number of less important or smaller relationships. These are likely to be as heterogeneous as the larger relationships, at least from the perspective of the counterpart, but each is less visible, less easy to understand and less easy to interact in. Many of the company's larger counterparts depend heavily on interaction with the CEO. The CEO's interactions with them may be long term and may involve well-developed mutual expectations and obligations. But many of the CEO's relationships as well of those of her company will have become *institutionalized*: They will have settled into a particular pattern of interaction through inattention or indifference and will fail to meet the requirements of either of the counterparts. There are no neat or predictable connections between the complexity of a relationship, its age, its volume, its profitability, its wider long- or short-term benefits, the efforts devoted to it, the learning it represents, its connections to other relationships or its potential for the company's future. All relationships are unique in their characteristics and the meanings that they have for all those involved in them. All have to be managed carefully. A company's relationships are among its prime assets: Without them it cannot buy and cannot sell. It cannot trade. A company's own resources, both tangible and intangible and its own activities are also part of a company's prime assets. But without its relationships, a company's resources and activities lose their value. Without the respective resources and activities of the counterparts, a company's resources and activities have no value. The core of the CEO's role lies in the connections between her company's resources and activities and its relationships. Through these relationships, its own and others' resources and activities are combined, developed, exploited and transformed. And it is through these relationships that the CEO's primary role in the transformation of the company can be achieved.

The days of a CEO in this environment are spent in 'relating' to others, assessing their pictures, problems and assets. They are also spent teaching and seeking to change the pictures of others or to lead or *coerce* them in areas of her expertise. They are also spent in learning from others and *conceding* to their expertise. In other words, the CEO is someone who chooses those areas in which she depends on others or seeks their dependence on her.

Many of the dependencies on others that the CEO needs to develop are with those in her own company. Therefore it is valuable for the CEO to relate the development of her leading team to the surrounding network, both in terms of who should be involved and where they should be positioned within the company. It is an advantage if the network is 'mirrored' in its different aspects in the leading team, so that it includes some people with intimate knowledge of significant counterparts and of the resource and activity structure of the network and how it relates to the company. It is important that the CEO knows the network pictures of these managers *and that these pictures are diverse*. But even more important is that the debate between the CEO and her management team is expressed in the language of the network and not of the company. This is one occasion when the cliché, 'think outside of the box', is worth repeating.

The Financial Accountant in the Business Rainforest

Financial accounting in the business rainforest presents major problems for the CEO and for accountants themselves. This is because accounting is usually restricted to a company and to its identifiably internal activities and resources. If we return to the analogy of the company as a 'box', then accounting is concerned with recording the dimensions of the 'box' and how these have changed over an arbitrary period of time. There are obvious constraints on accounting in a legal system that views commerce as something that is carried out by discrete and independent corporate entities, but it is important for the CEO and others to have financial information on which they can base their 'networking'. The issue of financial accounting does not stand alone. Instead it relates closely to two major aspects of contemporary business.

All companies face the pressures of increasing costs of developing and using the resources on which they depend in their interactions with others. Increased technological intensity has reinforced the need for the specialization of companies that has traditionally been the basis of their interdependent relationships with others. An important aspect of contemporary specialization is the separation between the development, production and use of technologies between different actors in the business network, as we discussed in Chapter 11. So for example, it is now common for some companies to concentrate solely on the design of offerings, whilst others make to the designs developed by counterparts and use dedicated intermediaries to provide supporting services and logistics specialists for deliveries. The enhanced dependence that arises from this specialization frees up a company to invest its scarce resources in more productive activities and resources. However, specialization places great emphasis on the appropriateness of decisions on technological investment. These decisions are always long-term and cover a time span greater than the life of single products. They are likely to involve major investments and, in some cases, require funding greater than the net worth of the companies making them. The time and costs involved in developing specialization mean that many specialization decisions involve companies in effectively forfeiting all other corporate directions.

The challenges for accounting of technologically and operationally specialized companies relate to the ways that the costs and returns of technological resources are calculated and presented as *assets*. Accounts reporting commonly takes place at the level of individual products or operating units and is based on costs and revenues for particular transactions or fixed periods of time. But accounting for technologically specialized companies involves consideration of the investments and returns on technological resources and investments that transcend individual products or operating units in time and in their possible multiple applications at different points in network space. Accounting for technological resources involves time periods relating to the life of the technology itself. While it is common for accounting to accommodate individual development projects or particular products, it is rare to find accounting that takes the broader perspective of return on technological investment over multiple products, multiple applications, multiple time periods and in combination with other types of technology.

The interdependence of companies in the business rainforest has implications for the concept, evaluation, use and accounting for business relationships as *assets*. We have emphasized the centrality of a company's relationship assets. But the valuation of these central assets is often subsumed under the generalized concept of 'good will'. Each of a company's relationships is unique. This means that companies need to financially evaluate each of these assets and re-evaluate them over time. Business relationships as assets are also important in relation to other assets. It is generally considered important for companies to apply a realistic value to their assets in market terms. However, in the current business landscape, many assets represent investments made as part of the development of specific relationships. Some of these assets have little or no value in other relationships or in some generalized or hypothetical market. Further, if many business assets have only relationship-specific value then that value is tied to the other assets of that relationship that are held on the books of a counterpart. The value of these assets relates to the continuing investments of both counterparts. Thus, asset value is often a property of a relationship, rather than of a company.

Business relationships take time to develop and involve considerable investment. A business relationship may be built round a single transaction as in the case of a major capital purchase or sale. Other relationships involve frequent and regular transactions whilst others may continue with infrequent and irregular purchases. In many of these cases, the cost and revenues that relate to a single transaction give an erroneous idea of the real profitability of that transaction, of the product or service involved in it, or of the customer. The development of a business relationship is likely to involve negative cash flows, particularly in its early stages as contacts are made, time is spent and adaptations and investments occur. Even long-established and well-developed relationships incur costs of operation, maintenance and adaptation. As a relationship develops, a vendor is likely to receive positive cash flow from the customer and the customer is likely to gain financial benefits from the relationship in terms of cost reductions or benefits in its other relationships. However, even though individual transactions may be profitable at any time in the relationship, the relationship itself only achieves profit for either counterpart when cumulative cash flow becomes positive. The time for this to be achieved is frequently measured in years. The importance to companies of small numbers of individually important relationships and the impact of time on them involves a reorientation in accounting theory towards performance over relationship time rather than over calendar time or for individual transactions or products.

The Consumer in the Business Rainforest

Consumers have not figured in our discussions in this book, but they underlie all of the interactions between business actors and without them there would be no network. Consumers have two connected roles in the business landscape: They are involved as individuals in both direct and indirect interactions with particular business actors and they may also participate in interaction in the business landscape as part of an organized collective.

The relationships between a single individual consumer and business actors may appear both individually insignificant and one sided, with the strength clearly on the side of the business. But a closer examination indicates some less obvious aspects of the interaction between a single individual and a business: We discussed asymmetry in business relationships earlier in this book and pointed out that it is unlikely to extend over the entirety of a relationship in favour of one of the counterparts. This is clearly the case in business–consumer interaction. The economic strength of the business is almost always greater than that of the individual consumer. But the situation of interdependence is reversed in the case of information. The consumer knows far more about his interactions with the business than does the business. Business actors now invest hugely in attempts to track individuals' consumption patterns and to interact with them directly via call centres, and so on. But business actors still have inadequate information about their interactions and particularly in how they relate to each consumer's interactions with other businesses and individuals. Because of this, they usually have to treat single individuals as members of a large and inevitably heterogeneous 'market segment'.

Consumers are not passive in their interactions with businesses. Like other business actors, consumers are very much the outcome of their interactions with others, in both social and business contexts. Also like businesses, consumers are adept at managing a portfolio of relationships with different business actors, using each for solving specific and different problems. For example, one major supermarket group saw itself as a direct competitor to two other major groups. It commissioned market research on how customers compared the three stores on a range of dimensions. But research showed clearly that many consumers did not see the stores as competitors. Instead, they had chosen to manage their relationship with the supermarket solely for the purposes of 'top-up' or emergency purchases. They had developed a quite different relationship with other retailers for their main or stock shopping. It was quite clear that the consumers were very adept at choosing relationships and developing their knowledge and schedules to capitalize on them appropriately. Finally, there is another non-trivial point on the relationship between a business and an individual consumer: The consumer has the power to walk away from the business but the business can't walk away from the consumer.

Consumers are increasingly organizing themselves to become powerful collective actors in the business rainforest. Over the years, many businesses have tried to become involved with and develop particular relationships with various social organizations, consumer clubs and associations, which, at least in some fields, have become interesting collective actors. Similarly, consumer pressure groups have developed particular relationships with different business actors that they see as important nodes in the network of businesses or the wider network of businesses and consumers. Well-known examples include the early targeting of Nestlé over its marketing of baby formula, pressure on Exxon over its stance on global warming, and pressure on companies trading with particular political regimes or involved in mining in sensitive areas.

In this book, we have described how efficient and innovative the network structure can be but also that it is extremely powerful, perhaps slow to change and capable of acting against the common good. Consumers are always part of this network structure and can easily become victims of it. But the network structure can also be used by consumers to effect change even against apparently powerful actors. Consumers can organize themselves into larger groups through networking as we saw in the election of President Obama and can counteract the financial strength of major actors. Many consumer groups are quite knowledgeable about the network structure of business and are able to exploit that knowledge, as we saw in Chapter 4 in our discussions of Greenpeace, Ikea and others. Even when it is disorganized, mass action by consumers can have powerful network effects, as we have seen in the decline of recorded music companies and the rapid transformation of an entire network precipitated by illegal downloading. This reconfiguring of the network has a clear logic from the perspective of (many) consumers and we are likely to see many more examples of consumers as major network actors now that they have access to the same information technology as other actors and the ability to become much better organized, often with a clearer network picture than their counterparts.

From a network perspective, this development should also be welcomed. The network as a totality can develop much better and be much more responsive if consumers are more powerful actors. The third network paradox points to the problems of restrictions on innovation and control that arise from the attempted or actual control of a network by single business actors. Powerful consumer actors can prevent any tendency towards unidirectionality in network evolution.

The Politician in the Business Rainforest

The issues of consumer power and unidirectionality of the network is an appropriate point to introduce politicians as actors in the business rainforest. Politicians have a well-developed interest in the business landscape and can be powerful actors within it. However their approach to business, or at least the language that they use when discussing it, appears to be very strongly influenced by a 'market perspective'. For example, many political efforts are concerned with 'enhancing competition', policies are developed for generic industries, many quasi-autonomous government organizations (quangos) are established to develop the business of particular industries towards generic markets such as Food from Britain or Fish from Norway, not withstanding the fact that the production and distribution of these products takes place within a network in which a small number of significant importers or distributors determine what is bought. Politicians are often closely involved in attempts to 'create' networks within particular geographical locations without an appreciation of how the network stretches across political and industrial boundaries, as we discussed in Chapter 11.

The business rainforest is perhaps rather like the natural rainforest: It is not a very robust organic system when faced with powerful external pressures and the interconnections between its different elements over space and time do not respond in predictable directions. Politicians can cause great damage to existing network structures, but they do have a number of potential roles to perform within the network. In order for these to be effective, they need to be based on a realistic view of its nature and of its light and dark sides.

Particular parts of the public sector are very active as individual actors in the network. Each has its own interdependencies, activities and resources. The way that they are manipulated by politicians has a major effect on their roles and is a strong indicator of political ideology. This is the case in the military sector as well as in the communications and construction sectors. Here government organizations, or organizations largely controlled by government, are both major customers and also sometimes large producers. In principle, these actors are subject to the same network phenomena as others: They usually have to follow the same principles as all other network actors. However, rules on public procurement often mean that normal network behaviour is restricted. When public funds are involved, it is inevitable that the nature of public–private relationships will come under scrutiny. But this means that public purchasers are often restricted in the relationships that they can build and benefit from and effectively have to assume that they are buying from 'markets'.

Politicians are also likely to become directly involved in the network in some particular situations: The interests of major business actors readily become the interests of politicians in times of crisis. But politician often find themselves in an uncomfortable position in these crises:

They have difficulty in relating individually to single business actors and they are often uneasy when interacting in unique relationships with companies in the way that private business actors do so commonly. This unease is reinforced by the need to preserve equity towards all those in a specific, or in some cases much wider, 'economic area'. But effective intervention cannot be based on broad approaches, political pressures, generalizations or restricted knowledge. Politicians rarely have detailed, relationship-specific, interaction experience and this severely limits their ability to 'pick winners'.

The internationalization of business networks causes further problems for the role of the politician as business actor. It is more difficult today for politicians to take general types of action across a range of actors because these actions are limited to the politician's own country while business actors are part of networks that are at least international and often global in scope. In these situations, the politician may have to attempt collaboration between governments, which adds to the problem, or be forced to deal directly with individual multinational business actors. The growing problem faced in the early 21st century in international banking, the car industry and elsewhere is likely to lead to attempts to develop support and control networks that mirror the business network across country borders.

Politicians are perhaps more comfortable in their important indirect role in the business rainforest. They are responsible for the rules within which business actors must develop their relationships and the network as a whole. Laws and regulations, educational and social institutions can support or limit the building of effective networks. As we concluded in Chapter 11, politicians cannot keep out of networks because those networks only self-regulate on the basis of the interests of those involved. However, it does not mean that the politicians will take over, just that they always have to be an active actor. As the full implications of the network economy become apparent, it is likely that we will see increasing involvement in a number of different forms as is currently the case in their interventions in research and development.

Conclusion

Each of the titles that we have used for people living in the business rainforest refers to an actor. All of these people are actors, each has access to resources and activities both their own and some belonging to others. None is complete, none is independent and none of these actors 'act' in any pure sense of the term: Everything they do follows from what has happened in the network before and provides an input into what will come. Each of their actions is part of a process of action and reaction that continues across the network in time and space.

Therefore, it is not possible to distil the role of each of the people with these different titles into the same set of behaviours. The business rainforest, like the natural rainforest, exists because nothing within it can live alone. Each individual element depends on the process of combining activities and resources between itself and others to transform these activities and resources, and transform itself and others into forms that can exist symbiotically together.

The rainforest teems with life and with death. Different species and individuals within them *simultaneously* depend on others as they seek to avoid the perils around them and at the same time struggle with these others for their share of light and nutrients.

We have argued in this book that the network form of business landscape is not a new phenomenon, but a description of an underlying structure that may produce different forms at different times. For example, it is only recently that business purchasing was viewed as a routine, clerical, cost-reducing function that was often seen simply as a way to 'screw suppliers'. That has changed and purchasing now has a major role in managing external resources and activities and integrating them in relationships with other counterparts. Other actors change and the network changes: For example, the role of politician and consumer is likely to expand, at least for the next few years. But all of this change and all of this continuity has one thing in common: It is interactive.

Go forth and interact . . .

APPENDIX: DISSERTATIONS RELATED TO IMP

Elling Homse, UMIST, Manchester, UK, PhD, 1981
Philip Rosson, University of Bath, UK, PhD, 1982
Lars Hallen, University of Uppsala, Sweden, PhD, 1982
Ian Strachan, University of Bath, UK, PhD, 1984
Malika Das, University of Bath, UK, PhD, 1984
Amjad Hadjikhani, University of Uppsala, Sweden, PhD, 1985
Mats Klint, University of Uppsala, Sweden, PhD, 1985
Nigel Holden, Manchester Business School, UK, PhD, 1986
Leo Leonidas, University of Bath, UK, PhD, 1986
Hans Benndorf, Stockholm School of Economics, Sweden, PhD, 1987
Bob Hardwick, University of Bath, UK, PhD, 1987
Luis Araujo, Lancaster University, UK, PhD, 1989
Alexandra Waluszewski, University of Uppsala, Sweden, PhD, 1989
Jens Laage-Hellman, University of Uppsala, Sweden, PhD, 1989
Ivan Snehota, University of Uppsala, Sweden, PhD, 1990
Nazeem Seyed-Mohammed, University of Uppsala, Sweden, PhD, 1990
Jan Åke Törnroos, Åbo Akademi University, Finland, PhD, 1991
Laurids Hedaa, Copenhagen Business School, Denmark, PhD, 1991
Anders Lundgren, Stockholm School of Economics, Sweden, PhD, 1991
Sören Kock, Swedish School of Economics and Business Administration, Helsinki, Finland,
    PhD, 1991
Phil Smith, Lancaster University, UK, PhD, 1992
Peter Naude, Manchester Business School, UK, PhD, 1992
Göran Liljegren, Stockholm School of Economics, Sweden, PhD, 1992
Louise Young, University of New South Wales, Sydney, Australia, PhD, 1992
Barbara Henders, University of Uppsala, Sweden, PhD, 1992
Susanne Herz, Stockholm School of Economics, Sweden, PhD, 1993
Anna Dubois, Chalmers University of Technology, Gothenburg, Sweden, PhD, 1994

Ragnar Hörndahl, Chalmers University of Technology, Gothenburg, Sweden, Ekon. Lic., 1994

Helen Andersson, Stockholm School of Economics, Sweden, PhD, 1994

Van Nguyen, University of New South Wales, Sydney, Australia, PhD, 1994

Maria Åsberg, University of Uppsala, Sweden, Fil. Lic., 1994

Mia Eriksson, University of Uppsala, Sweden, Fil. Lic., 1994

Aino Halinen, Åbo Akademi University, Finland, PhD, 1994

Asta Salmi, Helsinki School of Economics and Business Administration, Finland, PhD, 1995

Christopher Holland, Manchester Business School, UK, PhD, 1995

Peter Heydebreck, University of Karlsruhe, Germany, PhD, 1995

Jonna Sandell, Chalmers University of Technology, Gothenburg, Sweden, Tekn. Lic., 1996

Carlos Brito, Lancaster University, UK, PhD, 1996

AnnCharlott Pedersen, Norwegian University of Technology, Norway, PhD, 1996

Jan Frode, Norwegian University of Technology, Norway, PhD, 1996

Tim Torvatn, Norwegian University of Technology, Norway, PhD, 1996

Per Andersson, Stockholm School of Economics, Sweden, PhD, 1996

Desiree Blankenburg Holm, University of Uppsala, Sweden, PhD, 1996

Ulf Sjöberg, University of Uppsala, Sweden, PhD, 1996

Virpi Havila, University of Uppsala, Sweden, PhD, 1996

Roald Stole, Norwegian School of Economics and Business Administration, Bergen, Norway, PhD, 1997

Henrikki Tikkanen, Turku School of Economics, Finland, PhD, 1997

Achim Walter, University of Karlsruhe, Germany, PhD, 1997

Ariane von Raesfeld, University of Twente, The Netherlands, PhD, 1997

Annalisa Tunisini, University of Uppsala, Sweden, PhD, 1997

Lennart Bångens, Chalmers University of Technology, Gothenburg, Sweden, PhD, 1998

Oskar Jellbo, Chalmers University of Technology, Gothenburg, Sweden, Tekn. Lic., 1998

Finn Wynstra, Eindhoven University of Technology, The Netherlands, PhD, 1998

Rui DaSilva, Manchester Business School, UK, PhD, 1998

Carl-Johan Rosenbröijer, Swedish School of Economics and Business Administration, Helsinki, Finland, PhD, 1998

Gabi Helfert, University of Karlsruhe, Germany, PhD, 1998

Thomas Ritter, University of Karlsruhe, Germany, PhD, 1998

Lars Huemer, University of Umeå, Sweden, PhD, 1998

Sharon Purchase, Central Queensland University, Australia, PhD, 1999

Debbie Harrison, Lancaster University, UK, PhD, 1999

Stefanos Mouzas, Lancaster University, UK, PhD, 1999

Marketa Sumpikova, Prague University of Economics, Czech Republic, PhD, 1999

C-F Helgesson, Stockholm School of Economics, Sweden, PhD, 1999

Judy Zolkiewski, Manchester University, UK, PhD, 1999

Maria Duarte, Manchester Business School, UK, PhD, 2000

Mohd Omd, Manchester Business School, UK, PhD, 2000

Richard Brewar, University of Bath, UK, PhD, 2000

Catherine Pardo, University of Burgundy, France, PhD, 2000

Torkel Wedin, University of Uppsala, Sweden, PhD, 2000

Chris Medlin, Adelaide University, Australia, PhD, 2001
Damien McLoughlin, Lancaster University, UK, PhD, 2001
Sergio Rezende, Lancaster University, UK, PhD, 2001
Elsebeth Holmen, Southern University of Denmark, Denmark, PhD, 2001
Hans Kjellberg, Stockholm School of Economics, Sweden, PhD, 2001
Jana Tähtinen, University of Oulu, Finland, PhD, 2001
Bertil Markgren, University of Uppsala, Sweden, PhD, 2001
Martin Johanson, University of Uppsala, Sweden, PhD, 2001
Catherine Welch, University of Western Sydney, Australia, PhD, 2001
Fredrik von Corswant, Chalmers University of Technology, Gothenburg, Sweden, PhD, 2002
Kajsa Hulthen, Chalmers University of Technology, Gothenburg, Sweden, PhD, 2002
Peter Fredrikson, Chalmers University of Technology, Gothenburg, Sweden, PhD, 2002
Terje Våland, Norwegian School of Management BI, Oslo, Norway, PhD, 2002
Neeru Sharma, University of Technology, Sydney, Australia, PhD, 2002
Anna Löfmark Vaghult, University of Uppsala, Sweden, PhD, 2002
Neeru Sharma, University of Western Sydney, Australia, PhD, 2002
Subruto Roy, University of Western Sydney, Australia, PhD, 2002
Jesper Aastrup, Copenhagen Business School, Denmark, PhD, 2003
Magnar Forbord, Norwegian University of Technology, Norway, PhD, 2003
Karim Machat, University of Montpellier, France, PhD, 2003
Anna Bengtson, University of Uppsala, Sweden, PhD, 2003
Enrico Baraldi, University of Uppsala, Sweden, PhD, 2003
Espen Gressetvold, Norwegian University of Technology, Norway, PhD, 2004
Ricardo Morais, University of Jyväskylä, Finland, PhD, 2004
Frans Prenkert, University of Uppsala, Sweden, PhD, 2004
Daniel Hjelmgren, Chalmers University of Technology, Gothenburg, Sweden, PhD, 2005
Jens Geersbro, Copenhagen Business School, Denmark, PhD, 2005
Nina Veflen Olsen, Norwegian School of Management BI, Oslo, Norway, PhD, 2005
Cecilia Gilodi, University of Castellanza (LIUC), Italy, PhD, 2005
Sara Denize, University of Technology, Sydney, PhD, 2005
Robert Spencer, University of Uppsala, Sweden, PhD, 2005
Birgitta Forsström, Åbo Akademi University, Finland, PhD, 2005
Maria Elo, Åbo Akademi University, Finland, PhD, 2005
Fredrik Skarp, Chalmers University of Technology, Gothenburg, Sweden, PhD, 2006
Frida Lind, Chalmers University of Technology, Gothenburg, Sweden, PhD, 2006
Bente Flygansvaer, Norwegian School of Economics and Business Administration, Bergen, Norway, PhD, 2006
Lena Bygballe, Norwegian School of Management BI, Oslo, Norway, PhD, 2006
Annika Tidström, Swedish School of Economics and Business Administration, Helsinki, Finland, PhD, 2006
Rhona Johnsen, University of Bath, UK, PhD, 2006
Thomas Johnson, University of Bath, UK, PhD, 2006
Yvonne Zorzi, University of Lugano, Switzerland, PhD, 2006
Wendy van der Valk, Erasmus University, The Netherlands, PhD, 2007

Anne Vercauteren, Hasselt University, Belgium, PhD, 2007
Jens Hultman, Jönköping International Business School, Sweden, PhD, 2007
Florence Crespin-Mazet, Manchester School of Management, UK, PhD, 2007
Peter Dahlin, Mälardalens University, Sweden, PhD, 2007
Per Engelseth, Norwegian School of Management BI, Oslo, Norway, PhD, 2007
Chiara Cantu, Università Cattolica di Milano, Italy, PhD, 2007
Hanne Kragh, Aarhus University, School of Business, Denmark, PhD, 2007
Kostas Selviaridis, Lancaster University, UK, PhD, 2008
Markus Vanharanta, Lancaster University, UK, PhD, 2008
Fahad Awaleh, Norwegian School of Management BI, Oslo, Norway, PhD, 2008
Svein Minde, Norwegian University of Technology, Norway, PhD, 2008
Harri Terho, Turku School of Economics, Finland, PhD, 2008
Daniela Corsaro, Università Cattolica di Milano, Italy, PhD, 2008
Filipe J Sousa, University of Porto, Portugal, PhD, 2008
Bonnie Dawson, University of Technology, Sydney, Australia, PhD, 2008
Roberta Bocconcelli, University of Urbino, Italy, PhD, 2008
Anna-Greta Nyström, Åbo Akademi University, Finland, PhD, 2008
Salla Lutz, Copenhagen Business School, Denmark, PhD, 2009
François Scheid, Ecole Polytechnique, Paris, France, PhD, 2009
Andreas Brekke, Norwegian School of Management BI, Oslo, Norway, PhD, 2009
Carla Ramos, University of Bath, UK, PhD, 2009

REFERENCES

Achrol, R.S., 1991. Evolution of the marketing organisation: new forms for turbulent environments. *Journal of Marketing*, 55(October), pp. 77–93.

Achrol, R.S. and Kotler, P., 1999. Marketing in the network economy. *Journal of Marketing*, 63(Special issue), pp. 146–63.

Alchian, A.A. and Demsetz, H., 1972. Production information costs and economic organization. *American Economic Review*, 62(5) December, pp. 777–95.

Alderson, W., 1954. Factors governing the development of marketing channels. In R. Clewett, ed. *Marketing Channels for Manufactured Products*. Homewood (IL): Richard D. Irwin.

Alderson, W., 1957. *Marketing Behavior and Executive Action*. Homewood (IL): Richard D. Irwin.

Alderson, W., 1965. *Dynamic Marketing Behaviour: A Functionalist Theory of Marketing*. Homewood (IL): Richard D. Irwin.

Aldrich, H.E., 1979. *Organizations and Environments*. Englewood Cliffs (NJ): Prentice-Hall.

Aldrich, H.E. and Whetten, D.A., 1981. Organisation-sets, action-sets and networks: making the most of simplicity. In P.C. Nystrom and W.H. Starbuck, eds. *Handbook of Organizational Design*, Vol. 1. Oxford: Oxford University Press, pp. 385–408.

Allee, V., 2003. *The Future of Knowledge: Increasing Prosperity through Value Networks*. Oxford: Butterworth-Heinemann.

Allen, G.C., 1929. *The Industrial Development of Birmingham and the Black Country*. London: Allen & Unwin.

Almeida, P. and Kogut, B., 1997. The exploration of technological diversity and geographic localization in innovation: start-up firms in the semiconductor industry. *Small Business Economics*, 9(1), pp. 21–31.

Ammer, D., 1969. Materials management as a profit center. *Harvard Business Review*, 47(1), pp. 234–56.

Anderson, E. and Weitz, B., 1989. Determinants of continuity in conventional industrial channel dyads. *Marketing Science*, 8(Fall), pp. 310–23.

Anderson, J.C., Håkansson, H. and Johanson, J., 1994. Dyadic business relationships within a business network context. *Journal of Marketing*, 58, pp. 1–15.

Anderson, J.C. and Narus, J.A., 1990. A model of distributor firm and manufacturer firm working partnerships. *Journal of Marketing*, 54(Jan), pp. 42–58.

Anderson, J.C. and Narus, J.A., 1991. Partnering as a focused market strategy. *California Management Review*, 33(3), pp. 62–74.

Anderson, J.C. and Narus, J.A., 2004. *Business Market Management: Understanding, Creating and Delivering Value*. Englewood Cliffs (NJ): Prentice Hall.

Anderson, S.W., Glenn, D. and Sedatole, K.L., 2000. Sourcing parts of complex products: evidence on transactions costs, high-powered incentives and ex-post opportunism. *Accounting, Organization and Society*, 25, pp. 723–49.

Andersson, U., Johanson, J. and Vahlne, J.-E., 1997. Organic acquisitions in the internationalization process of the business firm. *Management International Review*, 37(2), pp. 67–84.

Ansoff, H.I., 1965. *Corporate Strategy*. New York: McGraw-Hill.

Araujo, L., 1998. Knowing and learning as networking. *Management Learning*, 29(3), pp. 317–36.

Araujo, L., Dubois, A. and Gadde, L.-E., 2003. The multiple boundaries of the firm. *Journal of Management Studies*, 40(3), pp. 1255–77.

Arndt, J., 1979. Towards a concept of domesticated markets. *Journal of Marketing*, 43(Fall), pp. 69–75.

Arthur, B., 1988. Self-reinforcing mechanisms in economics. In P. Andersson, K. Arrow and D. Pines, eds. *The Economy as an Evolving Complex System*. Reading (MA): Addison-Wesley.

Awaleh, F., 2008. *Interacting Strategically within Dyadic Business Relationships: A Case Study from the Norwegian Electronic Industry. (PhD dissertation)*. Oslo: Norwegian School of Management BI.

Axelrod, R.M., 1984. *The Evolution of Cooperation*. New York: Basic Books.

Axelsson, B. and Easton, G., eds. 1992. *Industrial Networks: A New View of Reality*. London: Routledge.

Axelsson, B. and Wynstra, F., 2002. *Buying Business Services*. Chichester: John Wiley & Sons.

Backhaus, K. and Büschken, J., 1999. The paradox of unsatisfying but stable relationships: a look at German car suppliers. *Journal of Business Research*, 46(3), pp. 245–57.

Baraldi, E., 2003. When information technology faces resource interaction (doctoral thesis no. 105). Department of Business Studies, University of Uppsala.

Baraldi, E., Fors, H. and Houltz, A., eds. 2006. *Taking Place: The Spatial Contexts of Science, Technology and Business*. Sagamore Beach: Science History Publications.

Baraldi, E. and Strömsten, T., 2006. Embedding and utilizing low weight: value creation and resource configuration in the networks around IKEA's Lack table and Holmen's newsprint. *IMP Journal*, 1(1), pp. 39–70.

Baraldi, E. and Waluszeski, A., 2007. Conscious use of others' interface knowledge: how IKEA can keep the price of the Lack table constant over decades. In H. Håkansson and A. Walusewski, eds. *Knowledge and Innovation in Business and Industry: The importance of using others*. Abingdon: Routledge, pp. 79–108.

Barkema, H.G. and Drogendijk, R., 2007. Internationalising in small incremental or larger steps? *Journal of International Business Studies*, 38(7), pp. 1132–48.

Barney, J.B., 2002. *Gaining and Sustaining Competitive Advantage*. Reading (MA): Addison-Wesley.

Basalla, G., 1988. *The Evolution of Technology*. Cambridge: Cambridge History of Science Series.

Belbin, M., 1993. *Team Roles at Work*. Oxford: Butterworth-Heinemann.

Bengtson, A., 2003. Framing technological development in a concrete context: the use of wood in the Swedish construction industry (doctoral thesis no. 99). Department of Business Studies, University of Uppsala.

Bengtson, A. and Håkansson, H., 2007. Introducing old knowledge in an established user context: how to use wood in the construction industry. In H. Håkansson and A. Walusewski, eds. *Knowledge and Innovation in Business and Industry: The importance of using others*. Abingdon: Routledge, pp. 54–78.

Bensaou, M., 1999. Portfolios of buyer–supplier relationships. *Sloan Management Review*, 40(4), pp. 35–44.

Best, M.H., 1990. *The New Competition: Institutions for Industrial Restructuring*. Cambridge: Polity Press.

Biemans, W.G., 1992. *Managing Innovation within Networks*. London: Routledge.

Biggart, N.W. and Hamilton, G.G., 1992. On the limits of firm-based theory to explain business networks: the Western bias of neo-classical economics. In N. Nohria and R.G. Eccles, eds. *Networks and Organisations: Structure, Form and Action*. Boston (MA): Harvard Business School Press, pp. 471–90.

Bijker, W.E, 1987. *Of Bicycles, Bakelites and Bulbs*. Cambridge (MA): MIT Press.

Blankenburg-Holm, D., Eriksson, K. and Johanson, J., 1996. Business networks and cooperation in international business relationships. *Journal of International Business Studies*, 27(5), pp. 1033–53.

Blau, P.M., 1964. *Exchange and Power in Social Life*. New York: John Wiley & Sons.

Bligh, P., Turk, D. and Porter, M., 2004. *CRM Unplugged: Releasing CRM's Strategic Value*. Chichester: John Wiley & Sons.

Blois K.J, 1972. Vertical quasi-integration. *Journal of Industrial Economics*, 20(3), pp. 253–72.

Blumer, H., 1969. *Symbolic Interactionism: Perspective and Method*. Englewood Cliffs (NJ): Prentice Hall.

Bocconcelli, R. and Håkansson, H., 2008. External interaction as a means of making changes in a company: the role of purchasing in a major turnaround for Ducati. *IMP Journal*, 2(2), pp. 25–37.

Borden, N.H., 1964. The concept of the marketing mix. *Journal of Advertising Research*, 4(June), pp. 2–7.

Bowman, D. and Narayandas, D., 2001. Managing customer-initiated contacts with manufacturers: The impact on share of category requirements and worth-of-mouth behavior. *Journal of Marketing Research*, 38(3), pp. 281–97.

Brekke, A., 2009. A bumper!? An empirical investigation of the relationship between the economy and the environment (PhD dissertation). Oslo: Norwegian School of Management BI.

Brandenburger, A. and Nalebuff, B., 1996. *Co-Opetition: A Revolution Mindset that Combines Competition and Cooperation*. New York: Doubleday.

Brennan, R. and Turnbull, P., 1999. Adaptive behavior in buyer–seller relationships. *Industrial Marketing Management*, 28(5), pp. 481–95.

Brennan, R., Turnbull, P. and Wilson, D., 2003. Dyadic adaptation in business-to-business markets. *European Journal of Marketing*, 37(11/12), pp. 1636–65.

Brunsson, N., 1989. *The Organization of Hypocrisy: Talk, Decisions and Actions in Organizations*. Chichester: John Wiley & Sons.

Bucklin, L., 1965. Postponement, speculation and the structure of distribution channels. *Journal of Marketing Research*, 2, pp. 26–31.

Burt, R.S., 1992. *Structural Holes*. Cambridge (MA): Harvard University Press.

Burt, R.S., 2004. Structural holes and good ideas. *American Journal of Sociology*, 110(2), pp. 349–99.

Buttle, F. and Naude, P., 2000. Assessing relationship quality. *Industrial Marketing Management*, 29(4), pp. 351–61.

Bygballe, L., 2005. Learning across firm boundaries: the role of organisational routines (PhD dissertation). Oslo: Norwegian School of Management BI.

Callon, M., 1980. Struggles and negotiations to decide what is problematic and what is not: the sociologics of translation. In K.K. Kron and R. Withley, eds. *The Social Process of Scientific Investigation*. De Reidel, pp. 197–200.

Carbone, J., 2004a. Motorola leverages its way to lower cost. *Purchasing*. http://www.purchasing.com/article/CA454052.html (accessed 29 April 2009).

Carbone, J., 2004b. Hewlett-Packard has slashed its direct materials cost. *Purchasing*. http://www.purchasing.com/article/CA426515.html (accessed 29 April 2009).

Carlisle, J. and Parker, R., 1989. *Beyond Negotiation: Redeeming Customer–Supplier Relationships*. Chichester: John Wiley & Sons.

Carlson, S., 1975. How foreign is foreign trade? A problem in international business research. *Acta Universitatis Upsaliensis: Studiae Oeconomia Negotiorum* 11. University of Uppsala.

Castells, M., 1996. *The Rise of the Network Society*. Oxford: Blackwell.

Chandler, A., 1977. *The Visible Hand: The Managerial Revolution in American Business*. Cambridge (MA): Harvard University Press.

Chandler, A., 1990. *Scale and Scope: The Dynamics of Industrial Capitalism*. Cambridge (MA): Harvard University Press.

Christensen, C., 1997. *The Innovator's Dilemma: When New Technologies Cause Great Firms to Fail.* Cambridge (MA): Harvard Business School Press.

Christopher, M., 1992. *Logistics and Supply Chain Management.* London: Pitman.

Christopher, M., 2005. *Logistics and Supply Chain Management: Creating Value Adding Networks.* London: Prentice Hall, Financial Times, Pearson Education.

Clark, F., 1923. *Principles of Marketing.* New York: Macmillan.

Collin, H. and Pinch, T., 1999. *The Golem: What You Should Know About Science.* Cambridge: Cambridge University Press.

Cook, K.S. and Emerson, R.M., 1978. Power equity and commitment in exchange networks. *American Sociological Review*, 43(5), pp. 721–39.

Cooper, R. and Slagmulder, R., 2004. Interorganizational cost management and relational context. *Accounting, Organization and Society*, 29, pp. 1–26.

Cox, R. and Goodman, C.S., 1956. Marketing of house-building materials. *Journal of Marketing*, 21(1), pp. 36–61.

Cunningham, M.T. and White, J.G., 1973. The determinants of choice of supplier. *European Journal of Marketing*, 7(3), pp. 189–202.

Cunningham, M.T. and White, J.G., 1974. The behaviour of industrial buyers in their search for suppliers of machine tools. *Journal of Management Studies*, 11(2), pp. 115–28.

Cyert, R.M. and March, J.G., 1963. *A Behavioural Theory of the Firm.* Englewood Cliffs (NJ): Prentice-Hall.

Dabholkar, P.A., Johnston, W. and Cathey, A., 1994. The dynamics of long-term business-to-business exchange relationships. *Journal of the Academy of Marketing Science*, 22(2), pp. 130–45.

Dahlquist, J., 1998. Knowledge use in business exchange: acting and thinking business actors (doctoral thesis no. 74). Department of Business Studies, University of Uppsala.

David, P.A., 1985. Clio and the economics of QWERTY. *American Economic Review*, 75(2), pp. 332–7.

Davidson, D., 1980. *Essays on Actions and Events.* Oxford: Oxford University Press.

Dekker, H.C., 2003. Value chain analysis in interfirm relationships: a field study. *Management Accounting Research*, 14(1), pp. 1–23.

Dekker, H.C., 2004. Control of inter-organizational relationships: evidence on appropriation concerns and coordination requirements. *Accounting, Organization and Society*, 29(1), pp. 27–49.

DiMaggio, P. and Powell, W., 1983. The iron cage revisited: institutional isomorphism and collective rationality in organizational fields. *American Sociological Review*, 48(2), pp. 147–60.

Dosi, G., 1982. Technological paradigm and technological trajectories: a suggested interpretation of the determinants and directions of technical change. *Research Policy*, 11(3), pp. 147–62.

Dosi, G., Freeman, C., Nelson, R. and Soete, L., eds., 1988. *Technical Change and Economic Theory.* London: Pinter.

Drucker, P., 1954. *The Principles of Management.* New York: Harper Collins.

Drucker, P., 1990. The emerging theory of manufacturing. *Harvard Business Review*, 68(3), pp. 94–102.

Dubois, A., 1998. *Organising Industrial Activities Across Firm Boundaries.* London: Routledge.

Dwyer, R.F., Shurr, P.H. and Oh, S., 1987. Developing buyer–seller relationships. *Journal of Marketing*, 51(April), pp. 11–27.

Dyer, J., Cho, D. and Chu, W., 1998. Strategic supplier segmentation: the next best practice in supply chain management. *California Management Review*, 40(2), pp. 57–76.

Dyer, J.H. and Singh, H., 1998. The relational view: cooperative strategy and sources of interorganizational competitive advantage. *Academy of Management Review*, 23(4), pp. 660–79.

Easton, G. and Lundgren, A., 1992. Changes in industrial networks as flow through nodes. In B. Axelsson and G. Easton, eds. *Industrial Networks: A new view of reality.* London: Routledge, pp. 88–104.

Eklund, M., 2007. Adoption of the innovation system concept in Sweden (doctoral dissertation). *Uppsala Studies in Economic History*, 81.

Ellram, L., 1995. Total cost of ownership: an analysis approach for purchasing. *International Journal of Physical Distribution and Logistics Management*, 25(8), pp. 4–20.

Ellram, L. and Edis, O., 1996. A case study of successful partnering implementation. *International Journal of Purchasing and Materials Management*, 32(4), pp. 20–28.

Emsley, D. and Kidon, F., 2007. The relationship between trust and control in international joint ventures: evidence from the airline industry. *Contemporary Accounting Research*, 24(3), pp. 829–58.

Englander, E.J., 1988. Technology and Oliver Williamson's transaction cost economics. *Journal of Economic Behavior and Organization*, 10(3), pp. 339–53.

Evan, W.M., 1966. The organization-set: toward a theory of interorganizational relation. In J. Thompson, ed. *Approaches to Organizational Design*. Pittsburgh: University of Pittsburgh Press.

Fai, F. and Cantwell, J., 1999. The changing nature of corporate technological diversification and the importance of organizational capability. In S. Dow and P.E. Earl, eds. *In Contingency Complexity and the Theory of the Firm Essays in Honour of Brian J.* Loasby. Cheltenham: Edward Elgar.

Farmer, D., 1981. Seeking strategic involvement. *Journal of Purchasing and Materials Management*, 17(Fall), pp. 20–24.

Ferrin, B. and Plank, R., 2002. Total cost of ownership models: an exploratory study. *Journal of Supply Chain Management: A Global Review of Purchasing and Supply*, 38(2), pp. 18–29.

Fill, C. and Fill, K., 2005. *Business to Business Marketing, Relationships, Systems and Communications*. Harlow: Prentice Hall, Financial Times.

Fligstein, N., 1990. *The Transformation of Corporate Control*. Cambridge (MA): Harvard University Press.

Forbord, M., 2003. New uses of an agricultural product? a case study of development in an industrial network (PhD thesis no. 36). Trondheim: Department of Industrial Economics and Technology Management, Norwegian University of Science and Technology.

Ford, D., 1976. An analysis of some aspects of the relationships between companies in channels of distribution (unpublished PhD thesis). Manchester: University of Manchester.

Ford, D., 1980. The development of buyer–seller relationships in industrial markets. *European Journal of Marketing*, 14(5/6), pp. 339–53.

Ford, D., ed., 1990. *Understanding Business Markets*. San Diego: Academic Press.

Ford, D., 2002. The development of buyer–seller relationships in industrial markets. In D. Ford ed., *Understanding Business Marketing and Purchasing*, 3rd ed. London: Thomson Learning, pp. 65–77.

Ford, D. and Håkansson, H., 2006a. The idea of interaction. *IMP Journal*, 1(1), pp. 4–27.

Ford, D. and Håkansson, H., 2006b. IMP: Some things achieved, much more to do. *European Journal of Marketing*, 40(3/4), pp. 248–58.

Ford, D. and Hardwick, B., 1986. Industrial buyer resources and responsibilities and the buyer–seller relationship. *Industrial Marketing and Purchasing*, 1(3), pp. 3–25.

Ford, D. and Rosson, P., 1982. Manufacturer-overseas distributor relations and export performance. *Journal of International Business Studies*, 13(2), pp. 57–72.

Ford, D. and Saren, M., 1996. *Technology Strategy for Business*. London: Thompson Business Press.

Ford, D. and Thomas, R., 1995. Technology strategy in networks. *International Journal of Technology Management*, 10(4), pp. 596–612.

Ford, D., Håkansson, H. and Johanson, J., 1986. How do companies interact? *Industrial Marketing and Purchasing*, 1(1), pp. 26–41.

Ford, D., Gadde, L.-E., Håkansson, H. and Snehota, I., 2003. *Managing Business Relationships*, 2nd ed. Chichester: John Wiley & Sons.

Ford, D., Gadde, L-E., Håkansson, H., and Snehota, I., 2007. *The Business Marketing Course: Managing in Complex Networks*, 2nd ed. London: Wiley

Forsgren, M., Holm, U. and Johanson, J., 1992. Internationalization of the second degree: the emergence of European-based centres in Swedish international companies. In S. Young, ed. *Europe and the Multinationals: Issues and Responses for the 1990s*. London: Edward Elgar.

Forsgren, M., Holm, U. and Johanson, J., 2005. *Managing the Embedded Multinational: A Business Network View*. Cheltenham: Edward Elgar.

Forsgren, M. and Kinch, N., 1970. Företagets anpassning till förändringar i omgivande system en studie av massa: och pappersindustrin. Acta Universitatis Upsaliensis: Studiae Oeconomia Negotiorum 2. University of Uppsala.

Forsström, B., 2005. Value co-creation in industrial buyer–seller partnerships: creating and exploiting interdependencies (PhD thesis). Åbo: Åbo Akademi University Press.

Frazier, G. and Antia, K., 1995. Exchange relationships and inter-firm power in channels of distribution. *Journal of the Academy of Marketing Science*, 23(4), pp. 321–6.

Frazier, G.L., Spekman, R.E. and O'Neil, C.R., 1988. Just-in-time exchange relationships in industrial markets. *Journal of Marketing*, 52(October), pp. 52–67.

Fredriksson, P. and Gadde, L.-E., 2005. Flexibility and rigidity in customization and build-to-order production. *Industrial Marketing Management*, 34(7), pp. 695–705.

Freeman, C., 1982. *The Economics of Industrial Innovation*. Cambridge (MA): MIT Press.

Freeman, C., 1991. Networks of innovator: a synthesis of research issues. *Research Policy*, 20(5), pp. 499–514.

Gadde, L.-E. and Araujo, L., 2007. Business recipes, historical narratives and the discovery of networks. *IMP Journal*, 1(3), pp. 2–25.

Gadde, L.-E. and Ford, D., 2008. Distribution research and the industrial network approach. *IMP Journal*, 2(3), pp. 36–52.

Gadde, L.-E. and Håkansson, H., 1993. *Professional Purchasing*. London: Routledge.

Gadde, L.-E. and Håkansson, H., 2001. *Supply Network Strategies*. Chichester: John Wiley & Sons.

Gadde, L.-E. and Håkansson, H., 2007. Teaching in supplier networks. In M. Gibbert and T. Durand, eds. *Strategic Networks*, Strategic Management Society Series. Oxford: Blackwell, pp. 40–57.

Gadde, L.-E. and Håkansson, H., 2008. Business relationships and resource combining. *IMP Journal*, 2(1), pp. 31–45.

Gadde, L.-E., Håkansson, H., Jahre, M. and Persson, G., 2002. More instead of less: strategies for the use of logistics resources. *Journal on Chain and Network Science*, 2(2), pp. 81–92.

Gadde, L.-E. and Mattsson, L.-G., 1987. Stability and change in network relationships. *International Journal of Research in Marketing*, 4(1), pp. 29–41.

Gadde, L.-E. and Snehota I., 2000. Making the most of supplier relationships. *Industrial Marketing Management*, 29(4), pp. 305–16.

Galison, P., 1997. *Image and Logic: A Material Culture of Microphysics*. Chicago: University of Chicago Press.

Ghemawat, P., 2002. Competition and business strategy in historical perspective. *Business History Review*, 76(1), pp. 37–76.

Ghoshal, S. and Bartlett, C., 1990. The multinational as an interorganizational network. *Academy of Management Review*, 15(4), pp. 603–25.

Gibbons, M., Limoges, C., Nowotny, H., *et al.*, 1994. *The New Production of Knowledge: The Dynamic of Science and Research in Contemporary Societies*. London: Sage.

Goffin, K., Lembke, F. and Szwejczewski, M., 2006. An exploratory study of close supplier–manufacturer relationships. *Journal of Operations Management*, 24(2), pp. 189–209.

Goffman, E., 1967. *Interaction Ritual*. Garden City (NY): Anchor.

Grabher, G., ed., 1993. *The Embedded Firm: On the Socioeconomics of Industrial Networks*. London: Routledge.

Granovetter, M., 1985. Economic action and social structure: the problem of embeddedness. *American Journal of Sociology*, 91(3) (November), pp. 481–510.

Grant, R., 1998. *Contemporary Strategy Analysis*, 3rd ed. Oxford: Blackwell.

Gressetvold, E., 2004. Developing relationships within industrial networks: effects of product development (PhD thesis). Trondheim: Department of Industrial Economics and Technology Management, Norwegian University of Science and Technology.

Gripsrud, G., 2004. The marketing discipline and distribution research: time to regain lost territory. In H. Håkansson, D. Harrison and A. Waluszewski, eds. *Rethinking Marketing Developing a New Understanding of Markets*. Chichester: John Wiley & Sons.

Grönroos, C., 1984. A service quality model and its marketing implications. *European Journal of Marketing*, 18(4), pp. 36–44.

Grönroos, C., 1997. From marketing mix to relationship marketing: towards a paradigm shift in marketing. *Management Decision*, 35(4), pp. 322–39.

Gudeman, S., 2001. *The Anthropology of Economy, Community, Market and Culture*. Oxford: Blackwell.

Guillet de Monthoux, P., 1975. Organizational mating and industrial marketing conservation: some reasons why industrial marketing managers resist marketing theory. *Industrial Marketing Management*, 4(1), pp. 25–36.

Gulati, R., 1998. Alliances and networks. *Strategic Management Journal*, 19(4), pp. 293–317.

Gulati, R., Nohria, N. and Zaheer, A., 2000. Strategic networks. *Strategic Management Journal*, 21(3), pp. 203–15.

Gummesson, E., 1979. The marketing of professional services: an organizational dilemma. *European Journal of Marketing*, 13(5), pp. 308–18.

Gummesson, E., 2002. *Total Relationship Marketing*. London: Butterworth-Heinemann.

Hägg, I. and Johanson, J., eds., 1982. *Företag i Nätverk. Ny syn på konkurrenskraft (Enterprise in Networks: New perspective on Competitiveness)*. Stockholm: SNS.

Håkansson, H., ed., 1982. *International Marketing and Purchasing of Industrial Goods: An Interaction Approach*. New York: John Wiley & Sons.

Håkansson, H., 1987. *Industrial Technological Development: A Network Approach*. London: Croom Helm.

Håkansson, H., 1989. *Corporate Technological Behaviour: Co-operation and Networks*. London: Routledge.

Håkansson, H., 1993. Networks as a mechanism to develop resources. In P. Beije, J. Groenewegen and O. Nuys, eds. *Networking in Dutch Industries*. Apeldoorn, NL: Garant.

Håkansson, H. and Ford, D., 2002. How should companies interact? *Journal of Business Research*, 55(2), pp. 133–9.

Håkansson, H. and Johanson, J., 1987. Formal and informal cooperation strategies in international industrial networks. In F.J. Contractor and P. Lorange, eds. *Cooperative Strategies in International Business*. Lexington: Lexington Books.

Håkansson, H. and Johanson, J., 1992. A model of industrial networks. In B. Axelsson and G. Easton, eds. *Industrial Networks: A new view of reality*. London: Routledge, pp. 28–34.

Håkansson, H. and Johanson, J., 1993. Network as a governance structure. In G. Grabher, ed. *The Embedded Firm: The Socio-Economics of Industrial Networks*. London: Routledge.

Håkansson, H. and Johanson, J., eds., 2001. *Business Network Learning*. Amsterdam: Pergamon.

Håkansson, H. and Lind, J., 2004. Accounting and network coordination. *Accounting, Organization and Society*, 29(1), pp. 51–72.

Håkansson, H. and Lind, J., 2007. Accounting in an interorganisational setting. In C.S. Chapman, A.G. Hopwood and M.D. Shields, eds. *Handbook of management accounting research*, Vol. 2. Oxford: Elsevier, pp. 885–902.

Håkansson, H. and Lundgren, A., 1997. Paths in time and space. In L. Magnusson and J. Ottosson, eds. *Evolutionary Economics and Path Dependence*. Cheltenham: Edward Elgar, pp. 119–37.

Håkansson, H. and Östberg, C., 1975. Industrial marketing: an organizational problem? *Industrial Marketing Management*, 4(2/3), pp. 113–23.

Håkansson, H. and Snehota, I., 1976. Marknadsplanering: Ett sätt att skapa nya problem? (Market Planning: A Way of Creating New Problems?). Lund: Studentlitteratur.

Håkansson, H. and Snehota, I., 1989. No business is an island. *Scandinavian Journal of Management*, 5(3), pp. 187–200.

Håkansson, H. and Snehota, I., eds., 1995. *Developing Relationships in Business Networks*. London: International Thomson.

Håkansson, H. and Waluszewski, A., 2002. *Managing Technological Development, IKEA, the Environment and Technology*. London: Routledge.

Håkansson, H. and Waluszewski, A., eds., 2007. *Knowledge and Innovation in Business and Industry: The Importance of Using Others*. London: Routledge.

Håkansson, H. and Wootz, B., 1975. Supplier selection in an international environment: an experimental study. *Journal of Marketing Research*, 12(February), pp. 46–51.

Håkansson, H., Harrison, D. and Waluszewski, A., eds., 2004. *Rethinking Marketing Developing a New Understanding of Markets*. Chichester: John Wiley & Sons.

Håkansson, H., Havila, V. and Pedersen, A.-C., 1999. Learning in networks. *Industrial Marketing Management*, 28(5), pp. 443–52.

Håkansson, H., Huysman, M. and von Raesfeld Meijer, A., 2001. Inter-organizational teaching. In H. Håkansson and J. Johanson, eds. *Business Network Learning*. Amsterdam: Pergamon.

Håkansson, H., Kraus, K. and Lind, J., eds., 2009a. *Accounting in Networks*. London and New York: Routledge.

Håkansson, H., Waluszewski, A., Prenkert, F. and Baraldi, E., eds., 2009b. *Use of Science and Technology in Business: Exploring the Impact of Using Activity for Systems, Organizations and People*. Bingley: Emerald Group.

Halinen, A., Havila, V. and Salmi, A., 1999. From dyadic change to changing business networks: an analytical framework. *Journal of Management Studies*, 36(6), pp. 779–94.

Halinen, A. and Törnroos, J.-Å., 1998. The role of embeddedness in the evolution of business networks. *Scandinavian Journal of Management*, 14(3), pp. 187–205.

Hallén, L., 1986. A comparison of strategic marketing approaches. In P.W. Turnbull and J.P. Valla, eds. *Strategies for International Industrial Marketing*. London: Croom Helm, pp. 235–49.

Hallén, L., Johanson, J. and Seyed-Mohammed, N., 1991. Interfirm adaptation in business relationships. *Journal of Marketing*, 55(2), pp. 29–37.

Hamel, G. and Prahalad, C., 1985. Do you really have a global strategy? *Harvard Business Review*, July–August, pp. 139–48.

Hamilton, G., ed., 1996. *Asian Business Networks*. Berlin and New York: de Gruyter.

Han, S., Wilson, D. and Dant, S., 1993. Buyer–seller relationships today. *Industrial Marketing Management*, 22(4), pp. 331–8.

Hannon, D., 2004. Sun shines by combining two supplier strategies. *Purchasing*. http://www.purchasing.com/article/CA416161.html?q=Sun+Microsystems (accessed 29 April 2009).

Harrison, D. and Waluszewski, A., 2008. The development of a user network as a way to re-launch an unwanted product. *Research Policy*, 37(1), pp. 115–30.

Hasselberg, Y. and Petersson, T., eds., 2006. *Bäste Broder! Nätverk entreprenörskap och innovation i svenskt näringsliv*. Hedemora: Gidlunds.

Haugland, S.A. and Reve, T., 1994. Price, authority and trust in international distribution channel relationships. *Scandinavian Journal of Management*, 10(3), pp. 225–44.

Hayek, F.A., 1945. The use of knowledge in society. *American Economic Review*, 35(September), pp. 519–30.

Hayek, F.A., 1967. *Studies in Philosophy, Politics and Economics*. London: Routledge and Kegan Paul.

Heide, J., 1994. Interorganizational governance in marketing channels. *Journal of Marketing*, 58(1), pp. 71–85.

Helander, A. and Möller, K., 2007. System supplier's customer strategy. *Industrial Marketing Management*, 36(6), pp. 719–30.

Helper, S. and Levine, D., 1992. Long-term supplier relations and product-market structure. *Journal of Law, Economics and Organisation*, 8(3), pp. 561–81.

Helper, S., 1987. Supplier relations and technical change: theory and application to the auto industry (doctoral dissertation). Boston (MA): Department of Economics, Harvard University.

Henders, B., 1992. Position in industrial networks: marketing newsprint in the UK (PhD dissertation). Department of Business Administration, University of Uppsala.

Henneberg, S.C., Mouzas, S. and Naude, P., 2006. Network pictures: concepts and representations. *European Journal of Marketing*, 40(3/4), pp. 408–29.

Hervey, R., 1982. Preliminary observation on manufacturer–supplier relations in the Japanese automotive industry. *The Joint US-Japan Automotive Study: Working Paper Series No. 5*. Ann Arbor: University of Michigan.

Hjelmgren, D., 2005. Adaptation and development of embedded resources in industrial networks (PhD thesis). Gothenburg, Sweden: Department of Industrial Marketing, Chalmers University of Technology.

Hollingsworth, J.R., 1991. The logic of coordinating American manufacturing sectors. In J.L. Campbell, J.R. Hollingsworth and L.N. Lindberg, eds. *Governance of the American Economy*. New York: Cambridge University Press, pp. 35–73.

Holmen, E., 2001. Notes on a conceptualisation of resource-related embeddedness of interorganizational product development (PhD dissertation). Institute for Marketing, University of Southern Denmark.

Holmlund, M., 1997. Perceived quality in business relationships (PhD dissertation). Swedish School of Economics and Business Administration.

Holmlund, M. and Törnroos, J.-Å., 1997. What are relationships in business networks? *Management Decision*, 35(4), pp. 304–9.

Homans, C.G., 1961. *Social Interaction*. New York: Harcourt, Brace and World.

Huemer, L., 1998. *Trust in Business Relations: Economic Logic or Social Interaction?* Umeå Borea.

Huemer, L., Håkansson, H. and Prenkert, F., 2009. Cermaq's entry and development in the international aquaculture sector. *IMP Journal* (submission).

Hughes, T.P., 1983. *Networks of Power: Electrification in Western Society (1880–1930)*. Baltimore: John Hopkins University Press.

Hughes, T.P., 1987. The evolution of large technical systems. In W. Bijker, T.P. Hughes and T.J Pinch, eds. *The Social Construction of Large Technological Systems*. Cambridge (MA): MIT Press.

Hughes, T.P., 2004. *American Genesis: A Century of Invention and Technological Enthusiasm, 1870–1970*. Chicago: University of Chicago Press.

Hulthén, K., 2002. Variety in distribution networks: a transvection analysis (doctoral dissertation). Gothenburg, Sweden: Department of Industrial Marketing, Chalmers University of Technology.

Hunt, S. and Goolsby, J., 1988. The rise and fall of the functional approach to marketing: a paradigm displacement perspective. In T. Nevett and R.A. Fullerton, eds. *Historical Perspectives in Marketing*. Lexington: Lexington Books/D.C. Health and Co., pp. 35–51.

Hutt, M. and Speh, T., 2007. *Business Marketing Management: B2B*. Mason (OH): Thomson South-Western.

Islei, G., Lockett, G., Cox, B., *et al.*, 1991. Modeling strategic decision making and performance measurements at ICI Pharmaceuticals. *Interfaces*, 21(6), pp. 4–22.

Ittner, C.D., Larcker, D.F., Nagar, V. and Rajan, M.V., 1999. Supplier selection: monitoring practices and firm performance. *Journal of Accounting and Public Policy*, 18(3), pp. 253–81.

Jahre, M., Gadde, L.-E., Håkansson, H. *et al.*, eds., 2006. *Resourcing in Business Logistics: The Art of Systematic Combining*. Malmö and Copenhagen: Liber and Copenhagen Business School Press.

Jarillo, C.J., 1988. On strategic networks. *Strategic Management Journal*, 9(1), pp. 31–41.

Jasanoff, S., ed., 2004. *States of Knowledge: The Co-production of Science and the Social Order*. London and New York: Routledge.

Jellbo, O., 1998. *Systemköp: en definitionsfråga.* (Licentiate dissertation). Gothenburg, Sweden: Division of Industrial Marketing, Chalmers University of Technology, p. 55.

Johanson, J., 1966. Svenskt kvalitetsstål på utländska marknader (Swedish Special Steel on Foreign Markets) (dissertation). Department of Business Administration, University of Uppsala.

Johanson, J. and Mattsson, L.-G., 1985. Marketing investments and market investments in industrial networks. *International Journal of Research in Marketing*, 2(3), pp. 185–95.

Johanson, J. and Mattsson, L.-G., 1986. Interorganizational relations in industrial systems: a network approach compared with a transaction cost approach. *International Studies of Management Organisation*, 17(1), pp. 34–48.

Johanson, J. and Mattsson, L.-G., 1992. Network positions and strategic actions: an analytical framework. In B. Axelsson and G. Easton, eds. *Industrial Networks: A new view of reality*. London: Routledge, pp. 205–17.

Johanson, J. and Vahlne, J.-E., 1977. The internationalization process of the firm: a model of knowledge development and increasing foreign market commitments. *Journal of International Business*, 8(1), pp. 23–32.

Johanson, J. and Vahlne, J.-E., 2009. The Uppsala internationalization process model revisited: from liability of foreignness to liability of outsidership. *Journal of Business Studies* (submission).

Johanson, J. and Wootz, B., 1986. The German approach to Europe. In P.W. Turnbull and J.P. Valla, eds. *Strategies for International Industrial Marketing*. London: Croom Helm.

Johanson, M. and Waluszewski, A., 2007. Handling resource interfaces in a planned economy: how Tipografiya solves interaction issues without direct interaction. In H. Håkansson and A. Walusewski, eds. *Knowledge and Innovation in Business and Industry: The importance of using others*. Abingdon: Routledge, pp. 109–26.

Johnsen, R. and Ford, D., 2008. Exploring the concept of asymmetry: a typology for the analysis of customer–supplier relationships. *Industrial Marketing Management*, 37(4), pp. 471–83.

Johnsen, T. and Ford, D., 2007. Customer approaches to product development with suppliers. *Industrial Marketing Management*, 36(3), pp. 300–308.

Jones, C.S., 1999. Hierarchies, networks and management accounting in NHS hospitals. *Accounting, Auditing and Accountability Journal*, 12(2), pp. 164–87.

Kaiser, A. and Hedin, M., eds., 1995. *Nordic Energy Systems: Historical Perspectives and Current Issues*. Mass: Science History Publications.

Katona, G., 1953. Rational behavior and economic behavior. *Psychological Review*, September, pp. 307–18.

Kauffman, S., 1995. *At Home in the Universe*. Oxford: Oxford University Press.

Keep, W., Hollander, S. and Dickinson, R., 1998. Forces impinging on long-term business-to-business relationships in the United States: an historical perspective. *Journal of Marketing*, 62(2), pp. 31–45.

Kent, R.A., 1986. Faith in four Ps: an alternative. *Journal of Marketing Management*, 2, pp. 145–54.

Kogut, B., 2000. The network as knowledge: generative rules and the emergence of structure. *Strategic Management Journal*, 21(3), pp. 405–25.

Kotler, P., 1967. *Marketing Management: Analysis, planning and control*. Englewood Cliffs (NJ): Prentice Hall.

Kraljic, P., 1982. Purchasing must become supply management. *Harvard Business Review*, September–October, pp. 109–17.

Kriesberg, L., 1955. Occupational control among steel distributors. *American Journal of Sociology*, 61(3), pp. 203–12.

Krugman, P., 1991. Increasing returns and economic geography. *Journal of Political Economy*, 99(3), pp. 483–99.

Krugman, P. and Venables, A.J., 1995. Globalization and the inequality of nations. *Quarterly Journal of Economics*, 110(4), pp. 857–80.

Kumar, N., 1996. The power of trust in manufacturer–retailer relationships. *Harvard Business Review*, November–December, pp. 92–106.

Kutschker, M., 1975. Rationalitat and Entscheidungskriterien komplexer Investitionsentscheidungen: ein empirischer Bericht. *Aus dem Sonderforschungsbereich 24 Der Universität Mannheim.* Mannheim.

Laage-Hellman, J., 1989. Technological development in industrial networks. In *Acta Universitatis Upsaliensis: Comprehensive Summaries of Uppsala Dissertations from the Faculty of Social Sciences,* 16. University of Uppsala.

Laage-Hellman, J., 1997. *Business Networks in Japan: Supplier–Customer Interaction in Product Development.* London: Routledge.

Lambert, D. and Cooper, M., 2000. Issues in supply chain management. *Industrial Marketing Management,* 29(1), pp. 65–83.

Lamming, R., 1993. *Beyond Partnership Strategies for Innovation and Lean Supply.* Hemel Hempstead: Prentice Hall.

Lamoreaux, N., Raff, D. and Temin, P., 2003. Beyond markets and hierarchies: toward a new synthesis of American business history. *American Historical Review,* 108(2), pp. 404–33.

Lampel, J. and Mintzberg, H., 1996. Customizing customization. *Sloan Management Review,* 38(1), pp. 21–30.

Langfield-Smith, K. and Smith, D., 2003. Management control systems and trust in outsourcing relationships. *Management Accounting Research,* 14(3), pp. 281–307.

Langlois, R.N., 2003. The vanishing hand: the changing dynamics of industrial capitalism. *Industrial and Corporate Change,* 12(2), pp. 351–85.

Langlois, R.N., 2004. Chandler in a larger frame: markets, transaction costs and organizational form in history. *Enterprise and Society,* 5(3), pp. 355–75.

Langlois, R.N. and Robertson, P.L., 1995. *Firms, Markets and Economic Change: A Dynamic Theory of Business Institutions.* London: Routledge.

Latour, B., 1984. *Science in Action.* Milton Keynes: Open University Press and Cambridge (MA): Harvard University Presss.

Latour, B., 1996. *Aramis or the Love of Technology.* Cambridge (MA): Harvard University Press.

Latour, B., Woolgar, S. and Salk, J., 1979. *Laboratory Life: The Construction of Scientific Facts.* London and Beverly Hills: Sage Publications.

Law, J., 1992. Notes on the theory of the actor network: ordering strategy and heterogeneity. *Systems Practice,* 5(4), pp. 379–93.

Law, J., 1994. *Organizing Modernity.* Oxford: Blackwell.

Lawrence, P. and Lorsch, J., 1967. *Organization and Environment.* Cambridge (MA): Harvard University Press.

Leek, S., Turnbull, P. and Naude, P., 2003. How is information technology affecting business relationships? Results from a UK survey. *Industrial Marketing Management,* 32(2), pp. 19–26.

Leenders, M., Johnson, F., Flynn, A. and Fearon, H., 2006. *Purchasing and Supply Chain Management.* New York: McGraw-Hill-Irwin.

Leonard-Barton, D., 1992. Core capabilities and core rigidities: a paradox in new product development. *Strategic Management Journal,* 13(Special issue), pp. 111–25.

Leonard-Barton, D., 1995. *Wellsprings of Knowledge: Building and Sustaining the Sources of Innovation.* Boston: Harvard Business School Press.

Levine, S. and White, P., 1961. Exchange as a conceptual framework for the study of interorganizational relationships. *Administrative Science Quarterly,* 5(4), pp. 583–601.

Lindberg, L.N., Campbell, J. and Hollingsworth, J.R., 1991. Economic governance and the analysis of structural change in the American economy. In J.L. Campbell, J.R. Hollingsworth and L.N. Lindberg, eds. *Governance of the American Economy.* New York: Cambridge University Press.

Lindblom, C.E., 1959. The science of muddling through. *Public Administration Review*, 19, pp. 79–88.

Lindqvist, S., 1984. *Technology on Trial: The Introduction of Steam Power Technology Into Sweden 1715–1736*. Uppsala Studies in History of Science 1. Stockholm: Almqvist and Wiksell.

Litwak, E. and Hylton, L.F., 1962. Interorganizational analysis: a hypothesis on coordinating agencies. *Administrative Science Quarterly*, 6(4), pp. 395–420.

Loasby, B.J., 1999. *Knowledge, Institutions and Evolution in Economics*. London: Routledge.

Luffman, G., 1974. The processing of information by industrial buyers. *Industrial Marketing Management*, 3(6), pp. 363–75.

Lundgren, A., 1994. *Technological Innovation and Network Evolution*. London: Routledge.

Lundvall, B-Å, 1988. Innovation as an interactive process: from user–producer interaction to national systems of innovation. In G. Dosi, C. Freeman, R. Nelson *et al.*, eds. *Technical Change in Economic Theory*. London: Pinter.

Lundvall, B.-Å., ed., 1992. *National Systems of Innovation: Towards a Theory of Innovation and Interactive Learning*. London: Pinter.

Macaulay, S., 1963. Non-contractual relations in business: a preliminary study. *American Sociological Review*, 28(1), pp. 55–67.

Malerba, F., 2002. *The Source of Technological Change*. MIT Press.

Malmberg, A. and Maskell, P., 2002. The elusive concept of localization economies: towards a knowledge-based theory of spatial clustering. *Environment and Planning*, 34(3), pp. 429–49.

March, J.G., 1988. *Decisions and Organizations*. Oxford: Blackwell.

March, J.G., 1999. *The Pursuit of Organizational Intelligence*. Oxford: Blackwell.

March, J.G. and Olsen, J.P., eds., 1976. *Ambiguity and Choice in Organizations*. Oslo: Universitetsforlaget.

March, J.G. and Simon, H.A., 1958. *Organizations*. New York: John Wiley & Sons.

Marglin, S.A., 2008. *The Dismal Science: How Thinking Like an Economist Undermines Community*. Cambridge (MA): Harvard University Press.

Marshall, A., 1920. *Principles of Economics*, 8th ed. London: Macmillan, http://www.econlib.org/library/Marshall/marP.html (accessed 29 April 2009).

Maskell, P., Eskelinen, H., Hannibalsson, I., *et al.*, 1998. *Competitiveness, Localised Learning and Regional Development: Specialisation and Property in Small Open Economies*. London and New York: Routledge.

Mattsson, L.-G., 1969. *Integration and Efficiency in Marketing Systems*. Economic Research Institute, Stockholm School of Economics.

Mattsson, L.-G., 1989. Development of firms in networks: positions and investments. In L. Hallen and J. Johanson, eds. *Advances in International Marketing, Vol. 3*: Networks of Relationships in Internaional Industrial Marketing. Greenwich (CT): JAI Press, pp. 121–39.

Mayer, J.W. and Rowan, B., 1977. Institutionalized organizations: formal structure as myth and ceremony. *American Journal of Sociology*, 83(2), pp. 340–63.

McCarthy, E., 1960. *Basic Marketing: A Managerial Approach*. Homewood (IL): Richard D. Irwin.

Mickwitz, G., 1959. *Marketing and Competition*. Helsinki: Societas Scientiarum Fennica.

Miles, R. and Snow, C.C., 1992. Causes of failure of network organizations. *California Management Review*, 34(4), pp. 53–72.

Milgram, S., 1967. The small world problem. *Psychology Today*, 2, pp. 60–67.

Mintzberg, H., 1987. The strategy concept I: five Ps for strategy. *California Management Review*, 30(1), pp. 11–24.

Mintzberg, H., 1993. The pitfalls of strategic planning. *California Management Review*, 36(1), pp. 32–47.

Mohr, J. and Spekman, R., 1994. Characteristics of partnership success: partnership attributes, communication behavior and conflict resolution techniques. *Strategic Management Journal*, 15(2), pp. 135–52.

Mol, M., 2003. Purchasing's strategic relevance. *Journal of Purchasing and Supply Management*, 9(1), pp. 43–50.

Möller, K. and Halinen, A., 2000. Relationship marketing theory: its roots and direction. *Journal of Marketing Management*, 16, pp. 29–54.

Möller, K. and Rajala, A., 2007. Rise of strategic nets: new modes of value creation. *Industrial Marketing Management*, 36(7), pp. 895–908.

Möller, K. and Svahn, S., 2006. Role of knowledge in value creation in business nets. *Journal of Management Studies*, 43(5), pp. 985–1007.

Möller, K. and Wilson, D., eds., 1985. *Business Marketing: An Interaction and Network Perspective*. Boston, Dordrecht and London: Kluwer Academic Publisher.

Mouritsen, J., Hansen, A. and Hansen, C.O., 2001. Interorganizational controls and organizational competencies: episodes around target cost management/functional analysis and open book accounting. *Management Accounting Research*, 12(2), pp. 221–4.

Mouzas, S. and Ford, D., 2006. Managing relationships in showery weather: the role of umbrella agreements. *Journal of Business Research*, 59(12), pp. 1248–56.

Narayandas, D. and Rangar, K., 2004. Building and sustaining buyer–seller relationships in mature industrial markets. *Journal of Marketing*, 68(3), pp. 63–77.

Nelson, R.R., ed., 1993. *National Innovation Systems: A Comparative Analysis*. New York and London: Oxford University Press.

Nelson, R.R. and Winter, S.G., 1982. *An Evolutionary Theory of Economic Change*. Cambridge (MA): Belknap Press of the Harvard University Press.

Nishiguchi, T., 1994. *Strategic Industrial Sourcing: the Japanese Advantage*. New York: Oxford University Press.

Nohria, N. and Eccles, R.G., eds., 1991. *Networks and Organizations: Structure, Form and Action*. Boston (MA): Harvard Business School Press.

Nonaka, I., 1991. The knowledge-creating company. *Harvard Business Review*, 69(3), pp. 27–38.

Nonaka, I. and Takeuchi, H., 1995. *The Knowledge-creating Company: How Japanese Companies Create the Dynamics of Innovation*. New York: Oxford University Press.

Norman, R. and Ramirez, R., 1993. From value chain to value constellation: designing interactive strategy. *Harvard Business Review*, 71(4), pp. 65–77.

North, D., 1981. *Structure and Change in Economic History*. New York: Norton.

North, D., 2005. *Understanding the Process of Economic Change*. Princeton: Princeton University Press.

Nowotny, H., Pestre, D., Schmidt-Assman, E., *et al.*, 2005. *The Public Nature of Science under Assault*. Hamburg: Springer.

Palamountain, J., 1955. *The Politics of Distribution*. Cambridge (MA): Harvard University Press.

Palmatier, R.W., 2008. Interfirm relational drivers of customer value. *Journal of Marketing*, 72(July), pp. 76–89.

Pasinetti, L., 1981. *Structural Change and Economic Growth: A Theoretical Essay on the Dynamics of the Wealth of nations*. Cambridge: Cambridge University Press.

Patel, P. and Pavitt, K., 1997. The technological competencies of the world's largest firms: complex and path-dependent but not much variety. *Research Policy*, 26(2), pp. 141–156.

Pavitt, K., 2004. Changing patterns of usefulness of university research: opportunities and dangers. In K. Grandin, N. Wormbs and S. Widmalm, eds. *The Science-Industry Nexus: History, Policy, Implications*. Sagamore Beach: Watson.

Pedersen, A.-C., Torvatn, T. and Holmen, E., 2008. Towards a model for analysing supplier relationships when developing a supply network. *IMP Journal*, 2(2), pp. 38–58.

Pelikan, P., 1988. Can the imperfect innovation systems of capitalism be outperformed? In G. Dosi, C. Freeman, R. Nelson *et al.*, eds. *Technical Change in Economic Theory*. London: Pinter.

Penrose, E., 1959. *The Theory of the Growth of the Firm*. Oxford: Oxford University Press.

Perez, C. and Soete, L., 1988. Catching up in technology: entry barriers and windows of opportunity. In G. Dosi, C. Freeman, R. Nelson *et al.*, eds. *Technical Change in Economic Theory*. London: Pinter, pp. 458–79.

Perrow, C., 1981. Markets, hierarchies and hegemony. In A. Van de Ven and W.F. Joyce, eds. *Perspectives on Organizational Design and Behavior*. New York: John Wiley & Sons, pp. 371–89.

Pinch, T.J. and Bijker, W.E., 1984. The social construction of fact and artefacts or how the sociology of technology might benefit each other. *Social Studies of Science*, 14, pp. 399–441.

Pine, B.J., 1993. *Mass Customization: The New Frontier in Business Competition*. Cambridge (MA): Harvard Business School Press.

Piore, M.J., 1992. Fragments of a cognitive theory of technological change and organisational structure. In N. Nohria and R.G. Eccles, eds. *Networks and Organisations: Structure, Form and Action*. Boston (MA): Harvard Business School Press, pp. 430–44.

Piore, M.J. and Sabel, C.F., 1984. *The Second Industrial Divide: Possibilities for Prosperity*. New York: Basic Books.

Podolny, J.M., 1994. Market uncertainty and the social character of economic exchange. *Administrative Science Quarterly*, 39(3), pp. 458–83.

Podolny, J.M., 2001. Networks as the pipes and prisms of the market. *American Journal of Sociology*, 107(1), pp. 33–60.

Polanyi, K., 1944. *The Great Transformation: The Political and Economic Origins of our Time*. Boston (MA): Beacon Press.

Porter M.E., 1980. *Competitive Strategy*. New York: Free Press/Macmillan.

Porter, M.E., 1990. *The Competitive Advantage of Nations*. New York: Free Press.

Portz, J., 1991. Economic governance of the American meatpacking industry. In J.L. Campbell, J.R. Hollingsworth and L.N. Lindberg, eds. *Governance of the American Economy*. New York: Cambridge University Press, pp. 259–92.

Powell, W.W., 1987. Hybrid organizational arrangements: new form or transitional development? *California Management Review*, 30(1), pp. 67–87.

Powell, W.W., 1990. Neither market nor hierarchy: network forms of organisation. In B.M. Staw and L.I. Cummings, eds. *Research in Organizational Behavior*, Vol. 12. Greenwich (CT): JAI Press, pp. 295–336.

Powell, W.W., 1998. Learning from collaboration: knowledge and networks in the biotechnology and pharmaceutical industries. *California Management Review*, 40(3), pp. 228–40.

Powell, W.W., 2001. The capitalist firm in the twenty-first century: emerging patterns in Western enterprise. In P. DiMaggio, ed. *The Twenty-First-Century Firm: Changing Economic Organization in International Perspective*. Princeton: Princeton University Press, pp. 33–68.

Powell, W.W., Koput, K.W. and Smith-Doerr, L., 1996. Interorganizational collaboration and the locus of innovation: networks of learning in biotechnology. *Administrative Science Quarterly*, 41(1), pp. 116–45.

Pugh, D.S., Hickson, D.J., Hinings, C.R. and Turner, C., 1968. Dimensions of organization structure. *Administrative Science Quarterly*, 13(June), pp. 65–105.

Quinn, J.B., 1999. Strategic outsourcing: leveraging knowledge capabilities. *Sloan Management Review*, 40(4), pp. 9–21.

Raesfeld, A., 1997. Technological Cooperation in Networks: A Socio-cognitive Approach (PhD dissertation). Enschede, NL: University of Twente.

Ramos, C. and Ford, D., 2009. The development of a research device to analyse actors' views of the world. IMP Annual Conference, Marseille, September.

Rasmussen, A., 1955. *Pristeori eller Parameterteori: Studier Omkring Virksomhedens Afsaetning (Price Theory or Parameter Theory: Studies of the Sales of the Firm)*. Copenhagen: Erhvervsokonomisk Forlag.

Raynor, M., 2007. What is corporate strategy, really? *Ivey Business Journal Online*, 71(8). http://www.iveybusinessjournal.com/article.asp?intArticle_ID=722 (accessed 29 April 2009).

Reve, T., 1990. The firm as a nexus of internal and external contracts. In M. Aoki, B. Gustayson and O.E Williamson, eds. *The Firm as Nexus of Treaties*. London: Sage.

Richardson, G.B., 1972. The organisation of industry. *Economic Journal*, 82, pp. 883–96.

Rigby, D.K., Reichheld, F.K. and Schefter, P., 2002. Avoid the four perils of CRM. *Harvard Business Review*, 80(2), pp. 101–9.

Rindfleish, A. and Heide, J.B., 1997. Transaction cost analysis: past present and future applications. *Journal of Marketing*, 61(4), pp. 30–54.

Ritter, T., 1999. The networking company: antecedents for coping with relationships and networks effectively. *Industrial Marketing Management*, 28(5), pp. 467–79.

Ritter, T. and Gemünden, H.G., 2003. Network competence: its impact on innovation success and its antecedents. *Journal of Business Research*, 56(9), pp. 745–55.

Robinson, P., Faris, C. and Wind, Y., 1967. *Industrial Buying and Creative Marketing*. Boston (MA): Allyn and Bacon.

Rogers, E.M. and Larsen, J.K., 1984. *Silicon Valley Fever*. New York: Basic Books.

Rokkan, A. and Haugland, S., 2002. Developing relational exchange: effectiveness and power. *European Journal of Marketing*, 36(1/2), pp. 211–30.

Roodhooft, F. and Warlop, L., 1999. On the role of sunk costs and asset specificity in outsourcing decisions: a research note. *Accounting, Organization and Society*, 24(4), pp. 363–9.

Rosenberg, N., 1982. *Inside the Black Box: Technology and Economics*. Cambridge: Cambridge University Press.

Rosenberg, N., 1994. *Exploring the Black Box: Technology, Economics, History*. Cambridge: Cambridge University Press.

Rosenbloom, B., 1995. *Marketing Channels: A Management View*, 5th ed. Forth Worth: Dryden Press.

Rumelt, R., 1988. The evaluation of business strategy. In J. Quinn, H. Mintzberg and R. James, eds. *The Strategy Process*. Englewood Cliffs (NJ): Prentice-Hall.

Sabel, C.F. and Zeitlin, J., 1997. Stories, strategies, structures: rethinking historical alternatives to mass production. In C.F. Sabel and J. Zeitlin, eds. *World of Possibilities: Flexibility and mass production in western industrialisation*. Cambridge: Cambridge University Press, pp. 1–33.

Sahal, D., ed., 1980. *Research Development and Technological Innovation*. Lexington: Lexington Books.

Sahlins, M., 2004. *Stone Age Economy*. London: Routledge.

Sanchez, R. and Heene, A., 1997. Reinventing strategic management: new theory and practice for competence-based competition. *European Management Journal*, 15(3), pp. 303–17.

Sartorius, K. and Kirsten, J., 2005. The boundaries of the firm: why do sugar producers outsource sugarcane production? *Management Accounting Research*, 16(1), pp. 81–99.

Saxenian, A., 1991. The origins and dynamics of production networks in Silicon Valley. *Research Policy*, 20(5), pp. 423–37.

Saxenian, A., 1994. *Regional Advantage: Culture and Competition in Silicon Valley and Route 128*. Boston (MA): Harvard University Press.

Scherer, C., 1991. Governance of the automobile industry: the transformation of labor and supplier relations. In J.L. Campbell, J.R. Hollingsworth and L.N. Lindberg, eds. *Governance of the American Economy*. New York: Cambridge University Press, pp. 209–35.

Schwartz, M. and Fish, A., 1998. Just-in-time inventories in old Detroit. *Business History*, 40(3).

Schwartz, M., 2000. Markets, networks and the rise of Old Detroit, 1920–1940. *Enterprise and Society*, 1(1), pp. 63–99.

Scranton, P., 1997. *Endless Novelty, Specialty, Production and American Industrialization, 1865–1925*. Princeton: Princeton University Press.

Seal, W., Cullen, J., Dunlop, A., *et al.*, 1999. Enacting a European supply chain: a case study on the role of management accounting. *Management Accounting Research*, 10(3), pp. 303–22.

Shapin, S. and Schaffer, S., 1985. *Leviathan and the Air-Pump: Hobbles Boyle and the Experimental Life*. Princeton: Princeton University Press.

Sheth, J.N., 1973. A model of industrial buyer behavior. *Journal of Marketing*, 37(4), pp. 50–56.

Sheth, J. and Parvatiyar, A., 1995. The evolution of relationship marketing. *International Business Review*, 4(4), pp. 397–418.

Shih, T., 2009. Scrutinizing a policy ambition to make business out of science: experiences from Taiwan (forthcoming doctoral dissertation). Department of Business Studies, University of Uppsala.

Skarp, F., 2006. *Adaptations of products to customers' use contexts* (doctoral dissertation). Gothenburg, Sweden: Department of Industrial Marketing, Chalmers University of Technology.

Snehota, I., 1990. Notes on a theory of business enterprise (doctoral dissertation). Department of Business Studies, University of Uppsala.

Sparling, S., 1906. *Introduction to Business Organization*. New York: Macmillan.

Speklé, R.F., 2001. Explaining management control structural variety: a transaction cost economics perspective. *Accounting, Organization and Society*, 26(4/5), pp. 419–41.

Spekman, R.E., 1988. Strategic supplier selection: understanding long-term buyer relationships. *Business Horizons*, July–August.

Spekman, R., Kamauff, J. and Myhr, N., 1998. An empirical investigation into supply chain management: a perspective on partnerships. *Supply Chain Management*, 3(2), pp. 53–67.

Spender, J.C., 1989. *Industry Recipes: An Enquiry into the Nature and Sources of Managerial Judgement*. Cambridge (MA): Blackwell.

Stabell, C. and Fjeldstad, Ø., 1998. Configuring value for competitive advantage: on chains shops and networks. *Strategic Management Journal*, 19(5), pp. 413–37.

Starr, M.K., 1965. Modular production: a new concept. *Harvard Business Review*, 43(6), pp. 131–42.

Stern, L., ed., 1969. *Distribution Channels: Behavioral Dimensions*. Boston (MA): Houghton Mifflin.

Stock, J. and Lambert, D., 2001. *Strategic Logistics Management*. New York: McGraw-Hill.

Storper, M., 1997. *The Regional World: Territorial Development in a Global Economy*. New York and London: Guilford Press.

Storper, M. and Venables, A., 2004. Buzz: face-to-face contact and the urban economy. *Journal of Economic Geography*, 4(4), pp. 351–70.

Strömsten, T. and Håkansson, H., 2007. Resources in use: embedded electricity. In H. Håkansson and A. Walusewski, eds. *Knowledge and Innovation in Business and Industry: The importance of using others*. Abingdon: Routledge, pp. 27–53.

Sturgeon, T.J., 2000. How Silicon Valley came to be. In M. Kenney, ed. *Understanding Silicon Valley: The Anatomy of an Entrepreneurial Region*. Stanford: Stanford University Press, pp. 15–47.

Takeuchi, H. and Nonaka, I., 1986. The new new-product development game. *Harvard Business Review*, January–February, pp. 137–46.

Teramoto, Y., 1990. *Network Power*. Tokyo: NTT Press.

Thibaut, J.W. and Kelly, H.H., 1959. *The Social Psychology of Groups*. New York: John Wiley & Sons.

Thompson, J.D., 1967. *Organizations in Action*. New York: McGraw-Hill.

Törnroos, J.-Å., 1991. Om företagets geografi: en teoretisk och empirisk analys (The geography of the firm: a theoretical and empirical analysis) (doctoral thesis). Åbo: Åbo Akademi University Press.

Torvatn, T., 1996. Productivity in industrial networks: a case study of the purchasing function (PhD dissertation). Trondheim: Department of Industrial Economics and Technology Management, Norwegian University of Science and Technology.

Tuli, K.R., Kohli, A.K. and Bharadwaj, S.G., 2007. Rethinking customer solutions: from product bundles to relational processes. *Journal of Marketing*, 71(3), pp. 1–17.

Tunisini, A., 1997. The dissolution of channels and hierarchies: an inquiry into the changing customer relationships and organization of the computer corporations (doctoral thesis no. 69). Department of Business Studies, University of Uppsala.

Turnbull, P., 1979. Roles of personal contacts in industrial export marketing. *Scandinavian Journal of Management*, 16, pp. 325–37.

Turnbull, P.W. and Valla, J.P., eds., 1986. *Strategies for International Industrial Marketing*. London: Croom Helm.

Twedt, D., 1964. How stable are advertiser–advertising agency relationships? *Journal of Marketing*, 28:(July), pp. 83–4.

Ulaga, W. and Eggert, A., 2006. Value-based differentiation in business relationships: gaining and sustaining key supplier status. *Journal of Marketing*, 70(1), pp. 119–36.

Utterback, J.M., 1994. *Mastering the Dynamics of Innovation*. Cambridge (MA): Harvard Business School Press.

Uzzi, B., 1997. Social structure and competition in interfirm networks: the paradox of embeddedness. *Administrative Science Quarterly*, 42, pp. 35–67.

Van de Ven, A.H., Emmit, D.C. and Koenig, R., 1975. Frameworks for interorganizational analysis. In A.R. Negandhi, ed. *Interorganizational Theory*. Kent (OH): Kent State University Press.

Van de Ven, A., Angle, H. and Poole, M.S., eds., 1989. *Research on the Management of Innovation: The Minnesota Studies*. New York: Ballinger/Harper and Row.

Van de Ven, A.H., Polley, D.E., Garud, R. and Venkatarman, S., 1999. *The Innovation Journey*. New York: Oxford University Press.

Van Der Meer-Kooistra, J. and Vosselman, E.G.J., 2000. Management control of interfirm transactional relationships: the case of industrial renovation and maintenance. *Accounting, Organization and Society*, 25, pp. 51–77.

van Weele, A., 2002. *Purchasing and Supply Chain Management*. London: Thomson Learning.

Vargo, S. and Lusch, R., 2004. Evolving to a new dominant logic for marketing. *Journal of Marketing*, 68(1), pp. 1–17.

Vercauteren, A., 2007. Inter-firm interaction for technology-based radical innovations (PhD dissertation). Belgium: Hasselt University.

von Corswant, F., 2003. Organizing interactive product development (PhD thesis). Gothenburg, Sweden: Department of Operations Management and Work Organization, Chalmers University of Technology.

von Hippel, E., 1976. The dominant role of users in the scientific instrument innovation process. Working paper. Sloan School of Management, pp. 764–75.

von Hippel, E., 1978. Successful industrial products from customer ideas: presentation of a new customer-active paradigm with evidence and implications. *Journal of Marketing*, 42(1), pp. 39–49.

von Hippel, E., 1988. *The Sources of Innovation*. New York: Oxford University Press.

von Hippel, E., 1998. Economics of product development by users: the impact of sticky local information. *Management Science*, 44, pp. 629–44.

Waldrop, M.M., 1992. *Complexity: The Emerging Science at the Edge of Order and Chaos*. New York: Touchstone.

Walter, A., Ritter, T. and Gemunden, H.-G., 2001. Value creation in buyer–seller relations. *Industrial Marketing Management*, 40(4), pp. 365–77.

Waluszewski, A., 1989. Framväxten av en ny massateknik: en utvecklingshistoria (The development of a new mechanical pulping technique) (dissertation). Acta Universitatis Upsaliensis: Studiae Oeconomia Negotiorum 31. Uppsala: Almqvist and Wiksell.

Waluszewski, A., 2004. A competing or co-operating cluster or seven decades of combinatory resources? What's behind a prospering biotech valley? *Scandinavian Journal of Management*, 20(1/2), pp. 125–50.

Waluszewski, A., 2006. Short time growth, the benefits of research: new aspirations for direct yields put old research ideals under pressure. Reprinted in *From Embracing Globalisation to the Limits of Tolerance: Themes from Axess Magazine 2006*. Viborg, Denmark: Nörhaven Paperback.

Waluszewski, A., Baraldi, E., Linné, Å. and Shih, T., 2009. Resource interfaces telling other stories about the commercial use of new technology: the embedding of biotech solutions in US, China and Taiwan. *IMP Journal* (submission).

Webster Jr., F.E., 1979. *Industrial Marketing Strategy*. New York: John Wiley & Sons.

Webster Jr., F.E., 1992. The changing role of marketing in the corporations. *Journal of Marketing*, 56, pp. 1–17.

Webster Jr., F.E. and Wind, Y., 1972. *Organizational Buying Behavior*. Englewood Cliffs (NJ): Prentice-Hall.

Wedin, T., 2001. Networks and demand: the use of electricity in an industrial process (doctoral thesis no. 83). Department of Business Studies, University of Uppsala.

Weick, K.E., 1979. *The Social Psychology of Organizing*, 2nd ed. New York: McGraw-Hill.

Weick, K.E., 1995. *Sensemaking in Organizations*. Thousand Oaks: Sage Publications.

Weightman, G., 2002. *The Frozen Water Trade: A True Story*. New York: Hyperion.

Welch, D. and Welch, L., 1996. The internationalization process and networks: a strategic management perspective. *Journal of International Marketing*, 4(3), pp. 11–28.

Welch, D., Welch, L., Wilkinson, I. and Young, L., 1996. Export grouping relationships and networks: evidence from an Australian scheme. *International Journal of Research in Marketing*, 13, pp. 463–77.

Westing, J., Fine, I. and Zenz, G., 1969. *Purchasing Management: Materials in Motion*. New York: John Wiley & Sons.

Wheelwright, S. and Clark, K., 1992. *Revolutionizing Product Development*. New York: The Free Press.

Whitaker, A., 1992. The transformation in work: post-Fordism revisited. In M. Reed and M. Hughes, eds. *Rethinking Organization: New Directions in Organization Theory and Analysis*. London: Sage, pp. 184–206.

Whitley, R., 1992. The social construction of organizations and markets: the comparative analysis of business recipes. In M. Reed and M. Hughes, eds. *Rethinking Organization: New Directions in Organization Theory and Analysis*. London: Sage, pp. 121–43.

Whitley, R., 1994. Dominant forms of economic organization in market economies. *Organization Studies*, 15(2), pp. 153–82.

Whitley, R., 2000. The institutional structuring of innovation strategies: business systems firm types and patterns of technical change in different market economies. *Organization Studies*, 21(5), pp. 855–86.

Widener, S.K. and Selto, F.H., 1999. Management control systems and boundaries of the firm: why do firms outsource internal auditing activities? *Journal of Management Accounting Research*, 11, pp. 45–73.

Wiley, J., Wilkinson, I. and Young, L., 2006. The nature role and impact of connected relations: a comparison of European and Chinese suppliers' perspectives. *Journal of Business and Industrial Marketing*, 21(1), pp. 3–13.

Wilk, R.R., 1996. *Economics and Cultures: Foundation of Economic Anthropology*. Oxford: Westview Press.

Wilkinson, I., 2008. *Business Relating Business, Managing Organisational Relations and Networks*. Cheltenham: Edward Elgar.

Wilkinson, I. and Yeoh, K., 2005. Value creation in Chinese and European business relationships. In D. Brown and A. McBean, eds. *Economy and Business in China*. London: Routledge, pp. 87–101.

Wilkinson, I.F. and Young, L.C., 1994. Business dancing: the nature and role of interfirm relations in business strategy. *Asia-Australia Marketing Journal*, 2(1), pp. 67–79.

Wilkinson, I. and Young, L., 2002. On cooperating: firms relations and networks. *Journal of Business Research*, 55(February), pp. 123–32.

Williamson, O.E., 1975. *Markets and Hierarchies: Analysis and Antitrust Implications*. New York: Free Press.

Williamson, O.E., 1979. Transaction cost economics: the governance of contractual relations. *Journal of Law and Economics*, 22(2), pp. 232–62.

Williamson, O.E., 1985. *The Economic Institutions of Capitalism*. New York: Free Press.

Williamson, O.E., 1991. Strategizing, economizing and economic organization. *Strategic Management Journal*, 12(Winter), pp. 75–94.

Williamson, O.E. and Masten, S.E., eds., 1999. *The Economics of Transaction Costs*. Cheltenham: Edward Elgar.

Wilson, D.T. and Jantrania, S., 1994. Understanding the value of a relationship. *Asia-Australia Marketing Journal*, 2(1), pp. 55–66.

Wilson, D.T. and Mummalaneni, V., 1986. Bonding and commitment in buyer–seller relationships: a preliminary conceptualization. *Industrial Marketing and Purchasing*, 1(3), pp. 44–58.

Wynstra, J.Y.F., 1998. Purchasing involvement in product development (dissertation). Eindhoven: Centre for Innovation Studies.

Young, L., 1992. The role of trust in interorganizational relationships in marketing (PhD dissertation). Sydney: University of New South Wales.

Young, L. and Wilkinson, I., 1989. The role of trust and cooperation in marketing channels: a preliminary study. *European Journal of Marketing*, 23(2), pp. 109–22.

Young, L. and Wilkinson, I., 1997. The space between: towards a typology of interfirm relations. *Journal of Business to Business Marketing*, 13(6), pp. 53–96.

Zajac, E.J. and Olsen, C.P., 1993. From transaction cost to transactional value analysis: implications for the study of interorganizational strategies. *Journal of Management Studies*, 30(1), pp. 131–45.

Zolkiewski, J., 2004. Relationships are not ubiquitous in marketing. *European Journal of Marketing*, 38(1/2), pp. 24–9.

INDEX

Printed and bound by CPI Group (UK) Ltd, Croydon, CR0 4YY

16/04/2025

14658512-0002